A Spectrum of Solutions for Clients with Autism

This book is a comprehensive resource to guide work with individuals on the autism spectrum. It reflects the true range of needs presented by individuals with autism, pulling together the most salient aspects of treatment with invaluable information from several disciplines synthesized to guide successful treatment.

Divided into topical parts with chapters from three field experts in each, this book features contributions from therapists, educators, and medical doctors, as well as financial planners, health advocates, and innovators. The diverse disciplines and backgrounds of each author lend a different voice and perspective to each chapter, reflecting the continuum of care necessary when working with clientele on the autism spectrum, and that, for clients on the spectrum, one solution does not fit all.

For use by psychotherapists, counselors, applied behavioral analysts, occupational therapists, social workers, teachers, and more, this text presents readers with expertise from various contributing disciplines to provide a valuable treatment resource that can inform and guide their daily work with clients on the autism spectrum.

Rachel Bédard, PhD, is in private practice in Fort Collins, Colorado. A long-standing advocate for those with autism, she primarily works with clients on the spectrum and has previously published two books about autism.

Lorna Hecker, PhD, is in private practice in Fort Collins, Colorado. She is a professor emerita of Purdue University Northwest and has published numerous books and articles on mental health-related topics and enjoys working with neurodiverse couples.

A Spectrum of Solutions for Clients with Autism

Treatment for Adolescents and Adults

Edited by Rachel Bédard and Lorna Hecker

Routledge
Taylor & Francis Group

NEW YORK AND LONDON

First published 2020
by Routledge
52 Vanderbilt Avenue, New York, NY 10017

and by Routledge
2 Park Square, Milton Park, Abingdon, Oxon, OX14 4RN

Routledge is an imprint of the Taylor & Francis Group, an informa business

Library of Congress Cataloging-in-Publication Data
Names: Bédard, Rachel (Psychologist), editor. | Hecker, Lorna L., editor.
Title: A spectrum of solutions for clients with autism : treatment for adolescents and adults / edited by Rachel Bédard, Lorna Hecker.
Description: New York, NY : Routledge, 2020. | Includes bibliographical references and index. |
Identifiers: LCCN 2020002460 (print) | LCCN 2020002461 (ebook) |
ISBN 9780367257446 (hbk) | ISBN 9780367280499 (pbk) |
ISBN 9780429299391 (ebook)
Subjects: MESH: Autism Spectrum Disorder–therapy | Transition to Adult Care | Self-Management–psychology | Interpersonal Relations | Adolescent | Adult
Classification: LCC RC553.A88 (print) | LCC RC553.A88 (ebook) |
NLM WS 350.8.P4 | DDC 616.85/882–dc23
LC record available at https://lccn.loc.gov/2020002460
LC ebook record available at https://lccn.loc.gov/2020002461

ISBN: 978-0-367-25744-6 (hbk)
ISBN: 978-0-367-28049-9 (pbk)
ISBN: 978-0-429-29939-1 (ebk)

Typeset in Bembo
by Swales & Willis, Exeter, Devon, UK

Contents

PART XV
Moving towards Adulthood: An Important
Developmental Step   **333**

Foreword

Michael John Carley

A true oxymoron exists in the words, "autism community." It's a term suggesting unity amongst autism parents, individuals, educators, and others, and a phrase that anyone in our clinical whereabouts hears ad infinitum.

And yet it is rather quite … the lie; albeit for very Darwinist, developmentally appropriate reasons.

Unlike other non-apparent disabilities, the word "autism" covers a great deal of territory. In the autism world you might have someone who will never acquire speech, enjoy a physically intimate relationship with a peer, or hold down a steady job for long. And on the other end of the spectrum you have all these famous people being diagnosed as autistic: Albert Einstein, Thomas Jefferson, Emily Dickinson, Beethoven … you can't get a wider spectrum than that! Furthermore, as opposed to the symptomology of (for example) Down syndrome, or obsessive compulsive disorder, our world is fraught with disagreements over language, medical vs. human models of disability, behavioral strategies of "Assimilate at all costs!" vs. boundary-absent versions of neurodiversity; and we especially duke it out over autism's origin – still alive are stalwarts who believe we got our autism from vaccines, and who scream "fake news!" at the millions of reputable studies proving otherwise.

We fight about research. "Walk for our organization and help average working families and their child with autism!" And yet engaging only in genetic research – pouring tens of millions of dollars to investigate serotonin levels, or nerve synapses – will not be helping the average working-class family with a child with autism … for 50 years. Organizations devoted to research that helps the living (i.e., with much-needed services) receive less than 2% of the funding because they don't have powerful, wealthy families behind them (wealthy families, you have to understand, have all their kids' service needs taken care of). The list of battlegrounds feels endless.

But here's the crux … these battles are inevitable … specifically because no condition presents with opposite extremes like autism. It is paradoxically right, and good that we so engage.

Intellectually, we have "stuff" to work out, and we won't work it out by sweeping the challenges under the rug. How we confront one another will be the measuring stick of whether we succeed or not. For to not confront each other (the contrarian and scared, not peaceful, spirit at work) will only further delay our ability to become that true community.

Back in 1994, the DSM-IV blew prevalence statistics wide open with the inclusion of Asperger's syndrome, in addition to an expanded criteria for traditional autism. This opened up diagnostic possibility itself in such a manner that liberated the hundreds of thousands of people like me, but that also overwhelmed the average Joe/Jane in the street. Public resentment, fueled also by a bull market for diagnosticians, then followed. And when a new definition of autism was bestowed on us by the DSM-5 (American Psychiatric Association, 2013), the disparity grew even more.

The new set of diagnostic criteria was supposedly intended to make it harder to misdiagnose, yet the new criteria did exactly the opposite, as the word "autism" not only now absorbed roughly 95% of those who had been previously diagnosed with "Asperger's syndrome." Additionally, much of our faith in the clinical world itself was further destroyed by the actual DSM committee, as they fought amongst themselves – publicly, I might add – working together only to repel the criticisms of faulty and unproven research trials, if not defend their questioned criteria. The end result was a populace that thought, "Look at the high-priced shrinks screwing this up!" and thereafter chose diagnostic anarchy, rejecting previously held clinical authority, and inventing new terms like "educational autism" – that are not in the DSM – as a means to get people the services they need. Involved heavily in autism politics at the time, I had a rather acidic conference call with the DSM committee in 2012 (after one of my organizations decided to honor Yale's Fred Volkmar, who acted as a whistleblower in revealing the committee's faulty practices and internal dysfunction), yet we actually got a laugh in when I remarked that no matter how solid or "unsolid" their criteria were, it wouldn't change the fact that there would always be "idiot clinicians."

Yet prior to 2013, during the days of DSM-IV, was there ever a defined line that separated autism and Asperger's syndrome? No, there was not, because we all grow, and change. We are not fixed in place and we will develop at varying rates of speed as time moves on. Therein the new definitions were right – we are not destined to be that community for quite some time.

And then there's Dr. Rachel Bédard …

I first met Rachel, a Colorado psychologist, online in 2017. She liked my books, and wrote me after hearing me speak for the first time. She was seeking some advice on sexuality for her spectrum clients. And as we talked, the relationship opened up. I discovered that she had (along with a fellow clinician Mallory Griffith) edited a book called *Raising a Child on the Autism Spectrum* (2017), a collection of parent stories from disparate parts of the autism parent universe. A second book that the two did together, *You've Got This* (2018), siphoned stories from individuals on the spectrum, as well as their parents, to tell unique tales about the journey from middle school to college.

What was clear about these books was that Rachel (and perhaps Mallory, whom I do not know) was a collector, maybe even a hoarder, of stories. My discovery didn't require much of a brain – it is evident on a very surface level once you dig into Rachel or her book projects.

The knowledge that had to be hard fought, however, was how revered Rachel was as a therapist, if not also the central focus of autism knowledge in her community of Fort Collins, Colorado. This more difficult discovery made sense only in the context of deferral, or the clinical version of grassroots organizing. If she'll permit me to speculate, I suspect Rachel has fervently sworn allegiance to the merits of involving all; even when she might not want to, and even those for whom she has little faith. She is a gatherer somewhat void of a selective mindset. Yet in her this is not laziness, it is discipline.

This past spring, after consulting for a couple of days at a school in Denver, I delayed my flight home and shot up to Fort Collins for a night to meet her. She had organized an informal "dinner" in my honor. At first I was a little bummed about the meal because she was so intriguing that I selfishly wanted more time to pick her brain. But easing into a lovely buffet of Thai takeout I laughed to myself that sharing me was the only option. This was who Rachel was and had to be. She shared me with her fabulous family (people like Rachel don't have "non-fabulous" families), and with denizens – some established, some starting out – from the clinical community of Fort Collins. It was a lovely evening, natch. And at times I surprised myself because I was sharing far more than I had expected to. It was only as I stood in line at a local 7-Eleven later that night, waiting patiently while the assumed homeless, or just hard-luck human, counted change in front of me, that I realized that it was Rachel, indirectly casting spells on me, who got me to share so much.

"Dude, I can cover," I said to the man.

Rachel has now teamed up with Dr. Lorna Hecker, an author/editor of nine books and a more than quarter-century veteran of clinical work at Purdue University. Their new baby is the book you hold in your hands. And as you can see, Bédard, helped by this new, prestigious teammate, has upped her hoarder game. From the relative nowheresville of Fort Collins they have accrued some of the world's most notable figures to contribute to a book published by an academic press that is by far more disparate in its contributors' belief systems than any other, multi-contributor autism book I have ever seen. Gone is the cohesive wallop that a multitude of philosophically united authors would have created. The result is that anyone whose autism values feel secured will really disagree with a couple of the dozens of chapters in here.

Instead, in the place of the anticipated, remains a book committed to sharing.

In an amazing 2018 interview with the *New York Times*, Anthony Romero, the head of the American Civil Liberties Union (ACLU), described how the ACLU was losing their fight with the National Rifle Association (NRA), and he couldn't understand why. For Romero, the ACLU's website was plastered with data and facts that for him should have won the public discussion hands-down. But Romero confessed that he one day went to the NRA's website, and quickly realized why the NRA was perceivably kicking his ass. There was no data on the NRA site. But there were lots of stories. Unlike the ACLU's, the NRA's website (in 2013, when Romera made this discovery) was about narrative. In the interview Romero cited one woman in an NRA video talking about how her father had hunted with her when she was a little girl, and that this bond/joyful memory had carried over into her life as an adult who now loved hunting with her children (Why the A.C.L.U. Wants to Be More Like the N.R.A, 2018, July 30).

It is the difference between experiences and opinions. Options vs. dogma. No, Bédard/Hecker don't have such open minds that their brains fell out – there is no promotion of ingesting bleach, chelation therapy, or vaccine theory herein. But for instance, as Applied Behavioral Analysis (ABA) continues its downslide as more humane behavioral strategies emerge, there are a few ABA professionals given voice within these pages.

And holy cow, what a recruiting/hoarding job! To start, Bédard/Hecker have herein scored icons Tony Attwood and Temple Grandin to contribute. I have also recognized names I haven't come across in a decade, like Gassner and Moravcik; new names that impressed, such as Turns, Eddy, Zuber, Townsend, Daniels, Lorenz, and Dow. Organized into three experiences/chapters within each subject, we get differing perspectives on siblings, employment, diet, etc. This is a book for and primarily by emotionally healthy clinicians that will present treatment options that will fit with their clients' needs more so than perhaps one person's (i.e., my) value systems. There's no other book like this available to clinical professionals.

Brava Bédard/Hecker. Those of us who have the luck and fortune to work with individuals one on one understand that the key to healthfully engaging in all these politics is to drop them when the singular individual walks into your office, or wants to talk to you after a speech. The fights, dogma – however righteous – go out the window. Now it's an upset human being, a damaged faith, or a beating heart that needs you. Now is not the time to threateningly yell "Put the knife down, sir, and step away from the door!" Now is the time to figuratively kneel, and say, "How can

I help?" to be the emotionally regulated hero, or the listener at peace … the person that they need, and not the person that we want. To hold multiple options, after listening? Now that's a Godsend.

References

American Psychiatric Association. (2013). *Diagnostic and statistical manual of mental disorders* (5th ed.). Washington, DC: Author.

Bédard, R., & Griffith, M. (2018). *You've got this! The journey from middle school to college, as told by students on the Autism Spectrum and their parents.* Camp Hill, PA: The Practice Institute (TPI) Press.

Griffith, M., & Bédard, R. (2017). *Raising a child on the autism spectrum: Insights from parents to parents.* Camp Hill, PA: The Practice Institute (TPI) Press.

Why the A.C.L.U. wants to be more like the N.R.A. (2018, July 30). Retrieved from www.nytimes.com/2018/07/30/podcasts/the-daily/aclu-nra-trump.html.

Introduction

Autism treatment traditionally focuses on the disabling aspects of living on the autism spectrum, while seldom focusing on the abilities. Autism can be seen as both a gift and a disability. We are starting to acknowledge the gifts of autism in our society, and this exposure to true "awetism" is beginning to change how we view people on the spectrum. In this book, we hold this duality, and help treatment providers harness these gifts while overcoming the disabling aspects of living on the spectrum of autism.

What you hold in your hand is the product of 49 authors, providing imperative insights about life on the spectrum and appropriate treatment interventions. While we know individuals on the spectrum hold special talents, they are thrust into an ableist world filled with neurotypically constructed demands. While society marches toward a more inclusive neurodiverse world, our autistic clients must traverse the neurotypical world that envelops their daily lives. This book is a product of many visionaries in our field, all trying to answer the question, "How can I help my client?" We have all struggled with figuring out how to help our clients on the autism spectrum lead their best lives. Many, many times clinicians call me (RB) and ask, "How can I help my client?" and I quickly realize they do not understand the breadth of the spectrum, the diversity of the spectrum, or the many needs of these clients. They are working in isolation, not referring for necessary services. I cannot count how many times I've asked, "Could your client be on the spectrum?" and the answer is, "No, because … she is female, he is smart, she is a professor, he is married." Generally, we find there is a lack of understanding regarding behaviors related to the autism spectrum; there are neurotypical assumptions about what is normal, and a general fumbling around the disability while overlooking the many strengths of their client. Lastly, many clinicians try to treat a client on the spectrum in isolation. They do not understand that, because of the depth of the spectrum, many professionals may need to be involved in order to provide adequate care.

This book reflects a multidisciplinary perspective in treating autism; it takes a village to support and nurture the unique abilities and frustrating disabilities of this clientele. As you will learn, success in treatment may mean integrating a speech language pathologist to teach social skills to your client, or coordinating with a medical professional around sleep issues, or integrating an occupational therapy around feeding issues or sensitivities.

Diversity of Expert Opinion

To attempt to reflect the full diversity of the autism spectrum, we as editors generated a list of topics to cover, and then asked three respected individuals to answer similar questions on the topic, like a panel at a conference, but in a book. For example, sleep problems are rampant in folks on the autism spectrum. We have three experts who can walk you through this concern and provide intervention ideas. Their ideas are similar, but the approaches and the interventions don't match perfectly (just like your clients, just like the spectrum!). The topics are intentionally wide ranging, as are the experts. What you hold in your hands is a book that is unique, creative, innovative, and reflects this diversity. It is intentionally an atypical book, which means that we all have atypical roles that play to our strengths. In the spirit of direct communication, transparency, cheerleading, and creating community, please allow us to share our roles.

As editors, we worked behind the scenes to convince people to join the team. We drew up a "dream team list" and asked people, fearlessly, repeatedly, and honestly, if they would join us. (A few invited guests said no due to time constraints – if your favorite professional isn't here, let's believe they said no due to time constraints!)

Each individual on the spectrum is different; in this book, each author brings a slightly different perspective on the same topic within specific parts of the book. Additionally, you will find that some chapters are written directly by people on the autism spectrum. We believe this is one of the most important features of this book: the voices of those on the spectrum must be heard, and this book is one of many ways to give voice to those who have too often been marginalized, even by therapists.

This book is rich with many authors sharing experiences of their clients so that you can better understand how to apply their suggestions and interventions. Please know that all client scenarios within the chapters are fictitious, and are typically compilations of many experiences with clients. Of note, every author in some way offered thanks to these many clients, from whom we have learned valuable lessons.

About the Editors

Lorna and I (RB) met on Craigslist. Our group needed an office mate, and Lorna, having just moved to Fort Collins (Colorado), responded to an ad, calling me on my day off. We arranged a time to tour the office a few hours after the phone call. While on the phone with Lorna, I googled

"Lorna Hecker" and found a college professor at Purdue who had written numerous books. Clearly "*my* Lorna Hecker" was not the professor, and as such I arrived in shorts and a tank top, suspecting that this would not work out. I did, however, arrive 10 minutes early, planning to get a random task done at the office. When I arrived at the office, Lorna was already there, with a one-page handout about who she was. I had met my match. Our 15-minute tour lasted an hour and a half. She took the office.

We discovered we had a mutual interest in autism spectrum clients. I (RB) spend the bulk of my week working with people on the spectrum. I have, hands down, the best client base in town: the most respectful, kind, creative, honest clients. In the span of my career, I am lucky to have witnessed the changing ideas, hopes, and expectations for individuals with autism. The bar is higher than it once was, and I hope to witness significant additional change before I retire; we continue to need to break stereotypes, challenge low expectations, address insufficient access to intervention, and improve professional training. As you will see in this book, terminology varies (autistic, individual with autism, autism spectrum disorder, neurodiverse), a controversy that initially seems like word choice, but really drives at a much deeper issue. We are witnessing a shift from normalcy defined by neurotypical traits; visibility of individuals on the spectrum is creating a cultural shift that is changing the notion that neurotypical is the only acceptable brain type. There is a growing appreciation for diversity, and you will see that reflected by struggles with terminology within these pages. We are in an evolution of sorts; please be patient with our terminology as this evolution unfolds.

After a 25-year academic career, I (LH) decided to start a private practice, and indeed, looked on Craigslist for space to set up shop. This was how I met Rachel Bédard. She was extremely serious and had an intensity I was not sure how to interpret; I now know she embodies unbridled energy and passions, and little did I know I would get further swept into the world of autism because of her energy and passions. I say further swept into this world as I have raised a wonderful son who was diagnosed on the spectrum. The world of individualized education programs (IEPs), food selectivity, sensory issues, and watching the amazing brain of a neurodiverse child develop (in spite of his neurotypically focused school system) is not far behind in my life. From this experience I know intensely the struggles family face; I intimately know the hopes of parents that the world truly see the talents of their child, and the hopes that they can develop to their fullest potential. And I understand their concerns when their child or young adult is wracked with anxiety that can impede them from putting one foot in front of the other to reach that potential. I understand the fears that their child may not have friends, and the hopes that they will. This book supports those working with individuals on the autism spectrum and their families, and helps build the community that can make these hopes reality.

Our Request of You, The Reader

One fact about academic books you may not know is that our authors volunteer their writing without renumeration. Know this book is a gift from them to you, in the hopes of bettering treatment for folks on the autism spectrum. We now have a request for you, an opportunity for your own atypical role: if you like what you read, please contact the specific author and tell them that they made a difference. Tweet, blog, skywrite, your call. Please, let this amazing team know that you appreciate the free work they offered this community, their time, their talents, their insights. Let them know it was worth it, because it helped you help a client, a member of the autism community, a family member. We are better together, and kindness and acknowledgment go a long way.

Part I

Individually Focused Treatment

It is vital that therapists know how to engage clients on the autism spectrum and create an effective treatment plan. These clients are often driven to therapy, both figuratively and literally! Adolescents are often brought by their parents, sometimes with the expectation that the therapist will just meet one on one with the adolescent and the parent will be uninvolved, taking a needed break in the waiting room. Other parents, in a twist of developmental irony, will want to be actively part of the treatment team for their *adult* children. Adults may be referred by others who see them struggling, sometimes they self-refer, or they, too, may be brought to therapy by their aging parents. As a therapist, you need to be prepared to connect with and nurture whatever team shows up in your office.

In this part, three experts share their wisdom about individual therapy. You will see that the experts agree that anxiety management, mood management, and social communication development are primary goals, but how each professional engages the client varies. Further, it is clear that some treatment teams intentionally engage parents, while other treatment teams work more directly with the client in a one-on-one setting to build skills. No matter the approach, you will find each author advocates for respect for neurodiversity and crafting a unique, individualized plan of action for the client.

1 Working with Individuals on the Spectrum

Tony Attwood

Autism occurs in approximately one in 59 adolescents and adults (Centers for Disease Control, 2019). Diagnostic criteria imply that someone who has autism will need support and guidance in social communication and interaction, reducing restricted and repetitive patterns of behavior, and coping with sensory sensitivity. Autism is also associated with mood, eating, learning, and personality disorders (Attwood, 2006). While we have the formal diagnostic criteria for autism (American Psychiatric Association, 2013), I have my own description of autism. The term autism describes *someone who has a different way of perceiving, thinking, learning, and relating and discovered interests that are more enjoyable than socializing.* Unfortunately, people who have autism are a minority in a world of social zealots. Those on the autism spectrum can benefit from having a therapist who understands both the challenges brought by their neurodiversity, but also the challenges of their being marginalized by a neurotypical dominant majority.

What Are the Top Concerns When Diagnosed With Autism?

Anxiety

Teenagers and adults who are on the autism spectrum appear to be vulnerable to feeling anxious for much of their day, often experiencing extreme anxiety in anticipation of, or in response to, specific events, such as socializing, sensory experiences such as the sound of a hand dryer, making a mistake, or a change in expected routine. Research has confirmed that an anxiety disorder is the most common mental health problem for adolescents and adults who have autism, with prevalence figures ranging up to 84 percent (Mattila et al., 2010; Van Steensel, Bögels, & Perrin, 2011; White, Oswald, Ollendick, & Scahill, 2009). An Internet survey of over 300 adults with autism indicated that over 98 percent ranked anxiety as the greatest cause of stress in their daily lives, greater than the stress associated with making and keeping friendships and relationships, finding and maintaining employment, and coping with daily living skills (Attwood, Evans, & Lesko, 2014) Sometimes, the level of anxiety may be perceived as actually more disabling than the diagnostic characteristics of autism.

All types of anxiety disorders are more frequent in teenagers and adults with autism in comparison to the typical population (Van Steensel et al., 2011). An assessment of the circumstances associated with, or that create, heightened levels of anxiety for the person who has autism can indicate an intolerance of uncertainty (Neil, Choque Olsson, & Pellicano, 2016; Wigham, Rodgers, South, McConachie, & Freeston, 2015) and a fear of judgment, being targeted for bullying, teasing, rejection, and humiliation, fear of making a mistake, and aversive sensory experiences (Attwood, 2006).

Socializing with peers is perhaps the greatest source of anxiety. Anxiety can frequently be associated with specific social situations, such as those circumstances where there are no apparent or previously experienced social rules, or where the social codes or conventions are being deliberately broken by others.

Depression

There are many reasons why an adolescent or adult with autism may become depressed, including feelings of social isolation, loneliness, and not being respected or valued, as well as internalizing and believing past criticisms. Another reason is the exhaustion experienced due to socializing, trying to manage and often suppress emotions, especially anxiety, and coping with sensory sensitivity. The person is constantly alert and anxious, trying to endure perpetual anxiety with a deficit in emotional resilience and confidence. The mental effort of intellectually analyzing everyday interactions and experiences is draining, and mental energy depletion leads to thoughts and feelings of depression.

The frequent and high level of bullying and humiliation by peers (Maiano, Normand, Salvas, Moullec, & Aime, 2016) can lead adolescents and adults with autism to believe they are indeed defective, and this belief affects how they will perceive themselves and their experiences. There is a heightened sense of self-blame and pessimism, and increased anticipation of a lack of social and academic achievement (Sharma, Woolfson, & Hunter, 2014). Problems with executive function, resulting in a degree of disorganization, can lead to feelings of underachievement, particularly when juxtaposed to the person's intellectual abilities. While typically developing teenagers and adults will have several close friends who can quickly and easily repair their emotions and provide reassurance and evidence that negative self-belief is not true, the isolation and lack of friendships of the person with autism can not only be a cause of depression, but also perpetuate the feelings.

Additional Concerns

Alexithymia

The term alexithymia describes the characteristic of having a diminished vocabulary of words to describe emotions; alexithymia includes struggling to identify one's own emotions as well as the emotions of other people and is a characteristic consistently associated with autism (Berthoz & Hill, 2005; Hill, Berthoz, & Frith, 2004; Milosavljevic et al., 2016; Samson, Huber, & Gross, 2012). Research suggests that the person can identify having an increased level of emotional arousal, but has great difficulty labeling and eloquently describing the level of emotion (Ketelaars, Mol, Swaab, & van Rijn, 2016). When asked how they are feeling at a particular time, or during a particular event, a teenager or adult with autism may reply, "I don't know," which typically means, "I don't know how to tell you." The person may therefore have difficulty telling a therapist how anxious they feel and why they are anxious.

Clinical experience has indicated that those who have autism have a greater eloquence and precision in expressing thoughts and feelings through the arts rather than conversation (Attwood & Garnett, 2016). Art, music, and writing can be used to explore the person's inner world of thoughts and emotions. A strategy that can be used in psychotherapy is to ask the person to create a play list of music with each song expressing the degree of emotion in the music or lyrics. Google Images can be used by asking the person to type a broad definition of a specific thought or feeling, and to select a number of images that eloquently and vividly express their thoughts and feelings. Other options include writing a poem or sending an email where we often observe greater insights through typing rather than talking. For example, if the client is an avid fan of a series of books such as the *Harry Potter* saga, we might ask them to select a passage or chapter that describes a particular thought or feeling; or we might ask them to choose a scene in the movies to describe their thoughts or feelings. Given the pull for musical or visual strengths, the multidisciplinary team could include an art and/or music therapist to aid with this expression.

Self-Identity

The sense of self of typical adolescents and adults is initially based on parental opinions and support, with the sense of self subsequently modified, and potentially reinforced or undermined by adolescent peers. Unfortunately, the sense of self of those with autism is often based on the criticisms and rejection of their adolescent peers rather than their compliments and acceptance. This can result in a propensity for an individual to self-blame and live in anticipation of failure and criticism. A negative self-identity can contribute to low self-esteem and depression. Clinically, when an adult who has autism is asked to "please describe to me who you are," clients with autism often will either be genuinely unable to answer the question or will describe the self in terms of knowledge and expertise rather than social network or personality descriptions.

The Need for a "Village" (Multidisciplinary Team)

Given the myriad of concerns those with autism face, adolescents and adults who have autism will greatly benefit from a multidisciplinary team; it indeed takes a village. Clearly, there is need for psychotherapy in terms of high levels of anxiety or depression and encouraging a positive sense of self. There is also a need for guidance and support in reading non-verbal communication and social cues and conventions, making and keeping friendships, and working effectively in a team at work. These abilities have been studied by psychologists, who may provide programs to improve and enhance specific social skills. However, other disciplines can contribute to achieving greater social skills and social cohesion. A speech language pathologist can focus on the pragmatic aspects of language, especially the art of conversation and prosody. An occupational therapist can focus on coping with sensory sensitivity and any movement disorders associated with autism such as dyspraxia. A psychiatrist can be a valuable member of the team in terms of prescribing and reviewing medication for an anxiety disorder or depression.

Clinical Interventions

With individuals with autism, conventional cognitive behavioral therapy "tools" can be used, such as physical and relaxation activities, and changing perception and thinking to manage emotions. Additionally, in Western cultures, there is a growing recognition by clinicians and academics of the value of awareness activities such as yoga and meditation for increasing self-awareness, as well as promoting a general sense of well-being, and providing an antidote to anxiety. We now have yoga activities specifically developed for those with autism to use at home (Bolls, 2013; Hardy, 2014; Harris, 2018; Mitchell, 2014; Rubio, 2008). Mindfulness is also being used in school settings to regulate attention toward the present moment, to accept and observe emotions, and cultivate an attitude of openness and acceptance using imagery, meditation, and yoga (Conner & White, 2018; De Bruin, Blom, Smit, Van Steensel, & Bögels, 2015).

Therapists can also help clients by aiding in the development of social tools. The strategy is to find, and be with, a person or an animal that can help repair the mood. The social experience will need to be enjoyable and without the stress that can sometimes be associated with socializing, especially when the interaction involves more than one other person. Clinical experience and research have indicated that young adults who have autism have found it easier to relate to other people on the spectrum because of shared understanding and experiences in a relationship in which atypical social behavior and interests are normalized (Sosnowy, Silverman, Shattuck, & Garfield, 2018). The social "tool" may be the creation of a social network of like-minded individuals, perhaps members of an autism support group.

There are social experiences that can actually reduce anxiety, for example, being with someone who accurately "reads" the teenager or adult's emotional state and intuitively knows what to say or do to reassure and calm them. Another social tool, in the broadest sense, is spending time with adoring pets who make the person feel safe. Pets are the best, nonjudgmental listeners and can be more forgiving than humans.

My favorite interventions in psychotherapy are the Emotional Tool Box (Attwood, 2004, 2006; Attwood & Garnett, 2016; Scarpa, Wells, & Attwood, 2012) and Energy Accounting (Attwood & Garnett, 2016), and I regularly utilize them in my clinical practice. The Emotional Tool Box aids clients in replenishing themselves and alleviating anxiety and depressive symptoms. Maja Toudal, an individual with autism, originally created the concept of Energy Accounting to help her cope with her cycles of depression; it is a useful tool to help clients understand how to both guard and replenish energy supplies.

Emotional Tool Box

Autism is associated with having a limited range of emotion repair mechanisms. However, adolescents and adults with autism can learn a broader range of strategies, and these can be conceptualized as acquiring more emotion repair tools. The approach is to identify different types of "tools" to fix the problems associated with anxiety and depression. For example, if a person is feeling socially anxious, we can identify strategies or tools to self-soothe and manage the anxiety in the moment. We can also identify some longer-term strategies that can be employed for social anxiety that may occur in the future. We might consider how to self-soothe, and who to turn to for soothing. Finally, we might identify instances where anxiety is bound to occur, and schedule the use of tools prior to the event, such as scheduling time for meditation or a trip to the gym for exercise prior to the anxiety-provoking event.

The range of tools can be divided into those that quickly and constructively release, or slowly reduce, emotional energy, and those that improve thinking or reduce sensory responsiveness. We can also identify tools that can make the emotions or consequences worse, such as violence, taking drugs, and self-harm.

Energy Accounting

The concept of Energy Accounting by Maja Toudal has been further developed and modified to treat depression in adolescents and adults who

Table 1.1 Energy Accounting: Withdrawals and Deposits

Withdrawal	Deposit
• Socializing	• Solitude
• Change in routine or expectations	• Special interest
• Making a mistake	• Physical activity
• Sensory sensitivity	• Animals and nature
• Coping with anxiety	• Computer games
• Negative thoughts	• Sleep
• Crowds	• Drawing
• Being teased or excluded	• Reading *Harry Potter* books
• Sensitivity to other people's moods	• Listening to music
• Over-analyzing social performance	• Favorite food

have autism (Attwood & Garnett, 2016). The approach is to encourage clients to imagine in their mind an energy bank account and that throughout the day there are withdrawals or deposits of mental energy. Table 1.1 shows possible withdrawals and deposits for someone who has autism; therapists can work with clients to help understand what causes withdrawals and deposits in their energy levels.

The withdrawals and deposits would probably be very different for someone not on the spectrum; for example, socializing and changes to routines and expectations may be perceived as being energizing and exciting. In the next stage of Energy Accounting, the client makes a list of their personal daily withdrawals and deposits and writes each type of withdrawal or deposit, as in Table 1.2.

There is the creation of a form of "currency", that is, a numerical measure or value of how much an activity or experience is mental energy draining or refreshing from day to day. For example, on some days, socializing can drain energy at a value of around 20 but on other days this could be 100. The client then adds all the numerical values in each of the two columns to see if their energy bank balance at the end of the day is in debit or credit, and determine if the account is in the "black" or the "red." If it is in the black, with more mental energy deposits than withdrawals, this is good energy accounting, and the person will have energy reserves and be more able to cope with energy-draining experiences over the next few days. If the account is in the red, with more withdrawals than deposits, the client will need to achieve more energy "income" over the next few days. If a healthy mental energy bank balance is not maintained, there will be an increase in the depth and duration of lethargy and depression.

Table 1.2 Energy Accounting: Personal Daily Withdrawals

Ledger Energy Account

Withdrawals		Deposits	
Activity/Experience	**(0–100)**	**Activity/Experience**	**(0–100)**
Grocery shopping	80	Looking up facts about the next eclipse	100
Returning a phone call	20	Video games	80
Returning an email	10	Time to think about my family	20
		Time with my cat	45

Strategies for Difficult or Unengaged Clients

One of the diagnostic characteristics of autism is a resistance to change and extreme distress at small changes (American Psychiatric Association, 2013). We know that people with autism generally prefer consistency and predictability. However, psychotherapy is based on the principle of accepting and benefiting from a change in perception and thinking. Thus, there may be resistance to believing that change can be a positive experience and should be embraced.

There can also be the issue of motivation to engage in therapy and it is important to explore the value system of the client. A potentially strong value system for those who have autism is intelligence. We sometimes find that appealing to a client's intellectual strength (rather than the altruistic desire to please the therapist) is more effective at increasing motivation for therapy and readiness for change.

Motivation can also be enhanced by incorporating a special interest in the therapy, such as an encyclopedic knowledge and enjoyment talking about Doctor Who. Therapy about managing anxiety can use the metaphor of Doctor Who encountering an alien on another planet who creates fear in humans to be able to manipulate and enslave them. The psychotherapist can ask the client, "What would Doctor Who do when encountering an alien that wants him to feel fear?" This strategy would achieve and maintain interest, and facilitate conceptualization and coping strategies.

Not to Erase Their Autism

Psychotherapy can alleviate the signs of an anxiety disorder and depression, but there is also the issue of self-identity. A valuable component of psychotherapy is to explore the positive attributes of autism and the client's qualities in their personality and abilities.

A diary can be used to record examples of achievements due to autism and the demonstration of personality qualities such as being kind and brave. Psychotherapy can be used to encourage self-acceptance and achieve greater resilience. The intention is to define autism by specific strengths such as determination, acquiring knowledge, pattern recognition, and innovative thinking, and to constructively use those strengths in psychotherapy and everyday life.

Summary

Common concerns faced by clients with autism include anxiety and depression, as well as alexithymia and self-identity issues. There are a range of modifications to psychotherapy that therapists can make to better accommodate the characteristics of autism. Changes therapist can make include accommodating the learning profile associated with autism (Attwood & Scarpa, 2013), enhancing rapport by having a positive conceptualization of autism, highlighting strengths and talents, avoiding idioms and figures of speech and not being offended by, and indeed grateful, when the person who has autism corrects your errors. By focusing on client strengths, building a multidisciplinary team, and being an advocate for neurodiversity, psychotherapists can be extremely important catalysts for better living with autism.

Recommended Resources for Professionals and Families

- Gaus, V. (2019). *Cognitive-behavioral therapy for adults with autism spectrum disorder* (2nd ed.). New York, NY: The Guilford Press.
- Greg, A., & Mackay, T. (2013). *The Homunculi approach to social and emotional wellbeing*. London, UK: Jessica Kingsley Publishers.
- *Ask Dr Tony*: YouTube videos for information and advice on a range of issues and therapy associated with autism.
- The CAT-kit to facilitate the communication of emotions: www.cat-kit.com/en-gb
- The Secret Agent Society to encourage social and emotional resilience: www.sst-institute.net

About the Author

Dr. Attwood is a clinical psychologist whose original qualifications were achieved in England and who now lives in Queensland, Australia. He has specialized in autism spectrum disorders since 1975, and achieved a PhD from the University of London in 1984. He currently works in private practice and is Adjunct Professor at Griffith University Queensland. His book *Asperger's Syndrome: A Guide for Parents and Professionals*, published in 1998, became the seminal book on Asperger's syndrome and his subsequent book, *The Complete Guide to Asperger's Syndrome*, published in 2006, has become the primary text book on Asperger's syndrome. He is the senior consultant at the Minds and Hearts clinic in Brisbane, Australia.

References

American Psychiatric Association. (2013). *Diagnostic and statistical manual of mental disorders* (5th ed.). Washington, DC: Author.

Attwood, T. (2004). *Exploring feelings: Cognitive behaviour therapy to manage anxiety.* Arlington, TX: Future Horizons.

Attwood, T. (2006). *The complete guide to Asperger's syndrome.* London, UK: Jessica Kingsley Publishers.

Attwood, T., Evans, C., & Lesko, A. (2014). *Been there. done that. try this!: An Aspie's guide to life on earth.* London, UK: Jessica Kingsley Publishers.

Attwood, T., & Garnett, M. (2016). *Exploring depression, and beating the blues: A CBT self-help guide to understanding and coping with depression in Asperger's syndrome [ASD-Level 1].* London, UK: Jessica Kingsley Publishers.

Attwood, T., & Scarpa, A. (2013). Modifications of cognitive-behavioral therapy for children and adolescents with high-functioning autism and their common difficulties. In A. Scarpa, S. W. White, & T. Attwood (Eds.), *CBT for children and adolescents with high-functioning autism spectrum disorders* (pp. 27–44). New York, NY: Guilford Press.

Berthoz, S., & Hill, E. L. (2005). The validity of using self-reports to assess emotion regulation abilities in adults with autism spectrum disorder. *European Psychiatry, 20*(3), 291–298. doi:10.1016/j.eurpsy.2004.06.013.

Bolls, U. D. (2013). *Meditation for Aspies: Everyday techniques to help people with Asperger syndrome take control and improve their lives.* London, UK: Jessica Kingsley Publishers.

Centers for Disease Control and Prevention. (2019). Prevalence and characteristics of autism spectrum disorder among children aged 4 years—Early autism and developmental disabilities monitoring network, Seven Sites, United States, 2010, 2012, and 2014. *Surveillance Summaries, 68*(2), 1–19. doi:10.15585/mmwr.ss6802a1.

Conner, C. M., & White, S. W. (2018). Brief report: Feasibility and preliminary efficacy of individual mindfulness therapy for adults with autism spectrum disorder. *Journal of Autism and Developmental Disorders, 48*(1), 290–300. doi:10.1007/s10803-017-3312-0.

De Bruin, E. I., Blom, R., Smit, F. M., Van Steensel, F. J., & Bögels, S. M. (2015). MYmind: Mindfulness training for youngsters with autism spectrum disorders and their parents. *Autism, 19*(8), 906–914. doi:10.1177/1362361314553279.

Hardy, S. T. (2014). *Asanas for Autism and special needs: Yoga to help children with their emotions, self-regulation and body awareness.* London, UK: Jessica Kingsley Publishers.

Harris, R. L. (2018). *Contemplative therapy for clients on the Autism Spectrum.* London, UK: Jessica Kingsley Publishers.

Hill, E., Berthoz, S., & Frith, U. (2004). Brief report: Cognitive processing of own emotions in individuals with autistic spectrum disorder and in their relatives. *Journal of Autism & Developmental Disorders, 34*(2), 229–235. doi:10.1023/B: JADD.0000022613.41399.14.

Ketelaars, M. P., Mol, A., Swaab, H., & van Rijn, S. (2016). Emotion recognition and alexithymia in high functioning females with autism spectrum disorder. *Research in Autism Spectrum Disorders, 21*, 51–60. doi:10.1016/j. rasd.2015.09.006.

Maiano, C., Normand, C. L., Salvas, M.-C., Moullec, G., & Aime, A. (2016). Prevalence of school bullying among youth with autism spectrum disorders: A systematic review and meta-analysis. *Autism Research, 9*(6), 601–615. doi:10.1002/aur.1568.

Mattila, M. L., Hurtig, T., Haapsamo, H., Jussila, K., Kuusikko-Gauffin, S., Kielinen, M., & Pauls, D. L. (2010). Comorbid psychiatric disorders associated with Asperger syndrome/high-functioning autism: A community-and clinic-based study. *Journal of Autism & Developmental Disorders, 40*(9), 1080–1093. doi:10.1007/ s10803-010-0958-2.

Milosavljevic, B., Leno, V. C., Simonoff, E., Baird, G., Pickles, A., Jones, C. R. G., ... Happé, F. (2016). Alexithymia in adolescents with autism spectrum disorder: Its relationship to internalising difficulties, sensory modulation and social cognition. *Journal of Autism & Developmental Disorders, 46*(4), 1354–1367. doi:10.1007/s10803-015-2670-8.

Mitchell, C. (2014). *Mindful living with Asperger's syndrome: Everyday mindfulness practices to help you tune in to the present moment.* London, UK: Jessica Kingsley Publishers.

Neil, L., Choque Olsson, N., & Pellicano, E. (2016). The relationship between intolerance of uncertainty, sensory sensitivities, and anxiety in autistic and typically developing children. *Journal of Autism & Developmental Disorders, 46*(6), 1962–1973. doi:10.1007/s10803-016-2721-9.

Rubio, R. (2008). *Mind/body techniques for Asperger's syndrome.* London, UK: Jessica Kingsley Publishers.

Samson, A. C., Huber, O., & Gross, J. J. (2012). Emotion regulation in Asperger's syndrome and high-functioning autism. *Emotion, 12*(4), 659–665. doi:10.1037/ a0027975.

Scarpa, A., Wells, A., & Attwood, T. (2012). *Exploring feelings for young children with high-functioning autism or Asperger's disorder: The STAMP treatment manual.* London, UK: Jessica Kingsley Publishers.

Sharma, S., Woolfson, L. M., & Hunter, S. C. (2014). Maladaptive cognitive appraisals in children with high-functioning autism: Associations with fear, anxiety and theory of mind. *Autism, 18*(3), 244–254. doi:10.1177/1362361312472556.

Sosnowy, C., Silverman, C., Shattuck, P., & Garfield, T. (2018). Setbacks and successes: How young adults on the autism spectrum seek friendship. *Autism in Adulthood, 1*(1), 1–8.

Van Steensel, F. J., Bögels, S. M., & Perrin, S. (2011). Anxiety disorders in children and adolescents with autistic spectrum disorders: A meta-analysis. *Clinical Child & Family Psychology Review, 14*(3), 302–317. doi:10.1007/s10567-011-0097-0.

White, S. W., Oswald, D., Ollendick, T., & Scahill, L. (2009). Anxiety in children and adolescents with autism spectrum disorders. *Clinical Psychology Review, 29*(3), 216–229. doi:10.1016/j.cpr.2009.01.003.

Wigham, S., Rodgers, J., South, M., McConachie, H., & Freeston, M. (2015). The interplay between sensory processing abnormalities, intolerance of uncertainty, anxiety and restricted and repetitive behaviours in autism spectrum disorder. *Journal of Autism & Developmental Disorders, 45*(4), 943–952. doi:10.1007/s10803-014-2248-x.

2 Challenging and Rewarding

Individual Psychotherapy for Adults and Adolescents with Autism

Brea M. Banks

Twenty-five-year-old Robert arrived with his mother for his first psychotherapy session. They were 30 minutes early so Robert could check out the clinic. Robert paced back and forth in the waiting area and asked the receptionist multiple questions. Robert's new therapist greeted them in the waiting room two minutes late. Robert looked down at the floor, grunted at the therapist, and walked slowly as the three made their way to the therapist's office. With prompting from his mother, Robert explained, "I'm not going to be able to come here any more. You were late." The therapist replied, "Thanks for telling me how you feel. I know that can be difficult when we're angry or disappointed. I'm sorry that I was late. Is there anything else you'd like to share before we get started?" His mother smiled because she knew Robert was wrong: This therapist was going to be a perfect fit!

Given the diverse needs of those diagnosed with autism, individuals may engage in many forms of treatment such as speech therapy, occupational therapy, applied behavior analysis therapy, and psychotherapy. Individual psychotherapy is often one of the first appointments for clients with autism, allowing therapists to set the tone for future interventions and a subsequent treatment team. Individuals diagnosed with autism often present with co-occurring or comorbid psychiatric disorders (e.g., depression), medical problems (e.g., seizures), and learning deficits (e.g., intellectual disability) that are sometimes the focus of therapy, and if not, must at least be considered (Doepke, Banks, Mays, Toby, & Landau, 2014). Service providers must bear in mind the intersections of systems that influence functioning, including family, school, work, and community and the multiple identities clients hold outside of their identification as an individual diagnosed with autism, as these identities together influence an individual's functioning across settings.

Intake

During my clinical practice, I most often encounter clientele on the spectrum presenting with the following concerns: anxiety, independent living and major life transitions, deficits in academic/occupational functioning, and difficulties with behavior and social relationships. Further, the techniques and strategies I discuss are most applicable to individuals who demonstrate well-developed verbal skills. Although psychotherapy can be beneficial for individuals with less advanced language abilities, these services more typically focus on the engagement of family and caretakers.

Establishing Rapport

Although it is imperative that clinicians utilize evidenced-based interventions when working with those on the autism spectrum, research suggests that therapeutic alliance offers greater contributions to fostering change in clients (Lambert & Barley, 2001). Because clients with autism may enter therapy with greater reservations, have difficulties with social interactions, be limited in their language skills, and have rigid thinking patterns, it is even more important for those counseling individuals with autism to focus on the development of the therapeutic relationship at the onset of therapy and as sessions progress. Clinicians may find that engagement in conversations about restricted interests, validation of client experiences and interpretations of difficult social interactions, scheduled breaks during session, and appropriate use of reinforcers are ways to foster alliance and trust in therapy. Clinicians working with those on the autism spectrum must be patient, as meeting treatment goals may involve the use of more resources (e.g., social stories, visual schedules), and therefore may take longer to accomplish. Although engagement in psychotherapy may be challenging because of social skills deficits, difficulties with flexibility, and so forth, I have found that successful psychotherapy with this population is more satisfying and rewarding than any other clinical experience.

Establishing rapport and a working alliance is also important with clients on the spectrum because of the difficulties clients may have with meeting new people, transitions, establishing new routines, and the overall work that is required in therapy. Further, any prior negative experiences with service providers or psychotherapy may make it difficult for individuals diagnosed with autism to reinitiate services. Initial psychotherapy sessions should involve the usual gathering of data surrounding presenting concerns, relevant developmental and medical history, and prior engagement in therapeutic services and goals for therapy. Clinicians working with individuals diagnosed with autism must always consider the developmental functioning of their clients, particularly relevant to expressive and receptive verbal language skills. Asking several questions, using imprecise or vague language, and expecting answers that neurotypically developing individuals would provide will likely produce frustration from clients. Nonetheless, questions that may be helpful during intake with individuals on the autism spectrum include questions around assessment of previous therapy experiences, and the intersectionality of the autism diagnosis with the client's other identities.

Assessment of Previous Therapy Experiences

First, in an effort to be mindful about clients' previous negative experiences in psychotherapy, clinicians might ask clients to discuss what has and has not worked previously in therapy so that they might disclose any issues they have had. This provides clinicians insight into clients' reservations about the therapeutic process; it also presents the opportunity to validate clients' feelings about prior experiences in therapy. Obviously, it is important for clinicians to refrain from expressing that therapy will be completely different from services they have engaged in previously, although clinicians may reassure clients that they will actively consider the shortcomings of their prior experiences when treatment planning. Further, some clients may enter therapy hoping that they will be cured, so clinicians must clearly state that therapy is intended to reduce symptoms and improve functioning, rather than providing a "cure" for autism.

Intersectionality of Autism with Other Identities

Clinicians might ask clients to consider how their diagnosis of autism spectrum disorder and their identification with other underrepresented groups (e.g., racial/ethnic background, sexual orientation, gender experience) impact their daily functioning. This question is often confusing, even for neurotypically developing clients, so clinicians might follow up with more pointed questions, such as, "Do things like your gender, race, sexuality, or religion impact your life? Just like having autism, being a certain race or gender can be difficult when other people treat you differently because of them." If this prompt does not offer clarity, clinicians might be more specific: "When others talk about you, should they say he, she, or they?," "Have you ever had a boyfriend or a girlfriend?," "Do people treat you differently because you have autism?," or "Do you practice a particular religion?" These questions can spark discussion surrounding client experiences as members of underrepresented groups, with particular focus on their identification as a person with autism.

Theoretical Orientation

In my own practice with individuals on the autism spectrum, behavioral and solution-focused orientations to therapy have been effective in fostering change in client behavior, especially when independent living is the referral concern. In these cases, I often foster conversations surrounding the clients' desires for change, collect and examine data, use immediate feedback for adaptive and maladaptive behavior, provide opportunities for multiple learning trials, and use schedules and visual aids. Consider the following case example:

> *Twenty-one-year-old Brad is a high school graduate living at home with his parents. During the intake interview with Brad and his parents, the clinician asks targeted questions to assess Brad's motivation to change, such as: "If you were to wake up and everything in your life was perfect, what would be different?" Brad answers: "I wish that I was able to live on my own," suggesting that he is ready to change, so goals are set to foster greater independence so that Brad may eventually obtain his own apartment. Specifically, the clinician and family agree that it would be beneficial for Brad to start with doing his laundry, shopping for his own groceries, and preparing his own meals. Given these goals, the clinician gathers data surrounding the baseline occurrences of these behaviors, barriers that make engagement in the preferred tasks difficult, and reinforcers and rewards that may produce adaptive behavior. Specifically, the clinician asks targeted questions during the session, such as, "Who usually does your laundry?," "What would make it easier for you to prepare your own meals?," and "Can you think of a reward you might like from your parents or me when you meet your goals?," and encourages Brad to think about and log his engagement in the given behaviors over the course of the week prior to the next session.*
>
> *Given the clinician's interpretation of the data and an assessment of Brad's motivation for change, they work together to establish the following attainable goals that are offered as homework in between sessions. Brad is to create a list of grocery items he would like to buy, go to the grocery store with a parent but shop for items and check out independently, study the bus schedule and/or download a rideshare application on his phone, use the bus schedule or rideshare application to travel to and from the grocery store with a parent, travel to the grocery store and shop independently. The clinician and Brad collaborate to develop schedules and/or visual aids that will help Brad complete tasks.*
>
> *Given Brad's interest in technology, he decides that it will be helpful to set a daily alarm on his cell phone that reminds him to do his therapy homework. He also decides to use his phone to develop a grocery list and to learn how to use rideshare applications. Continued collaboration with Brad's parents is essential, as the clinician will be unable to provide immediate feedback for Brad's behavior. With Brad's permission, his goals and assignments for the week are shared with his parents, and they are encouraged to provide daily reminders of the homework if Brad forgets and praise when they notice his engagement with the assigned homework,*

> *such as saying things like, "Great job doing your work for therapy." In session, the clinician also provides feedback for Brad's behavior and may provide small rewards when he meets goals, such as spending the last 10 minutes of the session watching YouTube videos.*

The amount of time spent in therapy on these tasks will vary, depending on the client's level of functioning and commitment to achieving the goals set forth. Individuals with autism may benefit from additional practice opportunities, so it is important that Brad's clinician not progress until Brad has mastered each skill.

Clients with autism attending therapy for internalizing concerns, such as anxiety and depression, may benefit from techniques, such as cognitive behavioral therapy (CBT), that help them recognize how distorted cognitions and emotional distress directly influence behaviors (Hofmann, Asnaani, Vonk, Sawyer, & Fang, 2012). Adaptations to CBT are made to best treat symptoms of autism. Consider the following case example, where CBT is adapted to best fit the client's needs.

> *Sherree is a 37-year-old woman diagnosed with autism who attends therapy to address her anxious symptomology. Her therapist decides to adapt CBT to address her faulty thinking patterns. For example, when providing psychoeducation to facilitate cognitive restructuring around identifying and refuting irrational thoughts, her therapist uses visual prompts and modeling. Specifically, the clinician uses handouts whenever she introduces a new concept. For example, a CBT triangle depicting the connection between thoughts, feelings, and behaviors is used as a visual tool for Sherree. The therapist then talks through several examples of how to apply the concepts. The clinician employs task analysis by dividing complex behaviors (e.g., diaphragmatic breathing) into manageable steps and prompt hierarchies to produce adaptive behaviors in session. For example, when introducing diaphragmatic breathing, significant time is first spent with Sherree in getting her to sit or lay comfortably with her eyes closed before introducing the breathing.*

In Sherree's example, the clinician is using a "prompt hierarchy," whereby the clinician first provides a great deal of verbalizations and physical prompts to help the client achieve the sought-out behaviors. As the client obtains mastery, these prompts are faded. Clinicians who are familiar with CBT may develop their own adaptations that fit the specific needs of their clients.

Summary

Psychotherapy can be effective for individuals with autism when clinicians are intentional about their selected interventions and recognize the importance of rapport and working alliance. Further, a holistic approach to learning about clients and their needs is essential, as autism spectrum disorder diagnosis is a characteristic an individual holds in conjunction with multiple intersecting identities. Although associated symptoms may present as challenging in most settings, clinicians who view difficulties from a strengths perspective will more likely see success in using such behaviors to foster change. These clinicians enter therapy with patience (e.g., waiting several seconds before repeating a prompt), consistency (e.g., use of the same language among clinicians), and in tune with their own reactions to difficult behavior (e.g., taking breaks when necessary), and find small victories most rewarding.

Recommended Resources for Professionals

- Scarpa, A., White, S. W., & Attwood, T. (Eds.). (2013). *CBT for children and adolescents with high-functioning autism spectrum disorders.* New York, NY: Guilford Press.
- Wood, J. J., Drahota, A., Sze, K., Van Dyke, M., Decker, K., Fujii, C., ... Spiker, M. (2009). Brief report: Effects of cognitive behavioral therapy on parent-reported autism symptoms in school-age children with high-functioning autism. *Journal of Autism and Developmental Disorders, 39*(11), 1608–1612. doi:10.1007/s10803-009-0791-7

Recommended Resources for Families

- The Autism Program of Illinois: www.tap-illinois.org/
- The National Autism Center: www.nationalautismcenter.org/

About the Author

Brea M. Banks, Ph.D. is a Licensed Clinical Psychologist and an Assistant Professor of Psychology at Illinois State University. Prior to her current position, she worked in private practice conducting psychological assessments and providing psychotherapy services. At the same time, she worked at a university counseling center, where she primarily engaged in therapy with students from underrepresented backgrounds. During her training and work in private practice, Dr. Banks has been dedicated to serving individuals with autism and their families. Her research interests include the cognitive consequences of microaggression and student of color experiences in higher education, while she has also published material focused on autism and other topics. Her teaching interests include cognitive assessment, multicultural counseling, and diversity in psychology. In her spare time, she and her spouse enjoy introducing sports and strategy games to their infant daughter and exploring the outdoors with their pup.

References

Doepke, K. J., Banks, B. M., Mays, J. F., Toby, L. M., & Landau, S. (2014). Co-occurring emotional and behavior problems in children with autism spectrum disorders. In L. Wilkinson (Ed.), *Autism spectrum disorders in children and adolescence: Evidence-based assessment and intervention in schools* (pp. 125–148). Washington, DC: American Psychological Association.

Hofmann, S. G., Asnaani, A., Vonk, I. J., Sawyer, A. T., & Fang, A. (2012). The efficacy of cognitive behavioral therapy: A review of meta-analyses. *Cognitive Therapy and Research, 36*(5), 427–440. doi:10.1007/s10608-012-9476-1

Lambert, M. J., & Barley, D. E. (2001). Research summary on the therapeutic relationship and psychotherapy outcome. *Psychotherapy: Theory, Research, Practice, Training, 38*(4), 357. doi:10.1037/0033-3204.38.4.357

3 Social Skills Treatment for Adolescents and Adults on the Autism Spectrum

Deanna Dow and Elizabeth Laugeson

> *Nathaniel is a 16-year-old adolescent boy with autism who was referred to our clinic by his individual therapist due to problems getting along with peers at school, lack of close friendships, and limited understanding of social cues and rules. He had a history of being teased and bullied, and he often expressed frustration over unintended conflict with classmates, as he never understood what he did wrong or why they reacted negatively to him. He reported that high schoolers were like "aliens," and he did not even know how to start a conversation with them. These difficulties led to the development of significant anxiety and avoidance of social situations; he hid in a band practice room during lunch every day so he would not have to interact with peers. His awareness of his social difficulties had also contributed to increasingly depressed mood, and Nathaniel had begun engaging in self-injurious behavior to cope with his low self-esteem, sadness, and frustration. Though he was taking all AP classes and had career aspirations to be a neurophysicist, his mother worried that he would be unable to cope with the stresses of attending college, living with a roommate, taking care of himself independently, and eventually holding a steady job.*

Nathaniel is only one example of a client we may see at the UCLA Program for the Education and Enrichment of Relationship Skills (PEERS®) Clinic, though his struggles are unfortunately not unique, given the social deficits that are characteristic of individuals with autism. Social impairment often remains a challenge over the lifespan, regardless of intellectual functioning or language abilities (Carter, Davis, Klin, & Volkmar, 2005). Social deficits rarely improve as a result of development or maturation alone (White, Keonig, & Scahill, 2007); in fact, they often worsen as youth transition into adolescence and adulthood as the complexity of social situations increases (Barnhill, 2007; Howlin, 2000). This may partially explain why symptom reduction commonly seen across childhood slows as individuals with autism reach adulthood (Taylor & Seltzner, 2010).

Autism is a spectrum disorder affecting individuals across a wide array of abilities from intellectually gifted to intellectually disabled. Arguably, social difficulties may be even more pronounced in adults with autism without intellectual disability (Taylor & Seltzner, 2010). Interestingly, those with less severe symptomatology and higher intelligence have an increased risk of experiencing social isolation, withdrawal, victimization, anxiety, and depression (Shtayermann, 2007; Sterling, Dawson, Estes, & Greenson, 2008). Because it is generally not socially acceptable to tease or bully someone who is visibly disabled, individuals with subtler, "camouflaged" deficits, who may seem "odd" rather than disabled, are at even greater risk for peer rejection (Laugeson, 2013). In addition, increased awareness of one's social differences, which is more characteristic of individuals without cognitive delays, likely contributes to greater anxiety and depression (Sterling et al., 2008). Moreover, adults with average or above-average intelligence are more likely than those with intellectual disabilities to be socially isolated, perhaps because they have fewer structured daily activities outside of the home, such as day programs or vocational training (Taylor & Seltzer, 2011). Although these individuals may have the skills and capability to meaningfully contribute in a work setting, adequate vocational support is rarely provided (Liptak, Kennedy, & Dosa, 2011).

Importance of Social Skills Treatment in a Comprehensive Treatment Program

Social deficits often lead to a range of concerns, including peer rejection, lack of social support, social isolation, loneliness, poorer quality of friendships, victimization through teasing or bullying, academic and occupational problems, and subsequent development of anxiety and mood disorders (Bauminger & Kasari, 2000; Capps, Sigman, & Yirmiya, 1995; Chamberlain, Kasari, & Rotheram-Fuller, 2007; Humphrey & Symes, 2010; Rao, Beidel, & Murray, 2008), as we saw in Nathaniel's case. Thus, it is of critical importance that adolescents and adults build their social competence as social demands and expectations increase. For this reason, social skills programs are a critical component of a comprehensive treatment plan for individuals with autism.

Social skills training is not only critical for improving current psychosocial functioning, but enhanced social skills may have longstanding positive implications to prevent or reduce future concerns (Spence, 2003). Evidence of good social functioning and sufficient social support is associated with better quality of life (Jennes-Coussens, Magill-Evans, & Koning, 2006) and increased involvement in social and recreational activities (Orsmond, Krauss, & Seltzer, 2004) in adults with autism. Having at least one close friend is also associated with improved self-esteem, greater independence, better adjustment, and decreased anxiety and depression (Buhrmester, 1990). Therefore, development and maintenance of reciprocal, supportive relationships should be prioritized in treatment for adolescents and adults with autism.

Considerations Regarding Intrinsic Motivation for Social Skills Treatment

Given that social interest and motivation vary in adolescents and adults with autism, it is important to ensure that individuals are open to learning social skills before embarking on treatment. For those who are not intrinsically motivated to learn social rules and customs, it may be helpful to discuss their understanding of why having good social skills will be necessary for their future goals and plans (e.g., attending college, living independently, obtaining and maintaining employment, making and keeping friends, or developing and maintaining romantic relationships). Individuals with autism may also have greater discomfort approaching new treatment settings; therefore, providing detailed information about what to expect may further encourage participation in social skills treatment. However, it is important to note that including those who are reluctant to participate could significantly impact their engagement and progress in treatment and lead to lack of group cohesion and higher attrition (Laugeson & Frankel, 2010). Additionally, under the lens of neurodiversity, one might argue that forcing social skills on someone uninterested in learning these skills would not only be futile, it may be unethical. Therefore, it is not recommended that adolescents and adults with autism be included in social skills training unless they convey willingness to engage in treatment.

Effective Treatment Delivery Strategies

While it is clear that social skills are an important treatment target for youth with autism, research suggests that most established social skills interventions demonstrate unclear or minimal treatment effects (Rao et al., 2008; White et al., 2007). Therefore, it is critically important to utilize an evidence-based approach when teaching social skills. Certain treatment strategies have been shown to promote more meaningful and successful social outcomes, including the use of behavioral methods of teaching, naturalistic techniques incorporated into everyday social settings, parent involvement, group treatment, and visual supports (Reichow & Volkmar, 2010). More specifically, effective social skills treatment delivery might include key ingredients, such as: (1) modeling and role play demonstrations of targeted social skills; (2) behavioral rehearsal practice exercises; (3) performance feedback through social coaching in a small-group setting; (4) use of scripts and social stories; (5) use of multimedia software; (6) video modeling; and (7) self-monitoring and self-management (i.e., recognition and modification of one's own behavior; Laugeson & Ellingsen, 2014).

It is also essential to teach ecologically valid social skills, which are behaviors exhibited by individuals who are socially accepted and successful. Social skills instruction is often based on what adults *think* is appropriate, rather than behaviors that are *actually used* by the dominant peer group. For example, many adults tell individuals to deal with teasing by ignoring the person, walking away, or telling an adult. In reality, typically developing teens handle this situation very differently by giving a short comeback that suggests what the teaser said did not bother them, such as comments like, "*Whatever,*" or "*And your point is?*" or "*Am I supposed to care?*" (Laugeson, 2014, 2017; Laugeson & Frankel, 2010). Teaching behaviors that deviate from social norms is problematic and ineffective if the goal is for the individual to be accepted and interact successfully within their peer group.

It is also important to focus on socially valid skills, or those that will meaningfully improve quality of life. Some essential social skills for adolescents and adults may include: (1) initiating and maintaining reciprocal conversations in order to develop meaningful relationships; (2) expanding one's social network; (3) promoting more successful peer interactions, leading to higher-quality relationships; (4) improving competence at handling peer rejection and conflict; (5) enhancing understanding of verbal and nonverbal social cues; (6) teaching perspective-taking to improve social cognition and emotion recognition; (7) changing one's bad reputation within the current peer group; and (8) improving emotion regulation in order to more effectively handle social conflict and rejection (Laugeson & Ellingsen, 2014). However, cognitive abilities, functioning level, and client goals should always be considered in treatment, as not all skills will be relevant for all individuals.

The PEERS Method

PEERS is an evidence-based social skills program that utilizes principles from cognitive behavioral therapy (CBT) to teach skills necessary for making and keeping friends and managing peer conflict and peer rejection (Laugeson & Park, 2014). It has been shown to improve social outcomes of adolescents and adults with autism across over two dozen clinical trials, as evidenced by significant improvements in overt social skills, frequency of peer interactions, and social responsiveness (Gantman, Kapp, Orenski, & Laugeson, 2012; Laugeson, Gantman, Kapp, Orenski, & Ellingsen, 2015; Schohl et al., 2013; Van Hecke et al., 2015). Long-term follow-up further shows that adolescents who participated in PEERS maintained treatment gains one to five years post-intervention (Mandelberg et al., 2014).

Summary

PEERS is one of the only empirically supported social skills programs for youth with autism that includes published treatment manuals for dissemination (Laugeson, 2014; Laugeson & Frankel, 2010). This international program is used in over 70 countries and has been translated into over a dozen languages. PEERS manuals are widely available and certified trainings are offered regularly for mental health providers and educators who are interested in learning how to implement the program into their clinical practice. With adolescence and adulthood known to be a time of great social change and increased social demand, the need for effective social skills interventions for youth with autism is critical in order for these individuals to lead healthy and successful lives.

Resources for Professionals

- Laugeson, E. A., & Frankel, F. (2010). *Social skills for teenagers with developmental and autism spectrum disorder: The PEERS treatment manual.* New York, NY: Routledge.
- Laugeson, E. A. (2014). *The PEERS® curriculum for school-based professionals: Social skills training for adolescents with autism spectrum disorder.* New York, NY: Routledge.
- Laugeson, E. A. (2017). *PEERS® for young adults: Social skills training for adults with autism spectrum disorder and other social challenges.* New York, NY: Routledge.
- To access the PEERS® library of role play videos and for information about certified training opportunities: www.semel.ucla.edu/peers/

Resources for Families

- Laugeson, E. A. (2013). *The science of making friends: Helping socially challenged teens and young adults.* San Francisco, CA: Jossey-Bass.
- To find a PEERS Certified Provider in your area: www.semel.ucla.edu/peers/certified-providers

About the Authors

Dr. Deanna Dow is a Postdoctoral Clinical Psychology Fellow and Clinical Instructor in the Department of Psychiatry and Biobehavioral Sciences at the UCLA Semel Institute for Neuroscience and Human Behavior. Dr. Dow has 15 years of experience working with individuals with autism and other neurodevelopmental disorders through assessment, intervention, and educational and research programs, and she has a particular interest in parent-mediated intervention for individuals with autism. Dr. Dow may be contacted at ddow@mednet.ucla.edu.

Dr. Elizabeth Laugeson is co-developer of the evidence-based social skills intervention for teens and young adults known as PEERS and the Founder and Director of the UCLA PEERS Clinic. Dr. Laugeson is a licensed clinical psychologist and Associate Clinical Professor in the Department of Psychiatry and Biobehavioral Sciences at the UCLA Semel Institute for Neuroscience and Human Behavior. She has been a principal investigator and collaborator on a number of studies funded by the National Institutes of Health and Centers for Disease Control and Prevention investigating social skills training for youth with autism spectrum disorder and other social challenges. Dr. Laugeson may be contacted through the UCLA PEERS Clinic at peersclinic@ucla.edu.

References

Barnhill, G. P. (2007). Outcomes in adults with Asperger syndrome. *Focus on Autism and Other Developmental Disabilities, 22*(2), 116–126. doi:10.1177/10883576070220020301

Bauminger, N., & Kasari, C. (2000). Loneliness and friendship in high-functioning children with autism. *Child Development, 71*(2), 447–456. doi:10.1111/1467-8624.00156

Buhrmester, D. (1990). Intimacy of friendship, interpersonal competence, and adjustment during preadolescence and adolescence. *Child Development, 61*(4), 1101–1111. doi:10.2307/1130878

Capps, L., Sigman, M., & Yirmiya, N. (1995). Self-competence and emotional understanding in high-functioning children with autism. *Development and Psychopathology, 7*(1), 137–149. doi:10.1017/S0954579400006386

Carter, A. S., Davis, N. O., Klin, A., & Volkmar, F. R. (2005). Social development in autism. In F. R. Volkmar, R. Paul, A. Klin, & D. Cohen (Eds.), *Handbook of autism and pervasive developmental disorders: Vol. 1. diagnosis, development, neurobiology, and behavior* (pp. 312–334). Hoboken, NJ: Wiley.

Chamberlain, B., Kasari, C., & Rotheram-Fuller, E. (2007). Involvement or isolation? The social networks of children with autism in regular classrooms. *Journal of Autism and Developmental Disorders, 37*(2), 230–242. doi:10.1007/s10803-006-0164-4

Gantman, A., Kapp, S. K., Orenski, K., & Laugeson, E. A. (2012). Social skills training for young adults with high-functioning autism spectrum disorders: A randomized controlled pilot study. *Journal of Autism and Developmental Disorders, 42*(6), 1094–1103. doi:10.1007/s10803-011-1350-6

Howlin, P. (2000). Outcome in adult life for more able individuals with autism or Asperger syndrome. *Autism, 4*(1), 63–83. doi:10.1177/1362361300004001005

Humphrey, N., & Symes, W. (2010). Perceptions of social support and experience of bullying among pupils with autistic spectrum disorders in mainstream secondary schools. *European Journal of Special Needs Education, 25*(1), 77–91. doi:10.1080/08856250903450855

Jennes-Coussens, M., Magill-Evans, J., & Koning, C. (2006). The quality of life of young men with Asperger syndrome: A brief report. *Autism, 10*(4), 403–414. doi:10.1177/1362361306064432

Laugeson, E. A. (2013). *The science of making friends: Helping socially challenged teens and young adults*. San Francisco, CA: Jossey-Bass.

Laugeson, E. A. (2014). *The PEERS curriculum for school-based professionals: Social skills training for adolescents with autism spectrum disorder*. New York, NY: Routledge.

Laugeson, E. A. (2017). *PEERS® for young adults: Social skills training for adults with autism spectrum disorder and other social challenges*. New York, NY: Routledge.

Laugeson, E. A., & Ellingsen, R. (2014). Social skills training for adolescents and adults with autism spectrum disorders. In F. Volkmar, J. McPartland, & B. Reichow (Series Eds.), *Autism in adolescence and young adulthood* (pp. 61–86). New York, NY: Springer.

Laugeson, E. A., & Frankel, F. (2010). *Social skills for teenagers with developmental and autism spectrum disorder: The PEERS treatment manual.* New York, NY: Routledge.

Laugeson, E. A., Gantman, A., Kapp, S. K., Orenski, K., & Ellingsen, R. (2015). A randomized controlled trial to improve social skills in young adults with autism spectrum disorder: The UCLA PEERS® program. *Journal of Autism and Developmental Disorders, 45*(12), 3978–3989. doi:10.1007/s10803-015-2504-8

Laugeson, E. A., & Park, M. N. (2014). Using a CBT approach to teach social skills to adolescents with autism spectrum disorder and other social challenges: The PEERS® method. *Journal of Rational-Emotive and Cognitive-Behavior Therapy, 32*(1), 84–97. doi:10.1007/s10942-014-0181-8

Liptak, G. S., Kennedy, J. A., & Dosa, N. P. (2011). Social participation in a nationally representative sample of older youth and young adults with autism. *Journal of Developmental & Behavioral Pediatrics, 32*(4), 277–283. doi:10.1097/DBP.0b013e31820b49fc

Mandelberg, J., Laugeson, E. A., Cunningham, T. D., Ellingsen, R., Bates, S., & Frankel, F. (2014). Long-term treatment outcomes for parent-assisted social skills training for adolescents with autism spectrum disorders: The UCLA PEERS program. *Journal of Mental Health Research in Intellectual Disabilities, 7*(1), 45–73. doi:10.1080/19315864.2012.730600

Orsmond, G. I., Krauss, M. W., & Seltzer, M. M. (2004). Peer relationships and social and recreational activities among adolescents and adults with autism. *Journal of Autism and Developmental Disorders, 34*(3), 245–256. doi:0162-3257/04/0600-0245/0

Rao, P. A., Beidel, D. C., & Murray, M. J. (2008). Social skills interventions for children with Asperger's syndrome or high-functioning autism: A review and recommendations. *Journal of Autism and Developmental Disorders, 38*, 353–361. doi:10.1007/s10803-0070402-4

Reichow, B., & Volkmar, F. R. (2010). Social skills interventions for individuals with autism: Evaluation for evidence-based practices within a best evidence synthesis framework. *Journal of Autism and Developmental Disorders, 40*(2), 149–166. doi:10.1007/s10803-009-0842-0

Schohl, K. A., Van Hecke, A. V., Carson, A. M., Dolan, B., Karst, J., & Stevens, S. (2013). A replication and extension of the PEERS intervention: Examining effects on social skills and social anxiety in adolescents with autism spectrum disorders. *Journal of Autism and Developmental Disorders, 37*, 354–366. doi:10.1007/s10803-013-1900-1

Shtayermann, O. (2007). Peer victimization in adolescents and young adults diagnosed with Asperger's syndrome: A link to depressive symptomatology, anxiety symptomatology and suicidal ideation. *Issues in Comprehensive Pediatric Nursing, 30*, 87–107. doi:10.1080/1091 1350802427548

Spence, S. H. (2003). Social skills training with children and young people: Theory, evidence and practice. *Child and Adolescent Mental Health, 8*(2), 84–96. doi:10.1111/1475-3588.00051

Sterling, L., Dawson, G., Estes, A., & Greenson, J. (2008). Characteristics associated with presence of depressive symptoms in adults with autism spectrum disorders.

Journal of Autism and Developmental Disorders, *38*(6), 1011–1018. doi:10.1007/s10803-007-0477-y

Taylor, J. L., & Seltzer, M. M. (2011). Employment and post-secondary educational activities for young adults with autism spectrum disorders during the transition to adulthood. *Journal of Autism and Developmental Disorders*, *41*(5), 566–574. doi:10.1007/s10803-010-1070-3

Taylor, J. L., & Seltzner, M. M. (2010). Changes in autism behavioral phenotype during the transition to adulthood. *Journal of Autism and Developmental Disorders*, *40*, 1431–1446. doi:10.1007/s10803-010-1005-z

Van Hecke, A. V., Stevens, S., Carson, A. M., Karst, J. S., Dolan, B., Schohl, K. … Brockman, S. (2015). Measuring the plasticity of social approach: A randomized controlled trial of the effects of the PEERS intervention on EEG asymmetry in adolescents with autism spectrum disorders. *Journal of Autism and Developmental Disorders*, *45*(2), 316–335. doi:10.1007/s10803-013-1883-y

White, S. W., Keonig, K., & Scahill, L. (2007). Social skills development in children with autism spectrum disorders: A review of the intervention research. *Journal of Autism and Developmental Disorders*, *37*(10), 1858–1868. doi:10.1007/s10803-006-0320-x

Part II

Marriage and Family Life

Autism does not occur in a vacuum. When a family member has been diagnosed with autism, it impacts everyone in the family. While historically we thought that having a *child* with autism impacts a marriage, we now realize that sometimes the person with autism is a *spouse*!

In this part we are reminded that listening very carefully, and providing space and time for a trusting therapeutic relationship to build, are necessary, but only entry-level therapeutic skills. We also see that, when you have a couple where one partner is on the spectrum, that couple has often tried to solve the relationship problems repeatedly over the years, leaving them feeling quite frustrated, betrayed, and genuinely confused. Highlighting the differences in brain patterns can be one of many ways to resolve that tension and return to the unique strengths that each partner brings to the relationship. Finally, we are reminded that we all hold expectations in relationships, and taking a circumspect look at those expectations of ourselves and others is an important part in building success in intimate relationships.

4 Taking the Time to Listen

Oliver's Story

Julie Ramisch

"Oliver is a very smart young man," reported Oliver's mother during our initial phone call. "He is really into robots," she continued, "and he would like for you to believe that he is *a robot. He gets into a bit of trouble when he's at school for not listening. He has a hard time engaging with other children appropriately." The phone call continued and I learned more about 12-year-old Oliver, his special interests, and the challenges facing the family.*

Listening

Each family with an adolescent with autism is unique and different. A parent may share with me that their adolescent has been diagnosed with autism with level 1, 2, or 3, but I believe that is only a piece of their story. Learning about an adolescent's level of functioning and behaviors is important, and so are listening for and learning about the family's history and dynamics. Often, when provided the space and asked the right questions, a family will share a complex story that includes a rich history of milestones, family changes, attempts to make life better, and other providers who have come and gone. I want to help as well as give families hope, which is why I listen and gather as much information as possible as we begin therapy.

For me, so I can best listen and learn, I invite the parent(s) to the first session alone. I want to learn about the family and the history. I also want them to view the therapeutic space. In that first session we talk about the developmental history of the adolescent, how school is going, interactions between family members, who is there to support the family, what stresses them out, and why they are seeking therapy with me. I also ask the parents to tell me more about the behaviors of the adolescent, special interests and hobbies, how they think their adolescent will do in my therapy space, and how we can use the therapy space to help the family to meet their goals for therapy. We work collaboratively as a team to map out a plan for success.

When families with adolescents with autism call me to initiate services, I remember that autism may not always the biggest challenge or the main stressor. Sure, it factors in and can contribute, but families with adolescents with autism experience many of the same stressors and challenges all other families face. I work with many families on adjusting to big life changes. I hear about parents trying to cope with work, financial stresses, and communication with each other and extended family. I help parents design and update parenting strategies, and I work with siblings so they can get along a little better. I see adolescents individually to help with problem-solving skills, social skills, and emotional development.

My work also involves collaboration with other professionals in the community. I have worked hard to build connections and networks with our primary care providers, specialists, and school professionals. It is important for me to know how systems work in my community so that I can make effective and efficient referrals and explain processes to families. Due to my relationships with these providers and educators, it is easier for me to connect with them when the course of treatment changes or when a new need arises. Having close relationships with other professionals also helps me to keep updated about programs and resources in our community.

During the first session with Oliver's parents they described a recent move from the Midwest to the West coast for dad's job. All extended family were left behind. They described that Oliver has one older brother, Sam, whom Oliver cherishes. Sam is 14 years old. They reported that Oliver was first diagnosed with autism at age 4 and he had been in speech therapy, occupational therapy, and counseling in the past. The robot fascination was not new and everyone in the family had just learned to accept it. Mom and dad described a charter school they found for Oliver in their neighborhood. The school is able to provide all accommodations that were in place before the big move. However, mom and dad noticed that Oliver is struggling to make new friends and get along with his peers. He especially gets upset if peers do not want to talk about robots with him.

Mom and dad liked our large play therapy room. They ensured I had some robots for Oliver. I let them know that Oliver was invited to bring his favorite toys to show me if he would like. We came up with a plan that I would meet Oliver alone at the second session. I wanted to make sure that I continued to get accurate reports about interactions with peers at school so I had mom and dad sign a release of information so I could collaborate with the school. I also gave the family resources so they could involve Oliver with his peers outside of school (local soccer and basketball leagues, a martial arts training center, a drama group for kids and teens, and a local art group that holds classes for youth in the community).

Observing

As a therapist it is important for me to watch and observe individual behaviors and family dynamics because a youth with autism may not be able to identify or communicate what is wrong or what could be improved at the beginning of treatment. How the youth interacts with me (most likely a stranger) and the therapy space can help me understand how they feel about meeting new people and going to new places. When family members join in for sessions, I am watching their interactions, the space between them, and the body language of each person, and the family as a whole, as it is all rich information that I gather to learn more about each family.

The first session with Oliver was ... energetic. He bounced from shelf to toybox, squealing joyfully when he found the box with the robots. Next thing I knew the child before me morphed from human to robot and I was flooded with facts about robots. He asked me to play with him and we created an elaborate plot about robots taking over the world and the planet's inhabitants abandoning planet dollhouse and relocating to planet sandbox. He appeared excited to be at my office and to have someone pay attention to him, and of course, play what he wanted. When his parents came to pick him up, he excitedly shared about our time together, the big relocation to planet sandbox, and the robot victory in taking over the world.

I asked mom and dad to bring Sam along for the next session and for them to also plan to participate. When Oliver and Sam came into the room together, Oliver took Sam by the hand and showed him all of the new toys and objects he discovered. First, he took Sam to the box with the robots and asked him to participate in an attack of "planet dollhouse." Sam engaged with Oliver for about 30 seconds before he took out his phone and detached from the interaction. Oliver's face sank and no attempt to distract Sam from his phone was successful. A robot even tried to take away Sam's phone but Sam growled and carried on with his phone. I asked mom and dad to join us for the rest of our session. I described what had happened and mom instantly sat down at the dollhouse and picked up where Sam had left off. Dad and Sam sat down at the table and joked about something unrelated. I observed as dad tried to reengage Sam by taking away his phone in a teasing manner.

Helping

As therapists we have been trained in a plethora of models for how to help our clients. There is no specific model that is *most* helpful for working with adolescents with autism or their families. Good therapy is about building relationships with clients and finding the best way to help them meet their goals, and therefore there are many ways to successfully help families with adolescents with autism. If a therapist does not understand autism and how it affects the individual and the family, it might be challenging for that therapist to know how to help (see *Recommended Resources for Professionals* below for additional information about treatment).

I believe that one of the first steps to effectively helping adolescents with autism and their families is to set appropriate treatment goals. Many of the treatment goals that I establish for adolescents with autism are often similar to what I establish for adolescents with other diagnoses. Youth with autism have specific challenges, but each youth is unique and may have different challenges than the next youth. The goals that I establish for adolescents with autism might include areas such as developing and using coping tools, making and keeping friends, managing anger or emotions in different situations and contexts, and taking responsibility for his/her actions. As a therapist who practices family therapy, I also try to weave in goals about enhancing and improving sibling relationships and the parental couple relationship, knowing these relationships can be strained (see *Recommended Resources for Professionals* for further information about the effects of autism on sibling and couple relationships).

I asked to see Oliver alone for our third session. As we restarted "Attack of Planet Dollhouse," I brought up his family's move, his relationship with his brother, and what was happening at school. At first, Oliver seemed frustrated that I wanted to talk about non-robot topics. I asked my questions again using robot language and Oliver was more interested. I described the situation of the particular robot in my hand (interestingly, that robot had a very similar situation to Oliver) and asked Oliver what his robot thought was wrong and what my robot should do. As I suspected, my robot was both having a hard time living on a new planet and was teasing friends at school to get their attention and to try to make friends. Oliver's robot told me that teasing was how he sees his dad laugh with Sam, so he thought if he teased other children, this would be a way to make friends.

Over the next few sessions I worked with Oliver and, through our robots, we were able to talk about his feelings regarding his family's move. Oliver talked about feeling sad that he does not get to see his old friends or his extended family any more. He was lonely. He was also sad that Sam did not want to play with him any more. He described feeling jealous that dad and Sam had a good relationship with each other. At one point we found a robot for each feeling and situation (the robots themselves all had similar experiences), and Oliver comforted them and gave them advice. We also used the robots to facilitate healthy new peer experiences such as making and keeping friends.

I asked mom and dad to join me for a session where I shared with them my progress with Oliver. I talked about the family's move to their new town and home. I relayed my thoughts that the move was hard on Oliver because he grew up in his old town and everyone there knew him. I talked about how moving to a new location is hard and it will take time to adjust and get connected. I shared the correlation between Oliver trying to make new friends and how he observed dad and Sam bonding and interacting. Oliver took observations from dad and Sam's relationship and used that as information on how to build new friendships. It would be important that we all worked with Oliver on how to make friends in a more positive way. Dad and Sam also could adjust or broaden their interactions to help with this. Ideally, mom and dad would help Sam to engage with Oliver to help facilitate a better relationship between the two brothers. Finally, I let mom and dad know that I would be collaborating with the school to see if they could help scaffold healthier and more positive interactions between Oliver and his peers during the school day.

Summary

Through thorough listening and observing each family, it is possible for therapists to learn how to become excellent helpers. Therapists who familiarize themselves about autism and how it affects families will be able to bring a more advanced view of the complex situations that families often face. Additionally, learning about and appreciating the uniqueness of each family will help therapists to design appropriate interventions to help families meet their goals.

Recommended Resources for Professionals

- Hock, R. M., Timm, T. M., & Ramisch, J. L. (2012). Parenting children with autism spectrum disorders: A crucible for couple relationships. *Child & Family Social Work, 17,* 406–415. doi:10.1111/j.1365-2206.2011.00794.x.
- Keller, T. E., Ramisch, J. L., & Carolan, M. (2014). Relationships of children with autism spectrum disorder and their fathers. *The Qualitative Report, 19,* 1–15. Retrieved from www.nova.edu/ssss/QR/QR19/keller66.pdf
- Ramisch, J. (2012). Marriage and family therapists working with couples who have children with autism. *Journal of Marital and Family Therapy, 38,* 305–316. doi:10.1111/j.1752-0606.2010.00210.x.
- Ramisch, J. L., Onaga, E., & Oh, S. M. (2014). Keeping a sound marriage: How couples with children with autism spectrum disorders maintain their marriages. *Journal of Child and Family Studies, 23,* 975–988. doi:10.1007/s10826-013-9753-y.
- Ramisch, J. L., & Piland, N. (2020). Systemic approaches for children, adolescents, and families living with neurodevelopmental disorders. In K. S. Wampler & L. M. McWey (Eds.), *The handbook of systemic family therapy* (Vol. 2). Hoboken, NJ: John Wiley & Sons.

- Ramisch, J. L., Timm, T. T., Hock, R. M., & Topor, J. (2013). Experiences delivering a marital intervention for couples with children with autism spectrum disorder. *American Journal of Family Therapy, 41,* 376–388.
- Turns, B., Eddy, B. P., & Smock Jordan, S. (2016). Working with siblings of children with autism: A solution-focused approach. *Australian & New Zealand Journal of Family Therapy, 37,* 558–571.
- Turns, B., Ramisch, J., & Whiting, J. B. (Eds.). (2019). *Systemically treating autism: A clinician's guide for empowering families.* New York, NY: Routledge.

Recommended Resources for Families

- Jackson, L. (2002). *Freaks, geeks and Asperger syndrome: A user guide to adolescence.* Philadelphia, PA: Jessica Kingsley Publishers Ltd.
- Sicile-Kira, C., & Grandin, T. (2006). *Adolescents on the autism spectrum: A parent's guide to the cognitive, social, physical, and transition needs of teenagers with autism spectrum disorders.* New York, NY: The Berkley Publishing Group.

About the Author

Julie Ramisch, Ph.D., LMFT, received her M.S. degree in Child Development and Family Studies with a specialization in marriage and family therapy from Purdue University Calumet and her Ph.D. in Human Development and Family Studies with a specialization in marriage and family therapy from Michigan State University. She was an assistant professor for a few years prior to moving to Oregon to start Coastal Center for Collaborative Health (www.coastal-center.com). She currently enjoys working in clinical practice, mentoring students and new professionals, and writing publications about working with families with children with autism. She recently co-edited *Systemically Treating Autism: A Clinician's Guide for Empowering Families* with Brie Turns and Jason Whiting. She can be reached by email at: julie.ramisch@gmail.com.

5   The Transformative Power of the Autism Spectrum Narrative

Marilyn J. Monteiro

"I'm here because my wife and I have had years of conflict. Recently, after she wondered if I had autism, I started reading about adults with Level 1 autism, and I saw myself in a lot of the descriptions I read. We both think that it might explain why she is so frustrated and angry with me most of the time, and why I feel like I am never able to get it right."

"Liam is a silo person," Anne explained.

"He takes me off the shelf when I get frustrated about how little time he's spending with me and the kids, but once he's done what I've asked him to do, he puts me right back on the shelf and goes on to the next thing. He's self-centered, unfeeling, and always needs to be right. When he isn't at work, he's working on his design projects, off by himself. I've been trying to get help for years, and recently I stumbled across a definition of Level 1 autism. It made me start to rethink how I was looking at Liam and how he acts in our relationship. I encouraged Liam to learn more about this from a knowledgeable therapist, and for us to come in together to work with someone who has experience with Level 1 autism. Maybe this is the missing piece."

A married couple with two children, Anne and Liam clearly loved each other, but they had no idea how to establish connecting ways to communicate. Conflict had built up between them over many years, as Liam was distant and avoidant, and Anne was angry and resentful of having to manage daily family decisions on her own. The traditional marital therapy they had tried in the past focused on encouraging the couple to express their feelings. This left Anne feeling increasingly alone and powerless, and Liam feeling incapable and anxious. They established a pattern of isolation and avoidance, with occasional outbursts of anger. One source of Anne's resentment was Liam's ability to effectively navigate social situations in his work setting, while lacking the ability to generalize those skills when participating in social events outside of work demands.

For verbally fluent adults with autism spectrum traits like Liam, it often takes a skilled therapist to explore whether the individual's maladaptive behavior patterns and mood challenges are a result of the presence of an underlying neurodevelopmental difference (autism spectrum disorder, Level 1). Most therapists are more proficient and comfortable identifying a mood or personality concern, and are either hesitant or unlikely to consider possible autism spectrum differences, despite the high prevalence rate (Centers for Disease Control and Prevention, 2018). For therapists working with adults, considering the possible presence of autism spectrum *differences* and framing those differences as the autism spectrum *brain style* is useful. Addressing Liam's possible autism spectrum brain style gave this couple a starting point in reframing their relationship. How does a therapist go about this process?

The first step is having a solid understanding of the multilayered and complex behavioral profile that makes up the autism spectrum brain style. Verbally fluent individuals have many areas of strength that professionals with a limited understanding of autism do not typically recognize as part of the autism spectrum brain style. Exploring the possible presence of autism spectrum differences is easily dismissed out of hand. It is important to understand that, in addition to areas of strength, verbally fluent individuals with autism have distinctive differences in the way in which they organize their behavior and regulate their emotions. Becoming familiar with an autism-specific visual framework with descriptive language empowers the therapist to recognize and support verbally fluent individuals with autism spectrum brain style differences. The visual framework for autism spectrum differences organizes the therapist's conceptualization into a descriptive triangle, as seen in Figure 5.1.

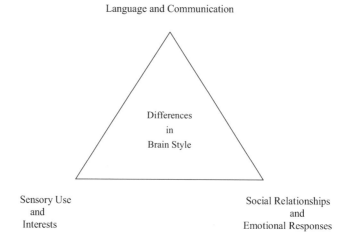

Figure 5.1 Language and Communication. © 2015 Marilyn J. Monteiro, Ph.D. All rights reserved. Reprinted with permission by author.

Verbally fluent individuals with autism spectrum brain style differences show a pattern of strengths and distinctive differences in the three key areas denoted in the visual framework. Therapists who become familiar with the descriptive language linked to each of the three key areas depicted in the visual framework are equipped to recognize and discuss individual presentations of autism spectrum differences in the individuals with whom they work. A comprehensive and accessible descriptive framework is available for clinicians and evaluators from several sources (Dilly & Hall, 2018; Monteiro, 2016, 2018).

With Liam, it was important to understand his areas of interest, and the sensory aspects of those interests. Both Liam and Anne described Liam's highly developed interest in design and building as his "obsession." This negative label closed the door on exploring the form and the function of Liam's interest, and implied that he needed to stop obsessing and start doing things the neurotypical way. In fact, Liam's interest in design held important clues about how to help Liam enter into Anne's social world in a supportive and meaningful way. Liam's passionate interest in design, including his job as an architect, showcased the form of his visual, three-dimensional thinking style, as well as how his preferred activities served the function of organizing his thinking and regulating his emotions, while blocking out incoming sources of stress. Discussing the form of Liam's thinking (organizing his thinking around visual and three-dimensional tasks as opposed to organizing around verbal processing and social exchanges) helped both partners understand that in the home setting and in family relationships, flexibly shifting from his visual, low-load language and low-load social thinking style, to process and respond to social communication requests, was stressful and challenging for him. Liam's "low-load" language and social thinking style are defined by his seeking out activities and situations in which the demand for sustained social communication is limited or not expected. In other words, what appeared as Liam's lack of interest in others was better understood as a difference in how Liam's brain managed input and organized his thinking and behavior. Liam consistently organized around his focus on objects and tasks, unlike his wife, who consistently organized around social communication and social exchanges. Anne was a social thinker and primarily a verbal processor. She processed incoming information quickly, while Liam required time and a clear context to shift his focus, organize his thoughts, and formulate his response.

Identifying and describing Liam's brain style pattern of strengths and differences was the bridge in therapy that led to this couple's ability to shift their thinking and make positive changes. In the area of language and communication, Liam and Anne were guided to describe Liam's obvious area of strength (well-developed language skills) along with his differences (hard work for Liam to shift his focus from objects and tasks to take in and respond to social communication information and demands; along with needing extra time to process social communication before responding to that input). In the area of social relationships and emotions, strengths for Liam included his feelings of love and deep attachment to his family, while his differences included his challenges in initiating social conversations and activities, and communicating both verbally and nonverbally regarding his thoughts and feelings. In the area of sensory use and interests, strengths for Liam included his highly developed visual thinking skills and his passionate interest in pursuing activities that used his visual and three-dimensional problem-solving skills. Differences for Liam included his challenges in managing multiple sources of sensory input (flexibly shifting from his agenda to follow the agenda of others; managing conversations, background noise, visual clutter, and unpredictability in the form of spontaneous activities and events). This reframing of Liam's behavioral profile, or brain style, shifted the conversation from negative labeling to identifying and changing patterns of behavior.

Anne noted: "Seeing Liam's interests as a way to better understand his thinking style opened up a whole new way of thinking about our communication for the first time. It helps me not get so reactive and resentful when he doesn't respond the way I think he should."

For the first time, Anne was given a way to see things from Liam's perspective. Liam was given the context and framework to identify his routines as having positive characteristics and value.

Once the descriptive, positive framework is introduced, what does the therapist do with that information? In Anne and Liam's case, it led to practical adjustments in how each partner viewed the other's communication strengths and needs. Anne had been frustrated for years with Liam's putting her off whenever she brought up topics that needed to be discussed. His avoidant behavior was interpreted in the past as a sign of lack of interest, when it actually was a sign of Liam's freezing in the face of incoming demands and having to flexibly shift to something he was not prepared to think about and comment on. Knowing that Liam's behavior did not reflect a negative intention helped Anne embrace doing something different: provide a context for substantive conversations with advanced notice. In other words, Anne was coached to pick one or two key points of discussion, write them in a list, and provide the list to Liam, along with several options for times to schedule the talk that would work for her. This provided Liam with the context, as well as time to organize his thoughts so that he was prepared to meaningfully discuss the topic with Anne.

In the work arena, Liam was able to help Anne understand that the social context was clearly delineated for him, in that a clear and consistent routine occurred in his job setting. Conversations were object-focused on the project at hand. In other words, when talking with others at work, there was a limited need for Liam to engage in social back-and-forth exchanges (social communication focus), as most of his conversations followed a pattern of discussing details related to his work projects (object-focused). The roles of his conversational partners were also consistently framed as expert and client, co-worker or boss. The routines were easy to map out, and followed a predictable pattern. Liam was able to add that, *although he appeared to manage the social aspects of his work life with ease, in fact, dealing with other people was a constant source of anxiety and an energy drain for him. After a full day at work, managing social communication and input, he had few reserves available to manage the onslaught of social communication demands from Anne and his children.*

In the social arena, Liam explained that he experienced a high degree of anxiety when in social situations, such as neighborhood dinners or even hosting dinners at their home. His anxiety blocked his ability to recall information about others, and he did not have a context to retain information others shared with him in social settings. Understanding his visual and organizational strengths led to suggesting that Liam design a schematic to organize and write down social information about individuals Anne wanted to socialize with as a couple. With the schematic in place, Liam was able to engage Anne in multiple conversations about other people, their interests, and what Anne's vision was for Liam in terms of participation at social gatherings.

"It took twenty years to feel hopeless about how to connect, but having us both better understand my brain style allowed us to make a monumental course correction." Liam was visibly more relaxed, engaged, and in sync with Anne, and Anne's entire manner towards Liam had softened considerably. They were in it together, partners in creating their narrative instead of silos existing side by side.

Four Key Emotional Shifts that Happen with the Autism Narrative Reframe

Without a context for understanding the autism spectrum perspective, and how that perspective shapes behavior routines, families often experience stress, a sense of powerlessness, and resentment towards one another. Therapists support four powerful emotional shifts (Figure 5.2) for families when they introduce the autism spectrum brain style narrative.

Shifting from Emotional Reactivity to Curiosity about Differences

The first emotional shift occurs when the therapist describes key aspects of the identified patient's brain style pattern of strengths and differences. Perceived deficits are reframed as differences. This neutral language moves the family conversation away from deficits, and the linked negative and reactive emotions, to style. Each family member is framed as having a brain style, with a pattern of areas of strength as well as areas of differences. Family members can shift from emotional reactivity to curiosity about each other and their differing brain style profiles. This first shift lays the groundwork for building new skills and new ways of thinking about one another.

The 4 Key Shifts

Shifting from Emotional Reactivity to Curiosity About Differences. Identification of the individual's pattern of strengths and differences shifts thinking from emotional reactivity to curiosity

Shifting to Appreciation of Complementary Styles and Perspective Taking. Perspective-taking of family members leads to letting go of negative assumptions and appreciation of differences

Shift from Negative Labeling of Neurodiverse Characteristics. Understanding the complementary nature of brain styles allows for a reframe of the individual's underlying emotional intentions as being positive

Shift to Feeling Empowerment leads to Mutual Understanding and Support. Empowerment and positive behavior change become possible when the individual with differences is heard and understood, mutual understanding and support occur

---

Figure 5.2 The Four Key Shifts When Families Introduce the Autism Spectrum Brain Style Narrative.

Shifting to Appreciation of Complementary Styles and Perspective Taking

As each person's patterns of strengths and differences is laid out in the therapeutic conversation, opportunities for perspective-taking unfold.

> *Anne was able to let go of her label of her husband as self-centered as she took his perspective of having a high need for solitary, sensory regrouping time to reset his brain and manage the demands of his job. Liam was able to let go of labeling his wife as angry and critical, as he took her perspective of managing multiple household decisions independently and feeling isolated while doing so.*

Instead of experiencing the familiar pattern of differing styles canceling each other out, leaving each partner feeling less capable, couples and families begin to experience the unfamiliar and energizing experience of finding ways to appreciate complementary styles, get needs met, and feel a sense of collaboration.

Shift from Negative Labeling of Neurodiverse Characteristics

The conversational shift to the complementary nature of their styles addresses the underlying assumption inherent in negative labeling: that the individual engaging in the behavior routines is doing so with negative intentions towards the other person. This is a social or neurotypical way of understanding behavior routines. When behavior routines are described and understood as part of the person's autism spectrum or sensory-based style of thinking, a shift occurs in the underlying emotional assumptions. For example, the negative labeling of Liam's disengaged behavior routines as "selfish," and "not caring" led to reactive and negative responses to him. Understanding the autism brain style reasons for avoidant behavior, and describing avoidance as being the most efficient way of managing unpredictable and unexpected incoming demands that require flexible thinking, leads to understanding that the behavior routines do not reflect underlying ill will. Unlinking assumptions about intention occurs with greater ease when style differences are described. When family members become educated about autism spectrum brain style differences and behavior routines, they are also able to shift their assumptions to crediting the family member with good will and good intentions towards others. Instead of focusing on negative intentions, the discussion shifts to identifying and teaching positive replacement behavior routines. Family members are more willing to problem-solve about replacement routines when they give up their belief that the individual with autism spectrum brain style differences has negative intentions.

Shift to Feeling Empowerment Leads to Mutual Understanding and Support

The fourth emotional shift occurs when individuals are able to feel empowered, heard, and understood as they work together to appreciate and use their brain style strengths to meet mutual needs. For example, Anne and Liam, with the help of their therapist, were able to identify ways to change their communication styles and to provide supports to one another to better match each other's styles and needs.

Application across Individuals and Families

This same process of reframing the autism spectrum narrative applies to therapy with young adults and their parents. Older adolescents preparing for the transition to college and adult life, young adults, and adults struggling in their primary relationships all benefit from reframing the narrative. Feelings of resentment and powerlessness dissipate with an understanding of brain style differences, and new avenues of communication become possible. Changing the language used in the family from negative labeling to describing behavior in neutral terms lays the groundwork for positive change. Just as negative labeling leads to ascribing negative intent, describing behavior leads to a shared understanding, and moves the discussion to sharing perspectives and making course corrections to accommodate differing styles. Connecting in a new way becomes possible.

Summary

Individuals on the autism spectrum typically have differences in how they understand and use language and communication, how they manage their sensory use and interests, and how they navigate their social relationships and emotional responses. Therapists who understand autism spectrum differences support individuals and their families as they make the shift from emotional reactivity to curiosity about these differences, develop an appreciation of how brain differences can be complementary, and shift away from negative labeling of these neurodiverse characteristics. The transformative power of the autism spectrum narrative leads to a feeling of empowerment for individuals, and a positive understanding and support in couple and family relationships.

Recommended Resources for Professionals

- Dr. Marilyn Monteiro: www.marilynmonteiro.com
- Dr. Tony Attwood: www.tonyattwood.com.au
- Social Thinking: www.socialthinking.com
- Monteiro, M. (2008). *Autism conversations: Evaluating children on the autism spectrum through authentic conversations*. Torrance, CA: Western Psychological Services.
- Attwood, T. (2006). *The complete guide to Asperger's syndrome*. London, UK: Jessica Kingsley Publisher.

Recommended Resources for Families

- Books on Autism: www.autismbookstore.com
- Wylie, P. (2014). *Very late diagnosis of autism spectrum disorder: How seeking a diagnosis in adulthood can change your life*. London, UK: Jessica Kingsley Publisher.
- Garcia-Winner, M. (2007). *Thinking about you, thinking about me*. Santa Clara, CA: Think Social Publisher.
- Smith, B. (2016). *Executive FUNction series*. Boys Town, NE: Boys Town Press.

About the Author

Marilyn J. Monteiro, Ph.D., a licensed psychologist and licensed specialist in school psychology, is an expert in the area of autism spectrum brain style differences. She is the author of the books *Autism Conversations: Evaluating Children on the Spectrum Through Authentic Conversations* and *Family Therapy and the Autism Spectrum: Autism Conversations in Narrative Practice*, as well as the *Monteiro Interview Guidelines for Diagnosing the Autism Spectrum, Second Edition (MIGDAS-2)*, a diagnostic test protocol to identify autism spectrum differences in children and adults. She maintains a practice in Dallas, Texas that specializes in supporting individuals with autism spectrum differences and their families. She thoroughly enjoys having conversations with individuals on the autism spectrum.

References

Centers for Disease Control and Prevention. (2018). Data and statistics on autism spectrum disorder. Retrieved from www.cdc.gov.

Dilly, L., & Hall, C. (2018). *Autism spectrum disorder assessment in schools*. New York, NY: Routledge.

Monteiro, M. (2016). *Family therapy and the autism spectrum: Autism conversations in narrative practice*. New York, NY: Routledge.

Monteiro, M. (2018). *Monteiro interview guidelines for diagnosing the autism spectrum* (2nd ed.). Torrance, CA: Psychological Services.

6   Neurologically Mixed Marriages and the Audacity of Social Compliance

David Finch

I am considered by some an "expert" on Asperger syndrome. It seems that all one has to do is write a best-selling book and embark on a seven-year, national speaking and media tour about a single topic, and voilà: suddenly, you're an expert.

That's how it happened for me. At the dawn of my third decade, my wife diagnosed me with Asperger syndrome. I'm told this is not an uncommon way people stumble into a diagnosis; frustrated spouses try to find some answer as to why they can't connect with their eccentric, seemingly disconnected partner. It's almost as if marriage causes autism. My wife in the heat of marital frustration wanted nothing to do with me. At the time of my diagnosis, my marriage with Kristen had unraveled so spectacularly that we couldn't even call each other friends. My moods, my rigidity, my routines – these things had all spiraled in our first five years of marriage, leaving Kristen to wonder who the hell she'd married.

Remarkably, as a speech therapist with an alphabet of credentials (MS, SLP, CCC) who happened to work exclusively with the autistic population, Kristen hadn't yet recognized Asperger's in me. When relating the story now, she admits that perhaps she should have spotted some of the indicators sooner. "But," she often says, "I wasn't looking at my husband through a diagnostic eye. Like any wife, I was just trying to get him to do some damn laundry."

I was later formally diagnosed by a psychologist, and from the moment of my diagnosis, I thought having Asperger's was great news. It gave me some insight into this life of mine, which I'd always felt was asynchronous with the rest of humankind. What's more, I used the information to learn a little more about my own behaviors and how they might be shaping my life as a husband, father, and person – for better or worse.

Asperger's never felt like a bummer diagnosis. If anything, I felt it gave Kristen and me a behavioral blueprint, of sorts. Almost like a user manual for my mind, which is a handy manual to discover in any marriage. The acknowledgment that I'd been horrible to live with, coupled with the recognition that I hadn't been willfully so, erased much of the agony of our troubled relationship, for both of us. With Kristen's support, I set out to learn some new behaviors that would improve our relationship. I penned a best-selling memoir of the story, traveled around the United States to talk about myself for seven years, and voilà: suddenly, I was an expert. More preposterous still was that, now, I was expected to give people advice.

Giving Advice on Relationships

I hesitated when asked to write for this book, mostly because they'd asked me to do it for free. What's more, I really don't like to provide advice to people in tricky relationships because I cannot possibly know enough of the couple's history to make a real impact. On paper I can be calculated and eloquent, but on stage I'm forced to improvise. My honesty and simplicity sometimes surprise people. "Leave him," I once said to a woman who'd burnt up 12 minutes of a Q & A publicly trashing her autistic husband, only to ask, "So, I guess my question is, what should I do?" Some gasped at my response so I clarified, "Not for your sake. For his."

And then there was Anders, a young man who'd stood in the back of an auditorium explaining that his last half-dozen love interests had filed restraining orders against him. He'd come to my keynote address specifically seeking some free counsel about this new guy he'd had his eye on. "Have you considered living out your remaining years a hermit?" I asked. "You know, find a nice, damp milk house on some abandoned mountainside farm where you can while away your hours befriending raccoons and naming spiders? Frankly, I don't see you changing and at least raccoons and spiders won't file for protections against you."

Despite the occasional lapse in social propriety, I really do enjoy speaking and working with individuals, couples, and professionals to provide some insight into the day to day of Asperger's and autism. That, in my opinion, brings far more value to the equation than spouting impromptu, dubious advice to strangers. I've found that most humans are capable of formulating their own strategies if they can understand their personal situation as well as those of the other people involved. When it comes to neurodiverse relationships, often what couples need most is access to one another's perspective. Being equal parts autistic and neurotypical, I can provide decent approximations of both those perspectives. The rest, as it ought to be, is up to the couple.

That said, there are two universal nuggets of advice that I'm happy to lend any couple, regardless of their neurological composition: don't be motivated by social compliance, and stay in your lane.

The Audacity of Social Compliance

Social compliance demands that we all demonstrate cognitive flexibility. *Put yourself in your partner's shoes. Stop being so black and white. Pay attention to this incredibly important topic.* Which is borderline insane behavior, especially in today's more enlightened age where we know that not everyone is wired the same. Demands such as these only serve the non-autistic members of our species. What I see creeping into people's relationships is a cultural insistence that the neurotypical order is the right one. So, in neurologically mixed marriages such as mine, we have one partner who's been culturally programmed to believe they're right because their style of thinking is in the majority, and one partner whose very genetics make it virtually impossible to assume they're wrong. Probably neither person is ever right or wrong in absolute terms, but that doesn't make coexisting easy for either of them. Which is why they show up to my lectures, wait until I'm done talking, and then ask me for tips on how to change each other.

Change in Relationships

The key to changing one's relationship, I've learned, is to change two things – and neither of those things is one's partner. Rather, to change one's relationship, one must first change one's relationship to oneself. Then, one must change one's relationship with the relationship. Most often – and, again, it is only observation and no hard evidence with which I make this claim – what dooms a relationship is not the behaviors or the attitudes of the people involved. It's not even the big-ticket items like infidelity or insistence on listening to Beyoncé in the car. No, what destroys relationships more surely than anything else are expectations.

If your relationship sucks and you're suffering because of it, then it is because you expected certain things. You expected your partner to be your best friend, your reliable confidante, your masseur, your business partner, your sexual partner, your road trip buddy, your date to every darned wedding for those doomed to repeat your mistakes, your laundry service, your cook, your parenting partner, your chauffeur, your perso-nal shopper, your kitchen cleaner, your bed-maker, your greeting-card selector, your primary source of comfort, laughter, joy, and affection. And then you have the gall – the absolute gall – to hold a grudge against that person when he or she fails to measure up. Who on earth could possibly fulfill all those roles? Who could live up to all those expectations? We choose different tires in our lives, based on need. The tires on your bike are great for bikes. They'd make terrible car tires, which is why you have tires specifically for your car. And those tires are way different than the tires on your lawnmower because you don't need your lawnmower rolling on all-season radials.

That's just tires, rubber rings that roll around in the same direction, and I've already identified three distinct categories. So, if we're careful about selecting the right tires for the job, why do we force one human to be good at all the things? It's because we haven't checked our expectations, and now they've gotten the better of us.

One doesn't *need* anything when one discovers that one is quite enough on one's own. That liberation from a perceived need is unbelievably freeing. It's empowerment that comes from the one person who can reasonably empower you: you. It frees you to enjoy and love your partner because it removes the shackles of contempt.

From there, it's an easy jump to changing one's relationship with the relationship. If you expected all these impossible things from your partner, then you've probably harbored some fairly corrosive expectations for the partnership as well. *It was supposed to last. It was supposed to feel special. It was supposed to look a certain way.* Aww, was it? It's not wrong to expect these things, but when they don't materialize and you're left suffering, it's clear that your precious expectations aren't serving you. And if something doesn't serve you, why hold on to it?

What Do Professionals Want to Know?

My conferences are often laced with professionals, sizeable groups of marriage and family therapists, clinicians, educators, and other professionals. When I relate the story of my own neurologically mixed marriage, they all seem to have similar questions.

They want to know about the behaviors and other factors that have had the greatest impact on my marriage. *Where do I begin?* I often wonder. *Over-the-top cognitive rigidity? Self-absorption? Obsessive thoughts and compulsive behaviors? Or, how about ignorance of the thoughts and feelings of other people, including my own kids? My knobby knees?*

Granted, only some of my idiosyncrasies can be attributed to Asperger's. The rest are more unique to me as a ridiculous person. My knobby knees, for example, are an unfortunate genetic legacy. As for the Asperger's, it turns out Kristen and I are not all that unique. Often my audiences nod in total recognition as I relate how challenging it can be for any two cultures to come together – especially neurological ones. This, I feel, is at the heart of it all: the neurotypical and autistic cultures are vastly different. From what I've seen of the hundreds of couples who've reached out to me, a mutual willingness to reconcile or at least make room for those differences is the most reliable indicator of positive outcomes.

Will tomorrow's therapists agree with this observation? Or am I over-simplifying things? I suppose time will tell. In the meantime, I think the more our therapists can try to access and normalize the neurodivergent perspective, the stronger they'll be when working with neurodiverse couples.

In one recent presentation, a young graduate student posed an interesting question. "I'll be entering the profession at the end of this year as a therapist," she began. I offered my condolences and she continued. "Do you have any advice for me? Is there anything I should know about working with couples where one or both partners is on the spectrum?" Indeed, I did. And indeed, there was. The problem, once again, was where to begin?

What I wanted the grad student to know – what I wanted every marriage and family therapist, counselor, pastor, rabbi, educator, partner, parent, friend to know – was that neurodiversity is the inevitable result of thousands of years of human evolution. Autism, one of the conditions that makes us a neurodiverse species, is just that: a condition, nothing more, nothing less. It is not something to be pathologized, it is something to be respected and understood. A diagnosis, then, does not reflect some deviation from a natural order. Rather, it explains how your brain works much of the time. A diagnosis can help to predict how a person might behave, but it will never characterize *who* a person is, or who they will become.

I wanted this grad student to understand that most evidence-based approaches to couples counseling have been built with a severe neurotypical bias. Atypical clients make atypical couples, and atypical couples may require atypical approaches. Most certainly, any professional working with individuals on the spectrum should seek, first and foremost, to understand the behaviors that are presenting challenges in that person's life. And, they should seriously reflect on whether those challenges must be corrected, or simply understood.

I wanted her to know that malice and premeditated cruelty are not characteristics of autism. That, generally speaking, partners on the spectrum are keenly interested in doing the right things the right ways. I also wanted her to know that having an autism spectrum condition does not get anyone off the hook. If a person has chosen to enter into a relationship, they have an obligation to it. Both parties have to act with reciprocity, autistic or not. That's just how it works.

But mostly, I wanted this grad student to understand that simply by showing up for her clients and seeking deeper understanding, she was already doing a hero's work.

And, who knows? If some day she writes a best-selling book and devotes the better part of a decade to lecturing around the country, maybe she, too, could be recognized as an expert in her field. And then she can go around writing other people's books for them, for free.

About the Author

David Finch is a writer, speaker, consultant, and author of the *New York Times* best-selling book, *The Journal of Best Practices: A Memoir of Marriage, Asperger Syndrome, and One Man's Quest to Be a Better Husband*. Mr. Finch consults on the hit Netflix series "Atypical" and has appeared on "This American Life," "The Howard Stern Show," ABC, CBS, NBC, CNN, O the Oprah Magazine, and other major outlets. He can be reached at david@davidjfinch.com.

Part III

Acknowledging and Including Siblings

As noted in the previous part, a family member with autism will indeed impact the entire family. This part takes a closer look at the important role of *siblings*. Siblings have a different role than parents: as multiple writers indicate, the sibling relationship will likely last longer than the parenting relationship, but often comes with less information, less power, and sometimes a sense of invisibility.

In this part we hear a poignant series of reasons why siblings should be provided with information, resources, and attention. We then learn what therapy might provide for these siblings, how therapists can intentionally include siblings, and the emotional impact of having a sister or brother on the autism spectrum on siblings. Finally, we consider resources both inside and outside of the therapy room that may be helpful for these important siblings.

7 Siblings

Unique Concerns, Unique Opportunities

Emily Holl

For many siblings, having a brother or sister with autism can bring both challenges and unique opportunities. Siblings share many, if not most, of the same concerns and opportunities as their parents regarding their sibling, as well as some which are uniquely theirs. The sibling relationship can easily exceed six or seven decades, and siblings will in all likelihood be relationally connected to their autism sibling for even longer than parents. This relationship may have additional complications as siblings age, such as the neurotypical sibling caring for their sibling with autism in later life (Hodapp, Sanderson, Meskis, & Casale, 2017).

Siblings often have fewer services and supports available to them than do parents of children with autism. Parents typically have access to information and support from medical professionals, social workers, therapists, teachers, and each other through parent-to-parent programs and parent support groups. If siblings are lucky, they receive some information about autism from their parents. All too often, family support services revolve around a functional definition of "family" that translates to "parents." The needs of non-autistic siblings who don't have legal caregiving responsibilities for their brothers and sisters have not traditionally been considered by service providers, and sibs are rarely connected with professionals or peers for information or support, often leaving them uninformed at best, and isolated at worst.

I direct the Sibling Support Project, which is a national program dedicated to the life-long and ever-changing concerns of millions of brothers and sisters of people with special health, developmental, and mental health needs. Our initiatives include books and publications for and by siblings, online communities, and workshops and trainings on sibling issues. We are probably best known for creating Sibshops, which are lively events for school-age siblings of children with special needs, offered throughout the United States, Canada, and in several other countries around the world. Sibshops provide young sibs with information and peer support in a recreational setting. Siblings can learn something about the diagnoses of their brothers and sisters, and meet other sibs of those on the spectrum, often for the first time. At Sibshops, siblings talk about the good, not-so-good, and everything-in-between of having a brother or sister with autism or other special developmental, health, or mental health concerns. Discussion activities are mixed with recreational activities—with an emphasis on wellness and fun! Our goal is to provide—and teach others how to provide—siblings of people with autism and other diagnoses with information, validation, encouragement, and support.

Unique Concerns

Siblings' needs change and evolve through the lifespan. Sibling support must therefore be flexible, timely, and focused on the most relevant issues for the individual. While no two sibling experiences are identical, if you listen to enough siblings over a long enough period of time—almost 40 years in our case—recurrent themes emerge.

Need for Information

The need for information about their brother or sister's diagnosis is one of the biggest ways that the sibling experience parallels the parental experience. Very young siblings need to know that they didn't cause and can't catch their brother or sister's autism. School-age children need to be able to explain their sibling's autism to themselves and to others, including peers who may ask questions in the not-so-nicest ways. We politely disagree with parents who choose not to use "the A word" when it comes to educating their children about autism. Having a name for the thing that makes your brother or sister "different" can be a big relief for young siblings.

One 11-year-old sister shared that, when she was younger, her mother said that her sister had a "handicap," and that she didn't really know what that meant. When she was a bit older, her mom found a book about autism in the library, and reading it helped her understand some of her sister's behaviors. She realized that her sister's brain worked differently, and that she wasn't being annoying on purpose (most of the time!). Most importantly, she had a name for what made her sister "different," and it was a word that most people seemed to understand when she explained it, which made doing so less uncomfortable.

Adolescent siblings are already thinking about the future care of their brothers and sisters, and what role they will play. One 17-year-old sister who was a competitive dancer feared that she would not be able to pursue a dancing career, because of the travel involved. She worried about not being available to help care for her sister with autism and their younger brother, and that she might not earn enough as a dancer to help to support her sister financially when their parents were gone. Like many siblings we know, she felt torn between pursuing her passion and staying close to home to help out. Teen sibs need to know that plans are being made by parents and others for the future of their siblings with autism, and they need to have opportunities to be part of these conversations with parents, providers, and their brothers and sisters.

Adult siblings thrust into the role of caregiver later in life are often just as overwhelmed as, if not more than, parents of newly diagnosed children. Navigating an unfamiliar and complex service system can be downright daunting. One brother whose brother with autism lived in another state was torn about whether or not to relocate his family or relocate his brother to live closer to each other. His brother had resided in a group home for many years, but as he aged, his list of health concerns grew, and this sibling felt that he needed to be nearby to help manage them. His wife was reluctant, to say the least, to uproot their family, which included teenage kids in high school, and they were equally overwhelmed by the idea of learning their state's service system and getting his brother on the necessary wait lists. Adult siblings can benefit from having access to information about local services for people with autism, and guidance in navigating these supports. Perhaps even more importantly, siblings need validation and reassurance. Supporting siblings in making life decisions that promote their own well-being is a powerful way to help them as both individuals and current or future caregivers.

Communication with siblings at every age is crucial. Sharing information on an ongoing basis, in age-appropriate written or spoken language, is key to helping siblings understand and feel part of their brother or sister's journey. We often urge parents to be proactive in sharing information with their non-diagnosed children, and providers to make themselves available to siblings.

Resentment

When the life of a family seems to revolve around one person, it is easy to understand why other family members might feel resentful. Often, a family's financial, social, and emotional resources are largely invested in the child with a diagnosis. In our social media groups and Sibshops, siblings often share their resentment about not receiving as much parental time and attention as their brothers and sisters, and about limitations on family outings, vacations, and activities. Siblings also resent unequal expectations for behavior and household chores, and often have a clear sense of which behaviors or limitations can be attributed to the diagnosis.

Many of the siblings we've met who reported little resentment tell us that all the kids in their family—including the kids with autism—were expected to do chores and treat each other with respect. These same sibs usually point to an external activity—camping, sports, music, belonging to a religious community—that family life centered around, not just the needs of their brothers or sisters. Siblings can also resent the aggressive behavior of their brothers and sisters with autism, particularly when there is physical violence involved. Too many sibs have told us over the years about the anxiety and fear caused by being the constant target of their brother or sister's aggression. One teen sibling who was the youngest in her family described coming home after a long day at school and having to dash into her bedroom and lock her door before she was seen by her brother, who was physically much larger and very strong, to avoid his frequent hitting, kicking, hair-pulling rage. While she understood that her brother's diagnosis contributed to his behavior, she nonetheless resented his physical abuse, and the fact that her parents were unable to recognize its impact on her, or stop the behavior.

Recognizing and validating siblings' resentment are crucial to supporting them in moving forward. Helping siblings sort through the many layers of resentment and accept these feelings as justified and normal is a powerful way that clinicians can facilitate self-efficacy and healing.

Guilt

Siblings experience guilt for many reasons. Young siblings may feel guilty if they believe they somehow caused the disability. Survivor's guilt is another typical response, and many siblings wonder, why their brother/sister has this diagnosis. Siblings experience guilt over natural, even healthy, conflicts with their brothers and sisters with autism. While most young people wouldn't think twice about being less than charitable to their typical brothers and sisters, young sibs often find reasons to regret and feel guilty about such behavior. Reaching developmental milestones is also a challenge for many siblings, particularly younger sibs who surpass their older brothers' and sisters' social development.

One 16-year-old sister, like many of her peers, was excited to learn how to drive. As she practiced with her learner's permit, she dreamed of getting her license and driving here, there, and everywhere with her friends. Then one day, she thought about her brother with autism, who happened to love cars, and how he would probably never drive, nor have friends to drive around with. Her excitement drowned in a sea of guilt.

Siblings also feel guilty about something that we, as a field, tout as a basic human right for all people: self-determination. Teen siblings, who eagerly flee to college, often lament a couple of years later that they really should be getting back home soon to help out. Young adults starting their own families and careers wrestle with living far from home, finding a partner who will accept a possible future caregiving role, and pursuing their own happiness along the way. Older adult sibs grapple with the guilt of falling short in some way as they juggle the demands of work and the needs of partners, kids, aging parents, and often, inevitably, caring for their autistic brother or sister.

Once again, sharing information in age-appropriate language is critical in helping to mitigate sibling guilt. Providing siblings with opportunities to talk about their feelings, and validating those feelings, is an important way to support them. What compounds feeling guilty is feeling guilty *and* wrong for feeling it.

Isolation/Loss

Like parents of children on the autism spectrum, siblings can feel isolated in many ways. Siblings often report feelings of loss of a "normal" relationship with their brother/sister; someone who they can confide in, and share hopes and dreams. Many siblings report envying their friends and relatives who share close bonds with non-autistic siblings. One adult sister lamented that, when friends talk about their non-autistic siblings' family or career milestones, she feels she has nothing to contribute to the conversation. Another sibling with young children shared her feelings of loss when friends told stories about their kids enjoying time with cousins.

Siblings can feel isolated from parents, whose time and attention are largely focused on their brothers/sisters. Sibs also experience isolation from friends and the greater community of seemingly carefree, "normal" peers and families who can enjoy outings and trips, and whose time isn't consumed by appointments with doctors, therapists, and teachers. Siblings' need to meet others who share similar experiences and for peer support parallels parents' needs, but siblings typically have fewer opportunities to meet each other.

Providing siblings with opportunities to meet and connect with each other is an important way to help them understand that they are not alone. For busy parents, creating even small windows of time to spend with each individual child can go a long way, and it can also be very helpful to have a trusted adult relative or friend that a sibling can call upon for support.

Pressure to Achieve

Many siblings talk about the pressure to play the "good kid role," and to excel in academics, extracurricular activities, and anything else they take on. Sibs tell us, and research confirms, that most often the pressure to achieve is self-imposed—an attempt to compensate for the perceived limitations and caregiving burden of their brothers and sisters. As one sister of a young man with autism put it, she felt internal pressure to be "perfect on demand." Another sibling attributed his high expectations of himself to his role as a caregiver for his sister with autism. Many sibs describe feeling exhausted by the constant need to deny and deflect any negative thoughts or emotions about their situation, and instead focus on the need to continually excel.

Future Concerns

Even young siblings worry about their brothers' and sisters' futures. One seven-year-old sister told us that she sometimes worried about her brother with autism, because she recognized, even at this young age, that he might not be able to take care of himself. A teen brother whose heart was set on becoming a doctor worried about balancing the demands of a career in medicine with the needs of his brother with autism later in life.

Siblings of all ages, particularly if their brothers and sisters live with parents, or have limited support services, wonder: What role will I play in taking care of my brother or sister? Will my sibling live with me? Will I be my sibling's guardian? What will my financial responsibility be for my brother or sister?

Siblings also worry about their own futures. Will they find a life partner who will accept a future caregiving role? One sibling fell in love and neglected to tell his partner about his two brothers on the autism spectrum, for fear that this information would jeopardize his relationship. The longer he waited, the more he agonized to find the right time to share this part of his life. Siblings also worry that they may themselves have children with autism. One sibling who had a brother with autism began to worry almost as soon as she said her wedding vows about not producing "perfect" grandchildren for her in-laws.

Planning for the future of the person with autism is an ongoing process that should begin early, be revisited often, and provide all family members— the person with the diagnosis, siblings, parents, and other family members/ friends who will be involved down the road—with the opportunity to discuss and weigh in on options and ideas. Families may not have all of the answers about the future, and talking about it together can provide siblings great relief.

Unique Opportunities

The good news is that, for as many unique concerns as siblings experience, there are just as many, if not more, opportunities and strengths that siblings and clinicians supporting them can build upon. Siblings are some of the most resilient, tolerant, resourceful human beings we know. Siblings of those with autism tend to be good at meeting people where they are, because all too often they've seen the repercussions of others not being as gracious toward their brothers and sisters. They recognize and take pride in the accomplishments of their brothers and sisters, and have the wisdom to acknowledge that all of us have strengths and areas for growth.

Many siblings we know tell us that they appreciate their health and opportunities to pursue their goals. Several end up in helping professions and attribute their desire to do good in the world to their experiences with their brothers and sisters. These loyal sibs also appreciate their families, and the friends they choose carefully, with whom they have been through thick and thin.

At the Sibling Support Project, we consider ourselves very lucky to work with siblings. We know that investing time, energy, and resources in supporting siblings has a positive impact on the entire family. We acknowledge that siblinghood, especially for brothers and sisters of people with disabilities, requires work, and a good support system. We are grateful for clinicians and other professionals who take the time to acknowledge, recognize, validate, and support siblings, the family members who will have the longest-lasting relationships with people with autism and other disabilities.

Recommended Resources for Professionals and Families

* The Sibling Support Project: www.siblingsupport.org (see "Our Books and Other Publications" on this site)
* What Siblings Would Like Parents and Professionals to Know: www. siblingsupport.org/documents-for-site/WhatSiblingsWouldLikeParents andServiceProviderstoKnow.pdf
* How to Let Young Siblings Know You Care: www.siblingsupport. org/documents-for-site/how-to-let-young-siblings-know-you-care
* The National Sibling Leadership Network: www.siblingleadership.org
* Meyer, D. (Ed.). (2009). *Thicker than water: Essays by adult siblings of people with disabilities.* Bethesda, MD: Woodbine House, Inc.

About the Author

Emily Holl is the Director of the Sibling Support Project, the first national program dedicated to meeting the life-long and ever-changing needs of siblings of people with special developmental and health concerns. Ms. Holl is a social worker, writer, and trainer who has provided workshops and groups for siblings and families, presented extensively on sibling issues, and researched and written about siblings. Ms. Holl contributed to *Thicker Than Water: Essays by Adult Siblings of People with Disabilities* and co-edited *The Sibling Survival Guide* (Meyer & Holl, 2014). Learn more at www. siblingsupport.org.

References

Hodapp, R. M., Sanderson, K. A., Meskis, S. A., & Casale, E. G. (2017). Adult siblings of persons with intellectual disabilities: Past, present, and future. *International Review of Research in Developmental Disabilities, 53,* 163–202.

Meyer, D., & Holl, E. (Eds.). (2014). *The sibling survival guide: Indispensable information for brothers and sisters of adults with disabilities.* Bethesda, MD: Woodbine House, Inc.

8 The Spectrum of Siblings' Experiences

Brie Turns and Brandon P. Eddy

The sibling relationship is one of the longest-lasting relationships in an individual's life. Siblings often grow up together, confide in one another, and share experiences together throughout their lives. An autism diagnosis for one child may drastically impact the experiences, perceptions, and relationship between siblings. In this chapter, we will discuss a variety of experiences we have had while treating siblings of children with autism. We'll also discuss common concerns reported by siblings and our favorite interventions. Due to the variety of symptoms, strengths, and challenges faced by the child with autism, siblings' experiences will often vary in much the same way. Understanding each sibling's unique experiences, thoughts, beliefs, and feelings is crucial for therapists in order to provide systemic, ethical treatment of families raising children with autism.

Siblings' Experiences

Excluded Siblings

When asking about the family unit, the parent's goals for treatment, and who they would like to attend therapy, some of the most common responses I (B.T.) have heard include: "We have other children, but we are seeking therapy for our child with autism. So, they [siblings] won't be coming," "Our other child is just fine. It's this child we need help with," and "If you can teach our child [with autism] how to behave appropriately, their sibling will be fine."

One of the most common experiences of siblings of children with autism is *exclusion*. I have found that if I do not openly invite siblings of children with autism into the therapy session, they are often left at home or with an extended family member. This overt exclusion can often send negative messages to the sibling, including: "You aren't important enough to be brought," "Your sibling is more deserving of receiving services," or worse yet, "You aren't a part of the family."

Therapists should be aware that, although the parents' primary concern may be with their child with autism, the sibling should be invited into therapy, even if it is for one session. This invitation tells the parents that each child's perspective and role in the family is important and should be evaluated. Next, therapists should ask about the sibling relationship and their relationship with each child, including challenges, strengths, and goals the parents have for enhancing both relationships. Again, this open discussion informs the parents that siblings are an important piece of the family.

Invisible Siblings

When siblings of children with autism do attend therapy, one of the most commonly reported experiences is feeling invisible or feeling as though they are treated differently than their sibling with autism. For example, one 15-year-old sibling stated: "My sibling gets away with *everything*! If I did half the things he does, I would be grounded for life. It's just not fair." Others have shared, "I can't invite my friends over because my parents are so focused on my brother/sister" and "I don't get to attend birthday parties because they don't have time to take me."

In addition to feelings of unfairness and invisibility, siblings often stated they wished their parents would spend more time with them. Siblings have stated that their parents will spend after-school hours managing their siblings' treatment activities, homework, or tantrums. By the end of the night, parents may be too tired to spend time with any child, leaving the neurotypical sibling feeling invisible.

From our experiences, the feelings of invisibility often spike from eight to fourteen years of age. One younger brother recently discussed experiencing anxiety because he did not believe his parents were aware of his challenges and needs. However, as children age, their perspectives typically change. Older teenagers and adult children will typically change their viewpoints into understanding. One teenager recently stated, "I was really angry as a kid, but looking back on it, my parents did the best they could. I know they love me; I just wish they would have showed it more."

One of our most common recommendations is the *The 5 Love Languages* quiz and book for children (Chapman & Campbell, 2016). Parents can spend time with their typically developing child by completing the quiz with them and asking them about how they like to receive love. After learning about each child's love language, parents can look for special times to provide that love to their child. For example, if a child's love language is physical touch, parents can spend two to five minutes at bedtime rubbing their child's back or giving extra hugs during the day. Learning a child's love language can decrease feelings of invisibility by gaining a deeper understanding of the child's needs. Additionally, providing love in the typically developing child's love language can enhance the parent–child relationship.

Embarrassed Siblings

Another topic that seems to present itself when working with siblings is the feeling of embarrassment. Siblings often make statements regarding how their siblings' behavior at home and in public can alter their lives: "I can't have my friends over because I am embarrassed by how my sibling acts." As a result, siblings may spend the majority of time playing at a friend's home instead of their own, or in some cases they do not play with friends at all and become more isolated from their peers.

Siblings also experience embarrassment while in public settings. Because children with autism often struggle with emotional regulation, they are more prone to temper tantrums and emotional outbursts, which can be embarrassing for siblings. One common report from siblings includes, "I get nervous every time I go out in public because I fear my sibling will act out and humiliate me." As a result, siblings may choose to avoid going out in public with their sibling or may distance themselves from their family during social events.

Therapists are advised to discuss these challenging situations with the typically developing sibling and his or her parents. Openly talking about their feelings and potential solutions can help the family identify options for how siblings can handle the embarrassment and also maintain friendships.

Proud Siblings

Although many siblings will state challenging experiences they have with their sibling with autism, not all experiences are negative. A common theme in therapy is siblings being proud of not only their brother or sister with autism, but also how they have developed a special connection or bond with their sibling. Many children with autism struggle with communicating their thoughts, opinions, and feelings. Due to the amount of time spent together, typically developing children are often able to understand and connect with their siblings more than others.

As a solution-focused brief therapist, I (B.T.) usually ask siblings what is going well in their sibling relationship. Many siblings state they are proud of how their sibling has cognitively or emotionally progressed and completed new tasks and challenges. For example, one sibling stated, "After struggling to pass the second grade a couple times, I was so excited for him when he was able to move to the third grade!"

Additionally, siblings report being proud of themselves in relation to their sibling with autism. Recognizing a child with autism's needs, emotions, and thoughts can be very challenging for family members. However, because the sibling bond is unlike any other relationship, siblings often learn how to recognize what their brother or sister needs and is thinking, which can further enhance their relationship: "A lot of people don't understand why my sister does what she does. I know how she feels, what she thinks, and why she does certain things." If therapists are having a difficult time identifying strengths within a family or sibling relationship, we recommend asking strength-focused questions, including: "What is your favorite characteristic about your sibling?", "What is your favorite activity to do with your sibling?", and "Tell me about a time when you felt close to your sibling."

Future Caregiver Siblings

Having a sibling with autism can also influence one's career path. Many siblings report something similar to "I want to go into the helping profession because of my experiences with my brother/sister." Siblings recognize the needs that families with autism have and possess a unique perspective on how to help. Their insight makes them especially qualified to provide aid to families similar to their own.

Siblings also mention that they have witnessed a lack of services available to their sibling and to their family. Many smaller communities lack the resources to provide support for families with autism. Due to experiencing a lack of services, many siblings state they would like to help families with autism by specializing in healthcare professions geared toward helping these families.

We advise clinicians not to push siblings into potentially helping others, but instead to encourage them to discuss their desire to help. Some siblings have stated that their parents often pressure them to pursue certain degrees or certifications in order to help their sibling, which could further the notion that the sibling's world should revolve around their sibling with autism.

Recommended Intervention

Sandtray

One of our favorite interventions for siblings who are struggling to connect with one another is a sandtray activity. At the beginning of session, we ask siblings to, "Create your world together using the figurines or miniatures you see on the shelf." Siblings will often discuss items they want to include and each pick their own special figurines. When we ask siblings to tell us about the world they created, we often see children smiling and laughing as they discuss the "dragons," "princesses," "wars," and "hidden creatures" that make up their life together. This is useful in understanding each child's perspective on the sibling relationship. The sand tray introduction goes something like this:

Therapist:	I would like to do an activity using this sandtray today. Is that OK?
Neurotypical Sibling (NS):	Yes, that sounds like fun.
Therapist:	Great. I would like you to use these figurines to create a favorite memory you have of you and your brother. Could you do that?
NS:	Yes. I will do that. *(Child places figurines in sand tray.)*
Therapist:	Can you explain what you created here?
NS:	Yes. This Captain America figure is standing between these mean dinosaur guys and me.
Therapist:	I see. Can you tell me more about that?
NS:	Captain America protects me when people are being mean to me or calling me names at school. The dinosaurs are mean guys because they scare me.
Therapist:	I see. So Captain America is like a hero and defends this guy from the dinosaurs?
NS:	Yeah. He makes sure nobody hurts this guy.

Additionally, therapists could ask children to create their favorite memory with their sibling and their worst memory with their sibling. By asking children to create their favorite memory therapists are able to highlight strengths and successes in the sibling's relationship. On the other hand, asking children to create a difficult experience with their sibling helps the therapist recognize areas of growth that can take place in the sibling relationship.

Sandtrays can be used with siblings together as well. Using figurines with children with autism is often helpful due to their ability to visually explain how they view their relationships. Individuals with autism often struggle with understanding, and then explaining, their relationships with others. Sandtray activities allow children to provide a visual picture in order to communicate their thoughts and feelings.

While completing this activity with children with autism, therapists should be aware of potential sensory issues. Some children with autism may experience discomfort regarding the way the sand feels. However, in our own personal experiences we have not encountered this sensory issue when working with children with autism. The therapist may need to adapt this intervention based on the individual needs of the child/children.

Summary

It's important to remember when treating families raising a child with autism that each family is unique and experiences different struggles, strengths, and growth areas. Sibling relationships are often complex and siblings of children with autism will rarely report the exact same experiences and feelings described by other siblings. Therapists should come from a curious standpoint, rather than an expert role, and attempt to understand each sibling's unique experiences, concerns, and feelings.

Recommended Resources for Professionals

- Goff, B. S. N., & Springer, N. P. (Eds.). (2017). *Intellectual and developmental disabilities: A roadmap for families and professionals.* New York, NY: Routledge.
- Turns, B., & Eddy, B. P. (2017). The use of puppets to externalize a child's "problem". In A. A. Drewes & C. Schaefer (Eds.), *Puppets and play therapy: A practical guidebook* (pp. 121–125). New York, NY: Routledge.
- Turns, B., Eddy, B. P., & Smock, S. (2016). Working with siblings of children with Autism: A solution focused approach. *Australian and New Zealand Journal of Family Therapy, 37*(4), 558–571.
- Turns, B., Ramisch, J., & Whiting, J. (Eds.). (2019). *Systemically treating Autism: A clinician's guide for empowering families.* New York, NY: Routledge.

Recommended Resources for Families

- Farmer, B., Farmer, M., & Neff, E. (2017). *What about me?: A book by and for an Autism sibling.* Cincinatti, OH: Farmer Publishing.
- Harris, S. L., & Glasberg, B. A. (2012). *Siblings of children with autism: A guide for families.* Bethesda, MD: Woodbine House.

About the Authors

Brie Turns, PhD, LAMFT is an Assistant Professor of Marriage and Family Therapy at Fuller Theological Seminary-Arizona. She recently co-edited the text *Systemically Treating Autism* and has published over a dozen articles and book chapters on families raising children with autism. Dr. Turns has spoken at state, national, and international conferences on the topic of families and autism. She also enjoys training clinicians how to effectively treat the entire family raising a child with autism and has spoken at Texas Tech, Brigham Young University, and Yale's Developmental Disability Clinic. For additional information, please visit www.TheFamilyTherapist. org or contact Dr. Turns at BrieTurns@Fuller.edu.

Brandon Eddy, PhD, MFT-I is an Assistant Professor in the Couple and Family Therapy Program at the University of Nevada Las Vegas. Dr. Eddy has published several journal articles and book chapters on medical family therapy topics such as postpartum depression, miscarriage, and autism spectrum disorder. Dr. Eddy has presented his research at international, national, and local conferences. He resides in Las Vegas, Nevada, with his wife and children. Dr. Eddy can be contacted at brandon.eddy@unlv.edu.

Reference

Chapman, G., & Campbell, R. (2016). *The 5 love languages of children: The secret to loving children effectively.* Chicago, IL: Moody Publishers.

9 Addressing the Needs of Siblings in Adolescence and Young Adulthood

Emily Daniels

By the time siblings of those with autism hit their teen years, they are all too familiar with the meltdowns, restricted or repetitive interests, social challenges, communication difficulties, and sensory issues that accompany having a sibling on the spectrum. Adolescents and young adults have well-established connections with their autistic brothers and sisters, though their relationship may change over time. Roles as caregivers, teachers, babysitters, advocates, friends, and siblings all intermingle and many young people observe that they must grow up more quickly than others who have typically developing brothers and sisters. While the aggregate of playing these parts can create a special bond, it can also lead to a lot of ambivalent feelings that bounce from appreciation to resentment, admiration to embarrassment, and patience to intolerance. Moreover, adolescence and early adulthood is a time of self-discovery and independence, often conflicting with supporting the needs of a brother or sister. Coupled with concerns about the future and the desire to establish oneself in the world, this can make siblinghood even more challenging to navigate and reconcile.

Autism is complicated and often unpredictable, and the realities of day-to-day life during this formative time of development for young people can be confusing and difficult to cope with for adolescents and young adults. Yet with positive parent attitudes about their children's differences, open communication and guidance, adolescent and young adult neurotypically developing (ND) siblings report being more empathetic, caring, tolerant, independent, responsible, able to commit, loyal, and resilient than if they didn't have a sibling with autism. In my clinical practice, these siblings express that they learn endlessly from their brother/sister, and that their relationship also contributes to valuing the important things in life and providing a deep and lasting bond.

What Adolescent/Young Adult Siblings Want You to Know

Ella, 17, is a bright, sociable girl who is active in school clubs and always willing to help out. Ella adores her 13-year-old sister with autism, Page, and says that she is not only inspiring, but has made Ella a better person. Still, Ella's parents encouraged her to come see me as she seemed to be worrying a lot and was experiencing occasional panic attacks at school. She had always been a good student, but recently found herself struggling in subjects that had once been easy for her. She had been spending a lot of time in her room, particularly when Page was having meltdowns (which were becoming more and more frequent). Mom and dad also expressed concerns about Ella's recent avoidance of activities she once found pleasurable and her increasing defensiveness when asked about her day. Since starting therapy, Ella has revealed that she is enormously stressed about her younger sister. In addition to the volatility that accompanies her sister's meltdowns, she reports being overwhelmed by pressure to live at home during college (for financial reasons as well as to help with her sister). Moreover, she is frustrated that her future (along with many missed opportunities from the past) is being determined by her sister's needs rather than her own. Since being in counseling, Ella has expressed that she feels significant relief, as these thoughts and feelings have caused her enormous guilt, and she has been ashamed to say them aloud.

Ella is just one example of the effects of having a sibling on the autism spectrum, though her story is not unusual. While siblings are unlikely to share a diagnosis of autism, a significant number demonstrate other clinically diagnosable issues such as attention deficit hyperactivity disorder, chronic depression, obsessive compulsive disorder, and generalized anxiety. Additionally, perspective taking, communication skills, and emotional sensitivity to others may not come as easily for some ND siblings. While symptoms may not present as obviously as their brother or sister on the spectrum, these conditions shouldn't be ignored. Aside from these concerns, ND siblings typically share numerous concerns, including worry, mixed emotions about their autistic sibling, and feeling invisible to their parents.

Pervasive Worry

Pervasive worry accompanies having a brother/sister with autism. Many ND siblings express that they feel a strong need to protect their brother/sister. This may range from shielding them from bullying and publicly defending their unusual behaviors to more directly protecting their sibling by preventing unsafe actions (eloping, self-harm, being taken advantage of, and so on). These lifelong concerns instill a sense of responsibility for the care of their brother/sister and ambivalence about how much time to spend with them.

Whether they like it or not, ND siblings are likely to be the longest relationship in the lives of their autistic brother/sister, leading to anxiety about what life may look like in the future. All of the ND siblings I've spoken with want a fulfilling life for their autistic brother/sister, but many are conflicted about their role in it. They worry about having to fill the parental role for their autistic brother/sister, express concerns about whether or not they are up to the task of serving as long-term caregiver, and worry about their ability to plan and find needed supports. Young adulthood is marked by numerous milestones towards independence, and many ND siblings feel stress about moving away (to college, for work, or for a relationship). Siblings typically state that they wish to be supported for whatever decisions they make and for whatever level of involvement they wish to have.

Mixed Emotions about Sibling

I have not met an ND sibling who hasn't felt a wide range of emotions about their brother/sister with autism. While siblings are comfortable with positive feelings such as love, admiration, and pride, they express guilt and worry over less "acceptable" feelings such as embarrassment, anger, resentment, shame, and exclusion. Several siblings have shared feeling disappointment that they don't have a brother or sister who can provide a reciprocal relationship or support and listen to *them*. And, when the sibling relationship *does* follow "normal" patterns (which include arguments) they feel guilt for the conflict. They may not want too much responsibility, but there is discord when they feel left out of decision-making for their brother's/sister's care.

Many ND siblings have shared that they find it challenging to reconcile the difficult thoughts they experience internally. Sometimes, they say that they do not feel their feelings are valid, and do not wish to stress their parents out with more problems. Still, feelings of caregiver burden, worry about doing the "right" thing, stress from unpredictability and emotional challenges, feeling "different," and a sense of isolation resonate inside. Many ND siblings state that they worry about their own inadequacies, that they may also be on the autism spectrum, or struggle with social or communication issues. This is coupled with the mixed emotions of needing to be independent, wanting to achieve, and loyalty and responsibility to their brother/sister, which can lead to depression, anxiety, and low self-esteem.

Feeling Invisible to Parents

When one child in a household has a special need (and a high-demand need such as autism) the family system shifts, making it a struggle to create normalcy as the world revolves around the brother/sister with autism. Some ND siblings say that they feel undervalued or underappreciated, and often view their own challenges as ignored or missed by their parents as if they are invisible. They also state that, even while understanding *why*, vastly different parental expectations for them vs. their autistic brother/sister can also be frustrating. Feelings of exclusion are also reported, as families frequently miss "typical" family outings and events because their brother/sister can't manage them. And, over time, these missed events turn into fewer invitations from extended family and friends, leading to a further sense of "otherness" and isolation.

How Practitioners Can Support Siblings

The range of concerns expressed by ND siblings is wide and extensive. Just as their autistic brothers or sisters need community support, so, too, do these siblings. Four core concepts repeatedly emerge suggesting ways to support adolescent and young adult siblings of someone with autism. These include *normalizing, educating, teaching coping skills*, and *encouraging future planning*.

Normalizing

One of the most difficult parts of having a brother or sister on the autism spectrum is the need for homeostasis. Autism can easily tip the scales of family systems with the immediate and continuous needs of the autistic child, creating chronic stress for families, while also directing family resources (energy, time, attention, money) to the child with autism. This can skew an ND sibling's idea of what family life is supposed to be, as reality may conflict with what they see in the families of peers or imagine through media. Many ND siblings report a strong desire to be "normal." They may find it difficult to explain the unusual and sometimes difficult behaviors of their autistic sibling, and often avoid situations or isolate in order to escape having to face these challenges. Some siblings report wanting an "ordinary" family – one in which they field less drama, receive comparable attention from parents, and have a more give-and-take relationship with their brother or sister. They often feel they are the only ones going through this experience, and that most people simply don't understand. Consequently, depression and anxiety are common in this population, and support is needed to normalize their experience and manage difficult emotions. ND siblings can benefit from finding others with shared experience, recognizing their experience is as valid and normal as any other, feeling understood for having complex feelings, and reducing the stigma of the diagnosis of autism spectrum disorder.

Educating

There are many benefits to education for ND siblings. One, learning about the autism spectrum encourages siblings to understand why their autistic brother or sister acts the way they do. Many siblings report that this helps them develop more empathy and patience, as they better comprehend the root of challenging behaviors. Education also helps them depersonalize these behaviors, so that they are less likely to internalize their autistic brother or sister's difficult and sometimes directed actions. Understanding autism also helps to *be* a better sibling, providing more ideas about how to both support their brother or sister as well as learn new and effective ways to spend time together. Additionally, education allows ND siblings to be better advocates. As young people grow into adolescence and young adulthood, they often seek to participate in the care of their brother or sister. Many express gratitude for being included in the process and feel empowered by knowing how they can help. This is especially meaningful as they may one day take over the parent's role of caregiver. It also allows them to understand how best to meet the needs of their autistic brother or sister and seek resources and support as they get older.

Teaching Coping Skills

Even typically developing adolescents and young adults need a toolbox of strategies to deal with the challenges of growing up through this dynamic stage of life. ND siblings experience all the confusion and chaos of other adolescents and young adults but compound their difficulties with the added and significant stress of having a sibling with autism in the family. Thus, they are often dealing with situations before they are developmentally prepared to do so. Caregiver burden and feeling responsible for their brother or sister can tip the scales of managing daily living. Therefore, having a solid set of coping skills is imperative for their mental health. Strategies for managing stress, regulating emotions, increasing self-care, handling difficult moments, and learning new ways to connect with those around them can make the difference between well-being and distress.

Encouraging Future Planning

Open family conversations about (and written lists) of community services such as respite care, emergency contacts, doctors, preferred therapists (occupational, physical, and speech language therapists), government support, day programs, and mental health support (be it group or individual) can help put an ND sibling's mind at ease about how to assist their brother or sister in times of need. ND siblings who express resilience and mental well-being say that they have been significantly helped by candid discussions with their parents, where future plans and supports for their brother or sister are discussed and determined. These families create formal plans to meet the needs of the autistic sibling, allotting resources for care and setting up contingencies so that the ND sibling doesn't feel overwhelmed by decision-making and caregiver burden, so they can retain their role as brother or sister.

What Support Can Look Like

A strengths-based, solution-focused approach enhances the abilities of siblings to manage the daily difficulties they face. This type of therapy also helps highlight the individual's unique strengths and empowers them to feel competent in their role. Helping young people feel valued both for their role as a sibling as well as for their own interests, enthusiasms, and dreams can be extremely impactful for maintaining a positive self-outlook and sense of meaning and importance. Family therapy can be beneficial to help to navigate relationships and needs with parents. All too often, ND siblings fail to bring their concerns to their parents for fear of being an added burden. Family counseling is ideal for providing a safe and manageable setting to allow ND siblings to express themselves. Additionally, parent psychoeducation, support groups, online support, and personal mentors can be useful adjuncts to treatment.

Parent Psychoeducation

One of the best predictors for sibling well-being is having parents who display positive, resilient attitudes towards their children. This comes from understanding the challenges faced and an acceptance of the differences involved. Two or three counseling sessions can go a long way in helping parents with their ND child. It has the added bonus of alleviating guilt for perceived neglect that many parents experience. Sessions are likely to include current research on sibling challenges, perspective taking, positive parenting strategies for sibling success, ways to help highlight and address the strengths of their ND child, discussions about future planning, and resources for sibling support, including available peer group opportunities and literature that speaks to the experience of the ND child.

Support Group

Support groups provide a safe place to process challenges and reduce isolation as siblings spend time with others who "get it." These can take the form of non-therapy (but therapeutic) Teen Sibshops; organized, informal monthly get-togethers for teens and/or young adult siblings of brothers or sisters with autism (scheduling around an activity or interest is often helpful); or a more structured setting with a facilitator (licensed counselor/therapist). The goals of the support group are threefold: (1) to normalize the experience by being around others who understand; (2) to provide a setting for problem solving and sharing ideas; and (3) to introduce information and strategies to help navigate the ND sibling journey within a safe group of peers. Most support groups provide the added benefit of long-standing friendships, and many siblings report that they appreciate having a place that is just for them.

Online Support

In adolescence and young adulthood, ND siblings may struggle to buy into the idea of belonging to a structured group. For these young people, having an online place to safely share their experiences and concerns can provide many of the benefits of group counseling, without the imposed structure (and with a sense of privacy and potential anonymity). This type of support is also not time-sensitive, and siblings can share thoughts and ideas whenever the mood strikes. There are also numerous websites that provide psychoeducation and personal stories that can be helpful to the ND sibling.

Personal Mentors

Having a close, personal mentor to help guide ND siblings through life events can be very impactful. Connections with slightly older peers who understand (and perhaps who have even lived through similar things) can be really helpful to make sense of experiences, safely share feelings, problem solve, and help feel connected and understood. Having a mentor can also help reduce loneliness and isolation. University programs, parenting groups and organizations like Big Brother/Big Sister can be good resources for finding mentors.

Summary

There is no one-size-fits-all approach to supporting ND siblings. The complications for supporting adolescents/young adults dealing with standard human development, identity, and social complexities mean that each sibling will experience their role differently as well as feel the need to process their challenges according to their unique outlook. Most important of all is to hear from the siblings themselves, and allow them to indicate where they would like help and guidance. Whether it be through reading, social media, face-to-face support, or family guidance, the mindful intention of looking through the lens of a sibling, truly listening to their concerns, helping them to feel valued, and working to meet their needs can be a great service to their well-being, and to their brother or sister on the autism spectrum.

Recommended Resources for Professionals

- Meyer, D. J., & Vadasy, P. F. (1994). *Sibshops: Workshops for siblings of children with special needs*. Baltimore, MD: P.H. Brookes Pub. Co.
- Orsmond, G. I., & Seltzer, M. M. (2007). Siblings of individuals with autism spectrum disorders across the life course. *Mental Retardation and Developmental Disabilities Research Reviews, 13*(4), 313–320. doi:10.1002/mrdd.20171

- Meadan, H., Stoner, J. B., & Angell, M. E. (2010). Review of literature related to the social, emotional, and behavioral adjustment of siblings of individuals with autism spectrum disorder. *Journal of Developmental and Physical Disabilities, 22*(1), 83–100. doi:10.1007/s10882-009-9171-7

Recommended Resources for Families

- Autism Speaks-A Siblings Guide to Autism: www.autismspeaks.org/sites/default/files/2018-08/Siblings%20Guide%20to%20Autism.pdf
- National Autism Association- ASD & Siblings Toolkit: http://nationalautismassociation.org/asd-siblings-toolkit/
- The Autism Community in Action-Teens with ASD: Siblings https://tacanow.org/family-resources/teens-with-asd-siblings/
- Organization for Autism Research-Resources: https://researchautism.org/resources/

About the Author

Emily Daniels, M.S.W., R.P., M.Ed. is a psychotherapist and social worker in Fort Collins, Colorado who supports families with children with disabilities. Ms. Daniels runs groups for young people on the spectrum and provides individual, sibling, parent, and partner counseling using a strengths-based approach. In addition, Ms. Daniels is the mother of a super-enthusiastic boy on the autism spectrum and a regular contributor to *Autism Parent Magazine*. You can find Ms. Daniels at www.danielscounseling.com and at www.thesociallearningproject.com.

Part IV

Enhancing Interpersonal Communication with Speech Language Pathology

Now that you have assembled a full team of participants in your office (identified client, parents, siblings, spouse, extended family), it is time to start making referrals to professionals *outside* of your treatment room. We observe that top referrals continue to be to speech language pathologists (SLPs), occupational therapists, and psychiatrists. The next two parts will cover speech language therapy and occupational therapy, with psychiatry later in the book.

While therapists are making more referrals to SLPs than we once did, there continues to be some mystery around what SLPs *do* in their offices. Parents wonder why they need to schedule an appointment with an SLP if they can understand their child perfectly?

In this part we hear three SLPs explain why highly verbal clients can and should be referred for therapy. (Hint: making friends and social connections requires the *language* piece of their training – and they are happy to do it!) We also learn how to prepare your clients for the referral, questions you might ask the family before making the referral, and some very specific goals that an SLP might target in treatment. Now that we have an SLP on our team, we will never work without one again!

10 Improving Quality of Life with Communication Coaching

Redefining Speech and Language Therapy

Gina-Marie Moravcik

While mental health therapists are increasingly making referrals to speech language therapists, there is clearly still a gap in knowledge regarding the role of speech language services in the treatment of autism. When most people are asked what a speech pathologist does, the typical response is that they help individuals to learn how to speak, or learn to speak more clearly due to poor articulation or speech impairments (e.g., stuttering). While those statements are true, that response does not capture the vast scope of language disorders treated within the autism spectrum and related disorders. Speech language pathologists (SLPs) are commonly referred to as "speech therapist" or "speech teacher" as opposed to "speech *language* pathologist." It is possible that when the word "language" is eliminated, people forget that we treat language disorders as well, not just speech impediments. As SLPs, our education and clinical training prepare us to treat impairments in the form, content, and use of one's communication abilities. The American Speech and Hearing Association (ASHA) defines language as the comprehension and/or use of spoken, written, and/or other communication systems. This includes *phonology* (the study of sounds), *morphology* (the study of grammatical inflections), and *syntax* (how sentences are structured), all of which SLPs address, as well as *semantics* (word meaning, relationships between words). SLPs also address use of language, referred to as *pragmatics*, which pertains to the rules associated with the language in conversation and broader social situations (ASHA, 1993). When treating autistic clients, SLPs also typically address higher-order language skills such as inferencing and comprehension of abstract language, as deficits in these higher-order language skills can have a significant impact on academic and social functioning.

How SLPs Help Individuals on the Autism Spectrum

Autism spectrum disorder includes persistent deficits in social communication and social interaction across multiple contexts, as manifested by deficits in social emotional reciprocity, nonverbal communication behaviors, and developing, maintaining, and understanding relationships. The severity of autism is determined by social communication impairments and the presence of restricted patterns of behavior (American Psychiatric Association, 2019).

Impairments in social communication are at the heart of an autism diagnosis. Common comorbid diagnoses treated in individuals with autism include traditional speech disturbances and learning disorders. For example, many students with autism struggle with a traditional speech disturbance. Speech disturbances may include *prosody* issues, which refers to differences in intonation, stress pattern, rate of speech and volume, dysfluency (i.e., stuttering), and oral/verbal *apraxia* (an inability to execute oral motor movements which negatively affects speech production).

The majority of school-age clients, as well as the increasingly recognized adult autistic population, are treated for comorbid dyslexia (language-based reading disorder), mixed receptive and expressive language disorder (difficulties in understanding language and being able to verbally and cohesively express thoughts, ideas, and so on) and social communication disorders. Individuals who experience social communication difficulties have difficulty using language to socialize, problem solve, and advocate for themselves when needed. The form and content of their language are considered to be within normal limits. Given their highly concrete way of thinking, these students often struggle in their ability to read between the lines or accurately process what is said. In light of the current autism spectrum disorder definition and the clear emphasis on language abilities, the SLP's role on the treatment team is not only necessary, but pivotal in ensuring the best possible outcome at any age. The majority (greater than 80%) of my current private practice clients are treated for mixed receptive and expressive language disorder and social communication diagnoses.

Goal of the SLP and the Three Cs

The crucial role of the SLP might be more widely known if others felt as strongly that communication (verbal and nonverbal), emotional regulation, and socialization go hand in hand in any context. For an individual who does not inherently use, recognize, interpret, or respond to communicative behaviors that would help them more successfully navigate social interactions across contexts, direct and concrete instruction is key. We continue to see the need for referrals for those individuals on the spectrum who are either diagnosed with or self-identify as having "Asperger syndrome," despite their seemingly average or above-average verbal abilities. Strong cognitive abilities do not exempt a person from experiencing communication problems.

A typical long-term therapy goal would be to develop what I like to refer to as the "three Cs": *competent, confident,* and *clear* communication. The three Cs are needed in order to assert yourself, express your thoughts/

feelings calmly and directly, and develop and maintain positive relationships through understanding another person's needs, communication behaviors, and perspectives. Typical goals pertain to the concrete and practical break-down of nonverbal and verbal behavior that will positively affect social, work, and peer relationships. Goal formation is driven by the observations made at the time of the comprehensive communication assessment (if done by the treating SLP) and/or input from the client and family member(s). Clients, family members, and additional treatment team members should be asked what is thought to be the greatest barrier to effective communication, academic/social success, and vocational endeavors. Referrals often come from the aforementioned sources and from the treatment team, with the client as the central focus of the team. Many adult clients have sought speech and language therapy due to their own awareness of their social communication difficulties and the impact it has had on their personal and work-based relationships.

What to Expect once a Referral to a SLP Is Made

Therapists should make referrals for a comprehensive communication assessment or treatment when they observe speech impairments, as well as when they observe language impairments affecting the use of language for social problem solving or relationship development and maintenance. Those individuals who are already receiving services in group social skills or individually in traditional psychological counseling formats, but who have yet to generalize the skills taught, would benefit from a closer look at underlying communication deficits. The best place to start is with a communication evaluation, but the client may have the ability to articulate their experienced communication impairments and want to begin treatment as soon as possible. Much collaboration happens during the evaluation process. Many times, an individual seen by a colleague (psychologist, neuropsychologist, psychiatrist) in search of a first-time diagnosis will be referred for a communication evaluation. Evaluation measures for children and young adults under the age of 22 years typically involve standardized and informal testing. Unfortunately, the current adult communication standardized test batteries do not meet the diagnostic needs of our aging/older autistic population. As a result, communication evalua-tions for adults who are potentially on the spectrum include a very detailed informal analysis of verbal and nonverbal communication obtained via real-time conversation, client interview, and family member interviews (if available). Findings are shared with the family and collaborating diagnosti-cians to provide the client and their families with the most accurate diagnosis possible and to inform treatment across disciplines.

The typical timeline for services ranges greatly based on several factors including, but not limited to, the severity of the targeted communicative behavior, the level of social motivation, communication, awareness they currently possess, and most of all, their level of active engagement in therapy (participation, ability to complete carryover exercises for the sake of generalization, and so on). A standard approach is a weekly 45-minute session at the onset of therapy. As the individual develops and applies those newly learned skills, they may shift to bimonthly appointments. As gains are maintained, the client may shift to monthly and eventually quarterly appointments. Communication is context- and transition-dependent, so clients are well informed that they may return at any time for additional support, if needed. For those clients who are newly employed, it is preferred that they remain consistent with their weekly therapy until they reach the end of their probationary period at work (typically three months).

The mode of service delivery varies based on the needs of the individual. While individual treatment allows for a deeper analysis/application of communication skills in a private setting, group work allows individuals to actively apply what they have learned in a semi-structured safe environment, where others are experiencing similar difficulties. Community-based programming is especially helpful for older individuals, particularly teens and adults seeking or entering vocational settings. For this population, specific feedback and guidance in applying contextually appropriate social communication are imperative. Due to technological advancements, SLPs also provide Health Insurance Portability and Accountability Act (HIPAA)-compliant telepractice sessions for those clients who want to pursue therapy, but lack access to a local provider. Telepractice sessions also allow for more flexibility for the schedules of adult clients.

How Can the SLP Aid in Employment-Related Needs?

Speech and language services should be innovative/creative and span several service delivery models. Ideally the SLP should work as part of a team with other treating clinicians from various fields and backgrounds (e.g., psychology, social work, psychiatry). A multidisciplinary evaluation and treatment team is highly beneficial in evaluations (internal or collaborative) and treatment. While SLPs are known to add value to the evaluation and traditional treatment services, we are needed in other areas as well. We continue to identify and diagnose adults as autistic, and to recognize the adult autistic population continues to experience communication challenges affecting gainful, competitive employment. There is a significant need for the SLP to support our client's employment or secondary education endeavors. For example, our group, Sunrise Speech and Language Services, has become New York State (NYS) Adult Career and Continuing Education Services-Vocational Rehabilitation (ACCES-VR) providers, further helping adults improve communication skills at their place of employment. NYS core rehabilitation initiatives are an encouraging sign that our government recognizes the adult autistic population and the need for continued support post high school graduation. According to current Autism Speaks (n.d.) data:

- 85% of college grads affected by autism are unemployed, compared to the national unemployment rate of 4.5%.
- Over the next decade 500,000 teens will age out of school-based services and enter adulthood.
- More than half of the adults with autism remain unemployed and unenrolled in higher education in the two years post high school.

Lastly, many services seem to "disappear" once a student with autism graduates from high school and no longer has an Individualized Education Plan (IEP). One of those services that tends to vanish even before high school graduation are social skills groups. Adults on the spectrum are in need of these services well into adulthood, yet there are very few services offered; Nevertheless we find our clients benefit from breaking down workplace interactions, interviewing skills, developing communication skills to support their employment and advance, interactions with possible romantic interests, and so on. Social skill groups are necessary to assist these adults with their personal, career, and independent living goals. These skills range from simple communicative initiation and turn taking (traits needed when conducting conversations); to more developed sensitivity to the listener and word association skills (needed for vocabulary development and development of topic relatedness); to advanced self-advocacy (a skill needed to aid individuals in speaking for themselves to explain their thoughts, feelings, and needs); to learning how to work and communicate on team-based projects or conversing with coworkers verbally or electronically (skills needed to maintain and advance in the workplace), and so on.

Intervention is provided at all ages. However, our largest client group consists of tweens, teens, and adults. Services delivered to these older age groups typically entail a higher level of self-monitoring and reflection, requiring a greater degree of perspective taking, and metalinguistic abilities. The current emphasis and usage of social media are also greater amongst this age range as opposed to working with children. Given the presence of social media (whether liked or not) and how frequently people communicate through these platforms, we would be amiss if we were to ignore teaching the hidden communication rules needed to successfully navigate the digital world. Many of our adults experience comorbid anxiety and depression, largely due to their past communication and social difficulties. As a result, we provide indepth counseling and self-advocacy services. We strongly encourage our adult clients to allow family involvement in their treatment regimen as much of communication is perceived by the communicative partner.

Summary

For those therapists who are new to treating individuals with autism, it would help you to anticipate collaboration with family members regardless of the age of your client. Communication with collateral contacts is quite valuable, as these family members can provide abundant insight and contextual information about your client's gifts and challenges. In addition, they can provide direct feedback in skill acquisition and generalization. Collaboration with other professionals will be required and will assist your client in reaching their goals. There are *always* gifts and strengths that are a direct result of autism. These strengths must be highlighted and employed as often as possible. It is imperative to link your communication goals to the emotions of your client and all who interact with him/her. Communication doesn't happen in a bubble. It is inseparable from socialization and emotional regulation. After all, we are treated based on how we make others feel. Individuals with autism want and deserve respect, opportunities, and understanding from the neuro-typical world.

Recommended Resources for Professionals and Families

- Adult Career & Continuing Education Services: www.acces.nysed.gov
- Asperger/Autism Network: www.aane.org
- Children and Adults with Attention-Deficit/Hyperactivity Disorder (CHADD): www.chadd.org
- Gaus, V. (2019). *Cognitive-behavioral therapy for adults with autism spectrum disorder* (2nd ed.). New York, NY: Guilford Press.
- *Global and Regional Asperger Syndrome Partnership*: www.grasp.org
- Sunrise Speech & Language Services: www.sunriseslpsvcs.com
- Wiley, L. H. (1999). *Pretending to be normal: Living with Asperger's syndrome*. London, UK: Jessica Kingsley Publishers.
- Zaks, Z. (2006). *Life and love: Positive strategies for autistic adults*. Kansas City, MO: Autism Asperger Publishing Company.

About the Author

Gina-Marie Moravcik, MA, CCC-SLP is a NYS licensed SLP who has worked with individuals on the spectrum of all ages, in a multidisciplinary setting and is the current owner of Sunrise Speech and Language Services. Although Ms. Moravcik has assessed and treated a variety of communication disorders, she is known among the autistic community for her evaluations and treatment of social communication disorders, focusing on higher-order language content and social use/problem solving. Ms. Moravcik has created and led social skills groups with an emphasis on conversation and perspective-taking abilities. She has also consulted to several school districts on Long Island. Ms. Moravcik is a contributing author to the book *Girls Growing Up on the Autism Spectrum*. She is an active presenter at the local, state, national, and international level for various professional organizations. She can be reached at Gmoravcik@sunriseslpsvcs.com or via www.sunriseslpsvcs.com.

References

American Psychiatric Association. (2019). *What is autism spectrum disorder?* Retrieved from www.psychiatry.org/patients-families/autism/what-is-autism-spectrum-disorder

American Speech-Language-Hearing Association. (1993). *Definitions of communication disorders and variations* [Relevant Paper]. Retrieved from www.asha.org/policy

Autism Speaks. (n.d.). *Autism facts and figures.* Retrieved from www.autismspeaks.org/autism-facts-and-figures

11 Everybody Communicates!

Kelly Lorenz

When contemplating the topic of communication skills in adolescents and adults on the autism spectrum, it is valuable to recognize that no two individuals with autism are the same; every individual has strengths and weaknesses in their ability to communicate. Referrals for speech language pathology evaluations occur as soon as it is suspected by a parent, caregiver, therapist, educator, or medical professional that an individual has a delay in their ability to understand or express language. The communication skills of individuals with autism can range from non-verbal to high-verbal. A speech language pathologist (SLP) will be involved in educational diagnostic evaluations as receptive, expressive, social/pragmatic language, articulation, and phonology skills are all areas in which an individual with autism may have deficits. A comprehensive assessment will provide information about an individual's vocabulary and language strengths and weaknesses gathered through formal (standardized tests) and informal (observation) measures.

What Areas Do SLPs Treat?

One area that SLPs assess and treat is articulation and phonology. *Articulation* (forming of sounds) and *phonology* (the rules and structure of speech sounds) error rates for individuals with autism who do not have accompanying severe disabilities resemble that of the general population (Hewitt, 2015). Individuals with deficits in speech sound development at the elementary education level will most likely be identified and assessed in the school setting. If it is determined that a student's speech is difficult to understand and if the student has a good chance of correcting speech sound errors, then the student will be diagnosed with a speech impairment and speech therapy services will be provided to correct speech sound errors.

Progress on remediation of speech sound errors can vary from person to person. In order to make effective progress, an individual must be able to hear the difference between a correct versus incorrect production, produce the sound in isolation, and accept a model by looking at the SLP's mouth in order to see how the sound is correctly produced. If an individual has difficulty making eye contact with others, consistently accepting a model may be difficult. There are also speech sounds that are more challenging to produce than others. For example, the /r/ sound can be difficult to produce as there is not a strong visual for the sound (production of the sound primarily occurs in the oral cavity) and there are many different types of /r/ sounds (e.g., /air/, /ear/, /or/, /er/). While persisting speech sound errors may not greatly affect an individual with autism's intelligibility, it may negatively impact their interactions socially and professionally (Hewitt, 2015).

Another area that SLPs assess and treat is language. Receptive language, which is the ability to understand language, precedes and develops prior to expressive language, which is the ability to communicate thoughts, feelings, and needs. We must understand before we can express. The levels of language include *pragmatics* (social language), *semantics* (word/sentence meaning), *syntax* (grammar rules), and *phonology* (sound rules). If a student's language abilities scores fall at or below the "below-average range," then the student will be diagnosed with a language impairment and speech therapy services will be provided to improve language abilities.

Augmentive and Alternative Communication (AAC)

Individuals who are non-verbal, have limited verbal skills, or have emerging verbal skills, may benefit from using AAC. A form of AAC is referred to as a Picture Exchange Communication System (PECS), in which a picture or symbol represents an object, item, or concept. SLPs use core vocabulary, or high-frequency words starting with actions such as "go," "stop," "give," and "more," as these words are more likely to elicit action and the opportunity to engage in reciprocal communication (for example, when the individual touches the "go" picture, the music turns on).

Social Language

As a student reaches middle or high school age and if they have demonstrated developmentally or age-appropriate language abilities, an SLP may transition to targeting more functional skills such as social language. Social language includes asking and answering questions, engaging in reciprocal conversation, and understanding idioms and figurative language. A student may be dismissed from speech therapy services in the educational setting if the student has reached all their goals, displays age-appropriate academic abilities, or is no longer making progress on their goals. Research suggests, however, that language difficulties, particularly in vocabulary and syntax, can persist into adolescence or adulthood for an individual with autism, even for those with IQ scores in an average range. Future research should include the examination of communication skills, as well as formal and informal measures of communication skills, for adults with autism as this currently is not a well-researched area (Hewitt, 2015).

Accessing Services

Speech language services are most easily accessed through school-based programming. As an individual gets older, it becomes more difficult to secure funding other than by privately paying for services regardless of the level of severity or need. However, as opportunities are being created for individuals to seek college degrees, the need for improving access to speech therapy services outside of primary and secondary education has been created (Alpern & Zager, 2007). Some examples of funding sources include insurance, grants, Medicaid, and Medicaid Waiver. If continued support for communication skills beyond high school is warranted, clinicians may need to get creative in order to access services for their clients. Some ideas for accessing services may include: contacting a local college with a communication disorders program to possibly receive reduced-fee or free services at a college clinic from student clinicians supervised by professionals, applying for grants, contracting with an SLP to provide a social skills group, teletherapy, or addressing communication skills through alternative treatment modalities such as music therapy.

Speech therapy services are provided based on the need of the individual, but can also be dictated by the funding source. Typically, insurance billed sessions are provided in a one-on-one basis if the individual is working on skills other than socialization. Services in the school setting are typically provided in a small group (2–4 students), or in a larger group depending on what kinds of goals are being addressed. In order to effectively address social/pragmatic language abilities, a small group of peers is warranted. Depending on the individual, addressing deficits in receptive and expressive language abilities may occur in a small group, where individuals can learn from each other, or otherwise in a one-on-one setting if an individual gets easily distracted by others or has behavior needs that may compromise the safety of others.

Considerations When Referring to an SLP

There are some specific things to consider prior to a clinician making a referral to an SLP, and a review of the individual's past history of speech therapy services is beneficial. Some potential questions to answer regarding an individual with autism's speech and language history include: How long did the individual receive speech therapy services? What were their standard scores on standardized speech and language measures? Were they dismissed from speech therapy services while in school? Why were they dismissed? Are there present needs that require the expertise of an SLP?

Individuals with autism, even those who have high-verbal skills, often continue to have deficits in areas of social/pragmatic language such as appropriate conversation skills and understanding figurative language (i.e., idioms and double meanings), as well as non-verbal communication such as eye contact and body language (Alpern & Zager, 2007). Generally, there is much room for growth when it comes to providing services for adults beyond high school. There currently appear to be few opportunities outside of the Medicaid waiver program where adults with autism can continue to work on their communication skills. Some families opt to pay privately for their adult child to receive services; however, this can become costly for a family. Continued deficits in social/pragmatic language also affect employability, with many individuals with autism struggling to maintain or gain employment even with a college degree. Job coaches also have a hard time locating opportunities for these individuals. Access to services for adults is definitely an area we need to work on, and it takes time, collaboration, and creativity to begin moving that process in the right direction.

Approaching Communication and Interaction with an Individual with Autism

It is vital to build a strong base of trust and positive rapport with individuals with autism; taking the time to build this relationship is one of the most effective tools for making progress. It may seem like taking the time to make a connection is time consuming, but the effort will pay off for the long term when that individual knows their voice has been heard, honored, and respected.

Through observation, as well as trial and error, we can learn valuable information on what makes our clients comfortable and encourages them to open up to us so we can effectively work together on their targeted goals. For example:

> *Carl was a 25-year-old with autism who used mostly single words and short phrases to communicate. He became anxious and shut down when I introduced a new activity to him. He shook his head and verbalized, "Nope!" I put the activity away and let him know I would bring the activity out during the following session. The next time he still said, "Nope!" I was feeling particularly humorous that day and in reply to his, "Nope!" I said, "Nope!" He laughed, appeared to relax, and began participating! I interpreted that interaction as if my acknowledgment of his "Nope!" was all he needed from me to validate his feelings related to my new activity.*

While not a one-size-fits-all approach, visual strategies can improve learning for individuals with autism. Examples of visual strategies include pictures, placing labels on common items to increase vocabulary, picture or written schedules for reference, and social stories. Providing information in a way that suits all learning styles is highly effective for learning and retaining information. When we hear it, see it, say it, write it, and do it, we increase our understanding and ability to express information. In my own speech therapy practice, I sit in front of a chalkboard with my students facing the board. Every session I am certain to put a word, picture, or both up on the board for students to have a visual for what I am teaching. I also do a lot of role-playing scenarios and modeling actions for my students, as well as verbally and visually reinforcing their correct responses (i.e., high-fives, "Yes, you got it!"). Regular use of visuals would be something to consider as you work with individuals with autism.

Setting up a routine and communicating clear expectations to clients will also increase your positive impact on individuals with autism. We all benefit from having routines (i.e., exercise, daily chores) and this holds true for individuals with autism. Sessions can include a combination of visual strategies and routine by writing out or drawing pictures of the tasks you intend to target. This session schedule gives your client an opportunity to feel comfortable in knowing what to expect, in what order, and allows them to predict how many tasks or activities there will be in which they will be expected to participate. As routines become comfortable, you can vary sessions by adding in a new task or activity. It is helpful to begin sessions with an easier task, move to a harder task, and then reinforce active participation by spending the last few minutes with an activity the client finds rewarding. This can be something as simple as playing a short game, having a dance party, or conversing about my student's preferred topics. Even though clients view it as "free" time, there are many ways to continue to work on positive social skills and conversation during this time.

Summary

When thinking about an individual with autism, step outside of what you've heard, what you've read, what you've seen, and what you've experienced. Yes, we often need "labels" to access funding, to provide proper placement within a school or facility, and to have a better understanding of general areas in which an individual may have strengths or deficits, but beyond that we need to look at the person sitting (or standing!) across from us in our places of treatment, just as we would any other individual who would be sitting there. Building a positive, therapeutic relationship with any individual is a key component to all therapies. Everyone wants the opportunity to be cared for, to be understood, and to have someone to whom they can express their thoughts, feelings, and needs. It's not any different for an individual with autism. Sometimes it just takes a bit more time, energy, and observation, but in the end all the effort will be worth it as you provide assistance to the client, and you too will be positively impacted by some amazing individuals!

Recommended Resources for Professionals

- American Speech-Language-Hearing Association: www.asha.org/
- Estay, I. A., & Paxton, K. (2007). *Counselling people on the autism spectrum: A practical manual.* Philadelphia, PA: Jessica Kingsley Publishers.
- Vicker, B. (2009). Social communication and language characteristics associated with high functioning, verbal children and adults with autism spectrum disorder: www.iidc.indiana.edu/pages/Social-Commu nication-and-Language-Characteristics-Associated-with-High-Function ing-Verbal-Children-and-Adults-with-ASD

Recommended Resources for Families

- Baker, J. (2006). *Social skills picture book for high school and beyond.* Arlington, TX: Future Horizons, Inc.
- Family Grant Opportunities: www.autismspeaks.org/family-grant-opportunities
- Patrick, N. J. (2008). *Social skills for teenagers and adults with Asperger syndrome: A practical guide to day-to-day life.* Philadelphia, PA: Jessica Kingsley Publishers.
- TEDx Talks. (2016, February 19). *What happens to children with autism, when they become adults.* Retrieved fromwww.youtube.com/watch? v=WtgGzKRHT-Y

About the Author

Kelly Lorenz, MHS, MT-BC, CCC-SLP, is a speech language pathologist for School City of Hammond in northwest Indiana. Ms. Lorenz is also a board-certified music therapist. She is passionate about using her expertise in both music and speech therapy to treat individuals with intellectual and developmental disabilities in one-on-one and group settings. You can find Ms. Lornez at steppingstonesmusictherapy@gmail.com.

References

Alpern, C. S., & Zager, D. (2007). Addressing communication needs of young adults with autism in a college-based inclusion program. *Education and Training in Developmental Disabilities, 42*(4), 428–436.

Hewitt, L. E. (2015). Assessment considerations for college students with autism spectrum disorder. *Topics in Language Disorders, 35*(4), 313–328. doi:10.1007/ s10803-005-0031-8.

12 My Client Has No Friends
Knowing When Your Client Needs a Good Speech Language Pathologist

Mallory Griffith

It's not uncommon for me to receive a call from a parent that a trusted colleague referred to my office. Frequently, it's paired with parent apprehension related to understanding what exactly a speech language pathologist (SLP) can provide for their highly verbose child. A typical call from a parent may sound something like this:

"John is a third grader; he has nearly perfect test scores across the board. He knows more about X topic than I do! His vocabulary is tremendous. John loves Minecraft, and is really an expert at it." Following probing questions, it may also be revealed, *"John talks at length about topics, seemingly disregarding the listener. He tells people things; John doesn't ask socially driven questions. He doesn't have any friends that he hangs out with outside of school. He struggles to talk casually to his peers. He is invading his classmates' personal space, and missing cues that they may not want to play with him."* The list goes on.

For most providers, it is fairly intuitive to send a child/adult with limited expressive or receptive language skills to an SLP. Similarly, if a child is difficult to understand, it is a natural referral. Communication skills are deeply meaningful skills to provide, and those with deficits warrant targeted support. However, recognizing social communication deficits and the role of an SLP for a child/teen/adult "who can talk just fine" but is unaware of social rules is slightly less intuitive. When you reframe the problem from someone "breaking all of the rules" or who "doesn't seem to care about their peers" to someone who likely cares deeply about their family and wants desperately to have friends, but has had no success with what they've tried on their own, it's a clear skill deficit. While in graduate school, SLPs receive specialized training to work on all areas of communication, including social and pragmatic communication. A diagnosis of autism generally comes with lifelong social communication deficits. An SLP can provide valuable insight and knowledge to support continued growth within this domain.

What's the impact of perseverating on topics and failing to read the listener's non-verbal cues? No friends. What's the impact of failing to recognize that you cannot give feedback to your boss? You're fired. These are life-altering mistakes related to skill deficits.

To provide an example of what a typical course of social communication therapy might look like, consider the eighth-grader who is struggling to establish school friends and obsessively talks about Minecraft. Social communication therapy would likely address conversational skills. Strategies incorporated may center around perspective taking (thinking about the listener), flexibility with topics, how to initiate a question outside of your interest, nonverbal skills (how close to stand and how to "read" the listener), possibly tone of voice, and how to use a "social fake." The concept of a "social fake," matching your behavior to the expectations of a situation, even when it may not reflect your inner state, is outlined in *Socially Curious and Curiously Social: A Social Thinking Guidebook for Bright Teens and Young Adults* (Winner & Crooke, 2011). *As soon* as I am confident my client can effectively apply the skill in a controlled setting, my goal is to jump them to a group setting. Groups are less structured than one-on-one sessions, but more structured than real life, so they provide a good practice arena for learned skills. Alternatively, it is important to create a realistic practice plan for applying skills outside of the therapy room if a group format is not available.

When considering whether or not a referral for speech language services is appropriate, it's initially important to differentiate the source of the social communication failure. If it is stress, anxiety, or difficulty with perspective taking that is impacting a client's ability to successfully navigate their social world, then psychological treatment will prove more fruitful. If it's an inability to read and apply non-verbal and verbal social communication, then an SLP may be helpful. Using our example, it may be important to consider, are you seeing John apply appropriate social skills around any of his same-aged peers? Or is he able to only interact with appropriate social skills with adults? Same-aged peers are the best metric of social competencies – whether your client is three or thirty-three. If you are not seeing the skill applied with peers in *any* settings, then consult an SLP to identify possible skill deficits.

This is where my passion lies. As an SLP who spends 90% of my day supporting highly verbal kids, teens, and adults on the spectrum, I cannot begin to emphasize the importance and impact of instilling social communication skills. Most of my work centers around providing some concrete strategies for our very abstract social world. Just as people do not generally discuss the complex social rules that are hidden within our environment, folks on the spectrum are often provided with abstract/vague feedback. When, "You're talking too loud," is quantified, and feedback is delivered instead as, "Using a 1–5 scale, where '1' is a whisper, and '5' is yelling, you're using a 4. I need you to use a 2. We're in a small space and we're sitting close together," skills become actionable, and clients are set up for more immediate success.

Evaluation

Some common social communication targets an SLP may be able to support include (but are not restricted to) the following:

Interpret/Use Facial Expression and Body Language

For example, is John able to read obvious facial expressions? What about more subtle changes? Can he identify what people are thinking/feeling when they are not using words? Is John's facial expression matching *his* words? Is he respecting personal space?

Interpret/Use Tone of Voice, Prosody, Volume

Does John use intonation appropriately? Is he regulating his own volume? Or does his volume elevate as his excitement rises? Can he interpret how another person is thinking/feeling based on their volume/tone of voice?

Interpret/Use Humor

Is John using humor? Does he like it when other people joke with him? Can he differentiate between friendly teasing and bullying? Is he telling jokes an appropriate number of times? Does he understand the deeper meaning behind jokes?

Initiate, Maintain, and Close a Conversation

Is John's timing appropriate for starting a conversation? Is he checking in with the listener? Is he showing flexibility with topics? Asking on topic questions? Showing preference to the other person's likes/interests? Does he end a conversation? Or continue to talk until the listener walks away? Can he identify when the listener is growing bored?

Identify the Hidden Rules Across Social Environment, and Modify Behavior Accordingly

There are millions of varying rules in different settings. One that may arise for John would include – we talk differently to our peers (classmates) than to authority figures (teachers/parents). Using very formal language with classmates may lead to a social reputation of being a "know-it-all." It's important to observe the subtle changes your classmates use, and learn how to emulate those.

Verbalize Social Problems and Develop Strategies to Solve Expectedly

Can John describe the problem? Does he view the problem as being a similar size as other people do? Can he identify why the other person took their actions? Does he have the tools to propose a solution or a compromise that is considerate and will not result in a larger problem?

Interpret Implied Meaning: Understand the "Bigger Picture" Academically and Socially

This line of questioning relates to higher-level language skill. Is John able to read a book and identify what the main characters' motives were? Can he describe the theme? Can John understand why his parents were so worried about him taking a piece of candy from the store when it was only worth 50 cents?

Identify How to Successfully Join and Participate in a Group Conversation

Is John's social timing appropriate? Is he included or ignored when he joins a group of his peers? Is he waiting to talk? Blurting? Matching the appropriate distance to stand? Tracking the conversation in real time? Or getting stuck on the initial topic?

Individual Treatment

Specific targets for individual therapy are identified within the initial evaluation. Once identified, individual sessions consist of generating strategies and practice opportunities to bridge the gap between a skill deficit and our target skill. For example, if John is practicing conversation skills specifically considering the listener, strategies for noticing and tracking the other person's interests would be introduced, paired with identifying opportunities to incorporate those into conversation. Following each session, a plan is identified for skill application within the week.

For most clients working on social communication skills, my goal is to target specific deficits in individual sessions for about six months. If too many skills are targeted at once, it can be overwhelming and consequently prevent success. Personally, I find that when I work for too long with a client, it sometimes starts to blend the line with counseling, rather than addressing targeted skills. Counseling or mental health therapy is outside of an SLP's scope of practice.

Group Therapy

For some people on the spectrum, identifying target skills and providing structured one-on-one practice is adequate for generalization. For *most* people I work with on the spectrum, that does not seem to suffice. I would work with clients, discontinue services, and then hear back from them in a couple of months because they continue to struggle applying the skill. For social communication therapy seeing clients in a structured, one-on-one setting simply does not consistently prepare them for real-world success.

A group that is appropriate for your client's specific skill set is a powerful thing. Beware, a group that is not a good match can be detrimental to confidence and willingness to use new skills. If you have two clients with similar skills and a third client with more significant social communication deficits, do not put them in the same group as no one will benefit. Good groups not only provide an opportunity to practice and develop skills, but they also come with a sense of camaraderie and instill confidence.

I run several weekly groups, and they are, without fail, the favorite part of my week. Within a group setting, I can quickly tell if that same Minecraft-loving eighth-grader, John (previously mentioned), has generalized his conversational skills (in which case, yay, time to take a break, or move on to another social communication skill), recognize that he is going to need more support to generalize skills, or identify anxiety that is heavily impacting his ability to use this skill and make an appropriate referral.

The groups I provide vary in structure and size. For younger kids and/or people just learning skills, smaller, more structured groups seem to provide the most benefit. For kids/teens/adults with more evolved social skills, larger, less-structured groups provide a more "real-life" practice opportunity. Most of my groups are client-driven, meaning we work on targets specific to social communication needs at that moment in time, rather than working through a curriculum.

Sometimes I co-facilitate groups with a counselor or psychologist, sometimes I facilitate on my own, depending on the needs of the group. Because I prefer focusing on a client-driven approach I do not prepare a list of topics. As the group arrives, we check in (and practice asking each person questions related to their story – conversational skills). Clients then proceed to generate a list of problems they've encountered during the week. In a recent high school group, we spent the majority of the time talking about how to (successfully) join a group. My goal is to have the participants share what has worked well (and has not worked well) and provide feedback to each other. I provide some structure by breaking it down into a series of steps that include how to identify a good group to join (the actual physical process), what to do/say when you're in the group, and how to judge whether it was successful or not. A flexible group can provide the opportunity for supporting numerous social communication targets in one setting which requires flexibility from the stance of facilitator as well.

The power of receiving and providing feedback to peers must not be underestimated and is a key component to a successful group. Not only does feedback seem to carry more weight than when coming from a peer rather than a professional, it starts to build friendships and develop a sense of togetherness. Groups help those who may be struggling to connect with a community of people with similar strengths and weaknesses.

Making the Referral to an SLP

When making a referral, it is always helpful to provide as much information as possible regarding your specific concerns. Which skills are you hoping to see addressed with your client? Understanding the support an SLP can provide, and positively framing that to your client prior to the evaluation, can positively impact the course of treatment. When a newly referred client does not acknowledge the skill deficit or refuses to work on identified skills, progress will not be made.

Services that are provided under this umbrella of speech language therapy are often reimbursable through private insurance or Medicaid, which can be beneficial for families. I encourage families to give it two to three sessions before making the choice as to whether or not speech language services are a good fit. Additionally, sometimes clients are referred when they are within a moment of crisis. Due to the nature of speech language therapy, opportunity to practice skills is necessary for acquisition. Mental health and safety takes priority over acquiring new skills.

Summary

There is no age that is "too late" for intervention, as a diagnosis of autism generally comes with lifelong social communication deficits. It's important to motivate and empower our clients to use the tools and strategies initially in a structured and coached setting, with the goal of gaining the ability to apply these skills on their own. This structured process allows us to step into the background and enable the client to thrive using their new skill set. Talking about and working on social communication skills requires bravery and vulnerability. Creating a successful transition to independent skills usage requires that we prepare our client for potential social bumps in the road and empower them to know how to successfully navigate them. An SLP can be a valuable treatment team member to aid your client in their efforts towards both independence and feeling connected to others.

Recommended Resources for Professionals

- Winner, M. G. (2007). *Thinking about you, thinking about me* (2nd ed.). London, UK: Jessica Kingsley Publishers.
- Winner, M. G. (2011). *Social thinking think sheets for tweens and teens.* Santa Clara, CA: Think Social Publishing.
- Wilson, A. (2018). *You've got this.* London, UK: Swirls Publishing Ltd.
- Dunn Buron, K., & Curtis, M. (2012). *Incredible 5-point scale: The significantly improved and expanded second edition; assisting students in understanding social interactions and controlling their emotional responses.* Shawnee Mission, KS: AAPC Publishing.

- O'Toole, J. C. (2012). *The Asperkid's (secret) book of social rules: The handbook of not-so-obvious social guidelines for teens with Asperger syndrome.* Philadelphia, PA: Jessica Kingsley Publishers.

Recommended Resources for Families

- Winner, M. G., & Crooke, P. (2011). *Socially curious and curiously social.* Great Barrington, MA: North River Press.
- Prizant, B. M. (2013). *Uniquely human, a different way of seeing autism.* New York, NY: Simon and Schuster.
- Griffith, M., & Bédard, R. (2017). *Raising a child on the autism spectrum: Insights from parents to parents.* Camp Hill, PA: The Practice Institute (TPI) Press.
- Bédard, R., & Griffith, M. (2018). *You've got this! The journey from middle school to college, as told by students on the Autism Spectrum and their parents.* Camp Hill, PA: The Practice Institute (TPI) Press.
- Robins, J. E. (2008). *Look me in the eye: My life with Asperger's.* New York, NY: Random House.
- Clark, J. (2010). *Asperger's in pink: Pearls of wisdom from inside the bubble of raising a child with Asperger's.* Arlington, TX: Future Horizons.

About the Author

Mallory Griffith, MA, CCC-SLP is a speech language pathologist living and working in Fort Collins, Colorado. In her private practice, she primarily works with people on the spectrum, coaching social communications skills. Ms. Griffith has co-authored two books with her colleague and friend, Rachel Bédard, PhD, including: *Raising a Child on the Autism Spectrum: Insights from Parents to Parents,* and, *You've Got This!: The Journey from Middle School to College, as told by Students on the Autism Spectrum and Their Parents.* Ms. Griffith can be found at www.mallorygriffithslp.com or mallorygriffithslp@gmail.com.

Reference

Winner, M., & Crooke, P. (2011). *Socially curious and curiously social: A social thinking guidebook for bright teens and young adults.* San Jose, CA: Think Social Publishing.

Part V

Addressing Executive Functioning and Sensory Needs

Some of the top concerns we hear about are time management, getting organized, and prioritizing, are all factors related to executive functioning (EF). One of the best referrals we can make is to a highly trained occupational therapist (OT). OTs can help with many things: finding success in tasks of daily living, executive functioning, and sensory concerns, to name only a few.

In this part we learn about how EF can impact virtually every facet of a daily routine, and we learn how diverse a simple struggle like "time management" can appear across several case examples. We then hear from two OTs about the combination of both sensory and EF interventions helping to make life better for folks with autism spectrum. Just as you would not treat only depression and ignore anxiety, an experienced OT will help clients find patterns in any life task that might be improved, including EF, daily schedules and routines, and sensory concerns.

13 Executive Functioning Needs

Valerie L. Gaus

Among the most perplexing and frustrating problems faced by people on the autism spectrum are those caused by impairments in executive functioning (EF). EF is an umbrella term used to describe the collection of cognitive operations that involve managing, integrating, coordinating, and utilizing multiple pieces of information in adaptive ways. As the term implies, these operations are necessary to successfully *execute* the tasks of daily living. If these functions are compromised, a person will have great difficulty with self-direction and adaptive behavior.

EF ability is not directly tied to intelligence, so it is possible for someone with a high IQ score to have impaired EF. The term "executive function" was first used in a description of patients with frontal-lobe brain damage (Duncan, 1986). Later these problems were described in patients with attention deficit hyperactivity disorder, obsessive compulsive disorder, schizophrenia, various forms of dementia (Ozonoff & Griffith, 2000), and more recently in people with autism (Ozonoff, South, & Provencal, 2005; Tsatsanis & Powell, 2014). Standard IQ tests are not sensitive enough to detect many of these deficits, but neuropsychological tests can assess for many types of EF problems.

Neuropsychological research has investigated EF in people with autism, producing evidence that these individuals are more prone to have relative weaknesses on tests of *flexibility*, *attention regulation*, and *planning*. Adults with autism without intellectual disability have difficulty making rapid alternations of attention between two different sensory modalities (Courchesne, Akshoomoff, & Ciesielski, 1990; Kleinhans, Akshoomoff, & Delis, 2005), and are slow to disengage from one visual cue to attend to another (Hill & Bird, 2006). Impaired working memory, or the ability to keep information in an online state to guide cognitive processing, adversely affects planning. Other findings involve difficulty with the ability to resolve conflicts between the target (long-range) goal and a sub- (short-range) goal (Ozonoff et al., 2005). Deficits in the ability to carry out response initiation (Hill & Bird, 2006) also have implications for planning ability.

These research findings may help to explain why people with autism are described as "rigid" and have difficulty with many independent living skills. The stress that is caused by this is often related to the reasons people with autism and their families seek professional help. The next section describes common presenting problems.

Daily Living Consequences of EF Impairment

Simple daily tasks and responsibilities are difficult to manage because of EF problems. The more cognitively able the individual is, the more stressful life can be because others expect more from people who appear "high-functioning." The discrepancy between intelligence and EF can be quite significant in people with autism, and the uneven profile of strengths and deficits may cause even more problems in adulthood than it did in earlier years, as the need for self-direction increases. In my practice, I work only with adults, and often their reasons for seeking treatment have something to do with the stress of managing tasks and responsibilities at home, work, school, or in the community. Clients describe how problems such as the examples below impact them every day:

- Getting distracted easily
- Difficulty completing tasks
- Losing things
- Procrastinating
- Difficulty "multi-tasking"
- Frustration with "never getting anything done"
- Difficulty setting goals
- Easily "thrown off" by unexpected changes
- Difficulty learning new routines
- Difficulty meeting deadlines
- Arriving late to meetings or events.

Not only do these issues interfere with the client's own goals, but they cause others to get annoyed and to express criticism. It is not uncommon for loved ones to attribute these behaviors to character flaws, with the worst-case scenario seen when the client is labeled as "lazy" or "unmotivated." This contributes to a sense of shame and can lead to isolation.

Clinicians working with this population should be aware of the many ways these issues can manifest themselves. Meet three people who are quite different from one another, yet all having some kind of problem that is driven by EF impairment. Consider the following case scenarios where the clients struggle with EF in their daily tasks:

Maria is a 27-year-old woman with autism who lives with her parents and works part-time at a bookstore. She drives herself the 3-mile distance between home and work, but is extremely anxious each time she has to do it. She is unwilling to drive anywhere else, and at times this holds her back from doing other things she would enjoy. Her anxiety increases when there are more cars on the road, and decreases when there are less. She described to her therapist that she feels like she is always attending to the wrong things *and is concerned she is missing important signs and signals. She also finds it* difficult to shift her attention quickly enough *to keep up with the ever-changing factors around her and her car.*

Bill is a 34-year-old man with autism who lives alone and works full-time as a lab technician. He loves his job, but is often struggling with getting his work done in a timely fashion. He runs behind schedule and his supervisor and co-workers have given him feedback many times about his slow pace. He has found himself staying 1–2 hours past the end of his shift just to finish his tasks to avoid being disciplined. He has tried to speed up, but finds he makes more mistakes if he rushes. He reported that it takes great effort to keep his attention on his tasks, *given the frequent interruptions that happen in the work setting. Each time someone calls his name to tell him something or to give him another task, he has great difficulty remembering where he left off in the task that was interrupted (*working memory*). He is worried that he will be fired if he does not improve.*

Janice is a 19-year-old college student with autism who lives in a dorm on campus. She is very bright and had excellent grades in high school. She is having great difficulty with managing her schedule and work because, she reported, she cannot keep things organized. She keeps losing her books and papers, has a messy desk in her dorm room, and often shows up to class missing things that she needs. She is falling behind on her work because she has difficulty planning *for her day and week and spends a lot of time looking for lost items. She realizes now how much she relied on her parents to structure her space and schedule when she lived at home. She is worried that she will get poor grades because of her lack of organization.*

Interventions to Address EF Impairment

Because EF problems are so varied and can appear so differently from one person to the next, the intervention plan that a clinician designs needs to be individualized. The strategies that the clinician will teach the client should be tailored to the unique profile of strengths and weaknesses. With that said, there are some basic components that every plan should include:

- Psychoeducation
- Self-assessment strategies
- Compensatory skills
- Self-advocacy skills.

Psychoeducation

First, the client should be provided with accurate information about EF problems. Educating the client about these problems and how common they are in people with autism can reduce shame and embarrassment. Janice, for example, could benefit from being told, "Some people with autism can have difficulty with organizing information, which involves sorting and categorizing. This can result in problems with setting up and/or maintaining organized spaces. Spaces that can be disorganized include pocketbooks, backpacks, desktops, or car interiors." My book, *Living Well on the Spectrum: How to Use Your Strengths to Meet the Challenges of Asperger Syndrome/High-Functioning Autism* (Gaus, 2011) can be used for this purpose, as the first half of the book is devoted to psychoeducation about many of the characteristics of the autism spectrum.

Self-Assessment Strategies

The more a client understands about the unique way his or her brain works, for better or for worse, the stronger position he or she is in to begin co-designing, with the therapist, a plan for success. As the old phrase goes, "Know thyself." In an ideal world, every client would come to therapy having had a neuropsychological assessment done, and then the report can provide a roadmap for understanding the client's profile of strengths and weaknesses. Because that is not always possible, other tools can be used to help guide the intervention plan. Helping the client to understand his or her learning style can often be helpful. The Dunn and Dunn learning styles assessment (Dunn & Dunn, 1999) can be a useful way to help the client go through the process of self-assessment. The resulting learning styles profile is not a substitute for a psychological evaluation, but is merely a tool that can be used to help clients become more comfortable thinking and talking about their own information-processing experiences and preferences. Online assessments for all ages can be found at www.learningstyles.net.

My self-help book (Gaus, 2011) also has many checklists and questionnaires designed to help people with autism become more aware of their own EF problems.

Compensatory Skills

Once the client and clinician have identified the EF difficulties that are most likely to be contributing to daily stress, skills for compensating and adapting can be taught. Though the plan will be individualized, some commonly helpful skill sets are *organization, time management,* and *problem solving,*

Organization and Time Management Skills

As mentioned, people with autism often report problems organizing spaces (e.g., living space, work space, carrying cases/bags). Closely connected to this are problems creating or following a schedule. Chronic lateness and/or a sense of "never getting anything done" contribute to stress. EF deficits contribute to some clients' poor awareness of how they are spending their time, or to their unrealistic ideas about what can be completed in an hour or a day. The following list from Gaus (2018) includes examples of strategies that can help patients manage space and time more effectively. These can be practiced by using a variety of materials and media, including smartphone applications. For example:

*   Use an organizational checklist to clean out and organize small spaces.
*   Make environmental modifications so spaces are "friendly" to the client's sensory or EF profile.
*   Build into the weekly routine times for discarding unneeded items.
*   Use a blank daily schedule template to take baseline data on how time is being spent.
*   Make a "to-do" list and put items in priority order.
*   Set small realistic goals for each day or week.
*   Use visual cues to help remind self about tasks.

Dawson and Guare (2016) provide a guide for any adult wanting to improve EF skills and have many more strategies like the ones listed above. Autism-specific organizational tools can be found in Gaus (2011).

Problem-Solving Skills

People with autism can be easily overwhelmed by the stressors described above. Teaching them a traditional problem-solving formula (D'Zurilla, 1986) helps them to modulate the intense emotional reaction they may have to an unexpected problem by learning to: (1) define the problem more objectively; (2) practice generating and choosing viable options; and (3) evaluate their own performance of solutions. In Gaus (2011), a modification of the traditional problem-solving model is presented in which some steps are broken down into smaller separate parts to appeal to the learning styles of people with autism.

Self-Advocacy Skills

An essential part of compensating for EF problems is knowing when and how to ask other people for help. Whether a client with autism needs to ask a family member to change something in the home or an employer to accommodate a need at work, self-awareness and assertive communication skills are necessary for success. If a client has gained a solid understanding of his or her unique ways of processing information and what types of strategies are needed, then learning to communicate that to others will be easier. Stephen Shore, a well-known professor, speaker, and author who himself has autism, wrote a very useful book about self-advocacy that can be recommended to clients for this purpose (Shore, 2004).

When to Make a Referral

For a better understanding of EF problems, a referral to a neuropsychologist who has experience with autism can be invaluable. A neuropsychological evaluation is the most thorough type of assessment to provide a better understanding of the specific ways EF problems are playing a role in the presenting problems.

Summary

EF problems are a common cause of stress for people with autism, as they are often at the root of the struggles they have with self-direction. Difficulties with flexibility, attention regulation, and planning interfere with tasks of daily living, even in people who have average or above-average IQs. Clinicians working with this population can help their clients by assessing these areas of functioning and then educating the clients and their families about EF skills. Intervention plans should be tailored to the unique profile of EF problems seen in each client, and include strategies for compensation and self-advocacy.

Recommended Resources for Professionals

- Gaus, V. L. (2018) *Cognitive-behavioral therapy for adults with autism spectrum disorder* (2nd Ed.). New York, NY: Guilford.

Recommended Resources for Clients and Families

- Dawson, P., & Guare, R. (2016). *The smart but scattered guide to success: How to use your brain's executive skills to keep up, stay calm and get organized at work and home.* New York, NY: Guilford.
- Gaus, V. L. (2011). *Living well on the spectrum: How to use your strengths to meet the challenges of Asperger syndrome/high-functioning autism.* New York, NY: Guilford.
- Shore, S. (Ed.). (2004). *Ask and tell: Self-advocacy and disclosure for people on the autism spectrum.* Shawnee Mission, KS: Autism Asperger.

About the Author

Dr. Gaus is a psychologist, licensed by New York State, who has been a practicing psychotherapist for more than 25 years. She specializes in individual psychotherapy for adults of all ages, from 18 to 98, with extensive experience serving people with disabilities, autism spectrum disorders, anxiety, depression, trauma, and stress-related problems. She approaches therapy using a cognitive-behavioral framework. She has written numerous articles, chapters, and books on these subjects, including *Cognitive-Behavioral Therapy for Adults with Autism Spectrum Disorder, 2nd Edition*, published in 2018 by Guilford Press, and *Living Well on the Spectrum: How to Use Your Strengths to Meet the Challenges of Asperger Syndrome/High-Functioning Autism*, published in 2011 by Guilford Press. You can find out more about Dr. Gaus at www.drvaleriegaus.com.

References

Courchesne, E., Akshoomoff, N. A., & Ciesielski, K. (1990). Shifting attention abnormalities in autism: ERP and performance evidence. *Journal of Clinical and Experimental Neuropsychology, 12,* 77.

Dawson, P., & Guare, R. (2016). *The smart but scattered guide to success: How to use your brain's executive skills to keep up, stay calm and get organized at work and home.* New York: Guilford.

Duncan, J. (1986). Disorganisation of behaviour after frontal lobe damage. *Cognitive Neuropsychology, 3,* 271–290.

Dunn, R., & Dunn, K. (1999). *The complete guide to the learning styles inservice system.* Boston: Allyn & Bacon.

D'Zurilla, T. J. (1986). *Problem-solving therapy: A social competence approach to clinical intervention.* New York, NY: Springer.

Gaus, V. L. (2011). *Living well on the spectrum: How to use your strengths to meet the challenges of Asperger syndrome/high-functioning autism.* New York, NY: Guilford.

Gaus, V. L. (2018). *Cognitive-behavioral therapy for adults with autism spectrum disorder* (2nd ed.). New York: Guilford.

Hill, E. L., & Bird, C. M. (2006). Executive processes in Asperger syndrome: Patterns of performance in a multiple case series. *Neuropsychologia, 44*(14), 2822–2835. doi:10.1016/j.neuropsychologia.2006.06.007

Kleinhans, N., Akshoomoff, N., & Delis, D. C. (2005). Executive functions in autism and Asperger's disorder: Flexibility, fluency, and inhibition. *Developmental Neuropsychology, 27*(3), 379–401. doi:10.1207/s15326942dn2703_5

Ozonoff, S., & Griffith, E. M. (2000). Neuropsychological function and the external validity of Asperger syndrome. In A. Klin, F. R. Volkmar, & S. S. Sparrow (Eds.), *Asperger syndrome* (pp. 72–96). New York: Guilford Press.

Ozonoff, S., South, M., & Provencal, S. (2005). Executive functions. In F. R. Volkmar, R. Paul, A. Klin, & D. Cohen (Eds.), *Handbook of autism and pervasive developmental disorders: Vol. 1. Diagnosis, development, neurobiology, and behavior* (3rd ed., pp. 606–627). Hoboken, NJ: Wiley.

Shore, S. (Ed.). (2004). *Ask and tell: Self-advocacy and disclosure for people on the autism spectrum*. Shawnee Mission, KS: Autism Asperger.

Tsatsanis, K. D., & Powell, K. (2014). neuropsychological characteristics of autism spectrum disorders. In F. R. Volkmar, S. J. Rogers, R. Paul, & K. A. Pelphrey (Eds.), *Handbook of autism and pervasive developmental disorders* (pp. 617–694). Hoboken, NJ: Wiley Publishing.

14 Achieving Health, Well-being, and Participation through Engagement in Occupation

Robin Seger

Occupations are the ordinary and familiar things that people do every day. They are the things you need to do, want to do, or are expected to do in daily life (Law et al., 2014). This includes all of the activities with which we pass time and make purpose out of our days. Occupational therapy (OT) helps individuals to learn and apply the skills needed to participate effectively in everyday activities and places by using *motivating activities* chosen *for specific therapeutic purposes.* Autistic individuals may struggle with occupational performance due to difficulty with movement planning, coordination, and control. They may have differences in how they notice and react to sensation, or there may be difficulties with how to pay attention to or organize a task. The environment or the expected task itself may impose barriers to performance. OT addresses specific occupations, client factors, performance and process skills, performance patterns, and contextual or environmental factors impacting performance of daily activities (AOTA, 2017).

Occupations include activities of daily living (ADL), such as dressing, bathing, grooming, or sleep; instrumental activities of daily living (IADL), such as caring for others or managing a home; play/leisure and health maintenance activities, such as identifying and participating in routine leisure pursuits; educational activities, including the ability to perform educationally related functions such as writing in and out of a classroom; and work, including activities related to finding and holding a job and social and community participation (AOTA, 2017).

Specific client factors impact occupations. Client factors are internal to the individual and may support or impede an individual's performance of daily occupations. Client factors include:

- Cognitive, sensory, or motor functions, as well as the consideration of how the individual's values and beliefs affect their ability to perform daily activities
- Performance and process skills, which are observable components of occupation that have a functional purpose

- Performance patterns, which are structures such as habits, routines, and roles that support or hinder occupational participation and performance (AOTA, 2017).

These factors are housed in a client's context and environment (interrelated physical, cultural, personal, temporal, and social factors) that affect occupational performance (AOTA, 2017).

Indicators for OT Referral

Referral for OT assessment is indicated any time a client has an identified occupational performance challenge they want to address (e.g., meal planning, shopping, and cooking) or an identifiable client factor (e.g., sensory reactivity, balance, motor control, strength), performance skill (e.g., lifting, carrying, organizing, pacing, completing), or context limitation (noise, tight spaces, expected speed of performance, social demands) that interferes with performance of daily activities. Some common referral considerations include motor performance difficulties, cognitive factors affecting daily performance, and emotional regulation.

Motor Performance Difficulties

Motor challenges in autism may be very subtle but can contribute significantly to anxiety and avoidance behaviors. Factors to observe include slumped posture, squirming and fidgeting, difficulty sitting still, lack of reciprocal arm swing when walking, limited rotational trunk movements, difficulty with balance, fine motor challenges, physical awkwardness, clumsiness, and restricted or no involvement in physical activity.

Cognitive Factors

Cognitive factors affecting daily performance may include impulsivity or distractibility, difficulties initiating or consistently completing self-care activities, difficulties organizing and performing instrumental ADL such as meal planning, shopping, and cooking, difficulties with speed of processing language affecting interactions and ability to follow directions, or difficulties establishing and maintaining daily routines.

Emotional Regulation

Emotional regulation challenges can be significantly affected by sensory processing deficits, as well as by any of the above-noted performance challenges. If the client demonstrates or reports challenges with functioning in noisy or busy places, pickiness about clothing or food, avoidance of or discomfort with physical activities, or a need for pressure through squeezing or seeking tight spaces or muscle work through activities involving pushing, pulling, lifting, or jumping, there is likely a sensory processing impairment affecting self-regulation. Poor frustration tolerance may be an indicator of motor planning and task organization challenges.

Most care systems operate on a deficits-based model and require identification of a deficit to be evaluated. ICD-10 diagnostic codes are now available that specifically address limits in performance of daily activities. A referral diagnosis of autism plus identification of a deficit to be evaluated is common practice. Some common diagnostic categories included in referral are lack of coordination, sensory processing deficits, and deficits in performance of ADLs.

The OT Process: Assessment, Planning, and Intervention

OT services begin with assessment. The tools and processes selected are specific to the individual's presenting occupational performance concerns. The occupational profile identifies the individual's occupational performance supports, strengths, and challenges, and guides further assessment. OT is client-centered with the autistic individual's priorities and preferences driving the process. The individual's family or designated support system is included to optimize understanding of the performance and contextual strengths and challenges and to support the intervention process. Assessment may directly evaluate an area of occupational performance (e.g., social interaction skills; self-care skills; food preparation skills) or characterize the body function skill deficits interfering with performance (motor assessments; assessments of sensory function; executive function assessment). OT assessment evaluates what is important to the client, and asks what their diagnosis or impairment means in their daily life. Once priorities are identified, the OT and the client work together to develop an intervention plan to improve the client's quality of life by addressing specifically identified occupational performance priorities (AOTA, 2017).

The OT then selects models and timelines for intervention, with the client's needs and priorities driving decision making. Evidence-based and informed practices help to define intervention strategies, but progress is individual and intervention is adjusted accordingly.

Interventions are likely more powerful and generalized when embedded in the individual's real performance environments. However, many OT practice environments and funding sources limit intervention in real-life contexts. Duration of care varies based on goals and progress and may range from a handful of consultative visits to a more intensive episode of care of weekly to twice-weekly visits for an average of 3–6 months.

The following case study illustrates the OT process as well as many of the indicators for referral listed above.

George is a 14-year-old young man recently diagnosed with autism spectrum disorder (ASD), level 1. Referral to OT was recommended to address sensory concerns. Evaluation of George's occupational history, patterns of daily living, interests, values, and needs (occupational profile) revealed that George had no reported difficulties with academics, thus he did not have an Individualized Education Plan (IEP) in place. However, George rarely participated in class and was not engaged with peers. At home, George was oppositional and resisted his parent's direction. He refused to do homework and became upset when required to stop playing video games. He wasn't performing his daily self-care routines consistently (e.g., bathing, combing his hair) and did not participate in any IADL such as simple meal or snack preparation, or assistance with household chores. He also had difficulty falling asleep. George was fussy about clothing and was a picky eater. George wanted to be able to hang out with friends after school and was interested in trying rock climbing and soccer. He also agreed that he would like things to be easier at home.

George's mother indicated her priorities for George included decreasing his yelling and refusal behaviors, and helping him to develop greater independence with self-care. She also wanted him to have friendships. She voiced concern about how much time George spent alone playing video games.

George and his mother identified several strengths and supports: school was flexible and allowed him to take breaks when needed; there were no penalties for incomplete homework assignments; George was comfortable with his school routines and never resisted going to school; he was driven to school by his mother and rode the bus home; George ate a good variety of foods and sat with his family for most meals; the family home provided George with quiet, personal spaces, and a porch swing and yard space which were calming for George.

George was observed to have difficulty sitting still and sitting upright. His movements were awkward and clumsy, and he had difficulty with shoe tying, cutting with a knife, and figuring out how to do multistep tasks. Standardized assessment identified difficulties with motor planning, postural control, balance and coordination, and fine motor precision. A sensory profile showed difficulties tolerating noise, the feel of clothing fasteners, and unanticipated touch. These challenges with body function and skills were contributing to George's resistance to performance of a variety of daily activities.

George's OT intervention plan addressed the following issues: he was having 4–5 daily tantrums which we wanted to see decrease, he had an absence of friendships, he evidenced inconsistency in performing daily self-care activities, and he had motor planning deficits (difficulty planning and executing unfamiliar motor actions) affecting performance of IADL.

Intervention began by addressing George's tantrums. The occupational therapist worked with George on self-regulation, which is the nervous system's ability to attain, maintain, and change levels of arousal or alertness (Williams & Shellenberger, 1994). A "sensory diet" approach was used to teach George about his regulatory states. A sensory diet is where the occupational therapist helps the client learn to calibrate the correct combination of sensory input they need to have in order to function optimally (Wilbarger, 1995). Sensory diets have nothing to do with food, but instead focus on giving the client the sensory input they need. For George, direct intervention, involving engaging him in specific trial activities in the clinic setting was used to design and test activities for use throughout the day.

Parent/client education was provided to develop understanding of George's sensory needs and the detective work needed to clarify specific types of sensory inputs most effective for George. George's sensory profile showed under-response to vestibular input, which contributed significantly to his difficulties maintaining an optimal state of arousal George's symptoms included poor postural stability and lethargy. Adding routine movement (vestibular) activities such as swinging and jumping on a trampoline several times per day helped George be more able to participate in daily activities. The home schedule and environment were adapted to establish routines and spaces in which George could use sensory diet supports to remain calm and participate in daily activities.

When George's parents began to understand his body function deficits, they were able to reframe his difficult behaviors as coping strategies rather than oppositional defiance. George's tantrums reduced to fewer than one per week within the first two sessions of intervention. This was likely due to both improved arousal regulation and responsive family interactions that included an understanding of what George needed to be ready to take on challenges.

To address George's goal to hang out with friends, the Adolescent Leisure Interest Survey (Henry, 2000) was used to guide George in thinking about what he would like to do, where, and with whom he would like to do it. Then the occupational therapist introduced the concept of a "Green Zone" of conversation (Shaul, 2015) to help George to think and plan how to negotiate conversations with his new friend. In this intervention, the occupational therapist helps the client visualize that their interests may be considered a "blue zone," and another person's (a potential friend) interests may be considered a "yellow zone," and that the goal is to find common ground, or a "green zone" that occurs when mixing blue and yellow, representing their shared interests.

George's priority was to go to a friend's house after school. He made a plan to ride the bus home with his friend and have his parents pick him up after 2 hours. With the encouragement of the occupational therapist, George planned to do whatever activities his friend wanted to do (joining the friend's yellow zone), even if it wasn't his preferred activity. George now understood that, in order to get to a "green zone," he may have to mix his "blue" activities with his potential friend's "yellow" activities. George and his mother contacted his friend's family and George talked to his friend at school and via text to plan a date, time, and activities. George completed this outing successfully and was elated at his success at making a potential friend.

To address self-care goals, a picture schedule was developed with George for morning and evening routines. The picture schedule is a list of the steps of a task or routine presented in picture format to support planning, sequencing, and communication skills needed to complete a task or routine. Picture supports were used despite George's ability to read, in order to ensure clarity of communication during times of dysregulation. Sensory diet activities were built into the schedule to ensure routine engagement in the sensory-based activities that helped George to maintain a calm, alert arousal state. The schedule was implemented at home. The initial goal was to establish twice-daily tooth brushing and bathing at least once every 2–3 days.

To establish routine participation in home maintenance activities, two simple chore routines were established (gathering and carrying laundry to the laundry room; sweeping the kitchen floor) that also provided needed physical activity to support regulation. Visual/picture schedules were used to establish the routines, and reinforcement with preferred activities was used to support the performance. Direct support, such as demonstrating and talking through the steps of the task, was provided by his parents initially to help George learn the tasks and this support was faded, with fewer verbal and physical prompts, as he became more adept with each task.

George was seen for six visits. He and his family reported they were very happy with the changes they had made and were ready to take a break and practice the new strategies they had learned. Follow-up recommendations and referrals included group sessions to address sensory issues to continue to aid in George's self-regulation, social skills group to build social interaction competencies, and life skills group to build George's skills for independent living.

Summary

Occupational therapists strive to create interventions that are intrinsically motivating for clients, and help them attain their occupational performance goals. The reasons for OT referral and the types of intervention are as varied as the individuals referred. OT referral is indicated when a client has difficulty performing routine daily activities. Reasons for referral often address client factors (e.g., sensory reactivity, balance, motor control, strength), performance skills (e.g., lifting, carrying, organizing, pacing, completing), or context limitations (noise, tight spaces, expected speed of performance, social demands) that interfere with this performance. The intended outcome of OT intervention is to improve the client's well-being and satisfaction with his or her quality of life through improved ability to meet occupational performance demands and priorities.

Recommended Resources for Professionals and Families

- Autistic Self Advocacy Network: autisticadvocacy.org
- Global and Regional Asperger Syndrome Partnership: grasp.org
- Thinking Person's Guide to Autism: thinkingautismguide.com
- The Spiral Foundation: thespiralfoundation.org

About the Author

Robin Seger, OTR/L is an outpatient pediatric occupational therapist at Children's Hospital Colorado working with children and adolescents with autism, sensory processing disorders, and feeding difficulties. Ms. Seger has practiced as a pediatric occupational therapist for 37 years, specializing in work with children with sensory integration and sensory processing disorders and autism. She is the OT Program lead for Social Skills programs at Children's Hospital Colorado and is certified in the Evaluation of Social Interaction (ESI), an OT-specific standardized assessment designed to evaluate social interaction in natural activities. Ms. Seger is passionate about expanding OT's role in helping autistic individuals to achieve full participation in all the routines, activities, and places they value.

References

American Occupational Therapy Association (AOTA). (2017, September). Occupational therapy practice framework: Domain and process (3rd ed.). *American Journal of Occupational Therapy, 68*, S1–S48. doi:10.5014/ajot.2014.682006

Henry, A. D. (2000). *Pediatric interest profiles: Surveys of play for children and adolescents, kid play profile, adolescent leisure interest profile*. San Antonio, TX: Therapy Skills Builders.

Law, M., Baptiste, S., Carswell, A., McColl, M. A., Polatajko, H., & Pollock, N. (2014). *Canadian occupational performance measure* (5th ed.). Ottawa, Ed., Ont: CAOT Publications ACE.

Shaul, J. (2015). *The green zone conversation book: Finding common ground in conversations for children on the autism spectrum*. Philadelphia, PA: Jessica Kingsley Publishers.

Wilbarger, P. (1995). The sensory diet: Activity programs based on sensory processing theory. *Sensory Integration Special Interest Section Newsletter, 18*(2), 1–4.

Williams, M. S., & Shellenberger, S. (1994). *How does your engine run? A leaders guide to the alert program for self-regulation*. Albuquerque, NM: Therapy Works Inc.

15 An Occupational Therapist Does What Exactly?

Megan Wolff

> *Jordan is a 17-year-old headed into her senior year in high school. She is patient, kind, quite talented in math and science, and hopes to attend college close to home, majoring in engineering. Jordan's therapist suggested that they meet with an Occupational Therapist (OT) at the college, part of a team of people who help college students with autism find success in college. Initially, Jordan's parents balked. "But she can hold a pencil just fine!" was the first objection. The therapist explained that an OT can help college students with far more than pencil grasp: they can help students learn to organize their schedules, figure out how to get themselves up on time and out the door, manage sensory input, and gain independent living skills, all of which will be necessary in college. Jordan's mom nodded sagely and wryly commented, "I did wonder who was going to tell her to put the video game down and get to studying."*

While mental health therapists are increasingly making referrals to occupational therapy, there is clearly still a gap in knowledge regarding the role of occupational therapy services in the treatment of autism. As noted above, a quality OT can help with executive functioning, planning a reasonable schedule, plotting out domestic chores, sensory issues, reducing barriers to social engagement, stress management, and more. If you have clients who want to live independently and engage socially, you want to have a high-quality OT on your team.

When Is It Time to Make a Referral for OT Services?

If an individual is experiencing challenges (or perceived challenges) with engaging in the activities that are integral to daily functioning and/or are important to the individual, a referral to occupational therapy services would be appropriate. All occupational therapy services focus on supporting performance and participation in valued activities for the individual. As the important activities or "occupations" change as youth age, so, too, does the focus of occupational therapy services. For example, OTs who work with children will often focus on the childhood "occupations" of play, learning, and social interaction. As they age into adulthood, primary occupations may focus more on independent living, executive functioning, and higher education and/or employment.

Typically, the earlier intervention starts, the better the prognosis/outcomes. With regard to supported education, transition planning should start around the age of 14 (which can include school-based occupational therapy), and we prefer to start working with college students on the autism spectrum as they make the transition to college during the summer prior to starting classes.

Oftentimes, pediatric occupational therapy clinics will work with transition-age youth and young adults up to age 26. We sometimes find, however, that a pediatric-focused practice is not prepared to help the college-bound client. Further, those college-bound clients sometimes feel uncomfortable in a pediatric setting. Referrals should be made with this in mind.

Institutions of higher education are also beginning to employ OTs to work with college students with disabilities through university health centers and/or supported education programs. In some cases, occupational therapy services can also be authorized by the Division of Vocational Rehabilitation (DVR) if someone is experiencing barriers to employment where occupational therapy is indicated and it is included in the person's individual plan for employment.

Though Jordan was encouraged by her parents and therapist to work with an OT in college, Jordan was determined to "make it on her own!" She declined to work with an OT. She struggled with a roommate (a novel situation, as she had always had her own room), got confused with an English Comp assignment and didn't know how to ask for assistance, and her stress was on the rise. She called her parents in distress, and they quickly learned that she hadn't left her room in days and was afraid to shower in the communal bathroom. After a series of frantic phone calls, Jordan's parents arranged for an emergency meeting with the therapist (a meeting that she was capable of making independently just months ago!). The therapist soothed the family, indicated that the first months of college can be rough, and again suggested working with an OT. The therapist again reviewed the many ways in which an OT can help, and again indicated that there was a top-notch program right on campus to help. The therapist offered to meet with Jordan and the OT together, and Jordan agreed that she would consider such a meeting. In meeting with the OT, it was determined that Jordan's executive functioning skills needed an upgrade to college-level skills.

What to Expect at the First Visit with an OT

OTs will start out with an assessment phase to gain an understanding of the individual's strengths, barriers, interests, and supports. One of the most important takeaways from completing assessments is developing an in-depth understanding of the activities/tasks (or "occupations") that the individual needs and wants to do, and if or how those tasks are currently being performed. OTs will often also observe the individual engaging in activities in order to ascertain their current level of performance to identify how we can support individuals as they improve their engagement and performance in the activities that are important to them. They may also administer specific assessments that help to further understand a person's needs, identify baseline of performance, guide intervention, and/or set goals.

The assessment phase allows OTs to develop goals focused on improving participation, engagement, and performance of their chosen or important occupations or activities. Areas that OTs tend to focus on with young adults on the autism spectrum include independent living (developing habits and routines to support daily living activities), education, and employment. While goals are typically "occupation"- or activity-specific, we often find that students who are on the autism spectrum experience barriers with executive functioning, social participation, sensory processing, and stress/anxiety management that impact their ability to engage in important activities. Thus, goals may also focus on those areas as they relate to participation in desired activities.

> *For example, with Jordan, during her senior year in high school we might prioritize some goals related to increasing independent living skills such as waking herself up, organizing her own schedule, being responsible for making her own doctor's appointments, and some domestic chores such as laundry and shopping. Because her schedule is so full during the school year, and because there are other children at home, Jordan's parents will continue to be responsible for the bulk of the cooking and cleaning, but they do want to be sure that she can do those things before she heads off to college. Once at college, we might propose working with Jordan to prioritize her own goals; the attention may focus on adjusting to living with a roommate, managing her own learning in classes of 200 students, and handling the freedom of her new schedule without being too rigid or too lax.*

"Typical" OT services will vary across settings, and this is often dependent on funding (insurance, self-pay, education, DVR), but OTs will often see someone on a weekly basis if needed. There is no set timeline for services; this is truly dependent on the individual's needs and goals, as well as stipulations set forth by funding sources.

OTs Can Help with Executive Function, Too!

Executive functioning is the skill set needed to be self-regulating and forward-thinking to accomplish a goal. This incorporates time management, organization, planning, prioritizing, prospective memory, and emotional regulation. Executive functioning takes place in the pre-frontal cortex, which is an area of the brain that isn't fully developed until around age 25. However, people who are on the autism spectrum (as well as those with other disabilities) can struggle with executive functioning skills throughout the lifespan.

It helps to provide a brief but thorough education to students/clients regarding the nature of executive functioning, how it changes over the lifetime, and how it fluctuates with stress. Despite having average to high intelligence, individuals on the autism spectrum can experience challenges/deficits in areas that others may take for granted, including being able to organize, prioritize tasks, and manage time. Young adults on the autism spectrum often require targeted instruction to develop these skills as they will not just "grow out of it." Reducing stress and self-blame is an important first step. The next steps involve self-awareness, and then actually finding tools and techniques to solve the problem!

Self-awareness regarding ability to plan, and recognition of how long activities actually take, is a tricky skill to learn. As a result, individuals with autism/attention deficit hyperactivity disorder have difficulty verbalizing challenges, and may not even realize that there is a deficit. Many college students underestimate how long tasks take, fail to budget adequate time to complete tasks, fail to budget time to ask for assistance, and then struggle, suffering debilitating anxiety or extremely high stress. Oftentimes, individuals on the autism spectrum also experience anxiety around the thought of even planning for long-term goals, as this can be abstract and overwhelming. OTs will support the individual with actionable objectives (e.g., actual support with getting into college and being successful in college) that are important/integral to success.

> *Jordan and her OT broke down tasks into actionable items (write this essay by Wednesday, go the grocery store at this time) until Jordan was able to write her own schedule for the semester and feel confident revising it when needed.*

Interventions that incorporate apps and technology (on a smartphone or tablet) tend to work well as these devices are mainstream and it is usually easy to get the "buy-in" from individuals to utilize them. For example, a great task management app is *Wunderlist*, which can be downloaded on to a phone and added on to the Google Chrome homepage.

We often find that parents substitute their own oversight to cover for their child's executive functioning defects while students are in high school. Unfortunately, the resultant gaps in knowledge and functioning are quickly exposed when students live apart from their parents' watchful guidance.

> *Jordan's parents, for example, did allow Jordan to run her own schedule while in high school, but the large family calendar and prompting of the other children in the household served as a prompt for Jordan, too. Further, Jordan's parents always made sure meals were on the table in a timely manner, and required Jordan to eat with the family. Once Jordan was living on campus, her anxiety level spiked, she didn't feel hungry, and her lack of eating contributed to additional executive functioning concerns. The OT helped Jordan stockpile some snacks that she could eat, and put reminders in her phone and in her schedule to eat regularly. They also scheduled a weekly check-in time to bolster her executive functioning skills while her stress was high.*

Overcoming Client Myths with Regard to OT Services

Many clients will be reticent to embark upon seeing yet another professional, and the therapist will likely need to do some myth-busting in order to aid the client (and their parents) in understanding why additional help may be warranted.

Myth #1. Sensory challenges are behavioral and will go away as the individual grows up. The reality is sensory challenges remain into adulthood, with many adults continuing to struggle with various sensitivities that impair their daily lives.

> *Jordan, for example, disliked the notion of working with an OT for many reasons, including her belief that she was "over" her sensory sensitivities. Yet moving from a high school, where she had found comfort over the years, to a new environment, with new noises and smells, was overwhelming for her. The therapist had to help Jordan understand these issues were not just going to "go away" or that she would "grow out of them." They were symptoms that could be reduced with proper treatment so Jordan could be more comfortable in daily living.*

Myth #2. Graduating from high school indicates you will be successful in college. The reality is that the development of self-advocacy skills is integral to success. With a much more supportive, individually tailored environment in high school, success has often been buttressed by educational supports.

> *Jordan had figured out how to advocate for herself within her family, but needed additional (generalized) skills to work things out with her roommate and to ask for help from her college instructors. Her instructors didn't check in with her, as they had in high school, and she was too intimidated to attend office hours by herself. Her OT went to office hours with her once, and then encouraged her to attend on her own – and she did!*

Myth #3. An autism spectrum disorder diagnosis automatically limits an individual. It is important for professionals to really see the person, not just the diagnosis!

> *Jordan's OT worked with her to highlight her personal strengths, made sure to budget adequate time to discuss hobbies and interests, and helped Jordan and others to understand that autism is one facet of her existence. Her neurodiversity brings many strengths that can help her succeed!*

Myth #4. College is a time for students learn to do things on their own. The ultimate goal of college is to have an educated, self-functioning adult *at the end* of the undergraduate career. The best treatment is a collaborative effort among multiple providers/services. Working in isolation rarely promotes success. Partnering with others and tapping into the strengths of other professions are imperative.

> *Jordan's team fluctuated, and included her parents, her OT, her therapist, sometimes her psychiatrist, and the occasional professor who invited her to work on research teams.*

All of us need to learn to function independently, but the timeline of demonstrating those skills varies considerably!

Summary

Mental health professionals typically help with *who you are* and address psychological aspects of symptoms or diagnosis. Typical mental health treatment goals for autistic clients include stress reduction and anxiety and depression management, and there is often a focus on social skills and relational issues. As a therapist, you must model flexibility in the room, advocate for your client, impart skills, encourage, teach, and also mind your boundaries. Conversely, OTs support individuals with *what clients do or what clients want to do* (i.e., support with getting from where clients are to where they want to be). The OT can be an integral part of the treatment team for an individual with autism; recognizing the need for a referral for these supportive skills can greatly enhance treatment of individuals with autism.

Recommended Resources for Professionals

- Guare, R., & Dawson, P. (2009). *Smart but scattered teens: The "executive skills" program for helping teens reach their potential.* New York, NY: The Guilford Press.
- Johnston-Tyler, J. (2014). *The CEO of self: An executive functioning workbook.* Scotts Valley, CA: CreateSpace Independent Publishing Platform.
- Warren, E. (2010). *Planning, time management, and organization for success.* Ossining, NY: Erica Warren Publications.
- Wolf, L. E, Brown, J. T., & Bork, G. R. K. (2009). *Students with Asperger syndrome: A guide for college personnel.* Shawnee Mission, KS: Autism Asperger Pub. Co.

Recommended Resources for Families

- Division of Vocational Rehabilitation (these are state by state resources that can be accessed at www.askearn.org/state-vocational-rehabilitation-agencies/)
- King, L., & Wolf, L. E. (2012). *The parent's guide to college for students on the Autism Spectrum.* Shawnee, KS: AAPC Publishing.
- Moss, H. (2014). *A freshman survival guide for college students with autism spectrum disorders.* Philadelphia, PA: Jessica Kingsley Publishers.
- Occupational therapy (Supported Education In Higher Education): www.aota.org/About-Occupational-Therapy/Professionals/CY/school-settings.aspx
- Panda Planners: https://pandaplanner.com/collections/planners?gclid=CjwKCAjw9dboBRBUEiwA7VrrzU6Vb-k5n8n7Cgik1BQFMXhmTMNA6fUhgajwgDFZexDE-4z_eQ-xKRoCo-QQAvD_BwE

- Student Disability Centers on college campuses (more information can be found at www.nccsdclearinghouse.org/disability-services-info-for-students.html)

About the Author

Megan Wolff, MOT OTR/L, received her Master's in Occupational Therapy degree from Colorado State University (CSU). She has spent the duration of her OT career working with transition-age youth and young adults in high school, in college, and in the workplace, providing supported education and supported employment services, particularly with the Opportunities for Post-secondary Success (OPS) program at CSU. She enjoys watching these students as they find success in their transition to adulthood. Ms. Wolff can be found at www.chhs.colostate.edu/ccp.

Part VI

Navigating Education Holistically

Students spend hours a day in school, for years and years. School is a significant time commitment for students, and this time commitment is reflected in the requests that parents and students make of schools. Debates have been held for years about the power of a 504 Plan versus an Individualized Education Plan (IEP), who qualifies, what services should be offered, how families can get what the student wants or needs, and the scarcity of resources in the public school system. Similar debates have raged about public schools versus private schools versus homeschooling (as if there is *one* answer that is the best answer for all students!).

Sidestepping much of those debates, in this part we learn about supporting neurodiverse students by changing the mindset of professionals who work with these students. We look at the role of empathy and appreciative inquiry. We consider lessons learned from the admissions office regarding the impact of anxiety, executive functioning, and social communication challenges. Finally, we start to explore the notion of college preparation – what to learn, when to start, and how to build self-awareness and resilience for college students. In this part we avoid the artificial debate of the IEP; instead we focus on how to prepare students to maximize their academic experiences.

16 Fall in Love with the Social World

Jennifer C. Townsend

We often assume others have a similar perception as ourselves and tend to surround ourselves with like-minded individuals, and there is a natural tendency to pass judgment on others who are different. Yet individuals on the autism spectrum have a brain that is wired with known differences; therapy first and foremost needs to focus on acceptance of these neurologically atypical individuals. Those with autism who find their way to your office may not yet have developed the skills necessary to discover an opportunity to garner social connections and develop social competence. The role of the therapist is to guide this learning through collaboration, appreciation of differences, and consideration of their atypical brain style.

Understand with Consideration (Not Emotions)

We are not socially competent at birth; we learn these skills as we grow and observe others around us. In fact, the brain has a lot of growing up to do in order to be socially able by *adulthood*. While the basics of keeping a child safe and providing good nutrition are critical, likewise the growth of a brain absolutely needs frequent and positive social connections. When a person's brain has "fallen in love" with people, developed communication skills, and acquired language, that person will likely have developed the ability to maintain relationships over time. This means that the individual's brain has developed in a manner that allows them to figure out the social rules, interact with friends, be a teammate, and so on. This ability to navigate social relationships and use executive functioning in relationships is the "skill" of social competence (Rubin, Townsend, & Vittori, 2015). As a therapist supporting an individual with autism, it will be important to specifically teach these skills, allow for practice and refinement of them, and provide support for the client in order to make a positive impact on social development and future success.

Individuals with autism often have limited social development, which can make connecting in typical manners challenging for the therapist. It is critical for therapists to understand that neurological development is atypical, and that connecting with autistic individuals may also require atypical means and methods. For example, therapists typically connect with clients in part by direct eye contact. However, individuals with autism may have difficulties making direct eye contact. Longitudinal research on visual fixation patterns of infants has found that infants later diagnosed with autism follow a different developmental path: at birth, infants who later are diagnosed with autism have eye fixation patterns similar to neurotypical infants, but this development diverges somewhere between two and six months of age. When researchers measured preferential attention to the eyes of others, they found that among infants later diagnosed with autism, eye fixation on others declines from two to six months of age (this pattern is not observed in infants who did not develop autism). Additionally, by two years of age, those later diagnosed with autism were more than twice as likely to focus on objects than their typically developing counterparts (Jones & Klin, 2013). Knowing this research about eye gaze and the tendency for someone with autism to focus on objects rather than people provides an opportunity for appreciation about how someone with autism will learn differently and the necessity to emphasize the skills associated with social competence.

Support with Empathy

For neurotypical individuals, social development consists of seeking social connections, using language (verbal and nonverbal) to connect with others, and ultimately "falling in love" with the social world. They connect with others through the social world, and it enhances their development. For individuals with autism, however, they seemingly tend not to connect with others, may have inhibited use of language to connect with others, and end up no longer seeking out social connections, but instead connect to objects or activities, and ultimately may fall out of love with the social world.

Often times, however, therapists attempt to "fix" the problem rather than first taking the time to appreciate the neurodiversity of the individual sitting in front of them. It is helpful to have an "appreciative inquiry" of what is going well for the client, and find out what's working for them rather than using a problem-focused approach that may magnify feelings of difference or defeat rather than understanding times the client has been able to connect with others. The therapist–client relationship is an important space to support with empathy, build a safe environment, and provide opportunities for growth and change. The therapist–client relationship can become a microcosm for success of other relationships. Learning how to discuss their thoughts and feelings, plan and reliably show up for appointments, and manage therapeutic boundaries all set the stage for success in other relationships. If you can connect with your autistic client, and your client can safely connect with you, s/he will actively seek out others, plan ahead, and maintain relationships with others over time. This support provides a crucial success of social competence.

When we provide support it is crucial to place the emphasis on the "skills" of social competence with strong consideration towards the information noted earlier in this chapter. Consider the following case of Julio as he struggles with social competence and the therapist supports him as he moves from social floundering to increasing mastery of skills. Julio comes to therapy with academic problems, but his issues are not just academic.

Julio is a high school student with autism and anxiety disorder. He is very bright, and historically has done well in school, although upon entering high school his self-advocacy skill set has become a challenge for educators to manage. Julio adamantly refuses to complete school assignments and comments that his teachers are disorganized and have minimal content knowledge. Julio also shared that he detests having to document his thinking. He agrees he does not turn in assignments, projects, or coursework. The teachers note that Julio does not complete his work, and that Julio frequently tells them that he knows how to do it, but dislikes any adult telling him what to do. His teachers also share that Julio does not seem to have friendships. His parents agree that he does not have strong friendships, though he does have acquaintances, and they do not see this adamant refusal to complete tasks at home. They see a smart young man who wants to get good grades, go to college, and become an engineer. Based on this information, the Individualized Education Plan (IEP) team believes that Julio needs more structure to break down the work assignments, as they are an important part of his grades, and suggests that he use an agenda book to help him keep track of his due dates for assignments, just like he manages his time to study for exams, so he can submit them in a timely manner.

Consider the skills of social competence. Specifically, consider the suggestion of an agenda book for Julio, who does not yet find the value in completing the projects assigned by his teacher. Why would using an agenda book be important to him if he can ace the exams? In talking further with Julio about how he would benefit from the use of self-monitoring tools and self-talk to guide his behavior, we discovered that he likes to learn by sharing facts, observation, and self-directed instruction, not collaboration or doing "busy work." Therefore, rather than telling Julio to use an agenda book to organize his projects, we use an appreciative inquiry process to discover, dream, design, and deliver a viable solution by: (1) considering his current skills in self-management; (2) discovering how he manages his time to study for exams; (3) modeling and/or discussing a variety of self-monitoring tool options for him to observe; (4) creating a clear understanding for why goal-setting and organizational skills are critical to Julio's future aspirations; and (5) letting Julio take the lead in the delivery for how this will look for projects, with the understanding that if his plans do not work, we will make some adjustments based on the principles of appreciative inquiry.

> *In further conversations with Julio, it became evident that he had not considered others' perspectives and did not realize there was more to getting a "good" grade than assessment scores. Appreciating his current skills and providing Julio a voice in the outcome, together we found a solution that was logical and made sense to support social competence skills in organization. The teacher also learned that fewer projects for Julio and more opportunities to show his knowledge on exams, tests, and quizzes could support their relationship and enhance the opportunities for Julio to feel success across a range of social settings, and help him understand that others are supportive of him.*

Note, for Julio to be engaged in using the solution, he needed to feel valued in the conversation. It was helpful to define the problem and narrow it down with specific discrete examples, so that all parties involved communicate their perceptions. The goal is for all involved individuals to understand their own perceptions about the identified problem, as well as to consider the perceptions of others, and then finally to develop a solution which is led by the learner (Julio), rather than the adults (IEP team). The goal is to provide support with empathy, to enhance the learner's sense of agency and social competence.

Energizing Growth

Appreciative inquiry, which includes focusing on client success, can specifically focus on how clients develop skills in social competence. This inquiry into even minor successes can help clients feel energized, and create a positive impact in therapy. It is important to note that sometimes we ask individuals to share their personal selves with us, as support professionals, but they do not know anything about us, which makes it a bit one-sided. When you have a social learning difference and are asked to do something with minimal support and limited relationship, the skill and/or task becomes more difficult and at times seemingly impossible. When diverse perspectives are included, respected, and valued we can start to get a full picture of the world: who we serve, what they need, and how to successfully meet people where they are (Brown, 2018, p. 109). Challenge yourself to think differently about those we support and to appreciate where the learner is in the moment. Where we enter their lives, not their past and not yet their future, it is important to appreciate the here and now. Recognize that we are all different and that is what makes us unique in our professions. With a belief in our collaborative efforts together we can do more than *make* a difference, we can *be* the difference. This writing is meant to challenge you to think differently, to be brave, and grow.

Resources for Professionals

- Rubin, E., Townsend, J., & Vittori, L. (2015). Social Emotional Engagement Knowledge and Skills (SEE-KS) Framework. Retrieved from www.see-ks.com
- Rubin, E., & Townsend, J., (2016, May 01). Social Emotional Engagement Knowledge and Skills. Retrieved from www.see-ks.com/
- Prizant, B. M. (2006). *The SCERTS model: A comprehensive educational approach for children with autism spectrum disorders*. Baltimore, MD: Paul H. Brookes Pub.
- Lives in Balance: www.livesinthebalance.org/

Resources for Parents

- Greene, R. W. (2014). *The explosive child: A new approach for understanding and parenting easily frustrated, chronically inflexible children*. New York, NY: Harper.
- Prizant, B. M., & Fields-Meyer, T. (2019). *Uniquely human: A different way of seeing autism*. London, UK: Souvenir Press.

About the Author

Jennifer C. Townsend, M.Ed., is an educational consultant with expertise in social emotional learning differences. Jennifer is a co-author of the Social Emotional Engagement Knowledge and Skills (SEE-KS) framework and presents internationally. Her approach uses appreciative inquiry coaching techniques with an emphasis on universal design for learning. Jen is a graduate of the Johns Hopkins University and a licenced educator in the state of Wisconsin as a special educator and Director of Special Education and Pupil Services. Jen is a dynamic influencer in the field of education and believes that together we can go beyond just making a difference; we can be the difference. To learn more visit www.universalaccessconsulting.com.

References

Brown, B. (2018). *Dare to lead: Brave work, tough conversations, whole hearts*. London, UK: Vermilion.

Jones, W., & Klin, A. (2013). Attention to eyes is present but in decline in 2–6-month-old infants later diagnosed with autism. *Nature, 504*(7480), 427–431. doi:10.1038/nature12715

Rubin, E., Townsend, J., & Vittori, L. (2015). Social Emotional Engagement Knowledge and Skills (SEE-KS) Framework. Retrieved June 1, 2019 from www. see-ks.com

17 Lessons from the Admissions Office

Lea Anne Paskvalich

In a quiet corner office, I listen to the parents of a seventh-grader describe how their once engaged and curious learner is now refusing to go to school. His mother explained:

> *"For the first few months of school we would get a call that Brayden was in the nurse's office at school with a stomach ache and that we needed to pick him up. For over a month now, he has been refusing to go to school in the morning. We can get him there on most days, but we have had to bribe him more and more. His teachers are telling us he is not turning in assignments and becomes argumentative with them and other students on a regular basis. He tells us he hates school and doesn't see the point in going because he thinks he is stupid, so why even bother?"*
>
> *She reaches for a tissue and Brayden's dad chimes in: "We are at a loss for what to do. We know he has his quirks, but he is smart! He loves aviation and history, especially World War II planes. His current escape is the History Channel documentary* World War II*. He will watch all 10 hours on repeat every weekend if we let him."*

Brayden was like countless other students I had come across in my eight years as the Admissions Director at the Temple Grandin School in Boulder, Colorado, These are students on the spectrum, who in elementary school generally did well, but for whom middle school presented a whole new and unforgiving environment.

> *Listening to these parents tearfully describe their son, a common theme emerged yet again. I sympathized and said, "I hear your concerns and think I know why Braden does not want to go to school. I think he feels disrespected and misunderstood when he is there." A sudden sense of recognition and a tinge of relief appeared on their faces after realizing "someone gets my kid?!"*

I see this all the time; that sense of relief quickly turns to a sense of urgency and questions about how to help their child. This family needs a road map marked with key interventions that will lead their son to increased respect and understanding from his teachers and peers. Without this valuing from teachers and peers, it is impossible for students with autism to thrive, or much less survive, in an educational setting.

Challenges for the Individual with Autism

The top concerns of parents I see who are seeking a more supportive educational setting for their child include worries about the child's anxiety, executive function deficits, social communication challenges, and academic progress. These concerns also impact how others understand a student on the autism spectrum, as the concerns are often misinterpreted as misbehavior or non-compliance.

Anxiety

Anxiety can manifest in numerous ways for students on the spectrum; it can be angry words hurled at teachers, pacing the classroom, incessant requests for reassurance, or a complete emotional shutdown with their head on the desk. Anxiety can look like disrespect to a teacher, when really it is a cry for help from the student. Similarly, executive function deficits can be detrimental to a student who "should just know by now how to use a planner!" Comments about executive functioning deficits can quickly increase feelings of anxiety in a student.

Anxiety management is often a life-long struggle for individuals on the autism spectrum. Teaching your young clients to understand and manage their anxiety can help reduce challenging behavior at school. All behavior is communication. When a student is feeling anxious at school, it may negatively impact their ability to communicate, focus, and learn. Maintaining their composure in the face of anxiety often feels impossible. Students on the spectrum with a higher number of behavior problems have been shown to have a lower-quality or strained student–teacher relationship (Robertson, Chamberlain, & Kassari, 2003). They feel the disrespect from the teacher, and students often sense that the disrespect will never change. These feelings may internalize into low self-esteem and lead to a feeling of hopelessness. These clients need assistance in identifying and developing coping strategies for school-related anxiety and its triggers. Whenever possible, communicate your client's anxiety triggers and coping strategies to parents and even to school staff.

Executive Functioning Deficits

Individuals with autism often have deficits in executive functioning skills. Brayden's dad related a story that is typical for students with autism:

> *"Last month Brayden wrote a short story for Language Arts class over several late nights and with lots of help from me. It was extremely difficult for him to get started and then when he finally finished it, he never turned it in! We found it in his locker at parent–teacher conferences last week. I just don't get it."*

When thinking about executive functioning and students on the spectrum, we often imagine a scatterbrained, overwhelmed teen with belongings strewn everywhere. Methods for teaching executive function must be overly explicit and directly taught to students on the spectrum. Teachers do not have the resources or time to do the intensive work on executive function skills that students on the spectrum require. Parents often describe lockers and backpacks as bottomless pits where unfinished assignments live. Student planners are blank, or lost. Most students receive a planner in the fourth or fifth grade. During this time, students on the spectrum are juggling increased academic and social demands, and often the planner is left in their desk or lost in the shuffle. By the time they reach middle school they are expected to "just know" how to use their planner.

Executive function coaches have emerged as a resource for teaching tools and strategies to students on the spectrum to address attention, focus, working memory, impulse control, and self-evaluation. Not all executive function coaches are going to be a good fit for a student on the spectrum. An important factor in determining the success of an executive function coach with an autistic student is whether or not the strategies being taught make sense to the student. Students with autism must be able to grasp *why* they are learning a skill. These students need to know the "why" and the why needs to matter to them. An executive function coach who prescribes organizational systems for students that do not make sense to the student will not be successful; an autistic student will not use a system they cannot conceptualize. Referring families to executive function coaches who have experience and success with students on the spectrum is imperative.

Social Communication Challenges

Social communication challenges play out as missed social cues and lack of perspective taking across the school setting. One of the greatest heartaches of parents and students is failed social connection with peers: no friends. While they all have their own unique set of challenges, I consistently observe that anxiety and executive function deficits impact all of the students I work with. Social communication challenges and academic progress can be more varied in terms of level of impairment and concern.

Again, Brayden's father provides a glimpse into this issue as he expresses exasperation with Brayden:

> *"Brayden can talk non-stop about D-Day during World War II, sometimes even going into a radio broadcast voice to recount the event. He doesn't even notice that the other person doesn't give a hoot about D-Day!"*

Focusing on building skills around social communication, and more specifically, perspective taking, will help students gain respect from teachers and peers. Social skills groups led by skilled speech language pathologists and occupational therapists can help students learn perspective taking, how to read body language, and how to pick up on conversational cues. For example, when Brayden does find a peer who shares his enthusiasm about World War II, he will still need to be a good conversational partner. Social skills groups can be most effective in teaching social communication skills when the participants in the group have a common interest or the group is centered around a preferred activity; these common-interest groups can promote authentic connection (i.e., cooking, *Dungeons and Dragons* game, model railroads). Recognizing and then using a child's strengths and interests to build social communication skills allows the child to have more buy-in to the interventions.

Academic Progress

Brayden's mom explains her concerns about Brayden's educational progress:

> *"His math grades have been all over the map. This year the biggest challenge has been to get him to show his work on problems. Brayden can often do the math problems in his head and get the correct answer, but he bombs the tests because he refuses to show his work."*

The families I meet with have children on the spectrum who often present with uneven cognitive profiles, which can impact academic ability or progress. When working with individuals on the spectrum, it is important to note these challenges can significantly impact the student in school. Parents are frequently concerned with at least one academic content area in their child's education. Gaps in learning, when they are not addressed in a timely manner, can expand to grand canyons by the time a student on the spectrum reaches high school. These gaps may exist for several reasons. A student on the spectrum may have missed content areas because of absences from the classroom due to anxiety or sensory overload. Undiagnosed learning disabilities or learning styles may play a role in how the student retains or does not retain information. These students tend to have a "leaky bucket" of learning; they have holes in their learning that need to be filled. Psychological testing using cognitive, academic, and executive function measures to get the full picture of the strengths and challenges of the student is recommended. The psychological assessment can be used as a guide to fill in the learning gaps. It is worth mentioning that Individualized Educational Plans (IEPs) often include academic and cognitive testing; however, these evaluations are often not updated regularly and frequently are just rolled over from the initial information and assessments that were collected to determine eligibility for special education services.

Additional learning support and remediation outside of the regular classroom can be a bridge to increased success for a student on the spectrum. An educational therapist or learning specialist who will work one on one with a student to build academic skills may be extremely useful. Parents should be cautioned not to just hire a "math tutor" or "reading tutor" to help with assignments. For the student to make progress it will require academic intervention with personalized instruction. The interventionist working with the student must understand how to work with a student on the spectrum.

Parents Are the Experts

"What does your child love to do or what are they into right now?" is how I start every conversation with a parent inquiring about admission to Temple Grandin School. This is where I learn the most valuable information about the student. The struggles of the student are important, *and* I want to know what motivates the student and what their strengths are. We want to understand the students' strengths, and not allow them to be defined by their challenges. Parents are the experts on their child and are excellent historians on their development. Many times students will have lost interest in things they once found pleasurable; the loss of respect and understanding by teachers and peers can strongly impact this discouragement.

Parents of students on the spectrum need to be just as involved in their child's education in middle and high school as they have been in the elementary years. The message from schools to all parents as students enter middle school and high school is: students need to learn how to advocate for themselves and parents need to stop doing things for them. Middle and high school students who are on the spectrum typically need their parents to be as much involved, or more so, in their education as in the early years, actively advocating for their child's education.

Summary

Parents often wonder if there are therapists out there who will actually understand their child. The answer to that question is a resounding yes! Students on the spectrum can be incredibly complex and therapists must not work in a vacuum. As noted, these clients often have concerns ranging from anxiety, to executive function deficits, to social communication and learning challenges that can impede academic progress without successful intervention. A therapist should consult and collaborate with parents, teachers, and other therapeutic professionals to address client concerns. There are wonderful educational success stories about students on the spectrum, and each one of those stories had a collaborative team behind the student with the parent leading the charge.

Recommended Resources for Professionals and Families

• Seth Perler, Executive Function Coach: www.sethperler.com
• Social Thinking: www.socialthinking.com
• Association of Educational Therapists: www.aetonline.org

About the Author

Lea Anne Paskvalich is Director of Admissions and Public Relations at the Temple Grandin School in Boulder, Colorado. The Temple Grandin School (www.templegrandinschool.org) serves students in sixth through 12th grade who have Asperger's syndrome and similar learning profiles. She is also the Founder of Next Steps Consulting LLC, a company that advises parents and adults on personalized resources for autism. She is a long-time volunteer in the local autism community, enjoys hiking and skiing in the Colorado mountains, and spending time in her backyard with her family and two rambunctious Australian Shepherds. You can find Ms. Paskvalich at www.nextstepsconsult.com.

Reference

Robertson, K., Chamberlain, B., & Kasari, C. (2003). General education teachers' relationships with included students with autism. *Journal of Autism and Developmental Disorders, 33*, 123–130. doi:10.1023/A:1022979108096

18 Being Prepared and Aware

Helping Individuals with Autism with Post-Secondary Education Goals

Amy Radochonski

Attending college for those with autism, once a "stretch goal," has become within reach for many. Universities, community colleges, and technical schools are increasingly providing opportunities for inclusion for students diagnosed with unique learning needs. While access to post-secondary education has increased, many wonder if students on the spectrum are able to persist and obtain their degrees. Indeed, fewer than 20% of college students with autism graduate or are on track to graduate five years after high school (Roux, Shattuck, Rast, Rava, & Anderson, 2015). Completion rates for students with disabilities of post-secondary education are lower than their non-disabled peers, with 41% of students with disabilities completing their education, compared to 52% of non-disabled similar-aged peers (Newman et al., 2011). No reports are yet available specifically comparing graduation rates of individuals with autism to neurotypical individuals (White et al., 2016). Challenges for those with autism include social communication difficulties, mental health concerns, poor emotional regulation, and executive functioning deficits such as difficulty managing competing demands (Roux et al., 2015; White et al., 2016).

Despite the grim statistics, there are many personal strengths that make college a viable and attractive option for individuals on the spectrum: their attention to detail, ability to memorize and retain information, and passionate interests (Anderson & Butt, 2017) can make individuals with autism able to thrive in an academic environment. Therapists are often asked to assist autistic clients with their unique academic and emotional needs that arise as they navigate post-secondary education. There is a significant transition that occurs after K-12 education to college education; what follows is a description highlighting some differences in rights and responsibilities between the two types of education, and what therapists can do to help prepare both the student and the family.

Lack of Preparation and Knowledge

Many students, not just those with autism, entering college are woefully under-prepared for the academic and emotional shift from high school to college (Harris Poll, 2015). Each student presents with a complex set of strengths and needs related to their overall college readiness including content knowledge, cognitive strategies, and transition challenges related to living independently. To make this shift even more difficult, while parental assistance is encouraged during primary and secondary education, at the college level parental involvement is significantly curtailed, leaving students to fend for themselves with little to no scaffolding to be on their own. Their overall knowledge of higher education culture and systems can also significantly impact retention.

In addition to the differing cultures of high school and college, we are observing a new set of generational norms. Current norms for college students include frequent changes in educational paths or majors; challenges in managing time and effort; increased prevalence of anxiety or mental health needs; and an increased need to self-advocate without necessarily having developed the tools to be able to do so. The executive functioning skills required to be successful in higher education are challenging for many students on the autism spectrum. This diverse presentation of student needs makes assessing educational interventions that can best support them a challenging task.

Supports in High School versus College

Students entering post-secondary education now have the opportunity to be in the driver's seat for potentially the first time in their life. As seen in Table 18.1, comparing high school education and the regulations of those schools to a higher education setting, a clear theme emerges. Supports once done for, around, or behind the scenes are now in the college student's control and can only be in place with self-advocacy.

How Therapists Can Help

As noted, expectations in college are very different than in the K-12 system. Adding a layer of challenge to the newfound autonomy is understanding that higher education pathways are not fixed. Therefore, how we teach an individual to be ready for the driver's seat cannot be a fixed approach either.

When transitioning to a new setting, the student's ability to know their needs is an area under their control. As the therapist, you can help the student to develop self-knowledge, self-advocacy, problem solving, and resiliency. These key skills can positively impact a successful higher education experience.

Table 18.1 Comparison of Disability Law and Supports: K-12 vs. Higher Education

K-12	College
Rules governed by Individuals with Disabilities Education Act (IDEA, 2004) or services provided by Section 504 (a civil rights law).	Legal requirements only protect students under the Americans With Disabilities Act (ADA), a much leaner set of laws than IDEA. The focus of ADA is to create an environment that does not discriminate against individuals with disabilities, a contrast from IDEA and 504.
Regulations in place allow for accountability and a systematic process to review student progress and educational interventions.	Review of student progress is generally simply a review of the student's transcript.
Adoption of district curricula and best practices for teaching and instruction in the classroom setting drive the focus of a student's education and classroom environment.	Some campus programs exist to provide additional assistance in common domains of education, socialization, or independent living, but these are not requirements and there is minimal infrastructure.
Resources within a school or district provide a wraparound model that supports individuals' domains, commonly impacting students on the spectrum, including occupational therapy, speech and language therapy, adaptive physical education, and social emotional supports.	If the student wants any services, they need to make a phone call, get appointments scheduled, request services, and often pay for services.
The educational pathway, goals, modifications, and accommodations are established based upon the assessment or analysis by professionals working with a student. Parents may also contribute heavily to the goals of a student and where the focus lies for an educational path.	Students choose their own classes, make their own goals, and find their own way. Parents may speak directly with their young adult (as parents do!), but parents are not consulted by the school.
Advocacy is done around the student. Accommodations are put in place *for* the student. Parents have a strong role to play.	Advocacy is done *by* the student. Accommodations are put in place at the student's request. Parents are not invited to participate.
Modifications are done ahead of assignment delivery.	The predominant accommodation is through offerings in a disability or accessibility office with additional resources such as taking tests in an alternate setting; on-campus tutoring from other students; assistive technology; and additional time available for test completion.

Self-Awareness

> *James always was permitted to stand up every 20 minutes in his high school classes thanks to his educational accommodations, as he has a difficult time sitting still. This break helped him to focus on academic content during his high school classes. However, when he got to college, he found he was expected to sit in the standard 50–70-minute lecture. He was tapping his feet to manage his discomfort, though he was oblivious to both the professor and fellow students being annoyed by his actions. When James could no longer manage to sit in the college classroom and he started to stand, the professor stopped her lecture, wondering what was happening. She thought he was leaving the classroom, and was upset that he interrupted her lecture. James was simply going to go to the back of the classroom to stand, unaware such an action would cause disruption. Now he is faced with stares from fellow students and a professor who erroneously thinks he is being disrespectful.*

Unfortunately, these scenarios play out repeatedly as those with autism enter college. Indeed, instructors find that students with autism tend to miss the instructor's non-verbal social cues, leading to behavior that violates group norms; they also find students on the spectrum tend not to follow conventional physical interpersonal boundaries (Gobbo & Shmulsky, 2014). Thus, therapists need to help students with both self-awareness and self-advocacy skills so that they can successfully navigate the classroom experience.

Self-awareness is a skill that therapists can help impart to clients. Self-awareness encompasses the ability to understand one's behaviors and attitudes. For individuals on the spectrum, self-awareness can be a particularly complex skill given the often mismatched intersection of chronological and developmental age of students. *All* teenagers are working on understanding themselves as individuals, and social-emotional learning can be confusing and hard to comprehend. Individuals on the spectrum require focused teaching since their chronological age may not match with the social-emotional maturity level they have developed. Self-awareness is an umbrella concept that includes: identification of strengths and areas of growth, exploration of the client's unique personality, knowledge of learning styles and preferences, and understanding triggers to anxiety or stress.

Everyone develops self-awareness through experiences, so there is fluidity in building self-awareness as growth and skill development occur. Strengths, abilities, and ownership of decisions are a constant evolution, yet a critical one for an individual with unique learning needs entering an unpredictable environment. Self-awareness needs to include cognizance of how the client's own behaviors, and their attitude towards these behaviors, helps to create self-efficacy and enhanced independence, and allows them to take control of their higher education experience. By increasing self-awareness while enhancing skills, clients develop increased comfort in advocating for their own needs.

James noticed which classes or times of day are most comfortable for him, and when he is most likely to want to fidget or move. He worked to lengthen the time he is able to sit relatively still in class. James also decided to meet with his instructors at the beginning of the semester to let them know about his needs, and highlight possible coping skills he might want to employ (getting up to stretch his legs in the back of the class, sitting near an aisle, sitting in the back of the room). James also worked to learn to understand the perspective of his instructors and classmates: some people are genuinely bothered by motion in the classroom, or instructors may feel disrespected by these actions if they don't understand the need for accommodations.

Talking about their needs, perspectives, and respect early in the semester is a strategy that many students employ with great success.

Self-Advocacy

The development of a student's self-advocacy skills may initially focus on developing insights, identifying patterns, and crafting ways to help them get their needs met. It would be best if students can practice these skills before they head off to college. Therapists can help clients become aware of a need for a particular accommodation (insight, observing patterns), requesting it (behavior), and why the accommodation is important (attitude). More specifically, a student who needs to move around in class may observe that they fare better in smaller classrooms, or at a certain time of day. The student first sees the pattern, and uses insight to identify behaviors to make life better. The student might then communicate (behavior) to their professor that sitting in the back of the class allows for the chance for a movement break (also a behavior/solution) that will positively impact attendance. The student should communicate to the professor that they can move around *and* accept the professor's feedback on how this occurs (attitude). For example, if James had discussed his situation with the professor ahead of class, she likely would have taken his movement in stride, supported it, and James would not have felt the burning embarrassment of being singled out for his behavior. As a professional, you are in a unique position to help students learn these skills and practice them prior to heading to college.

Problem Solving

Students need to develop problem-solving skills to face the challenges of higher education (and adulthood). Being in the driver's seat means problem solving on their own. As a therapist, you can help to identify the opportunities to build the skill set of problem solving in the educational or community setting. You might gently guide your client from solving simpler problems to intentionally solving problems that involve discomfort. These are opportunities for reflection, growth, and skill building. For example, when in a safe community space such as an indoor mall, how can a student respond when they are lost? Do they possess the ability to scan the environment for cues? Read a map? Identify an appropriate individual who can assist? Ask the person for that assistance? These skills mirror the challenges of getting lost on a college campus, and resiliency can come from a knowledge of the discomfort it can cause as well as the ability to problem solve out of it.

Problem solving and planning for failure help students develop necessary skills. Examples of safe places to experience an obstacle that requires some flexibility and that mirror common educational challenges ahead are:

- Wake up independently for a preferred activity or event. The student can be helped to understand the costs of not waking up, including potentially missing out on part of the activity.
- Independently requesting a classroom accommodation; without doing so the accommodation is not provided, and a grade may reflect that lack of accommodation.
- Conveying to a new person at the school or at work about their strengths and needs as a means of practicing articulation of their skills without the assistance of a teacher or family member. This skill will be required at college or work.

Building Resilience

Resiliency is about the ability to recover from and have some grit to keep going after facing difficulty, and there is a need for resiliency due to the changes that are inevitably ahead. Taylor and DaWalt (2017) reported that, in the two to three years following high school, half of the participants experienced "disruption" in their vocational or educational experience, including failing out of a post-secondary education program or being fired from a job. Failure or "disruption" may occur. Expect it. Plan for it. Help your clients learn resiliency skills. Failure in college or the workplace can carry a different weight, consequences can potentially be more significant, and this may be the first time a parent cannot intervene in the capacity that may have been available throughout K-12 education. For example, a student can be responsible for tracking, completing, and submitting assignments independently (perhaps by starting in a singular class). If the student slips up, the parents can coach the student on how to remediate the situation by talking to the instructor, requesting timely assistance, asking for an extended timeline, or asking for additional opportunities to demonstrate learning. The consequences of missing an assignment at high school level tend to be less serious than missing an assignment at college level. To accomplish this, parents and student alike must understand that failure is part of the learning experience, and that when parents "rescue" students they solve the problem in the short term (the grades look better), but create a different problem in the long term (lack of problem-solving skills).

If failure has never occurred before or the student has been sheltered by others around them, the ability to dust themselves off and get back on track is compromised. Experiencing natural consequences in a safe space is a good starting point, with family members only intervening when necessary for safety. Resiliency does not mean the goal of success through every obstacle. Resiliency can also be the recognition that a new path or solution may emerge. A new major may serve a student better; a different degree track may be of higher interest; or a job someone wants to attain may not require a degree, and therefore work experience is the most valuable investment of time and energy.

Summary

Ultimately, preparing for college (and life) involves building a sense of self-awareness, increasing self-advocacy and problem solving, and developing the ability to act with resiliency when an environment is not meeting their needs. The keys to developing these skills are clear communication, being provided with the opportunity to develop self-awareness, being provided with support as self-advocacy skills are practiced, and being offered emotional support as resiliency skills are developed. While we all go through this developmental phase as we learn to advocate for ourselves, our students with autism need more structure, support, and opportunity to practice. Therapists are in a unique position to highlight opportunities for practice and celebrate both attempts and successes.

Recommended Resources for Professionals

- College Autism Network: www.collegeautismnetwork.org
- Think College: https://thinkcollege.net/

Recommended Resources for Families

- Bedard, R., & Griffith, M. (2018). *You've got this! The journey from middle school to college, as told by students on the autism spectrum and their parents.* Camp Hill, PA: TPI Press.
- I'm Determined: www.imdetermined.org

About the Author

Amy Radochonski, Vice President of College Living Experience (CLE), has dedicated her career to providing new opportunities for individuals with disabilities and a belief that all students deserve access to meaningful educational that promotes the life they deserve. Ms. Radochonski's background in special education across settings for 20 years highlights her commitment and desire to help students and their families. Ms. Radochonski's keen analytical skills and ability to design individualized programming based on each student's needs have driven CLE to be a continued trend-setter within the industry of post-secondary education. Learn more about the scope of transition services at www.ExperienceCLE.com.

References

Anderson, C., & Butt, C. (2017). Young adults on the autism spectrum at college: Successes and stumbling blocks. *Journal of Autism and Developmental Disorders*, 47 (10), 3029–3039. doi:10.1007/s10803-017-3218-x

Gobbo, K., & Shmulsky, S. (2014). Faculty experience with college students with autism spectrum disorders: *A qualitative study of challenges and solutions. Focus on Autism and Other Developmental Disabilities*, 29(1), 13–22. doi:10.1177/1088357613504989

Individuals with Disabilities Education Act, 20 U.S.C. § 1400 (2004).

Newman, L., Wagner, M., Knokey, A.-M., Marder, C., Nagle, K., Shaver, D., … Schwarting, M. (2011). The post-high school outcomes of young adults with disabilities up to 8 years after high school: A report from the National Longitudinal Transition Study-2 (NLTS2) (NCSER 2011-3005). Menlo Park, CA: SRI International. Retrieved from www.nlts2.org/reports/

Poll, H. (2015). The first-year college experience: A look into students' challenges and triumphs during their first term at college. Retrieved from www.theharrispoll.com/in-the-news/client-polls/College-Experience-Emotional-Readiness.pdf

Roux, A. M., Shattuck, P. T., Rast, J. E., Rava, J. A., & Anderson, K. A. (2015). *National autism indicators report: Transition into young adulthood*. Philadelphia, PA: Life Course Outcomes Research Program, A.J. Drexel Autism Institute, Drexel University.

Taylor, J. L., & DaWalt, L. S. (2017). Brief report: Postsecondary work and educational disruptions for youth on the autism spectrum. *Journal of Autism and Developmental Disorders*, 47(12), 4025–4031. doi:10.1007/s10803-017-3305-z

White, S. W., Elias, R., Salinas, C. E., Capriola, N., Conner, C. M., Asselin, S. B., … Getzel, E. E. (2016). Students with autism spectrum disorder in college: Results from a preliminary mixed methods needs analysis. *Research in Developmental Disabilities*, 56, 29–40. doi:10.1016/j.ridd.2016.05.010

Part VII

Preparing for the World of Work

As you will quickly see, employment statistics for individuals on the autism spectrum are grim: most autistic individuals are underemployed or unemployed. There is clearly much work to be done in the employment arena, from helping clients manage anxiety around applying for jobs or asking for support at work to radically changing the employment landscape so that employers can tap into the strengths of their autistic employees. We all need to do our part on this one, from therapist to client to parent to employer.

We see in this part that preparation for employment starts early by learning to drive and encouraging parents not to overprotect their children (though the temptation is strong!). We learn how to address concerns related to anxiety, including the use of mindfulness-based therapy and phone apps that can be accessed any time, anywhere. We hear repeated directions to employers regarding what they can do differently to be more inclusive, modify the environment at work, and improve their communication with autistic employees. Employment warrants its own book, and this part is a reminder that work-related goals must be addressed in many locations, including in your office.

19 Job Preparation and How to Help People on the Spectrum Have Successful Employment

Temple Grandin

I am a person with autism who has had a career in the livestock industry for over 45 years. In 1990, after I completed my Ph.D. in animal science, I joined the faculty at Colorado State University. Today I am a full professor of animal science at Colorado State University. During a long career, I have designed livestock handling systems for large meat companies and worked as a consultant with major restaurant companies on implementing their animal welfare programs (Grandin, 2005, 2015; Langert, 2019). I've come a long way since I was three, when I had no speech (cf. Cutler, 2004; Grandin, 1995; Grandin & Scariano, 1986).

The statistics are grim for individuals with autism seeking employment. Many people who are formally diagnosed with autism are either unemployed or underemployed (Coleman & Adams, 2018; Shattuck et al., 2012). It is imperative that we help people with autism prepare for and find success at work. In this chapter I will speak about how, as an individual with autism, I had early work experiences that gave me valuable skills, and I will encourage employment experiences for those with autism prior to graduation from high school. I will discuss how autistic people think differently than neurotypical individuals, and how knowledge of these thinking types can inform employment/career selection. The importance of college internships and vocational training will also be highlighted. The role of parents in launching their child into the world of work will also be discussed. Lastly, I provide tips for employers who want to entice and retain valuable employees who have autism.

Learn Working Skills before Graduating High School

When I was freshman in high school, I started learning how to work by doing a task on a schedule that was outside the family. My mother set up a summer job for me doing hand sewing for a seamstress who worked out of her home. I learned to really like the money I earned and got satisfaction from doing a task that another person appreciated.

These early job experiences seem to fuel successful jobs and careers. For example, during my many lectures about autism, I have met many grandparents who discovered that they were on the autism spectrum when their grandchildren were diagnosed. In most cases, the grandparent had a good career in engineering, accounting, skilled trades, or as a musician or journalist. It is likely that there are several reasons why these grandparents were successful. Most of them learned working skills when they were young. Many had a paper route before their teenage years. They also had many other jobs when they were still in high school. Some of their jobs were working in a bowling alley, mowing lawns, as a lifeguard at a beach, and working at a restaurant or retail store. Many successfully employed individuals who got diagnosed later in life gained a better understanding of their relationship issues. In my book *Different Not Less*, fourteen fully employed individuals on the spectrum describe their experiences (Grandin, 2012). All fourteen of these people had many different jobs when they were young. Their careers range from computer programmer to veterinarian, tour guide, and retail positions. All of these successfully employed individuals had jobs outside the home before they graduated from high school.

Additionally, scientific studies show that learning to work before high school graduation improves the rate of employment for fully verbal teenagers with autism (Coleman & Adams, 2018). In one successful program, high school students did internships in the Project SEARCH program. The rate of successful employment was 73% for Project SEARCH and only 17% for the control group with autism (Wehman et al., 2014).

Parents and teachers can easily create work programs in their own homes or school. Jobs outside the home can be easily started in the local neighborhood such as walking dogs, washing cars, church volunteer jobs (such as ushers), and volunteering at a nursing home. It is important for the teenager to learn how to do a scheduled task that is outside the home. When the teenager turns legal working age he/she should get a real paid summer job.

Choosing Careers by Thinking Types

In my book *The Autistic Brain*, I describe three different thinking types for individuals with autism (Grandin & Panek, 2014). Cognitive research provides evidence that these three types of mind really exist (Kozhevnikov, Hegarty, & Mayer, 2002; Mazard, Mazoyer, Crivello, Mazoyer, & Mellet, 2010). The three types are: (1) visual thinkers (object visualizers); (2) pattern/math thinkers (visual spatial); and (3) word thinkers (see Table 19.1). New research provides evidence for all three types (Höffler, Koć-Januchta, & Leutner, 2016).

It is helpful to know an individual's thinking types when it comes to choosing employment or career opportunities.

Table 19.1 Three Types of Thinking (Grandin & Panek, 2014)

Visual Thinkers	Pattern/Math Thinkers	Word Thinkers
Tend to think in pictures, and process information by seeing things in their mind or by physically seeing objects	Think in patterns (mathematical, musical, geometrical)	Enjoy words, literature, speech. Often have a large memory of facts

Visual Thinkers

Some good jobs involve skilled trades, such as plumber, electrician, welder who can read blueprints, and all types of mechanics. Some of these people also excel in graphics, photography, and industrial design. I am a visual thinker and algebra makes no sense to me. Most skilled traders do not need algebra and I am concerned that educational algebra requirements may lock out qualified individuals.

Pattern/Math Thinkers

Suitable jobs are computer programming, statistician, physics, math teacher, and engineering. I have visited several tech companies in Silicon Valley and it is obvious that some of the programmers are on the autism spectrum. In the book *Coders*, Thompson (2019) describes several prominent programmers who were autistic.

Word Thinkers

These are the individuals who love history and facts. They will know everything about their favorite thing. Parents and teachers have told me that several teenagers with autism were very good at selling cars. They were appreciated for their knowledge of this complex specialized product. Other successful careers were in selling auto parts, business insurance, painting, and being a history teacher.

College Internships

I often get asked about my entry into the cattle industry, since I came from a non-agricultural background. Students become interested in things they get exposed to; my interest in cattle arose from working on my aunt's ranch; this is why internships at college are so important. When students try new jobs, they will discover what they like and it is equally important to discover what they do not like.

While in college, I did two different internships which taught me further working skills. The first internship was being an aid for a severely autistic child, and the second internship was working in a research lab. During the internship at the research lab, I had to rent a house and live with a new roommate. By the time I had graduated with a bachelor's degree in psychology I had lots of work experience.

Vocational Training

Today there is a shortage of people to work in the highly skilled trades, such as plumbers, electricians, mechanics, welders, and heating and air conditioning technicians. Most of these jobs require a two-year associates degree or skills can be learned on the job (Checiak, 2018; Gross & Marcus, 2018). Department of Labor occupational outlook shows that the following jobs are expected to grow: plumbing (16%), electrician and truck mechanic (9%) and welders (6%) (United States Department of Labor, 2019).

During my work as a designer of livestock equipment I worked with many skilled trades people who were probably (or should have been) diagnosed with autism, dyslexia, or attention deficit hyperactivity disorder (ADHD). In fact, autism and ADHD have shared genetic influences (Stergiakouli, et al., 2017). The skilled trades folks I worked with were the weird quirky kids. They had good careers that started after they took a skilled trades class in high school, such as welding, auto shop, or carpentry. I know older folks in the livestock and meat industry who would certainly be diagnosed with autism if they were a child today. One man, who is now in his sixties, owns a successful metal fabrication company. He has a severe stutter and has ADHD, dyslexia, and probably autism.

It is never too late to learn. Adults can still be successful in getting jobs after high school. Research also shows that good vocational training and employment support can move an autistic individual to needing less intensive support (Brooke et al., 2018). Services that can improve success are customizing the first job, and lateral job moves.

The Role of Parents

Often, opportunities arise out of parental "stretching," where parents put their child in places of opportunity that may not necessarily be comfortable at first. For example, I had been kicked out of a large high school for throwing a book at a girl who bullied me; I was required to start cleaning the stalls at the horse barn at my boarding school at age 15. This ended up in me cleaning the stalls, feeding the horses, and putting them in and out of the barn, giving me tangible skills! I also learned job-related skills during summers on my aunt's ranch in Arizona. She had guests and my job was to take them on trail rides and wait on tables.

Today I have talked to many parents who overprotect their teenager with autism. Overprotection prevents the teenager from learning basic skills such as shopping, driving, or managing a bank account. Some parents have difficulty letting go and allowing their child to learn the simplest skills. My mother had a really good instinct on how to "stretch" me just outside my comfort zone. Teachers, parents, and therapists have to work on "stretching" these kids without throwing them in the "deep end of the pool." Placing an 18-year-old girl who has never worked in a chaotic store during the Christmas rush is a recipe for disaster. Starting the same job during a slower time of year is recommended. It is best to provide some choices for early job experiences. An example may be a choice between trying different skilled trades or a choice of tasks in a store.

I have found that even the incentive of money cannot motivate some people to get a job, especially if the person has high levels of anxiety. A question that parents often ask is how to help their child deal with debilitating anxiety. I had this problem. There is a point where, despite anxiety, you simply have to move forward. Parents may need to give limited choices. When I was afraid to go to my aunt's ranch, Mother gave me a choice: I could stay all summer at the ranch, or I could come home after one week. She provided two choices, but not going to the ranch at all was not a choice. After I got out to the ranch, I loved it. Going to the ranch helped start my career in the cattle industry. Parents have to "stretch" their child in order for them to become successful, especially when anxiety is a barrier to success.

In my many discussions with parents and teachers, I have seen two distinct pathways for fully verbal adults with autism. The pathways are that individuals learn how to work and have a career, *or* they end up in the basement or bedroom playing video games. Autistic individuals are more prone to video game addiction (Grandin & Moore, 2016). Unfortunately, I have observed several autistic individuals with advanced university degrees fail in the workplace. To help prevent this, they should be counseled to gain work experience *before* they graduate with the advanced degree. This provides a slow transition from the world of school and study to the world of employment. A slow transition from school to work helped me to be successful in a career. Sudden changes are very difficult. Parents can help by both limiting video games and encouraging employment opportunities.

Learning to drive was essential for my employment success. Lack of transportation is a major barrier to employment (Coleman & Adams, 2018). Learning to drive will take longer for teens with autism than without autism. I drove 36 miles a week to and from my aunt's mail box on ranch dirt roads. This enabled me to fully learn to operate the car before learning to cope with traffic. I recommend starting learning to drive in a totally safe place, such as a large empty parking lot or a dry field. After the teenager has learned how to operate the car he/she can graduate to a deserted office park on the weekend or back roads. Driver's education often throws the kids into traffic too quickly. It may be best to do lots of safe practice before a formal driver education class.

Tips for Employers Who Have an Employee with Autism

Employers are becoming more aware of accommodating autistic individuals in the workplace. Some tips to enhance this accommodation include the following:

Avoid Long Verbal Instructions. Employers should avoid long verbal instructions on how to do a task that has a sequence of steps. A better approach is to demonstrate the task and then provide a "pilot's checklist." I am absolutely terrible at remembering a sequence of steps for a task such as cleaning and reassembling a piece of equipment. The checklist should have one to three keywords for each step to jog the person's memory. Checklists also help allistic people at work (Gawande, 2011).

Help Autistic Individuals Understand Social Mistakes. Correct individuals in private when they make a social mistake. Tell them what they should do instead of just reprimanding them. For example, you may tell the individual with autism to watch how another specific employee interacts with customers and learn from him.

Be Specific In Your Instructions to the Employee. Tasks need clear, well-defined goals and endpoints. Telling an autistic employee to develop new software is too vague. Be specific about what the code is supposed to do, and when it has to be completed.

Interview Potential Employees by Asking the Individual to Show You Their Accomplishments. Individuals with autism need to learn how to sell their work during an interview. I sold livestock design to major companies by showing them drawings, photos of completed projects, and articles I had written. You might need to modify the questions you ask in an interview, and instead ask your potential employee to show you what they have done, or demonstrate competence for a hands-on task at work.

Provide Step-by-Step Training and Avoid Multitasking. Try to avoid multitasking. Many individuals on the spectrum become overwhelmed in noisy chaotic environments such as busy fast-food restaurants. Many individuals have been successful at fast-food restaurants by starting the job on an easier, slower shift. As they become skilled, they may be able to work into the busier shifts and handle competing demands. Some individuals will require more time to train, but they can be very successful after they are trained.

Have Zero Tolerance for Bullying. Individuals with autism can appear quirky or different, and yet can be loyal, model employees. Employers need to provide a safe environment in order for the autistic individual to thrive; bullying should not be tolerated, and differences in approaches should be encouraged.

Be Aware of Potential Sensory Issues. Accommodating sensory issues can aid the individual with autism to thrive. Some individuals will require a quiet place to do work, other may benefit from being allowed to wear noise-reducing earplugs, still others may benefit from changes to non-fluorescent lighting.

Summary

In this chapter I have emphasized the importance of learning working skills before graduating from high school, and have discussed how for me, seamstress work, cleaning horse stalls, and working on my aunt's ranch were all pivotal experiences that helped me become a successfully employed adult with autism. Thinking differences for those with autism were discussed; knowledge of these thinking differences can help guide careers. The roles of college internships, vocational training, and parents all can be pivotal in successful transition into the world of employment. It is essential for both work and life skills to be learned *before* the individual with autism leaves the educational environment. Finally, I provided tips for employers to accommodate and retain employees with autism.

Recommended Resources for Professionals

- Grandin, T. (2015). *The way I see it.* Arlington, TX: Future Horizons.
- Grandin, T. (1996). *Thinking in pictures.* New York, NY: Vintage (Random House).
- Grandin, T., & Panek, R. (2013). *The autistic brain.* New York, NY: Houghton Mifflin Harcourt.

Recommended Resources for Parents

- Grandin, T., & Moore, D. (2016). *The loving push.* Arlington, TX: Future Horizons.

About the Author

Temple Grandin is Professor of Animal Science at Colorado State University. During a long 45-year career, she has designed livestock facilities for many major livestock and meat companies. She was non-verbal until age four. She had an HBO film made about her life. Some of her awards include: Women's Hall of Fame, American Academy of Arts and Sciences, and World Organization for Animal Health. You can learn more about Dr. Grandin at https://www.templegrandin.com/.

References

Brooke, V., Brooke, A. M., Schall, C., Wehman, P., Mcdonough, J., Thompson, K., & Smith, J. (2018). Employees with autism spectrum disorder achieving long-term employment success: A retrospective review of employment retention and intervention. *Research and Practice for Persons with Severe Disabilities, 43*(3), 181–193. doi:10.1177/1540796918783202

Checiak, A. (2018, June 26). The skilled trades shortage is real. The Stream. Retrieved from https://stream.org/skilled-trades-work-shortage-real/

Coleman, D. M., & Adams, J. B. (2018). Survey of vocational experiences of adults with autism spectrum disorders, and recommendations on improving their employment. *Journal of Vocational Rehabilitation, 49*(1), 67–78. doi:10.3233/jvr-180955

Cutler, E. (2004) *A thorn in my pocket.* Arlington, TX: Future Horizons.

Gawande, A. (2011) *Checklist manifesto: How to get things right.* Surrey, UK: Picador Press.

Grandin, T. (1995). *Thinking in pictures.* New York, MY: Vintage Press (Random House).

Grandin, T. (2005). Maintenance of good animal welfare standards in beef slaughter plants by use of auditing programs. *Journal of the American Veterinary Medical Association, 226*(3), 370–373. doi:10.2460/javma.2005.226.370

Grandin, T. (2012). *Different not less.* Arlington, TX: Future Horizons.

Grandin, T. (2015). *Improving animal welfare: A practical approach.* Wallingford, Oxfordshire: CAB international.

Grandin, T., & Moore, D. (2016) *The loving push.* Arlington, TX: Future Horizons.

Grandin, T., & Panek, R. (2014) *The autistic brain.* New York, NY: Houghton Mifflin Harcourt.

Grandin, T., & Scariano, M. (1986) *Emergence labeled autistic.* Novato, CA: Academic Therapy Publications.

Gross, A., & Marcus, J. (2018, April 25). High-paying trade jobs sit empty, while high school grads line up for university. National Public Radio. Retrieved from www.npr.org/sections/ed/2018/04/25/605092520/high-paying-trade-jobs-sit-empty-while-high-school-grads-line-up-for-university

Höffler, T. N., Koć-Januchta, M., & Leutner, D. (2016). More evidence for three types of cognitive style: Validating the object-spatial imagery and verbal questionnaire using eye tracking when learning with texts and pictures. *Applied Cognitive Psychology, 31*(1), 109–115. doi:10.1002/acp.3300

Kozhevnikov, M., Hegarty, M., & Mayer, R. E. (2002). Revising the visualizer-verbalizer dimension: Evidence for two types of visualizers. *Cognition and Instruction, 20*(1), 47–77. doi:10.1207/s1532690xci2001_3

Langert, B. (2019) *The battle to do good.* Bingley, UK: Emerald Publishing, Ltd.

Mazard, A., Mazoyer, N. T., Crivello, F., Mazoyer, B., & Mellet, E. (2010). A PET meta-analysis of object and spatial mental imagery. *European Journal of Cognitive Psychology, 16*(5), 673–695. doi: 10.1080/09541440340000484

Shattuck, P. T., Narendorf, S. C., Cooper, B., Sterzing, P. R., Wagner, M., & Taylor, J. L. (2012, June). Postsecondary education and employment among youth with an autism spectrum disorder. *Pediatrics, 129*(6), 1042–1049. doi: 10.1542/peds.2011-2864

Stergiakouli, E., Smith, G. D., Martin, J., Skuse, D. H., Viechtbauer, W., Ring, S. M. … St. Pourcain, B. (2017). Shared genetic influences between dimensional Autistic and ADHD symptoms during child and adolescent development. *Molecular Autism, 8*, 18. doi:10.1186/s13229-017-0131-2

Thompson, C. (2019) *Coders: The making of the new tribe and the remaking of the world.* New York, NY: Penguin Press.

United States Department of Labor, Bureau of Labor Statistics (2019). *Occupational handbook.* Washington, DC: Author.

Wehman, P. H., Schall, C. W., McDonough, J., Koegel, J., Brooke, V., Molinelli, A., … Thiss, W. (2014) Competitive employment for youth with autism spectrum disorders: Early results from a randomized clinical trial. *Journal of Autism and Developmental Disorders, 44*(3), 487–500. doi: 10.1007/s10803-013-1892-x

20 Working Together

Empowering the Autistic Voice

Barb Cook

Autistic adults have very low employment rates, and more specifically, the lowest rate of employment amidst all disability groups (Roux, Rast, Rava, Anderson, & Shattuck, 2015). Additionally, despite their ambition to work and, more so, the capacity to work, employed autistic adults are often in low-paying positions with limited hours. These positions are often well below the capacity and educational level of the individual and do not provide meaningful or fulfilling employment. Low and underemployment affirms the necessity to recognize what the barriers are, and that we must collaborate and take decisive action in investigating solutions, strategies, and tools that can effectively support these individuals in gaining meaningful and sustaining employment.

To understand the barriers and difficulties experienced by autistic adults in attaining and maintaining employment, you must gain first-hand experience from these individuals to truly appreciate the obstacles that lay before them. As a person on the autism spectrum myself, I have unique insight into just how difficult gaining employment is, and when employed, how complex workplace dynamics are. From my decades of failures and successes, I have become somewhat of an "expert" in navigating the employment scene in a multitude of sectors. It is with this life experience that I have found myself in the position of being an employment mentor to autistic adults, a consultant to employers, and an independent workplace assessor.

Helping Clients Take Control of Their Anxiety

In my experience mentoring one on one with autistic adults, I have encountered a common theme of anxiety when applying for jobs, understanding how to fill out applications forms, knowing how to "perform" in the interview, and, if successful in landing a job, the anxiety of what is expected of them in the workplace. Those who are employed express fear of asking for support at work, or not knowing how to ask for needed support.

Effective communication also poses a significant barrier for autistic individuals, who have great difficulty in conveying not just their needs and concerns, but also their worth and value. This barrier of effective communication adds to their anxiety and begs the question, does anxiety increase communication problems, or do the communication barriers increase the levels of anxiety? It is postulated that providing supports and interventions prior to the autistic adult embarking on employment seeking will help improve pathways in communicating their worth through employment application and the interview process. Plus, dependent on the intervention, this type of help can reduce anxiety levels. It is assumed that anxiety reduction will have a wider effect on the autistic individual's wellbeing and socio-communicative experiences.

The significant prevalence of anxiety among autistic individuals, in conjunction with substandard employment prospects, requires serious consideration as to how best to support and manage the individual. In my experience and research, one of the more effective tools an autistic person can implement is that of mindfulness-based therapies (MBTs) for reducing anxiety (Spek, van Ham, & Nyklíček, 2013). Once taught, MBTs can be self-implemented as either a daily practice in an individual's home life, or implemented when faced with an upcoming stressful situation (e.g., job interview) as a preventative method. MBT can be a great tool that autistic people can use in a variety of situations, with immediate positive effects.

Costs of MBTs are relatively low and do not require long-term training. There are inexpensive MBT apps, such as *Smiling Mind* (2019), that an individual can add to their phone or iPad and listen to when they require support in reducing their anxiety. The individual can listen privately with headphones when traveling on public transport without drawing attention to themselves, or during a lunch break to help them reduce their anxiety. This tool can effectively be implemented anywhere, at any time, and discreetly. Ideally, prior to using the app, training by a certified therapist will give the autistic person extra tools in learning when to see the signs within themselves that suggest their anxiety levels are rising and that they should implement MBT for maximum support (see *Recommended Resources for Professionals and Families* below for more information on implementing MBT).

Based on the speed of effectiveness, cost, and ease of implementation, MBT has a considerable amount to offer in terms of personal support to autistic people with anxiety. Implementing mindfulness practices within their daily routine would ideally provide some relief from elevated anxiety levels, plus mindfulness can prepare the individual for anxiety-inducing situations they may encounter. Teaching the individual how to implement these practices themselves and educating them on how to recognize when their anxiety levels are increasing gives the individual a sense of ownership of how to best help themselves. Empowering the individual in knowing the signs, the feelings, and the emotions connected with rising anxiety will effectively give them the power to stop or reduce it within a short time. When the autistic person has control of a situation, they are more likely to feel safe and calm. An example of how to implement MBT can be seen in Table 20.1.

Table 20.1 Implementation of Mindfulness-Based Therapy (MBT) for Anxiety Reduction Prior to Applying for a Job

Setting of Intervention	Applying for a job.
When to initiate the intervention	MBT and self-centering using *Smiling Mind* app one hour before applying for a job. Duration 30 minutes.
Preparation steps required	Finding a quiet place to implement mindfulness strategy one hour prior to filling out job application. This can be in a personal space at home. If traveling by public transport to fill out job application, put on headphones and listen to *Smiling Mind* app on journey. Set alarm on phone to remind individual of upcoming stop for them to get off the public transport when listening to mindfulness app. If being transported by family or friend, listen to *Smiling Mind* app in car, and advise the person taking them to the place where they are applying for the job that they need to listen to this app without interruption.
Materials required	Qualified mindfulness therapist to teach autistic person how and when to implement mindfulness strategy. Another material might be literature such as *Mindful Living with Asperger's Syndrome*, by Chris Mitchell (2013), for reference on how to apply mindfulness techniques.
Procedure	The individual needs to prepare/allow for 60 minutes prior to filling out job application to use the first 30 minutes of this time for MBT. Plan quiet space and/or setting if traveling for up to 30 minutes of listening to *Smiling Mind* app on phone or iPad. 15–30 minutes prior to job application and upon completion of MBT, autistic person should be ready and calmly waiting to fill out job application.
Desired outcome	Autistic person will be feeling less anxious about filling out job application and have clearer thought processes to complete application. It is anticipated that, feeling less anxious about filling out the job application, the autistic person will feel more confident about portraying their worth and skills through the job application. The individual will also be more likely to complete the application form and with reduced stress.

Support in the Workplace – Embracing True Inclusion

As a research assistant at the University of Wollongong in Australia, I have worked on projects that encompass the collaborative approach of a community of practice, working together with a variety of stakeholders for a common goal in brainstorming ideas, solutions, strategies, and tools to help autistic adults find their voice through self-advocacy and self-determination. It is through taking these collaborative approaches that as a community we can work together in re-evaluating a variety of environments to become more inclusive of diversity.

In the workplace environment, employers can take the lead by embracing the qualities that autistic people often have to offer, such as attention to detail, following the rules, providing out-of-the-box thinking and loyalty, and being hardworking and dedicated individuals. When these individuals are set up for success, valued for their difference in thought, and truly included within the workplace setting, it can not only bring forth work satisfaction to the employee, but also strengthens the outlook, opportunities, and vision of the business in which they are employed.

So how do we set up the workplace to be inclusive of all employee needs? And more so, how do we do this cost-effectively and efficiently? Firstly, the employer must become autism- aware and gain an understanding of what the autism spectrum means. This can be done via workplace training with a skilled trainer, preferably one who is also on the autism spectrum themselves, to give the employer and current staff knowledge of autism and how to best support a colleague or employee.

Often, we see autistic people have sensory problems. Inviting an autism-specific workplace assessor can create a pathway for bringing the employee and employer together in mutually learning how to implement accommodations in the workplace. Further, the team can learn how the autistic individual can implement strategies to support themselves at work. When an employer is open and supportive of encompassing inclusivity for the employee, this lays the foundations to opening dialogues and ways of working together to creating successful outcomes for all stakeholders.

Case Study: Accommodating Sensory Issues

As an example of how workplaces can accommodate autistic individuals, we will look at some simple solutions for a light-sensitive individual.

Sharon was recently diagnosed autistic and is sensory-avoidant. She has difficulty staying focused at work and makes recurring minor mistakes. Sharon often suffers from headaches and feels overwhelmed and exhausted at the end of the working day. She has experienced meltdowns at home, especially if her train is late or extremely crowded heading home, tipping her "over the edge." She is often anxious and depressed due to her constant mistakes at work. She is extremely anxious she will lose her current position in administration, but is afraid to ask for support and feedback on her progress due to previous job losses.

Sharon's workplace is an office space that is brightly lit with large double-tubed fluorescent lighting and three medium-sized windows on the far-left side of the room. Sharon's cubicle is positioned furthest away from the windows in a line of three. Her desk has a white gloss surface and her computer screen is 21 inches in size.

Sharon is being visually overwhelmed with bright lighting, computer screens, and light-colored reflective surfaces. This is leading to her difficulty in retaining information from assigned tasks as the day progresses. It is also contributing to her regular headaches, feeling of being overwhelmed, and exhaustion at the end of the working day. A combination of these factors contributes to making Sharon hyper-vigilant and extremely anxious, and her low threshold for bright lighting is compounded through the day.

Individuals on the autism spectrum experience visual irregularities in sensory integration and can vary enormously in how they perceive and process visual experiences (Bakroon & Lakshminarayanan, 2016). Overhead fluorescent lighting is cited as problematic for autistic people who can detect flicker rates (Robertson & Simmons, 2013), causing mental fatigue.

Sharon's workplace can turn off sections of lighting and it is recommended that the employer discuss with the other employees within the room what their preference is as regards level of lighting. If one row prefers less lighting, the lights above this row could be turned off.

Another consideration is that Sharon's workstation could be moved to the end of the row, nearest the windows, to allow for more natural lighting and to benefit from the afternoon sunlight after a morning of artificial lights. This could reduce some of her mental fatigue and onset of headaches. The option for each individual workstation to have access to a lamp with lower wattage and warm color should be available to provide more lighting, for example, when reading paper documents.

Each workstation allows for individual changes to décor and it is suggested that Sharon could use a dark-colored cloth or covering for her white glossy desk. This will reduce the glare from the surface of the desk.

Computer monitors should be adjusted to a lower brightness. Current software programs used have a significant amount of white-space working area and can be adjusted by changing the theme colors to a more suitable color. For example, having dark-blue text on a light-blue background aids individuals to read (Evett & Brown, 2005).

The advised accommodations and rearranging of where Sharon's workstation is placed in respect to ceiling and natural lighting will not incur equipment costs. Redesigning the layout will benefit Sharon and her colleagues as they will be working in light conditions that they prefer. A lamp for each workstation is an inexpensive implementation.

Helping Sharon to understand how to adjust her monitor screen light intensity and to personally tailor software program background colors and themes will also help reduce light sensory input. Combined with a new workstation position and dark covering to Sharon's desk, this will reduce her visual issues significantly.

As we can see, by mutually working together, both employee and employer will benefit from implementing small changes that are of very little cost and disruption to the workplace. When an employee feels they are being valued and supported within the workplace, it encourages confidence and promotes a sense of satisfaction for them. Empowering autistic individuals to self-advocate, to determine and voice their needs and supports, plus supporting and educating them in the acquisition of skills of how to best support themselves provides a solid framework of knowledge, strategies, and tools that will equip them in attaining a future that they aspire to and one that they most certainly deserve.

Recommended Resources for Professionals and Families

- Barb Cook: www.barbcook.com.au
- Cook B., & Garnett, M. (Eds.). (2018). *Spectrum women: Walking to the beat of autism.* London, UK: Jessica Kingsley Publishers.
- Mitchell, C. (2013). *Mindful living with Asperger's syndrome.* London, UK: Jessica Kingsley Publishers.
- Spectrum Women: www.spectrumwomen.com

About the Author

Formally identified as on the autism spectrum, along with having attention deficit hyperactivity disorder and phonological dyslexia at age 40, Barb Cook is editor and co-author of the internationally acclaimed book *Spectrum Women: Walking to the Beat of Autism*, and editor in chief of *Spectrum Women Magazine*. Ms. Cook is an internationally recognized speaker and writer and was awarded a Special Commendation in the 2017 Autism Queensland Creative Futures Awards by the Queensland Governor. Ms. Cook completed a Master of Autism (Education and Employment) and is a Research Assistant at the University of Wollongong, Australia. She is a registered Developmental Educator and provides consulting, workplace assessments, and mentoring services for the neurodiverse community. Ms. Cook recently was the keynote speaker and a panel participant for a special event, "A Woman's Voice: Understanding Autistic Needs" for the National Institute of Mental Health (NIHM) in Washington, DC, USA. You can connect with Ms. Cook at www.barbcook.com.au.

References

Bakroon, A., & Lakshminarayanan, V. (2016). Visual function in autism spectrum disorders: A critical review. *Clinical and Experimental Optometry, 99*(4), 297–308. doi:10.1111/cxo.12383.

Evett, L., & Brown, D. (2005). Text formats and web design for visually impaired and dyslexic readers—Clear text for all. *Interacting with Computers, 17*(4), 453–472. doi:10.1016/j.intcom.2005.04.001.

Mitchell, C. (2013). *Mindful living with Asperger's syndrome.* London, UK: Jessica Kingsley Publishers.

Robertson, A. E., & Simmons, D. R. (2013). The relationship between sensory sensitivity and autistic traits in the general population. *Journal of Autism and Developmental Disorders, 43*(4), 775–784. doi:10.1007/s10803-012-1608-7.

Roux, A., Rast, J., Rava, J., Anderson, K., & Shattuck, P. (2015). *National autism indicators report: Transition into young adulthood.* Philadelphia, PA: Life Course Outcomes Research Program, A.J. Drexel Autism Institute, Drexel University.

Smiling Mind. (2019). Retrieved from www.smilingmind.com.au

Spek, A., van Ham, N., & Nyklíček, I. (2013). Mindfulness-based therapy in adults with an autism spectrum disorder: A randomized controlled trial. *Research in Developmental Disabilities, 34*(1), 246–253. doi:10.1016/j.ridd.2012.08.009.

21 Autism Spectrum Job Readiness Challenges and Possibilities

Sara R. Colorosa

Adults with autism experience high unemployment and underemployment, change jobs more often, make less money than their counterparts, and have issues adjusting to the workplace (Hendricks & Wehman, 2009, p. 81). Adults on the spectrum frequently encounter painful rejection in job interviews, and if hired, they tend to have troubled relationships with their employers (Wolf, Thierfeld Brown, & Kukiela Bork, 2009). Temple Grandin notes that people with autism can get jobs, but often have difficulty keeping them. She observed that the reasons those on the spectrum get fired include having a new or unsympathetic boss, and/or that the employee was promoted to a job where the social skills and social interaction did not match the individual's abilities (Grandin, 2008, p. 238). Individuals with autism need to learn the skills to understand workplace dynamics, social/office etiquette, and office politics (Grandin, 2008). Therapists can help with these challenges as they help clients with autism navigate the world of work.

In my practice, clients seek advice as they are starting career exploration. They are either looking for part-time summer work or have just finished college and are looking for their first job. As a human resources professional there are two challenges they typically come to talk with me about: identifying what they want to do for work, and how to present themselves on paper through application materials and interviews.

Fearing the Unknown

When starting on this journey to find employment, many clients get anxious about all the unknowns which can be daunting; worrying about how much money they will make, who they will work with, whether they will get along with their supervisor and co-workers, and whether they will have to talk with a lot of people. I encourage my clients not to worry about the details that are way down the road yet, and instead focus on what we can control in the moment. It is important to match communication needs with a job which will increase retention in a position and reduce anxiety (Grandin & Duffy, 2004; Hendricks & Wehman, 2009; Hurlbutt & Chalmers, 2004), and encourage those with autism to talk about their needs and disability with potential employers when appropriate.

Getting Comfortable with Uncomfortable Feelings

Throughout early childhood and young adulthood, many individuals with autism have had support systems in place and are now being encouraged to develop independent thinking skills and behaviors so they can transition to living on their own and get jobs. Many of the jobs that clients will encounter will not have similar support systems that clients were accustomed to while in school, and clients will be required to solve problems, communicate in teams, and be timely and organized, just to name a few. This transition to independence can cause significant discomfort. I ask my clients probing questions about what their emotions are about employment, and how they would describe them. The emotion I hear most often is fear, with thoughts such as, 'what if I do something wrong?,' 'I'm worried I will let someone down,' 'I don't know what to say,' and so on. Clients feel unprepared and worried about the unknown. These fears and anxieties can be attributed to the changes that come from being supported throughout school and then transitioning to somewhat unsupported environments when living independently and in the workplace. Clients find themselves having to make independent judgements about day-to-day processes they are about to transition into. Together we work through those feelings, getting to know what those feelings are, and how through these changes, clients will learn from their feelings and experiences. For most clients, this process is uncomfortable, yet it is part of the transition and growth process. I help to normalize this discomfort and assist clients in becoming comfortable with this discomfort as part of the process of independent living.

Skill Building

There are numerous skills to obtaining employment that need to be taught. I ask clients to try things and see what works, as many of these skills are new to them. I frame the tasks as part of a journey, and that this is not a quick sprint. Instead it is a process of exploration, of trial and error. During each session, we discuss specific skills, I provide time to think and process what they are learning, see what we need to adjust or strengthen, and give homework assignments. First, we break the large goal, getting a job, into small, obtainable tasks and specific skills as follows.

Focusing on a Path

When exploring career options, many clients struggle with concrete thinking interfering with deciding on a career path. Many clients enjoy doing one or two things, as they tend to hyper-focus on topics that bring them joy and are naturally easy, or they have been doing for a long period. In my practice, I ask clients to make a list of things they enjoy doing, such as hobbies, and determine if those hobbies could be careers. To help distinguish between hobby and career, we discuss if they could do these activities for up to 40 hours per week and earn a wage doing them. These discussions tend to bring some perspective to clients as their hobbies may not align with career options, so they have to consider alternatives. Many times clients have to explore additional education and build on their skillsets in order to find jobs; this realization can be a challenge.

Recommending that clients volunteer or intern for a short period will allow young professionals to gain and improve skills, align hobbies with career options, and enhance communication and professional skills. There is a lot of value in starting early, trying different strategies, or exploring interests. I tell my clients this process is like trying on hats − try things on, find what fits; if it does not fit, find something else. It is easier to change volunteer positions and internships than to change jobs or a career.

Developing a List of Strengths and Skills

During each session, clients are asked to develop a list of their strengths and tangible skills. Often clients struggle with envisioning their goals, so I ask about their favorite classes and why they enjoyed those courses. This helps to develop their list of strengths and skills. Having a visual list of their strengths and skills helps clients get more comfortable in knowing who they are as a future professional. In addition to discovering strengths and skills, we talk about what they did not enjoy in school or extra-curricular activities to help the client understand their limitations as well. These lists help with internet job database key word searches when clients are ready to look for jobs that align with their career interests.

Verbalizing Their Strengths and Skills

Once clients have a list of strengths and skills, we practice talking about their specific strengths and skills. Some clients find this difficult, so I create a safe space, letting them know that no one is judging them, and we are only practicing before they meet potential employers. Clients are encouraged to work on their 'elevator speech.' The elevator speech is an opportunity for clients to briefly tell someone they meet about themselves in about 30 seconds. Typically, this includes four points about them: their name, where they went to school, what they want to do for work, and why they are interested in a certain field. Some clients have a hard time remembering these details, especially when encountering a new person, or when they are in a new situation. A simple trick I encourage my clients to use to remember the four talking points is to press their fingers into their thigh as they talk through their 'elevator speech.' For each talking point, subtly press one finger into their thigh as they talk about each specific item. To make this exercise feel as real as possible with clients, we discuss, visualize, and practice the situation they will be in when meeting someone for the first time to share their story.

Practicing New Skills

Local job fairs are a good mechanism for getting clients to take their new skills for a test drive. Prior to attending these events, clients and I talk about what organizations will be at the event, so we can research about the company and the types of positions available. To lessen the fears of walking into a career fair, clients and I attempt to predict what to anticipate and how to communicate with the recruiters and hiring managers. During many of our sessions leading up to the career fair, I ask the client what they expect to see, hear, smell, and feel when we walk into the room with other attendees and the recruiters. Visualizing the event helps reduce some of the uncomfortable feelings and we can discuss strategies for how to handle situations that the client may encounter during these types of events.

As we talk about the event, we role-play during our sessions; I act as the recruiter standing behind a table while the client approaches me ready to talk about job opportunities. We might work on shaking hands, saying hello, and avoiding awkward silences. I often offer to attend a job fair with the client to help coach them and facilitate conversations between them and the recruiters.

Clients are encouraged to practice their 'elevator speech,' including the four talking points. Part of the planning process is also to develop open-ended questions to encourage dialogue between a recruiter and the client; an example of a question a client could ask of a recruiter would be, 'What are you looking for from future employees?' Walking through these specific expectations and giving clients tangible tools to use decreases anxiety and they can feel more confident in approaching employers.

As clients build confidence in talking about their skills and practice talking about themselves, they learn critical advocacy skills that transfer to the workplace. Knowing who they are, what they value, their learning and communication styles, how to say no, and asking for an alternative, will in turn make them successful in the workplace. These skills need to be developed, as working in a team in school may look different than it will in the workplace. The demands, expectations, and assistance of supervisors may be different from what teachers provided.

Professional Dress and Readiness

Making a first impression is important as this can set the tone for future interactions; clients need to look the part of an employee. Clients and I discuss what their physical appearance should be when interviewing and attending career fairs. I ask clients what they think professional dress should be for a situation professionally and ask them what this means to them. When they describe this, we talk about collared shirts, ironed dress pants, and appropriate footwear (i.e., not their everyday tennis shoes).

Part of being ready for the workplace is having the right materials. Clients are encouraged to bring copies of their updated resumes in a pad folio to hold the resumes, a note pad, pen, and place to hold business cards from the recruiters. Some clients are worried about costs for new clothing; I encourage the use of local consignment shops where professional clothing can be purchased at reduced cost. I also keep extra pad folios and handbags that clients can borrow when attending interviews and career fairs. Looking the part helps clients feel better and once again lessens the emotions of these stressful situations.

Making Introductions and Using Communication Skills

Some clients have shared their concerns about how to address their autism with the recruiters or potential employers. During our conversations, clients tell me that they are not sure how they feel about sharing their diagnosis with others, especially people they have just met. In some cases, clients share that they feel like they need to tell people why they 'act weird,' how they may not make eye contact or may take longer to respond to questions. We discuss that everyone has strengths and it is up to them to decide how they share their stories with others. Each client is different in how they determine what, when, and how much information they share about their autism.

To help with introductions to new people, I have suggested to clients that we make business cards. On the front of of the card is the client's information, name, phone number, email address, and statement that says, 'To learn more about me, please see other side of card' (Figure 21.1). On the back of the card, we list traits about the client to help with social skills and first impressions. These items come from the client; this is one of the homework assignments: I ask clients what they would want to share with someone so they know how to communicate and interact with them.

Clients who use these cards have found the first interactions between everyone they meet to be very pleasant and communication flowed much easier.

Summary

Therapists can assist clients in visualizing what to anticipate in these new settings, making the unfamiliar a little more familiar. Therapists can encourage their clients to try some of the skill development listed above and see what works for the client. Exploring career options can

Front	Back
Client Name Phone: 555.555.2222 Email: dclient@yahoo.com To learn more about me, please see other side of card	• I may take longer to respond to questions so please do not interrupt me; • I may not make eye contact, but I am still paying attention; • I may make notes on paper instead of verbally communicating with you.

Figure 21.1 Sample of a Client Card to be Used to Help With Introductions.

be challenging and overwhelming for many, yet breaking the process into more manageable pieces may lessen the emotional aspects that can create barriers to success. Through this process, the practitioner can assist the client with building their confidence and self-advocacy skills, improve how they communicate about their skills and strengths, explore alternative career paths, and determine if additional schooling is needed. To lessen the employment challenges for adults with autism, practitioners can implement interventions that enhance their client's communication, social skills, self-advocacy, and self-awareness.

Recommended Resources for Professionals

- Colorosa, S. R. (2016). *Case study of performance management techniques: Voices of managers and employees* (Order No. 10138067). Available from Dissertations & Theses @ Colorado State University; ProQuest Dissertations & Theses Global. (1803939361). Retrieved from https://search-proquest-com.ezproxy2.library.colostate.edu/docview/1803939361?accountid=10223
- Wolf, L., Thierfeld Brown, J., & Kukiela Bork, G. (2009). *Students with Asperger syndrome: A guide for college personnel.* Shawnee Mission, KS: Autism Asperger Publishing Co.

Recommended Resources for Families

- Grey, C. (2010). *The new social story book.* Arlington, TX: Future Horizons.
- Tammet, D. (2006). *Born on a blue day: Inside the extraordinary mind of an Autistic Savant.* New York, NY: Free Press.

About the Author

Sara R. Colorosa, Ph.D., is the owner of The Engagement Catalyst, LLC. She has completed a research study in an organization where employees and managers shared their experiences about aligning with people's diverse skills, abilities, and interests with career opportunities. Dr. Colorosa understands the gap between theory and practice, and focuses on adult learning styles, diversity in the workplace, and leaders' roles in organizational success. She is passionate about helping individuals develop their executive functioning, organizational skills, and studying habits to achieve career goals. To learn more about Dr. Colorosa and her practice, visit www.theengagementcatalyst.com.

References

Grandin, T. (2008). *The way I see it: A personal look at autism and asperger's.* Arlington, TX: Future Horizons.

Grandin, T., & Duffy, K. (2004). *Developing talents: Careers for individuals with Asperger syndrome and high-functioning autism.* Shawnee Mission, KS: Autism Asperger Publishing Co.

Hendricks, D. R., & Wehman, P. (2009). Transition from school to adulthood for youth with autism spectrum disorders: Review and recommendations. *Focus on Autism and Other Developmental Disabilities, 24*(2), 77–88. doi:10.1177/1088357608329827

Hurlbutt, K., & Chalmers, L. (2004). Employment and adults with asperger's syndrome. *Focus on Autism and Other Developmental Disabilities, 19*(4), 215–222. doi:10.11177/10883576040190040301

Wolf, L., Thierfeld Brown, J., & Kukiela Bork, G. (2009). *Students with Asperger syndrome: A guide for college personnel.* Shawnee Mission, KS: Autism Asperger Publishing Co.

Part VIII

Addressing Nutrition and Eating Concerns

Read any forum for parents living with a family member with autism and you will quickly note concerns related to eating: parents worry about their children eating well, eating nutritious foods, and eating diverse foods. Parents report that children and adolescents with autism often eat very restricted items (chicken nuggets – the right brand, perfectly prepared) and wonder how to find the magic solution to get their child to eat differently. Adults with autism acknowledge that there is a problem, but sometimes feel as though they have "tried everything" without relief.

In this part we hear from a variety of professionals about how to address eating concerns. It is clear that eating problems are a top concern, and professionals are trying to bring relief to these families. Learn more about what you could be asking your clients about eating habits (including sensory concerns such as textures, smells, attempts they have made to solve the problem, and who is motivated to solve the problem). This part also helps us understand that it may take several team members to help solve the eating issues: developmental pediatrician, occupational therapist, gastroenterologist, allergist, nutritionist, dietician, swallow specialist. No wonder parents are confused! You can help them solve the eating puzzle by making the proper referrals.

22 Why So Picky?

Food Selectivity and How It Impacts Eating

Nicole A. Withrow

It is well established that feeding disorders occur in approximately 25–35% of typically developing children and as many as 90% of children with developmental disorders (Bandini et al., 2017). It is generally agreed upon in the literature that the most predominant feeding problem for children on the autism spectrum is that of food selectivity (Bandini et al., 2010). Individuals with autism are reported to have problematic eating behaviors such as food refusal, unwillingness to consume a large variety of foods, repetitive and ritualized eating behaviors, motor impairments, and sensory processing abnormalities (Schreck, Williams, & Smith, 2004). Four domains have been identified in the literature and clinical practice that are associated with food selectivity surrounding autism: sensory processing difficulties, aberrant mealtime behaviors, motor skills issues, and dietary intake. Although picky eating is not uncommon in children, it appears that individuals with autism may be more food-selective and, without treatment, this selectivity can extend into adulthood. Due to the complexities of problematic eating behaviors, individuals with autism should have early and regular screening for nutritional risk.

Sensory Processing Difficulties and How They Can Impact Eating

Researchers began investigating sensory processing theories in individuals with autism during the 1970s in relation to eating and nutritional status (Baranek, Foster, & Berkson, 1997). Sensory processing impairments are often discussed in conjunction with food selectivity and food refusal with autistic clients. Commonly avoided textures include: frozen, cold, hot, wet, slimy, colorful, strong smells, and hard-to-chew foods (meat) (Withrow & Alvidrez, 2019). These sensitivities can interfere with the child's ability to consume an adequate amount and variety of foods necessary for healthy growth and development. If a child is exhibiting any of these symptoms, they should be referred to a registered dietitian to be screened for nutritional risk.

How Oral Motor Impairments Can Impact Eating for Those with Autism

Individuals with motor impairments may not be able to properly chew foods, by potentially causing swallowing issues. Also, individuals who suffer from motor impairments may not be able it to use utensils, may struggle to grab food with fingers and bring it to their mouths, have difficulty in using a cup and a straw, pocket food without swallowing, and/or keep liquids in their mouth (Field, Garland, & Williams, 2003; Mayes & Zickgraf, 2019). Screening of oral motor and fine motor skills at any age can provide helpful information when treating individuals with autism suffering from food selectivity. Individuals with autism who experience motor delays should be referred to a registered dietitian to screen for nutritional risk.

Aberrant/Atypical Mealtime Behaviors and How They Can Impact Eating for Those with Autism

Higher rates of atypical mealtime behaviors for individuals with autism are associated with increased food selectivity for all ages. It has been reported that individuals with autism experience more grazing, leave their seats during meals/snacks, develop a strong preference for specific brands, refuse new foods, exhibit self-injurious behaviors when offered non-preferred foods, and consume large quantities of sugary beverages (Mayes & Zickgraf, 2019; Withrow & Alvidrez, 2019). Parents often report that meals/snacks are stressful and look for suggestions to increase the variety of foods while decreasing aberrant mealtime behaviors. Schreck and colleagues reported that children with autism who presented with more problematic eating behaviors consumed fewer servings of fruit, vegetables, dairy, non-dairy proteins, and starches (Schreck et al., 2004). These problematic eating behaviors by individuals with autism may have implications for nutritional risk at every age and should be screened by a registered dietitian (Herndon, DiGuiseppi, Johnson, Leiferman, & Reynolds, 2009).

Nutritional Connection in Autism

Dietary and nutrient intake in individuals with autism appear to differ from neurotypical individuals (Geraghty, Bates-Wall, Ratliff-Schaub, & Lane, 2010). It has been reported that individuals with autism consume a limited variety of foods and that up to 93% of children with autism do not meet the recommended intakes for macronutrients and some micronutrients (Eaves & Ho, 2008). Individuals with autism suffering from food selectivity can have long-term consequences to their nutritional status if they are not identified and treated early in life (Schreck et al., 2004). In clinical practice, parents/caregivers often report that individuals with autism consume fewer servings of fruits, vegetables, dairy, meat, and whole grains, and within each food group consume a narrower variety of foods. For example, they may eat applesauce, but that is the "only" fruit they will consume, so a narrower variety is also an issue in nutritional risk assessment. Individuals with autism may also be at a higher risk for being overweight and obese due to the limited variety and decreased consumption of fruits, vegetables, lean meats, and low-fat dairy products and whole grains (Bowers, 2002). Often, individuals grow into their food selectivity. It is more challenging to treat the older the individual. Early intervention and screening of nutritional risk by a registered dietitian are paramount.

Dietary Interventions

Today, the use of complementary and alternative medicine (CAM) has steadily increased in western society, especially in the pediatric population. CAM interventions have been reported to occur at a rate as high as 85% in families who are treating autism (Wong, 2009). Despite a lack of evidence-based trials, these treatments continue to gain in popularity among families and providers. Within the last decade, dietary interventions have become increasingly popular in treating autism. Survey results indicate that 15–38% of families have tried and are currently using a dietary intervention to help treat symptoms of autism (Green et al., 2002). Most dietary interventions used to treat symptoms of autism involve eliminating at least one or more types of food from the individual's diet such as wheat (gluten), milk (casein), soy, yeast, additives, sugar, eggs, and yeast (Mulloy, O-Reilly, Sigafoos, Lancioni, & Rispoli, 2010). The most common dietary intervention is a gluten-free and casein-free (GFCF) diet.

Families often receive information regarding diet and nutritional therapies from other parents, internet sites, unpublished sources, autism organizations, and CAM providers (Arnold, Hyman, Mooney, & Kirby, 2003). Many dietary interventions have shown little, if any, evidence supporting or refuting their efficacy and effectiveness; however, these dietary interventions continue to gain in popularity. There is a small body of evidence linking the GFCF diet to suboptimal bone development, specifically reduced cortical bone thickness (Mulloy et al., 2010). Some dietary interventions also add additional stress due to the financial burden, time commitment, and possible increase in social isolation caused by food restrictions. Individuals with autism who have specialized dietary interventions should be screened for nutritional risk, especially nutritional deficiencies.

How Therapists Can Assist

Therapists can assist clients with autism and their families by helping with screening for eating issues, setting small nutritional goals, reinforcing positive eating behavior, and making appropriate physician referrals as needed.

Screening

First, individuals should be screened using a validated eating screening inventory. The Sensory, Aberrant Mealtime behaviors, Motor Inventory for Eating (SAMIE) has been developed so providers can identify nutritional risk (Withrow & Alvidrez, 2019). This inventory will allow the professional to make immediate referrals to providers who can address the primary reason(s) the individual is struggling to eat.

Start with Small Goals

If a patient is not able to see another provider and nutritional risk is identified, the current provider should start with small goals. For example, if an individual does not eat vegetables or fruit, but likes crunchy foods that are red and orange, then encourage the individual or parents to purchase dried strawberries or dried carrots and start by offering a bite size portion to the individual with food selectivity. Repetition and consistency are key to introducing new foods since it may take an individual 25 times or more of seeing that food item before they will touch/lick/taste and eventually eat it. Keep consistent and only offer bite sizes of the targeted food.

Reinforce Positive Behavior

When an individual looks at, touches, or licks a new food, the behavior should be positively reinforced to encourage eventual consumption of the food. Focus on one change at a time. For example, if the individual eats shoestring french fries from McDonald's, then encourage the individual/parent to buy a bag of frozen shoestring french fries and serve a few with the preferred McDonald's french fries. It may take several exposures, but that is OK; consistency and patience are critical for acceptance of a new food. Also, pair language such as "same but a little different" when introducing a new food. Changing a sensory component (texture/color/shape/brand) may be a big enough change for a while, but once the individual is in the habit of seeing "same but a little different" foods, the feeding program can gradually launch and new foods can be integrated in the diet.

When Physician Referrals are Appropriate

If the individual is not consuming any fruits or vegetables, a multivitamin at night may be helpful. For more complex issues, physician referrals may be warranted. For example, if restlessness or sleepless nights occur, the individual should see their primary care physician to check iron levels. A full iron study may be recommended because for some individuals, repletion of iron assists in improving sleep cycles. If an individual is on a GFCF diet or other dietary interventions, calcium (800–1200 mg/day) and vitamin D (400 international units) supplements may be recommended. These supplements can be split up during the day and should be eaten with a source of fat since vitamin D is a fat-soluble vitamin. If bowel movements are a problem, especially constipation, have the individual see their primary care physician for a bowel movement regimen and possibly a referral to a specialist and a registered dietitian. However, water and fiber aid in healthy bowel movements. If a fiber supplement is needed it is typical to start with 5 grams/day and increase slowly to maintenance (25–35 grams/day). *Fiber One* snack foods and whole grains (fortified breakfast cereals) are sometimes the easiest way to increase fiber if the individual is extremely food-selective.

Summary

Problematic eating behaviors reported in individuals with autism appear to be longstanding and without proper screening, diagnosis, and treatment they could be life-long and can have serious health consequences. Early identification and screening of eating problems surrounding autism is crucial given that delayed treatment can have deleterious effects on an individual. For example, after the age of eight, eating problems have been associated with growth rates falling below average (Schwarz, 2003) as well as with above-average obesity rates when compared to typically developing populations (Curtin, Bandini, Perrin, Tybor, & Must, 2005).

Recommended Resources for Professionals

- Berry, R., Novak, P., Withrow, N., Schmidt, B., Rarback, S., Feucht, S., Criado, K., & Sharp, W. G. (2015). Nutrition management of gastrointestinal symptoms in children with autism spectrum disorder: Guideline from an expert panel. *Journal of the Academy of Nutrition and Dietetics, 115*(12), 1919–1927. doi:10.1016/jand.2015.05.016
- Thomas, J. J., & Eddy, K. T. (2019). *Cognitive-behavioral therapy for avoidant/restrictive food intake disorder: Children, adolescents, and adults.* Cambridge, UK: Cambridge University Press.
- Withrow, N., & Alvidrez, L. (2019). The Sensory Processing, Aberrant Mealtime Behavior, Motor, Inventory for Eating (SAMIE). *Advances in Autism* (volume ahead of print). doi:10.1108/AIA-08-2018-0025.

Recommended Resources for Families

- Fraker, C., Fishbein, M., Cox, S., & Walbert, L. (2007). *Food chaining: The proven 6-step plan to stop picky eating, solve feeding problems, and expand your child's diet.* Boston, MA: De Capo Press.

- Harris, G., & Shea, E. (2018). *Food refusal and avoidant eating in children including those with Autism Spectrum.* Philadelphia, PA: Jessica Kingsley Publishers.
- Hart, M., & Lutz, K. (2009). *The everything guide to cooking for children with autism.* Avon, MA: Adams Media, a division of F+W Media, Inc.

About the Author

Nicole Withrow is a Registered Dietitian and expert in understanding the struggles with eating in individuals with autism and other complex medical conditions. She works at the Colorado Children's Hospital in Developmental Pediatrics. Dr. Withrow's research addresses the complexities in food selectivity, gastrointestinal issues, and weight management in individuals with special needs and their families. She is an Assistant Professor and educates nutrition students and dietetic interns to work with families and individuals with autism and other medical conditions. She is a well-recognized national speaker and works as a consultant for the Center for Discovery. She is a proud mother to two wonderful teenagers. You can contact Dr. Withrow at nicole.withrow@unco.edu.

References

Arnold, G. L., Hyman, S. L., Mooney, R. A., & Kirby, R. S. (2003). Plasma amino acids profiles in children with autism: Potential risk of nutritional deficiencies. *Journal of Autism and Developmental Disorders, 33,* 449–454. doi:10.1023/A:1025071014191

Bandini, L. G., Anderson, S. E., Curtin, C., Cermak, S., Evans, E. W., Scampini, R., ... Must, A. (2010). Food selectivity in children with autism spectrum disorders and typically developing children. *Journal of Pediatrics, 157*(2), 259–264. doi:10.1016/j.jpeds.2010.02.013

Bandini, L. G., Curtin, C., Phillips, S., Anderson, S. E., Maslin, M., & Must, A. (2017). Changes in food selectivity in children with autism spectrum disorder. *Journal of Autism and Developmental Disorders, 47*(2), 439–446. doi:10.1007/s10803-016-2963-6

Baranek, G. T., Foster, L. G., & Berkson, G. (1997). Sensory defensiveness in persons with developmental disabilities. *Occupational Therapy Journal of Research, 17*(3). doi:10.1177/153944929701700302

Bowers, L. (2002). An audit of referrals of children with autistic spectrum disorder to the dietetic service. *Journal of Human Nutrition and Dietetics, 15*(2), 141–144. doi:10.1046/j.1365-277X.2002.00345.x

Curtin, C., Bandini, L. G., Perrin, E. C., Tybor, D. J., & Must, A. (2005). Prevalence of overweight children and adolsecents with attention deficit hyperactivity disorder and autism spectrum disorders: A chart review. *BMC Pediatrics, 5,* 48. doi:10.1186/1471-2431-5-48

Eaves, L. C., & Ho, H. H. (2008). Young adult outcome of autism spectrum disorders. *Journal of Autism and Developmental Disorders, 38*(4), 739–747. doi:10.1007/s10803-007-0441-x

Field, D., Garland, M., & Williams, K. (2003). Correlates of specific childhood feeding problems. *Journal of Paediatrics and Child Health, 39*(4), 299–304.

Geraghty, M. E., Bates-Wall, J., Ratliff-Schaub, K., & Lane, A. E. (2010). Nutritional interventions and therapies in autism: A spectrum of what we know: Part 2. *Infant, Child, & Adolescent Nutrition, 2*(2), 120–133. doi:10.1177/1941406410366848

Green, D., Baird, G., Barnett, A. L., Henderson, L., Huber, J., & Henderson, S. E. (2002). The severity and nature of motor impairment in Asperger syndrome: A comparison with specific developmental disorder motor function. *Journal of Child Psychology and Psychiatry, 43*(5), 655–668. doi:10.1111/1469-7610.00054

Herndon, A. C., DiGuiseppi, C., Johnson, S. L., Leiferman, J., & Reynolds, A. (2009). Does nutritional intake differ between children with autism spectrum disorders and children with typical development? *Journal of Autism and Developmental Disorders, 39*(2), 212–222. doi:10.1007/s10803-008-0606-2

Mayes, S. D., & Zickgraf, H. (2019). Atypical eating behaviors in children and adolescents with autism, ADHD, other disorders, and typical development. *Research in Autism Spectrums Disorders, 64*, 76–83. doi:10/1016/j.rasd.2019.04.002

Mulloy, A., O-Reilly, L. R. M., Sigafoos, J., Lancioni, G., & Rispoli, M. (2010). Gluten-free and casein free diets in the treatment of autism spectrum disorders: A systematic review. *Research in Autism Spectrum Disorders, 4*(3), 328–339. doi:10.1016/j.rasd.2009.10.008

Schreck, K. A., Williams, K., & Smith, A. F. (2004). A comparison of eating behaviors between children with and without autism. *Journal of Autism and Developmental Disorders, 34*(4), 433–438. doi:10.1023/B:JADD.0000037419.78531.86

Schwarz, S. M. (2003). Feeding disorders in children with developmental disabilities. *Infants and Young Children, 16*(4), 317–330.

Withrow, N., & Alvidrez, L. (2019). The Sensory Processing, Aberrant Mealtime Behavior, Motor, Inventory for Eating (SAMIE). *Advances in Autism.* doi:10.1108/AIA-08-2018-0025

Wong, V. C. N. (2009). Use of complementary and alternative medicine (CAM) in autism spectrum disorder (ASD): Comparison of Chinese and western culture. *Journal of Autism and Developmental Disorders, 39*(3), 454–463. doi:10.1007/s10803-008-0644-9

23 Feeding and Nutrition in Individuals Diagnosed with Autism

Dannah G. Raz and Abigail S. Angulo

The role of a developmental behavioral pediatrician in the nutrition and eating habits of clients on the autism spectrum is multifaceted. First and foremost, the goal is to understand the etiology of a client's eating habits so that we can determine what is the best intervention or treatment option needed to support the client and their family. We need to assess if a client's different eating habits are attributable to a medical condition or need, or if it is primarily behavioral. We try to understand the underlying issue that is driving a client's picky eating practices so we can direct the client and their family to the right intervention and treatment.

As part of our assessment we obtain a thorough medical history and conduct a physical examination. The medical history includes an in-depth history of the challenges related to eating. We ask the client and caregivers when the problem started and if it occurs every day. We obtain a detailed feeding history that includes where the client eats their meals (which will include questions around physical location of meals, table setting, and chair height and support), what foods the client will eat and what foods the client will refuse, and what is the environment in which the client is eating their food (are there others at the table, is there TV use?).

We also review questions that will point us to specific medical concerns that can lead to selective eating, such as gastroesophageal reflux disease (GERD), constipation, eosinophilic esophagitis (EoE; inflammation of the esophagus), and dental pain, among others. Along these lines, it is important to ensure that there is no pain or discomfort associated with feeding that can lead to a potential cause for food avoidance. McElhanon, McCracken, Karpen, and Sharp (2014) note that there is a higher prevalence of gastrointestinal (GI) symptoms among children with autism. This highlights the need for a thorough investigation into possible medical causes for selective eating.

A detailed history helps guide the physician; this includes a detailed birth history, early life feeding history, medical and surgical history, family history, and social history which could lead to a specific diagnosis. A physical examination is performed to identify any physical factors leading to picky eating. Additionally, height, weight, body mass index (BMI), and vital signs are monitored closely for clients who present with selective eating. Sometimes, a medical professional will need to refer to another specialist, such as a gastroenterologist, for diagnosis and management of medical causes for picky eating.

It is important to note that clients who are selective eaters are not necessarily underweight (low BMI). Frequently, however, clients who are selective eaters are either overweight or meet criteria for obesity. Must et al. (2017) found that there is a higher prevalence of obesity among adolescents with autism, ages 10–17, than a control matched group. Often times weight gain occurs as a result of a selective food repertoire that includes unhealthy and overprocessed foods. When we see overweight or obese clients with autism, in addition to ascertaining a feeding history, it is important to obtain screening labs to look for disease processes such as diabetes and hyperlipidemia (high fats, cholesterol, and triglycerides). Often times there is a family history of obesity, as well. For these clients, understanding the barriers to healthy eating habits and exercise is important. Barriers to healthy eating and exercise can be due to financial strains or lack of a safe environment in which they can exercise. Nevertheless, it is important to understand that selective eating can present across the range of BMI, and proper screening and counseling should follow.

Another role of a medical provider is to ensure that the client is not deficient in any nutrients. This can be difficult to ascertain in many cases if there is not clear avoidance of specific foods. However, if there is any concern for a potential nutrient deficiency, it is important to screen with bloodwork for the appropriate nutrient or nutrients that may be lacking in the diet. Fortified food, such as milk enriched with vitamin D, may be recommended to prevent nutrient deficiencies.

Barriers to Healthy Eating

There are a variety of barriers that contribute to poor nutrition for picky-eating clients with autism. One significant factor relates to the insistence on sameness for those on the spectrum. The sameness is part of the autism spectrum disorder criteria of repetitive behaviors and rigidity with changes in routine. The insistence on sameness can involve a variety of factors when it comes to food. First, there may be an insistence on sameness with regards to the color of the food that the client eats. If a food does not match the color that they prefer, the client may avoid eating it. There may also be an insistence on sameness with regards to food presentation. Some clients have described that they insist that sandwich ingredients be put on the sandwich in a specific order. If the ingredients are not in the specific order they prefer, they may avoid eating that food. Additionally, many clients insist on the sameness of the brand of foods. Many clients will only eat specific name brands of chips, frozen chicken nuggets, and so on.

Others will only eat foods from specific food or fast-food establishments. Other ways that insistence on sameness can present, with respect to food, is insisting on sameness of placement at the table, utensils that are used, or people who are present during the meal. These rigidities may make every meal difficult to manage within any household.

Sensory processing differences also can significantly contribute to selective eating. This can present in a variety of ways. A client may be sensitive to the smell of certain foods and avoid foods with that smell. Sensory challenges with foods relate to the texture of foods. Clients may avoid foods that are too soft or mushy, or foods that have hidden foods inside of them with a variety of textures in each bite. There are other clients who may avoid foods that are too crunchy or chewy. Other sensory aversions present as visual aversions. Clients may avoid foods that are touching other foods or foods that are mixed together, such as spaghetti bolognese or lasagne. A thorough history should elucidate what sensory aversions a client may have when it comes to food. This will help professionals work to tailor their approach to clients with selective eating.

It is important to highlight that there are a number of diet regimes out there for clients with autism. Many of them promise to improve aggression, irritability, mood, sleep, and other symptoms in clients with autism. Numerous studies have examined the benefits of gluten-free/casein-free diets and found that there is no evidence to support the use of this diet in clients with autism (Hyman et al., 2016; Lange, Hauser, & Reissmann, 2015; Piwowarczyk, Horvath, Lukasik, Pisula, & Szajewska, 2018). Furthermore, these diets can further limit an already limited repertoire of food. If a client chooses to try a specific diet, it may be beneficial for them to do so under the guidance of a nutritionist to ensure proper nutrients are being consumed.

Interventions for Selective Eating

There are a variety of interventions for selective eating in clients with autism. One approach is called the Sequential Oral Sensory approach to feeding (the SOS approach) that desensitizes a client to food textures in a play-based, non-stressful context (Toomey Kay & Ross Erin, 2011). The Autism MEAL plan is a parent-training intervention that aims to teach caregivers how to implement feeding interventions that are behaviorally based (Sharp, Burrell, & Jaquess, 2014). The BUFFET program is a cognitive behavioral approach to treatment of selective eating that targets older clients with autism who have developed anxiety or maladaptive habits around eating. The goal is to utilize an approach that improves anxiety and flexibility around eating (Kuschner et al., 2017). These are just to name a few. There are many professionals who care for clients with autism who have developed their methods of improving selective eating. There are non-intensive outpatient approaches, intensive outpatient approaches, and inpatient approaches. It can be helpful for a multi-disciplinary team to evaluate the client initially in order to understand the challenges the client faces related to eating. Ultimately, a professional caring for a client with autism should aim to identify what is leading to selective feeding to best tailor the intervention to their client's needs.

Importance of Medical Care

When a professional encounters a client with autism who is a selective eater, they should ensure that their client is receiving appropriate medical care. This is important for two reasons. First of all, a medical professional should be monitoring their height, weight, BMI, and vital signs to ensure that there are no changes related to their eating habits. Second, a medical provider will be able to monitor for any medical diagnoses that contribute to picky eating. Beyond this, a professional should refer for any other eating-related issues that are beyond their scope of practice. We frequently refer clients to occupational and speech therapists for further evaluation of the issues contributing to selective eating, such as sensory and oral motor challenges, and so on. We also refer to nutritionists and dieticians for an in-depth assessment of their nutritional intake and recommendations for improving their overall nutrition within the context of a child who has a limited variety of food intake.

Summary

Selective eating is not uncommon with autism, and there may be numerous reasons that contribute to eating problems. Autism symptoms can contribute, such as the insistence on sameness and routine in food, and sensory processing difficulties. There are specific interventions to increase optimal feeding behaviors; therapists can help by making appropriate medical referrals. Medical care is important to monitor the overall well-being of the individual with autism, especially as related to the individual's nutrition and eating habits.

Recommended Resources for Professionals and Families

• Autism Speaks-Autism Treatment Network Toolkit: Exploring Feeding Behavior in Autism: www.autismspeaks.org/tool-kit/atnair-p-guide-exploring-feeding-behavior-autism

About the Authors

Dannah G. Raz, MD, MPH is a board-eligible Developmental-Behavioral Pediatrician. She graduated from medical school at the University of Arizona College of Medicine and received her Masters in Public Health with a concentration in Maternal and Child Health at the Colorado School of Public Health. During her fellowship, Dr. Raz developed an interest in understanding feeding difficulties in clients with autism. She is passionate about helping people with developmental disabilities live their best lives. Outside of work she loves spending time with her husband, daughter, and sweet dog.

Abigail S. Angulo, MD, MPH is an Assistant Professor and board-certified Developmental-Behavioral Pediatrician in the Department of Pediatrics Division of Developmental Pediatrics at the University of Colorado School of Medicine. She received her Doctorate of Medicine from the University of Illinois at Chicago – College of Medicine. She also received her Masters of Public Health with a concentration in Maternal and Child Health from the Colorado School of Public Health. Dr. Angulo has a special clinical interest in the integration of developmental specialists within the medical home. Outside of work she enjoys spending time traveling the world with her husband.

References

Hyman, S. L., Stewart, P. A., Foley, J., Cain, U., Peck, R., Morris, D. D., … Smith, T. (2016). The gluten-free/casein-free diet: A double-blind challenge trial in children with autism. *Journal of Autism and Developmental Disorders*, *46*(1), 205–220. doi:10.1007/s10803-015-2564-9

Kuschner, E. S., Morton, H. E., Maddox, B. B., de Marchena, A., Anthony, L. G., & Reaven, J. (2017). The BUFFET program: Development of a cognitive behavioral treatment for selective eating in youth with autism spectrum disorder. *Clinical Child and Family Psychology Review*, *20*(4), 403–421. doi:10.1007/s10567-017-0236-3

Lange, K. W., Hauser, J., & Reissmann, A. (2015). Gluten-free and casein-free diets in the therapy of autism. *Current Opinion in Clinical Nutrition and Metabolic Care*, *18*(6), 572–575. doi:10.1097/mco.0000000000000228

McElhanon, B. O., McCracken, C., Karpen, S., & Sharp, W. G. (2014). Gastrointestinal symptoms in autism spectrum disorder: A meta-analysis. *Pediatrics*, *133*(5), 872–883. Retrieved from www.ncbi.nlm.nih.gov/pubmed/24777214

Must, A., Eliasziw, M., Phillips, S. M., Curtin, C., Kral, T. V., Segal, M., … Bandini, L. G. (2017). The effect of age on the prevalence of obesity among us youth with autism spectrum disorder. *Child Obesity*, *13*(1), 25–35. doi:10.1089/chi.2016.0079

Piwowarczyk, A., Horvath, A., Lukasik, J., Pisula, E., & Szajewska, H. (2018). Gluten- and casein-free diet and autism spectrum disorders in children: A systematic review. *European Journal of Nutrition*, *57*(2), 433–440. doi:10.1007/s00394-017-1483-2

Sharp, W. G., Burrell, T. L., & Jaquess, D. L. (2014). The autism MEAL plan: A parent-training curriculum to manage eating aversions and low intake among children with autism. *Autism*, *18*(6), 712–722. doi:10.1177/1362361313489190

Toomey Kay, A., & Ross Erin, S. (2011). SOS approach to feeding. *Perspectives on Swallowing and Swallowing Disorders (Dysphagia)*, *20*(3), 82–87. doi:10.1044/sasd20.3.82. doi:10.1044/sasd20.3.82

24 Occupational Therapy for the Treatment of Selective Eating

Melanie A. Hunt

Seth is a 16-year-old who is being treated for anxiety, social skills, school performance, and flexibility. After several months of treatment, Seth's mother contacts his psychologist and states:

"Seth is so funny about food. Every morning, since he was 6 years old, he has eaten two chocolate toaster pastries. Seth won't eat the broken ones, so I end up sharing those with the neighbor kids. I pack a lunch each day: a peanut butter sandwich, white bread, crusts off with a drizzle of honey, chips, and a sports drink. I figure at least he's getting something with the sports drink. I don't think Seth eats a lot because he comes home starving and eats a bowl of cheese crackers. By dinnertime, I can sometimes get him to eat chicken nuggets, cooked to perfection. If I get them too done, he won't eat them. He usually is on his video game or doing homework upstairs when we are eating. If he does join us, he is usually bouncing up and down in his seat and distracts everyone. I don't know, maybe I'm over-reacting, his physician doesn't seem to be concerned. He looks OK and he's always in the 90th percentile for weight at his check-ups."

When Picky Eating Becomes a Problem

Seth's mother's recount of his day is common for adolescents and adults who have autism. A staggering 67–90% of people with autism have mealtime challenges, including difficulty sitting at the table, trying new foods, fear, and overall "picky eating" (Kodak & Piazza, 2008; Twachtman-Reilly, Amaral, & Zebrowski, 2008). Overwhelmed parents often report their child "used to eat everything" and then little by little they started refusing foods.

Seth's teacher also reports the following about his behavior in school:
"For the most part he's enjoyable to have in class but he comes into class almost hyper, bouncing around the room. He loves math and science and is interacting more with peers. He has difficulty organizing his thoughts and he usually forgets his homework. I noticed in the afternoon he can be quite cranky with his friends and he's often laying his head on his desk by sixth period. This is typically when he takes a break or becomes easily upset. He must be hungry, because he's typically chewing on his shirt and pencils. We're working on regulation but having a hard time with anything really sticking."

At first glance, the teacher's recall of the day doesn't seem out of the ordinary for a 16-year-old. But, after hearing about the concerns with his mother, could his challenges getting through the day, problematic regulation, and difficulty with attention be related to his poor diet? All professionals and parents have heard of or witnessed first-hand the so-called "typical" picky eater. But when does a "picky eater" turn into something more serious? The following are signs that may warrant further evaluation.

Leaving Out Entire Food Groups

When we review Seth's case, he is primarily eating crackers, breaded foods, and sugary carbohydrates. These foods are generally preferred in the autistic population since they are processed and predictable in the way they feel, taste, or look. Variety in proteins, fruits, or vegetables can be so limited that the person only has a handful of foods that they eat in total.

Leaving Out Certain Textures

We can see that Seth seems to prefer crunchy foods like crackers and toaster pastries. We all have food preferences, but when these preferences become so narrow and rigid that we are leaving out all wet foods, like fruits, or combination textures like cheeseburgers, then variety becomes a challenge.

Food Jagging

This is a term used when we only want one specific food item, for example Seth's penchant for chocolate toaster pastries every day. Food jagging is risky both because frequently the food will then be dropped and the individual's repertoire becomes further restricted.

Signs of Weight Loss, Discomfort, Low Energy, or Mood Swings that Could Be a Result of Poor Nutritional Intake or Physiological Issues

In our case study, Seth's teacher recounts that he can fluctuate between hyperactive in the morning to cranky and even lethargic. Seth's diet is primarily made up of carbohydrates that turn into sugar; the sugar leads to insulin spikes, which in turn can lead to additional cravings of sugar and subsequent mood swings. Seth also complains of stomach pains which can be a sign of gastrointestinal issues that are prevalent among the autistic population. Because Seth is eating a diet high in carbohydrates his weight is not in jeopardy of being too low, however, this can sometimes create a false sense of the adolescent being "OK" despite a diet of poor nutritional value.

Resistance, Behaviors, or Avoidance of Mealtimes

In Seth's case, he is avoidant of sitting with the family at mealtimes. Mealtimes can be stressful and create anxiety for the person who has challenges. This stress can then trickle down to the entire family and even impact peer relationships if the person has difficulty eating around others or is unable to eat what is offered at social events.

Impact of Sensory Processing on Eating

Now, let's take a look through Seth's eyes. He reports:

> *I eat just fine. I just like my food the way I like it. I don't like it when my toaster pastries are broken or when it has weird marks on it. The lunch area is really loud and I have about 10 minutes to eat. I drink the sports drink and eat a few bites of sandwich but sometimes my stomach hurts. I don't really like when mom cooks, it smells weird. I don't like fruits, they feel weird and slimy in my mouth. I don't know, I wished I ate pizza though because we have pizza parties after basketball games.*

A reported 96% of the autism population has extreme hypo- or hyper-responsivity in at least one sensory system (Marco, Hinkley, Hill, & Nagarajan, 2011). Eating could arguably be considered one of the most complex daily activities, involving all eight sensory systems. Beyond the five common sensory systems – tactile, visual, olfactory, auditory, gustatory – there are three internal sensory systems, including proprioception (muscle/joint or body sense), vestibular (movement), and interoception (internal body sensations). During the eating process, all eight sensory systems are working together or "integrating" by taking in information from the environment and body. Therefore, inefficient sensory processing will then have a vast impact on the development of feeding skills.

Let's take a very basic look at how the sensory systems may be contributing to Seth's challenges.

Visual

Usually a strength in the autistic population, this makes Seth very good at reading and math. However, it is hindering him in eating because he notices the tiniest changes in the visual properties of his food (grill marks or change of shape of his pastries) and he rejects it. Foods that are "amorphous" or without shape such as pudding or crumbled crackers may also be challenging to look at.

Touch

Seth mentions that wet foods (i.e., fruit) feel "slimy" and he prefers crunchy foods. Our touch system encompasses not only touching things with our hands but also how foods feel in our mouth. Some people are sensitive or cannot tolerate sticky foods (i.e., BBQ chicken), crumbly foods (i.e., breaded foods), or wet foods (i.e., puddings) on their hands or in their mouths and then avoid those foods, require utensils, or even have a gag reflex.

Smell

Seth has difficulty being in the kitchen while his mother cooks and therefore avoids participating in mealtimes. Imagine the multitude of smells that occur during any one meal and how impactful it would be if this sense was magnified. Challenges with this system can limit a person's desire to go to restaurants and therefore limit social interaction.

Sound

Seth mentions that the cafeteria is very loud. For some people, even the sound that they hear chewing particular textures can be overwhelming.

Movement

Seth's mother recounts that he bounces in his seat. People with challenges in this area may have difficulty sitting still for meals and may have distracting behaviors at meals such as leaning on the table.

Muscle/Joint Sense

In Seth's case, he seems to be seeking this input by chewing on things excessively, a common tool that people use to calm themselves. However, challenges in this area can also contribute to difficulty sitting, using utensils, and knowing where food is in the mouth, causing a person to overstuff.

Interoception

Seth has challenges with timing of meals and getting full/hungry at inopportune times. Many people with difficulty in this area do not recognize hunger/full cues and may under- or over-eat.

Although sensory-based theories may not explain every feeding challenge, they can certainly contribute to the person having extreme fears and rigidity regarding food. To keep their sensory systems from being disrupted or challenged, maintain their body's homeostasis, and create a sense of predictability they can develop feeding habits and rituals around food. In turn this rigidity around food contributes to compromised nutrition and then can be a contributing factor to poor regulation and other cognitive skills.

Professionals Who Can Help

When any of the above-mentioned feeding challenges exist, a referral to a feeding therapist, a professional who specializes in the treatment of feeding concerns, is recommended. A feeding therapist is trained to address underlying sensory, oral motor, or behavioral components affecting feeding, thereby expanding variety and/or increasing volume. Professionals who commonly specialize in feeding therapy include speech therapists, with focused training in oral motor and swallowing functions, and occupational therapists, with focused training in sensory motor aspects of feeding. Although entry-level professionals may have their respective knowledge base, there can be overlap in training and frequently experienced therapists can meet both needs. Behavioral therapists and psychologists may also practice in feeding therapy and will be knowledgeable in managing fears and anxieties as well as setting up behavior supports. While some programs utilize only behavior approaches in treatment, these approaches can be stringent and may not be a good fit for all individuals.

Although the feeding therapist will be an integral part of treatment and resolution of feeding concerns, they are likely not the only professional who should be involved. Feeding disorders in people with autism are highly complex and there are a myriad of compounding factors that can make feeding challenging. Additional support may be needed by integrating one or more of the following professionals into the treatment team:

- **Gastroenterologist.** A gastroenterologist may be needed to evaluate stomach pain, diarrhea, poor weight gain, reflux, and constipation, which has a higher incidence in the autistic population (Haiao, 2014).
- **Allergist.** An allergist may be utilized to evaluate food or environmental allergies that may contribute to eczema, rash, and stomach pain.

- **Nutritionist/Dietician.** A nutritionist or dietician may be needed to evaluate growth and nutritional needs and recommend appropriate ways to get calories and nutrients.
- **Swallow team**. This is usually of lesser concern; however, an evaluation of swallow is important if coughing, choking, or a "stuck" feeling is present when eating/drinking.

Expectations of Therapy

The Individual Will Have to Be "On Board" and Motivated for Therapy to Be Successful

While it is frequently parents and caregivers who are the most concerned about the adolescent's or even adult's eating, therapy can be a slow, arduous process and the individual has to be willing to participate. In Seth's case, he starts out ambivalent about his need to change his eating habits; however, there is a glimmer of wanting to change to stay engaged with friends at basketball. This small desire to change for peer interaction can be used in therapy sessions to help promote change.

The Occupational Therapist Will Do a Thorough Evaluation to Assess Sensory, Motor, Developmental Level, and Behavioral Components that are Impacting Feeding

A comprehensive evaluation will be essential in order to tailor intervention and utilize a strengths-based approach. For example, in Seth's case he's often overwhelmed by visual ("I don't like marks on my food" or "I don't like broken foods") and tactile components of food ("I don't like wet foods") and therefore intervention should include gradual exposure to changing these properties of currently accepted foods and moving towards totally new and unfamiliar foods. Depending on developmental, cognitive, and behavioral components, additional visual or behavioral supports may be necessary.

Team Members Will Need to Collaborate in order to Understand Physiological and Psychological Needs

In Seth's case, it will be important for his mother, psychologist, feeding therapist, and teacher to collaborate to understand if this rigidity exists elsewhere, if his anxiety is a component of his challenges, and what strategies have been effective in other areas. To be effective, they will also need to collaborate across environments to provide consistent routines and exposures in other settings besides therapy sessions.

The Family Will Need to Be Willing to Make Changes to Their Routines and Mealtimes

Therapeutic strategies only occurring during 1-hour therapy sessions once a week will likely not be effective in meeting therapy goals. The family, friends, and other caregivers may need to make changes in order to support the individual.

Ongoing Evaluation of Progress Will Occur to Insure Treatment Is Working

The individual, family, and therapist will be evaluating progress throughout treatment. Although feeding therapy can be laborious and grueling, particularly if the history is long-standing and complex, there should be small and incremental gains throughout the therapy process.

With additional support from skilled feeding therapists, individuals like Seth and their families can get support to improve flexibility with new foods and gradually expand their food repertoire and subsequently improve their quality of life.

Recommended Resources for Professionals

- Tanner, A., & Andreone, B. (2015). Using graduated exposure and differential reinforcement to increase food repertoire in a child with autism. *Behavior Analysis in Practice, 8*(2):233–240. doi:10.1007/s40617-015-0077-9
- Volkert, V. M., & Petula, C. M. (2010). Recent studies on feeding problems in children with autism. *Journal of Applied Behavior Analysis, 43*(1), 155–159. doi:10.1901/jaba.2010.43-155

Recommended Resources for Families

- Fraker, C., Fishbein, M., Cox, S., & Walbert, L. (2007). *Food chaining: The proven 6-Step plan to stop picky eating, solve feeding problems, and expand your child's diet.* Cambridge, MA: Da Capo Press.
- Miller, L.J., & Fuller, D. A. (2006). *Sensational kids: Hope and help for children with Sensory Processing Disorder.* New York, NY: G.P. Putnam's Sons.

About the Author

Melanie A. Hunt, MOT, OTR/L, is an Occupational Therapist and serves as the Feeding Sensory Integration/Autism Spectrum Disorder Team Lead at Children's Hospital Colorado. A special thanks to: Lucy Jane Miller, PhD, OTR, for your mentoring in Sensory Processing Disorder, Kay Toomey, PhD, for your mentoring in feeding, and Kim Korth, OTR, for your facilitation of this project.

References

Haiao, E. Y. (2014). Gastrointestinal issues in autism spectrum disorder. *Harvard Review of Psychiatry.*, *22*(2), 104–111. doi:10.1097/HRP.0000000000000029

Kodak, T., & Piazza, C. C. (2008). Assessment and behavioral treatment of feeding and sleeping disorders in children with autism spectrum disorders. *Child and Adolescent Psychiatric Clinics of North America.*, *17*(4), 887–905. doi:10.1016/j.chc.2008.06.005

Marco, E. J., Hinkley, L. B., Hill, S. S., & Nagarajan, S. S. (2011). Sensory processing in autism: A review of neurophysiologic findings. *Pediatric Research*, (5 Pt 2), 48–54. doi:10.1203/PDR.0b013e3182130c54

Twachtman-Reilly, J., Amaral, S. C., & Zebrowski, P. P. (2008). Addressing feeding disorders in children on the autism spectrum in school-based settings: Physiological and behavioral issues. *Language, Speech, and Hearing Services in Schools*, *39*(2), 261–272.

Part IX

Finding Solutions for Sleep Concerns

Got autism? Got sleep problems! Most individuals with autism report difficulties with sleep: falling asleep, staying asleep, and getting deep and restful sleep. Adolescents and adults are more independent in solving their needs, but sleep problems in any family member have the potential to impact the entire family. You may find that families don't even mention the sleep problems because they have tried without success to solve the problem, or they don't realize that a solution is possible.

In this part we learn why sleep problems likely exist for people with autism, and the importance of sleep. We learn about what additional team members you may wish to invite to your team (more referrals!), behavioral interventions (yes, screen time will be discussed!), and the anxiety that any change in sleep routines might prompt in other family members. We need sleep to be healthy but accessing it can be so challenging. Help your clients build the successful team that will help them access restful sleep.

25 Sleep Challenges for People with Autism

Karen Landmeier

Sleep problems are pervasive in individuals on the autism spectrum, substantially impacting both the individual and the family. Sleep problems occur in 40–80% of children and adolescents with autism vs. 25–40% of typically developing peers (Cohen, Conduit, Lockley, Rajaratnam, & Cornish, 2014). The most commonly occurring sleep problems in this age group are: highly irregular sleep–wake cycles; difficulty settling and delayed sleep onset; frequent, prolonged, and disruptive nighttime awakenings; short sleep duration; and early-morning waketimes.

Sleep data from adults with autism demonstrate a sleep latency twice as long as controls, lower sleep efficiency index, and prolonged waking after sleep onset (Tani et al., 2003). In other words, autistic adults take twice as long to fall asleep and they spend more time lying in bed *awake* than their typical peers. Therapists often hear about sleep problems, but may struggle to identify all the factors that impact sleep, implement effective solutions, and know when to refer for further evaluation.

A Brief Medical Primer on Sleep Issues

Several theories attempt to explain the increase in sleep problems in patients with autism. Researchers postulate that circadian entrainment may be disrupted for those on the autism spectrum (Cohen et al., 2014). Circadian entrainment is the synchronization of one's internal biological clock through recurring exogenous markers, predominantly light–dark signals. The entrainment of the circadian rhythm usually develops around 12 weeks of life, but for those with autism, variations in light sensitivity and decreased awareness of environmental sleep cues may impair this naturally occurring process. Melatonin is a hormone involved in the circadian rhythm and is released by the body in response to light–dark cues. Melatonin has sometimes been referred to as the "Dracula hormone," because it only comes out in the dark. When melatonin is present in the bloodstream it causes physiological changes that promote sleep. Changes in melatonin production and secretion have been clearly demonstrated in autistic individuals (Tordjman et al., 2013). Abnormalities in rapid eye movement (REM) sleep have also been identified (Devnani & Hegde, 2015), but the clinical impact of this physiological difference is not yet understood.

In addition to differences in mechanisms directly related to sleep, physiological differences in other organ systems contribute to sleep problems. Individuals with autism are more likely to have gastrointestinal problems, such as gastroesophageal reflux disease, constipation, and diarrhea, all of which can impact and impair sleep (Chaidez, Hansen, & Hertz-Picciotto, 2014). Similarly, seizures are more common in this population (Spence & Schneider, 2009). Seizures can adversely affect sleep architecture, and sleep deprivation can facilitate seizures. Anxiety and attention deficit hyperactivity disorder (ADHD) can heighten pre-sleep arousal, thus causing delayed sleep onset. Finally, the medications used to treat many co-existing medical problems can directly impact sleep, e.g., selective serotonin reuptake inhibitors and antipsychotics. Challenging behaviors during the daytime and before bed can also impact sleep.

Importance of Sleep for Overall Functioning

Sufficient sleep is paramount to improving daytime functioning in autistic individuals. Thus, it is crucial for those working with these individuals to both recognize and address sleep problems. Sleep problems impair cognitive and executive functions, worsen school performance overall, and are associated with increased internalizing and externalizing behaviors (Astill, Van der Heijden, Van IJzendoorn, & Van Someren, 2012). Insufficient sleep is associated with worsening of pre-existing behavioral problems and increasing severity of core symptoms of autism—of which peer interactions are impaired most significantly (Veatch et al., 2017).

As a developmental and behavioral pediatrician, my work commonly involves identifying and diagnosing autism in children and adolescents. My role in the evaluation of patients with developmental delays is first and foremost to assess for all causes of their developmental, learning, social, and behavioral challenges. On occasion, after identifying a significant sleep problem, I will inform a family that the sleep problem must be remedied before I can determine what other diagnoses the patient may have. Sleep problems can mimic learning disorders, executive functioning disorders—especially ADHD, behavioral problems, and other health problems.

Identifying Sleep Problems and Contributing Factors

Professionals working with patients with autism must inquire about sleep and must explore the topic in depth. In my experience working with autistic individuals, there are many other pressing needs and sleep is seldom a topic addressed without specific inquiry. I find it is helpful to inquire about why a family or individual is utilizing their chosen approach to sleep. Often, I hear: "it's working" or "we've been doing it this way forever." Some adolescents have trained themselves into deleterious sleep rituals that they are resistant to changing. Many families have a fear of upsetting their teen by changing the sleep rituals or even broaching the topic of potential solutions, such as decreased use of electronics in the evening or removing screens from the bedroom. These families are dealing with many stresses and sleep problems can feel like a Jenga piece that, if upset, may demolish their sanity. Adults indicate that they have suffered from sleep problems "for years" and feel that there are no solutions available to them. Finally, some may not know that their sleep is problematic unless a professional identifies issues by investigating all areas of sleep.

Screen use is one of the most ubiquitous obstacles to good sleep. The blue light emitted by screens inhibits release of melatonin, thereby causing a sense of alertness equal to that caused by the noontime sunlight and impairing physiological changes to initiate sleep. Individuals with autism spend more time using electronic devices than their typical peers (Mazurek, Shattuck, Wagner, & Cooper, 2012), and often struggle to discontinue use when they should be sleeping. Worse, if the person uses the device while in bed, they further compound the obstacles to achieving normal sleep by diminishing the association between *being in bed* and *sleeping*.

Because the causes of sleep problems are myriad and can be multi-factorial, using a standardized screening instrument is the most effective and efficient way to identify symptoms. (A list of specific instruments can be found at the end of this chapter.) These tools can help tease apart medically based disorders, such as sleep-disordered breathing or move-ment disorders; substance-contributing factors, such as caffeine, medica-tion, drugs, or alcohol; or behaviorally related factors such as sleep hygiene, sleep environment, or sleep-onset associations. Likewise, having the individual complete a sleep diary for 2 weeks prior to initiating treatment will help identify problematic sleep patterns. Given the high prevalence of sleep disorders for those on the autism spectrum and the negative impact of sleep deprivation on all areas of functioning, I would argue that therapists should be screening all individuals with autism for sleep problems.

When to Refer

If medically based factors are identified, the therapist should refer to a medical specialist for further evaluation. If substances or behaviors are thought to be the problem, a therapist should proceed with implementa-tion of strategies discussed later in this chapter. Medications may be utilized as an adjunct to behavioral strategies, but medications should always be instituted as a bridge to aid in the process and not as a permanent fix for sleep problems. As with all medications, individuals with autism may be more sensitive to dosing and more likely to demonstrate adverse effects from the medication. Nighttime safety concerns that are not remedied by basic behavioral strategies or home monitoring systems also necessitate a referral to a sleep specialist, in order to explore other safety devices such as modified beds.

Preparation for Addressing Sleep Problems

In addition to determining the reasons for the sleep behaviors and gauging readiness for change, it is imperative to specifically determine what changes an individual or family can try to implement. For example, some adolescents may still need a caregiver to actively be involved with the bedtime routine, enforcing rules around access to electronic devices, or helping with implementing behavioral modification strategies. For autistic individuals independent in their self-care for sleep, rigidity and anxiety around sleep patterns and potential changes may need to be addressed prior to implementation of strategies. It is important to concretely explain the reason for the change and allow the individual to direct the types and pace of changes. For example, if an electronic device is in the room and impairing sleep, a fading process may be necessary rather than immediate extinction.

When discussing behavioral sleep modification with a family or autistic individual, I explain the goal I am trying to achieve, describe the options for how to achieve that goal, and ask them to choose what feels most comfortable and feasible. Finally, I describe the potential challenges to the modification (e.g., need for some trial and error with sensory modifications, or extinction burst with removal of electronic devices) and ask them to pick a date that will be ideal to begin and is not close to a time of transition such as travel, move, family visit, or holiday. During this process, the use of a sleep diary is again important, in order to accurately document behaviors and effects, since recall of events is often skewed and interferes with successful treatment recommendations from the professional.

Summary

Sleep is a stressful aspect for both the individual with autism and their family. A non-judgmental approach is helpful to elicit honest reporting of sleep circumstances and to partner with the individual to implement changes. It is important to advise families that making changes with sleep is an ongoing process and not a quick fix. Unfortunately, different sleep challenges often arise and problems that have been corrected can recur. A new sleep problem does not indicate failure on behalf of the family, but a time for reassessing current functioning and implementing new strategies if necessary.

Recommended Resources for Professionals

- Sleep Diary: www.sleepfoundation.org/sites/default/files/inline-files/SleepDiaryv6.pdf
- Sleep Diary: http://yoursleep.aasmnet.org/pdf/sleepdiary.pdf
- Mindell, J. A., & Owens, J. A. (2015). *A clinical guide to pediatric sleep: Diagnosis and management of sleep problems* (3rd ed.). Philadelphia, PA: Wolters Kluwer/Lippincott Williams & Wilkins.

Sleep Screening Instruments:

- *Sleep Habits Survey* (ages 10–19): Wolfson, A. R., Carskadon, M. A., Acebo, C., Seifer, R., Fallone, G., Labyak, S. E., & Martin, J. L. (2003). Evidence for the validity of a sleep habits survey for adolescents. *Sleep, 26* (2), 213–216.
- *Pediatric Sleep Questionnaire* (ages 2–18): Chervin, R. D., Hedger, K., Dillon, J. E., & Pituch, K. J. (2000). Pediatric sleep questionnaire (PSQ): Validity and reliability of scales for sleep-disordered breathing, snoring, sleepiness, and behavioral problems. *Sleep Medicine, 1*(1), 21–32.
- *Adolescent Sleep Wake Scale* (ages 12–18): LeBourgeois, M. K., Giannotti, F., Cortesi, F., Wolfson, A. R., & Harsh, J. (2005). The relationship between reported sleep quality and sleep hygiene in Italian and American adolescents. *Pediatrics, 115*(1 0), 257.
- *Cleveland Adolescent Sleepiness Questionnaire* (ages 11–17): Shahid, A., Wilkinson, K., Marcu, S., & Shapiro, C. M. (2011). Cleveland Adolescent Sleepiness Questionnaire (CASQ). In *STOP, THAT and one hundred other sleep scales* (pp. 127–130). New York, NY: Springer.
- *Global Sleep Assessment Questionnaire* (adults): Roth, T., Zammit, G., Kushida, C., Doghramji, K., Mathias, S. D., Wong, J. M., & Buysse, D. J. (2002). A new questionnaire to detect sleep disorders. *Sleep Medicine, 3*(2), 99–108.
- *Holland Sleep Disorders Questionnaire* (adults): Kerkhof, G. A., Geuke, M. E., Brouwer, A., Rijsman, R. M., Schimsheimer, R. J., & Van Kasteel, V. (2013). Holland sleep disorders questionnaire: A new sleep disorders questionnaire based on the International Classification of Sleep Disorders-2. *Journal of Sleep Research, 22*(1), 104–107.
- *Sleep-50* (adults): Spoormaker, V. I., Verbeek, I., van den Bout, J., & Klip, E. C. (2005). Initial validation of the SLEEP-50 questionnaire. *Behavioral Sleep Medicine, 3*(4), 227–246.

Recommended Resources for Families

- Durand, V. M., (2014). *Sleep better! A guide to improving sleep for children with special needs* (Rev. ed.). Baltimore, MD: Paul H. Brookes Publishing.
- Katz, T., & Malow, B. (2014). *Solving sleep problems in children with autism spectrum disorders: A guide for frazzled families*. Bethesda, MD: Woodbine House.
- ATN/AIR-P Sleep Strategies for Teens with Autism: www.autism speaks.org/tool-kit/atnair-p-sleep-strategies-teens-autism

About the Author

Karen Landmeier, MD, is a Developmental and Behavioral Pediatrician who currently works at The Youth Clinic in Fort Collins, Colorado. Prior to starting her current clinical work, she trained at The University of Chicago, and has also spent time training at The Sie Center for Down Syndrome Children's Hospital Colorado and in the Department of Developmental and Behavioral Pediatrics at Cincinnati Children's Hospital. Dr. Landmeier is passionate about helping with early diagnosis of autism, and helping families understand and support their child on the spectrum.

References

Astill, R. G., Van der Heijden, K. B., Van IJzendoorn, M. H., & Van Someren, E. J. W. (2012). Sleep, cognition, and behavioral problems in school-age children: A century of research meta-analyzed. *Psychological Bulletin*, *138*(6), 1109–1138. doi:10.1037/a0028204

Chaidez, V., Hansen, R. L., & Hertz-Picciotto, I. (2014). Gastrointestinal problems in children with autism, developmental delays or typical development. *Journal of Autism and Developmental Disorders*, *44*(5), 1117–1127. doi:10.1007/s10803-013-1973-x

Cohen, S., Conduit, R., Lockley, S. W., Rajaratnam, S. M., & Cornish, K. M. (2014). The relationship between sleep and behavior in autism spectrum disorder (ASD): A review. *Journal of Neurodevelopmental Disorders*, *6*(1), 44. doi:10.1186/1866-1955-6-44

Devnani, P. A., & Hegde, A. U. (2015). Autism and sleep disorders. *Journal of Pediatric Neurosciences*, *10*(4), 304–307. doi:10.4103/1817-1745.174438

Mazurek, M. O., Shattuck, P. T., Wagner, M., & Cooper, B. P. (2012). Prevalence and correlates of screen-based media use among youths with autism spectrum disorders. *Journal of Autism and Developmental Disorders*, *42*(8), 1757–1767. doi:10.1007/s10803-011-1413-8

Spence, S. J., & Schneider, M. T. (2009). The role of epilepsy and epileptiform EEGs in autism spectrum disorders. *Pediatric Research*, *65*(6), 599–606. doi:10.1203/PDR.0b013e31819e7168

Tani, P., Lindberg, N., Wendt, T. N., Wendt, L. V., Alanko, L., Appelberg, B., & Porkka-Heiskanen, T. (2003). Insomnia is a frequent finding in adults with Asperger syndrome. *BMC Psychiatry*, *3*(1). doi:10.1186/1471-244x-3-12

Tordjman, S., Najjar, I., Bellissant, E., Anderson, G. M., Barburoth, M., Cohen, D., … Vernay-Leconte, J. (2013). Advances in the research of melatonin in autism spectrum disorders: Literature review and new perspectives. *International Journal of Molecular Sciences*, *14*(10), 20508–20542. doi:10.3390/ijms141020508

Veatch, O. J., Sutcliffe, J. S., Warren, Z. E., Keenan, B. T., Potter, M. H., & Malow, B. A. (2017). Shorter sleep duration is associated with social impairment and comorbidities in ASD. *Autism Research*, *10*(7), 1221–1238. doi:10.1002/aur.1765

26 Approaching Sleep Problems in Adolescents with Autism

Kathleen Kastner

> *Ben is a 13-year-old with autism who presents with difficulty waking up in the morning. Parents describe that he is often late for school because it takes over an hour to get him up. Ben describes that he doesn't fall asleep until midnight, even if he tries to go to sleep earlier, and he wakes up 2–3 times each night. He is often fatigued during the day.*

Sleep is an essential daily activity that can have remarkable influences on cognitive, emotional, social, and physical functioning. Sleep difficulties are a common co-morbidity for individuals on the autism spectrum, with more than half of children with autism reporting sleep problems (Krakowiak, Goodlin-Jones, Hertz-Picciotto, Croen, & Hansen, 2008). The period of adolescence can pose particular challenges, as teenagers experience a delayed sleep phase, or later sleep onset time, due to changes in circadian rhythm. Simultaneously, they may also have increasing independence in managing their daily routines. As a result, sleep issues become a prominent concern for adolescents. Inadequate sleep can significantly impact daytime functioning, quality of life, and mental health. Sleep difficulties are often multi-factorial, and therefore frequently require an interdisciplinary team to be fully addressed. Often therapists may be the first provider to learn of an individual's sleep difficulties, and therefore can serve an important role in helping adolescents and their families navigate sleep challenges, including by providing behavioral intervention and by referring to other team members when appropriate.

A Team Approach

Given the multifactorial influences on sleep, management of sleep difficulties often requires an interdisciplinary team. It is important to recognize indication for referral to another team member when appropriate. Physician referral for medical evaluation should be considered for all individuals with sleep difficulty, especially those whose symptoms persist after a brief behavioral intervention. Physician evaluation may include screening for and identifying underlying medical issues, providing behavioral intervention to improve sleep hygiene, and in some cases, prescribing medications. Other possible referrals should also be considered. Psychotherapy referral should be considered when there are concerns regarding anxiety or depression. Occupational therapy referral could be helpful if sensory sensitivities are disrupting sleep onset or maintenance. Behavioral therapist referral can be important if implementation of initial behavioral strategies has not been successful. However, in order to determine which referrals are appropriate, it is necessary to first learn more about the nature of the sleep problem.

Characterizing the Sleep Problem

Sleep concerns can be divided into several different categories, including difficulties with sleep onset, difficulties staying asleep, inadequate total sleep, and restless sleep. In order to develop an effective sleep intervention, it is essential to accurately characterize and diagnose the sleep problem with a thorough clinical history. The BEARS screening acronym has been shown to be an effective clinical tool in obtaining a sleep history (B: bedtime issues; E: excessive daytime sleepiness; A: night awakenings; R: regularity and duration of sleep; S: sleep-disordered breathing/snoring [Owens & Dalzell, 2005]). Some adolescents and their parents may have difficulty characterizing their sleep patterns in detail, especially if their sleep cycles are irregular and sleep is generally unmonitored. It can therefore be very helpful for therapists to encourage use of a sleep log for a couple weeks prior to a sleep evaluation in order to obtain more detailed information. This information can identify areas of primary concern, which can then guide management and referral.

What to Expect during the Medical Evaluation

A medical evaluation is important to assess for an underlying medical condition when working to address sleep problems in individuals with autism. Physician referral is appropriate in all patients with sleep difficulties that do not resolve with brief behavioral intervention. Sleep difficulties can arise in the context of a number of medical conditions, including primary sleep disorders, mental health conditions, gastrointestinal conditions, pain, skin discomfort, neurological disorders, or respiratory conditions. Several such conditions occur more frequently in individuals with autism than in typically developing peers, including mental health conditions, constipation, and seizures. Primary sleep disorders include several different conditions that can impact sleep, such as parasomnias (sleepwalking, sleep talking, night terrors), narcolepsy, restless-legs syndrome, and obstructive sleep apnea. Individuals with restless-legs syndrome may report itching, tingling, or crawling sensations on their legs, an irresistible urge to move, or extremely restless sleep. Restless-legs syndrome can sometimes be associated with low iron stores, so this is especially important to consider if the individual has limited dietary iron intake. Signs of sleep apnea include snoring, gasping/pauses in breathing during sleep, and unusual sleep positions. In addition, children and adolescents who have obstructive sleep apnea may present with daytime behavioral symptoms, such as hyperactivity, impulsivity, inattention, or irritable mood, which can mimic behavioral conditions such as attention deficit hyperactivity disorder (ADHD). Therefore, when children or adolescents present with behavioral concerns, a thorough sleep history should be obtained to identify any sleep problems which could be contributing to the behavioral concerns.

Mental health conditions can also significantly impact sleep, and adolescents with autism disproportionately experience co-morbid mental health conditions in comparison to their typically developing peers. ADHD can make it challenging for adolescents to settle their bodies for sleep at the end of the day. Anxiety and depression can both make it difficult to fall asleep as well as cause nighttime awakenings and early rising. Many medications, including those used to treat mental health conditions, can affect sleep, such as antihistamines, seizure medications, stimulants, selective serotonin reuptake inhibitors, alpha-agonists, tricyclic antidepressants, and benzodiazepines. Finally, other health conditions, such as gastrointestinal, respiratory, skin, and neurological disorders, dental conditions, and untreated pain, can worsen sleep. A comprehensive medical evaluation should assess for all of these possible contributors to sleep problems.

It can be beneficial for therapists to help families anticipate what a medical evaluation might entail. In addition to a comprehensive history to better characterize the sleep problem, a physician evaluation will include a physical exam. Current medications will also be reviewed in detail to identify if the individual is taking any medications that could be contributing to sleep difficulties. Laboratory evaluation will be guided by symptoms on history and physical. And ultimately, the primary care physician may refer to additional specialty physicians in some circumstances. Individuals may be referred to neurology if there are concerns for seizures, including atypical sleep movements/behaviors during sleep. If there are signs of obstructive sleep apnea, referral to either otolaryngology or sleep medicine, depending on local resources, would be appropriate. Any other indicators of a primary sleep disorder may prompt referral to sleep medicine. Sleep medicine providers may order additional testing, including polysomnography (sleep study) or actigraphy (wristwatch device that monitors movement at night) to further characterize sleep concerns.

Behavioral Interventions

Once therapists help connect families to a medical evaluation to rule out medical co-morbidities, then attention should turn to behavioral intervention as the first-line strategy for addressing sleep concerns. Sleep hygiene, or the set of habits/practices associated with daily sleep, can be an important contributor to one's ability to fall asleep and an important target for intervention. Sleep hygiene not only includes sleep and bedtime routine, but also daytime and evening routines which can significantly influence sleep. Consistent daytime physical activity can be very helpful in improving sleep.

In addition, evening screen usage can be associated with worsening difficulty falling asleep. Screen time should end approximately 30 minutes before bedtime. For many families, it is often most successful if the entire family implements a "screens off" policy at the same time each night. It can also be helpful to designate a "parking lot" for all screens (e.g., phones, tablets, computers, and so on) in a common area of the house, so that devices are not available in the bedroom overnight. If a phone/tablet is in the bedroom, it may be more likely that adolescents will use the device when they wake up overnight and subsequently have difficulty settling back to sleep. Negotiating screen time rules can be challenging for many families, so clinicians can serve a valuable role in helping adolescents and their parents work together to set family rules.

Food and drink consumption in the evening also has a direct effect on sleep. Some people find that eating heavy meals late in the day can contribute to difficulty sleeping. Caffeine and nicotine use, especially in the last several hours before bedtime, can make it more difficult to fall asleep. In addition, a number of medications, both prescription and non-prescription, can impact sleep.

A consistent bedtime routine can help with falling asleep and staying asleep. An ideal bedtime routine consists of quiet, calming activities lasting about 15–30 minutes. It is often helpful if the bedtime routine remains consistent from night to night. Teenagers should be encouraged to identify which activities might be most calming for them, such as reading, drawing, puzzles/board games, listening to music, or talking with family. In addition, the bedtime routine should include the steps necessary to prepare for sleep, such as changing into pajamas and brushing teeth. Some people may find bathing/showering to be an uncomfortable experience, in which case it may be helpful to move that activity to the morning routine. A visual schedule outlining the bedtime routine can be useful for some individuals with autism, but this may not be helpful for others.

It is also very important to maintain a consistent sleep schedule. This can be especially difficult for adolescents, who often prefer to sleep later on weekends. However, this variability in sleep schedule can make it more difficult to settle for sleep on weeknights. Therefore, it is often best to limit bedtime and wake-up time variability to 1 hour. Recommended sleep quantity for teenagers is 8–10 hours of sleep a night, so it is essential that bedtime and wake-up time are set accordingly (Paruthi et al., 2016). If an adolescent experiences a prolonged sleep latency (time to sleep onset), it can sometimes be helpful to temporarily move bedtime later to the time when they are typically falling asleep. Once the individual is falling asleep more quickly on a consistent basis, bedtime can then be pushed earlier in small increments (15–30 minutes) until the goal bedtime is established.

An ideal sleep environment is another important area of intervention. For most people, characteristics of an ideal sleep environment include a dark, cool, and quiet room. White noise can be helpful, such as a fan or white-noise machine, as long as the sound remains consistent throughout the night. Use of variable background noise, such as music or TV, should be discouraged, as this can lead to nighttime awakenings. Adolescents with autism may experience sensory sensitivities in regards to the sleep environment. It can be helpful to consider the type of sheets, blankets, pajamas, pillows, and so on that would be most comfortable. Another important strategy can be encouraging adolescents to avoid using their bed for activities other than sleeping, such as reading, listening to music, or watching TV.

Use of Medications

If behavioral interventions are not successful in managing sleep disorders, and sleep symptoms remain significant, pharmacological interventions may be a consideration. Overall, evidence is limited in regard to use of medications to manage sleep disorders in children with autism spectrum disorder. There are currently no medications approved by the US Food and Drug Administration (FDA) for treatment of pediatric insomnia. Commonly used medications for sleep disorders in children with autism spectrum disorder include melatonin and alpha-agonists, though there are a variety of other medications also used in clinical practice, including antidepressants, gabapentin, and atypical antipsychotics (Blackmer & Feinstein, 2016; Malow et al., 2016). It is important to carefully weigh the possible risks and benefits of any pharmacological interventions for sleep disorders, given the relative lack of evidence-based treatment guidelines. Even when medications are used, behavioral intervention is still essential to help maximize the effectiveness of the intervention.

Inadequate sleep can have far-reaching consequences in the day-to-day functioning of adolescents with autism spectrum disorders and their families. It is important for all providers who work with adolescents with autism spectrum disorder to proactively recognize and address sleep concerns. Often appropriate management involves support from an interdisciplinary team of providers, with a strong emphasis on use of behavioral strategies as a first-line intervention.

Ben's therapist encouraged use of a sleep log which revealed he was sleeping an average of 6.5 hours per night with two night awakenings. They also discovered that Ben was often on his phone while trying to fall asleep and when he woke up overnight. He reported anxiety symptoms which made it hard to fall asleep. Ben then saw his primary care doctor for evaluation and there were no concerns about underlying medical conditions. With behavioral intervention, Ben successfully moved his bedtime to 10:30 pm and slept through the night. He continues to work with his therapist on managing anxiety symptoms.

Recommended Resources for Professionals

- Malow, B. A., Byars, K., Johnson, K., Weiss, S., Bernal, P., Goldman, S. E., ... Sleep Committee of the Autism Treatment, N. (2012). A practice pathway for the identification, evaluation, and management of insomnia in children and adolescents with autism spectrum disorders. *Pediatrics, 130*(Suppl 2), S106–S124. doi:10.1542/peds.2012-0900I
- American Academy of Sleep Medicine (AASM) Practice Guidelines-https://aasm.org/clinical-resources/practice-standards/

Recommended Resources for Families

- Autism Speaks Toolkits (*Sleep Strategies for Teens with Autism; Strategies to Improve Sleep in Children with Autism*): www.autismspeaks.org
- Malow, B. A., & Katz, T. (2014). *Solving sleep problems in children with autism spectrum disorders.* Bethesda, MD: Woodbine House.

About the Author

Kathleen Kastner, MD, is an assistant professor of pediatrics at University of Wisconsin-Madison. Dr. Kastner is a board-certified developmental and behavioral pediatrician who cares for children and teens with autism spectrum disorder in the Autism and Developmental Disabilities Clinic at the Waisman Center. Dr. Kastner also has a passion for medical education, including expanding opportunities for medical trainees to learn more about providing compassionate, family-centered care for children with developmental disabilities.

References

Blackmer, A. B., & Feinstein, J. A. (2016). Management of sleep disorders in children with neurodevelopmental disorders: A review. *Pharmacotherapy, 36*(1), 84–98. doi:10.1002/phar.1686

Krakowiak, P., Goodlin-Jones, B., Hertz-Picciotto, I., Croen, L. A., & Hansen, R. L. (2008). Sleep problems in children with autism spectrum disorders, developmental delays, and typical development: A population-based study. *Journal of Sleep Research, 17*(2), 197–206. doi:10.1111/j.1365-2869.2008.00650.x

Malow, B. A., Katz, T., Reynolds, A. M., Shui, A., Carno, M., Connolly, H. V., ... Bennett, A. E. (2016). Sleep difficulties and medications in children with autism spectrum disorders: A registry study. *Pediatrics, 137*(Suppl 2), S98–S104. doi:10.1542/peds.2015-2851H

Owens, J. A., & Dalzell, V. (2005). Use of the 'BEARS' sleep screening tool in a pediatric residents' continuity clinic: A pilot study. *Sleep Medicine, 6*(1), 63–69. doi:10.1016/j.sleep.2004.07.015

Paruthi, S., Brooks, L. J., D'Ambrosio, C., Hall, W. A., Kotagal, S., Lloyd, R. M., ... Wise, M. S. (2016). Recommended amount of sleep for pediatric populations: A consensus statement of the American Academy of Sleep Medicine. *Journal of Clinical Sleep Medicine, 12*(6), 785–786. doi:10.5664/jcsm.5866

27 Catching Some ZZZs
Helping Individuals Sleep Better

Terry Katz

Many individuals on the autism spectrum have sleep problems that start in infancy and last throughout their lives. Families and individuals with sleep problems can grow weary of attempts to find success, and often end up feeling as though their situation is not fully understood. As referenced in the previous chapters, critically important behavioral factors that are addressed when assessing sleep problems include daytime diet and activities, evening schedules, bedtime routines, sleep-onset associations, an individual's sleep environment, and what happens if an individual wakes up during the night. Psychiatric factors such as anxiety and mood are also important to consider. Individuals with autism often have difficulty falling asleep, going to sleep much later than the rest of the family, waking up during the night, and waking up much earlier. Finally, a number of medical issues may impact sleep and need to be considered. These include constipation, reflux, seizures, pain (including dental pain), restless-legs syndrome, sleep-disordered breathing, allergies, and medications. As a therapist, you will be referring out for medical evaluations and behavioral interventions that go beyond the scope of your expertise.

If you have concerns about an individual's sleep, it will be important to determine whether working on sleep is a priority for the family. If not, the first step in intervention may be educating the family about the importance of sleep. You also need to have a good understanding of a family's strengths and challenges and the obstacles they may face when addressing sleep. Many families describe working with professionals who have given them suggestions that are based on scientific evidence, but are not realistic for that individual or his or her family. Often, providers will be able to make helpful changes if they adopt a gradual approach that is supportive and family-friendly. Thus, families and individuals need to agree about primary sleep concerns and the ways in which these problems will be addressed.

The Cases of Penny and Diego

Penny, an adolescent with autism, an intellectual disability, and a seizure disorder, is a good example of the importance of addressing a family's stated concerns. Penny is not able to fall asleep independently and needs to sleep with a family member. She takes a long time to fall asleep (more than 20 minutes) and wakes up frequently during the night. Her family notes that Penny loves to drink caffeinated soda and does not engage in any exercise during the day. She does not have a bedtime routine and engages in stimulating activity until it is time to go to sleep. While her family describes many behavioral factors that are likely contributing to her poor sleep, they believe that her seizure disorder is causing her sleep problems.

Through discussions with the family, it is clear that they do not want to work on changing Penny's sleep habits until they are sure that there is not a medical explanation for the sleep problems. Thus, the first step will be a referral to Penny's medical team. Once medical concerns have been addressed, the therapist can work with the family to decrease her intake of caffeinated beverages and increase her physical activity. Therapy can help them develop a calm and consistent bedtime routine and suggest using visual supports to help Penny learn this routine. Once these steps have been achieved, the therapist can work with the family to help Penny fall asleep independently. This might involve having a parent sit in a chair in Penny's room while she falls asleep. Then gradually over time, her parents can move the chair farther away from Penny's bed and closer to her bedroom door until she is falling asleep without any parental presence.

While Penny needs considerable support from her family in order to improve her sleep, many adolescents and adults need to be responsible for changing their own sleep habits.

Diego likes to stay up late playing on his tablet and likes to keep the lights on until it is time for him to fall asleep. He often stays up very late and then has great difficulty waking up in the morning. After assessing all relevant medical and behavioral factors, it is determined that Diego has a delayed sleep phase disturbance. In order to make the necessary changes to his daytime and evening habits, Diego needs education about the importance of sleep. Diego will need to be actively involved in making decisions about his daily routines and the strategies he will use to establish new sleep practices. His family can also support Diego by using visual reminders and rewards to reinforce Diego's efforts to maintain his new habits. A referral to a sleep specialist may be needed if Diego successfully develops new habits but continues to have trouble falling asleep at an appropriate time. He may need to work with someone who has expertise in chronotherapy (moving bedtime sequentially by 1–3 hours or more later on successive nights) or bright-light therapy (using a lightbox) to reset his body's internal clock. It may also be helpful to talk with a sleep specialist about the use of melatonin or other sleep medications.

Technology and Sleep

Many of Diego's sleep difficulties have been exacerbated by his use of computer technology. The ubiquitous nature of technology in our society is one of the main barriers to adequate sleep because of the difficulty involved in disengaging from technology-based activities at bedtime. In addition to the challenges posed by being overstimulated before bed, the use of technology exposes us to bright light which interferes with our melatonin production and thus our ability to sleep well. The light from electronic devices is particularly disruptive because the blue light emitted by electronic devices interferes the most with our ability to sleep (Chellappa et al., 2013). Solutions include turning off all electronic devices about an hour before bedtime and using tools that filter out blue light. This may include apps that are already programmed into a device, uploading an app, or using plastic orange screen coverings or orange-tinted glasses.

Societal Devaluing of Sleep

Another barrier to restful sleep is our society's general devaluing of a good night's sleep. Sleep is frequently seen as a barrier to accomplishing important tasks. Many high schools ignore the fact that adolescents naturally shift to a later sleep schedule and require teens to come to school much too early in the morning. Difficulties with sleep impact daytime functioning (Sikora, Johnson, Clemons, & Katz, 2012), but this is not always acknowledged. Additionally, many providers do not think to ask about sleep, and in a busy practice with little time to address pressing problematic behaviors, sleep is often overlooked. Even when a family or an individual is concerned about sleep, they may not think to bring this up because they are used to the problem or do not think anything can be done. So, even when an individual has significant difficulties with sleep, the problem is not addressed. Providing more education about the importance of sleep and the relative ease with which many sleep problems can be solved should help address this issue. Ideally, providers will routinely ask about sleep and address difficulties as they arise.

Providing Hope

In addition to knowing that they need to ask about sleep, providers need to know that sleep problems can get better, and communicate this to families. Medical issues can be solved (Reynolds & Malow, 2011) and behavioral strategies to address sleep are highly effective (Malow, MacDonald, Fawkes, Alder, & Katz, 2016). Some providers and families do not think an individual will be able to cooperate with a sleep study or comply with medical interventions such as continuous positive airway pressure (CPAP). Individuals can, however, be desensitized to sleep study procedures and can learn to tolerate devices such as CPAP (Slifer, Tunney, & Paasch, 2019).

Top Sleep Concerns

Some of the top sleep concerns that families discuss include irregular sleep–wake cycles, difficulty settling for bed, delayed sleep onset, night wakings, short sleep duration, and early-morning wake times. Many of these difficulties are inter-related. For example, the family of an adolescent who has significant difficulty settling for bed may let the teen play on their tablet at bedtime to avoid conflicts. This may then lead to an even later bedtime, short sleep duration, and night wakings. Conversely, some families have a bedtime that is too early. We all have natural circadian rhythms and experience an increase in alertness in the evening. If someone goes to bed during this time, it is very difficult to fall asleep. Thus, correct timing of bedtime is essential.

Difficulties with sleep maintenance are often due to problems with sleep onset associations. These associations are the behaviors individuals engage in while falling asleep. Individuals can have helpful and unhelpful sleep-onset associations. If an individual's sleep-onset associations include electronics, he or she is much more likely to wake up during the night. This is because we all cycle through phases of sleep throughout the night and we are much more likely to wake up during the night if we cannot replicate the way we have fallen asleep at the beginning of the night. So, individuals who fall asleep while playing on a tablet are more likely to wake up during the night.

Psycho-educating Families about Sleep

When addressing sleep-onset associations and other sleep concerns, it is always important to provide education about why specific behaviors may be of interest. The next step is to determine a family's priorities and ability to make necessary changes. It is best to tell families that it is up to them to decide whether and when to implement suggested strategies. Since some families need to make many changes, it is often helpful to start with some of the easier problems. This often gives families a sense of accomplishment and makes it easier to subsequently tackle tougher issues.

Learning to work collaboratively with families is imperative. While new professionals need to know the key components of successful sleep (e.g., daytime habits, evening routines, timing of bedtime, sleep environment, and bedtime patterns) as well as evidence-based interventions, they also need to understand how to be an effective consultant. An empathic understanding of how difficult some of these changes may be and a collaborative approach when working with individuals and their families are key aspects of a successful sleep program. While many of the strategies can be immediately effective, some families are just not ready to make any changes even when they know there is a problem. It is always important to keep the door open and allow families to make needed changes when they are ready to do so. Their days are challenging and they are doing the best they can. They want help and want to make things better, but they cannot always follow a therapist's preconceived time frame.

First-Step Interventions

There are a number of first-step interventions that are relatively easy to implement. These include decreasing caffeine use and increasing daytime exercise (but not too close to bedtime). Walking, yoga, mini trampolines, and swimming are often great forms of exercise. Light exposure is a critically important component of good sleep. Exposure to natural light first thing in the morning and throughout the day is very important. Finding the right bedtime and keeping the lights down as low as possible the hour before bedtime are also essential. Night lights help with fears of the dark and can also be used instead of bright lights if someone does get up in the middle of the night. Visual schedules for bedtime routines are highly recommended. The routine should consist of easy and relaxing activities and each step should be followed in the same order each night. The use of visuals may include a written list that can be checked off, a visual schedule (using either photographs or icons), or an object schedule. An example of a bedtime routine might include the following: putting on pajamas, brushing teeth, getting a drink, reading a book, and getting into bed. Consider providing families with a starter kit that includes photos, icons, Velcro, and laminate so that they can make their own schedule. This helps emphasize the importance of using visuals while acknowledging how hard it is to find the time and energy to gather the needed materials.

Summary

While it is essential to address sleep-onset associations if night waking is a problem, it is best to do so once other good sleep habits have been established. Focusing initially on daytime habits and bedtime routines is a good place to start. It will be easier for everyone to address this more challenging aspect of sleep once they have had success implementing easier suggestions and these easier suggestions will make it less challenging for the individual to eventually fall asleep independently.

Recommended Resources for Professionals

- Accardo, J. (Ed.). (2019). *Sleep in children with neurodevelopmental disabilities: An evidence-based guide.* Switzerland: Springer Nature Switzerland, AG.
- Meltzer, L. J., & McLaughlin Crabtree, V. (2015). *Pediatric sleep problems: A clinician's guide to behavioral interventions.* Washington, DC: American Psychological Association.
- Mindell, J. A., & Owens, J. A. (2015). *A clinical guide to pediatric sleep: Diagnosis and management of sleep problems* (3rd ed.). Philadelphia, PA: Wolters Kluwer.

Recommended Resources for Families

- Durand, V. M. (2014). *Sleep better!: A guide to improving sleep for children with special needs* (Rev. ed.). Baltimore, MD: Paul H. Brooks Publishing, Co.

- Katz, T., & Malow, B. A. (2014). *Solving sleep problems in children with autism spectrum disorders: A guide for frazzled families.* Bethesda, MD: Woodbine House, Inc.
- Sleep Strategies: www.autismspeaks.org/tool-kit/atnair-p-strategies-improve-sleep-children-autism
- Sleep Strategies for Teens: www.autismspeaks.org/tool-kit/atnair-p-sleep-strategies-teens-autism
- Sleep Tips: www.autismspeaks.org/sites/default/files/2018-09/Sleep%20Quick%20Tips.pdf
- Visual Supports: www.autismspeaks.org/tool-kit/atnair-p-visual-supports-and-autism
- Melatonin: www.autismspeaks.org/tool-kit/atnair-p-melatonin-and-sleep-problems-guide-parents

About the Author

Terry Katz, PhD is a Psychologist and Senior Instructor with Distinction at Children's Hospital Colorado, University of Colorado School of Medicine. She has worked with individuals with autism for over 30 years. She is the co-author of a book on sleep and autism: *Solving Sleep Problems in Children with Autism Spectrum Disorders: A Guide for Frazzled Families* (Woodbine House, 2014). Dr. Katz co-founded the Sleep Behavior Clinic in Developmental Pediatrics at Children's Hospital Colorado. She was the co-leader of the Sleep Committee of the Autism Speaks Autism Treatment Network. She provides sleep consultation to agencies and gives workshops on sleep and autism throughout the country, and has developed numerous toolkits, videos, and other educational material for families of children with autism.

References

Chellappa, S. L., Steiner, R., Oelhafen, P., Lang, D., Götz, T., Krebs, J., & Cajochen, C. (2013). Acute exposure to evening blue-enriched light impacts on human sleep. *Journal of Sleep Research, 22*(5), 573–580. doi:10.1111/jsr.12050

Malow, B. A., MacDonald, L. L., Fawkes, D. B., Alder, M. L., & Katz, T. (2016). Teaching children with autism spectrum disorder how to sleep better: A pilot educational program for parents. *Clinical Practice in Pediatric Psychology, 4*(2), 125. doi:10.1037/cpp0000138

Reynolds, A. M., & Malow, B. A. (2011). Sleep and autism spectrum disorders. *Pediatric Clinics, 58*(3), 685–698. doi:10.1007/s10803-013-1866-z

Sikora, D. M., Johnson, K., Clemons, T., & Katz, T. (2012). The relationship between sleep problems and daytime behavior in children of different ages with autism spectrum disorders. *Pediatrics, 130*(Supplement 2), S83–S90. doi:10.1007/s40675-015-0012-1

Slifer, K. J., Tunney, M. A., & Paasch, V. (2019). Behavioral intervention for positive airway pressure (CPAP/BPAP) desensitization. In J. Accardo's (Ed.), *Sleep in children with neurodevelopmental disabilities* (pp. 373–382). Springer Nature Switzerland AG: Springer, Cham.

Part X

Acknowledging and Addressing Medical Concerns

Individuals on the autism spectrum appear to have complex medical conditions that impact daily living. We often hear about allergies and seizures, as well as adverse reactions to medications, dosing issues, and general issues that appear to stem from the differing biology of individuals with autism.

In this part we hear from a psychiatrist, who suggests timely referrals to psychiatry, and offers some entry-level education about the types of symptoms that medication might address, preferably in combination with therapy. We also learn about underlying medical conditions that may impact daily living, such as seizures, allergies, and genetic conditions. Finally, we have a personal account from a talented writer who shares her harrowing experiences and offers direct guidance about how we can invite our autistic clients who excel at researching to partner with us, and how to listen better to our clients who are plagued with numerous sensitivities.

28 The Role of Medication for Children on the Spectrum, from the Perspective of a Child and Adolescent Psychiatrist

Aaron G. Meng

> *Charlie is a 12-year-old boy diagnosed with autism. He was brought to my office by his parents due to concerns about irritability and aggressive behaviors. Both the family and teachers have commented that Charlie has a difficult time sitting still and paying attention; he is also quite anxious and has engaged in increasing self-stimming behavior over the past five or six months.*

In my experience working with Charlie and other children and teens on the spectrum, as well as with their parents, I have found that medication can be extremely helpful for indications such as hyperactivity/inattention, irritability and aggression, anxiety, and depression. While therapy is an integral aspect of treatment for these children, knowing when to make a referral for medication management can potentially help these children move towards wellness at a faster pace. Just as children and teens on the spectrum can react differently than other children to symptoms of psychiatric disorders such as depression and anxiety, and as their responses to therapy and intervention can differ from their neurotypical counterparts, their reactions to medications can differ as well. As such, it is important to refer to a child and adolescent psychiatrist who is knowledgeable regarding working with people on the spectrum.

Common Presenting Problems

In the following paragraphs I will discuss the most common presenting problems for which I am consulted in my practice, how these often present (spoiler alert: irritability will be a common theme), and how I typically use medication as a tool to treat these children. As such, the following is not meant to be an exhaustive review of the literature on this topic, but a brief summary of my experience. There are psychiatrists whose sole focus of their career in academic medicine is researching this topic. My experience, however, is that of a child psychiatrist in community mental health and private practice settings, ranging from rural areas in central Maine to large towns/small cities where resources are often limited, and demands usually outstrip those resources. The following is not meant to be exhaustive, and is not meant to be a full treatise regarding my treatment algorithms when approaching these children or teens, but rather some general thoughts, philosophies, and observations that I hope might be helpful.

When working with children on the spectrum, one of the most common symptom clusters I am asked to treat is attention and focus problems, with or without hyperactivity. Oftentimes these symptoms cooccur with irritability, which, as I mentioned above, is a common theme when treating children in general, and especially children on the spectrum.

In terms of irritability and aggression in the context of inattention/hyper-activity symptoms, I see two frequent causes: the first cause is low frustration tolerance, and the second cause is impulsivity. I have found that it is extremely important to consider whether anxiety is present, as well as whether the anxiety may be triggering the lack of attention and low frustration tolerance.

To complicate matters further, problems with attention and focus may trigger anxiety. Children and teens who have trouble with attention and focus will often have insight that they are not able to perform up to expectations or to the level of their peers, and this insight can lead to significant anxiety — academically, vocationally, and socially — as well as trigger depressive symptoms.

In counterpoint, however, an anxious child or teen may experience this anxiety and worry as physical restlessness and find their ability to attend to task and focus overwhelmed by anxious and worried thoughts.

I have found taking a thorough history in terms of the timeline at which symptoms first presented to be extremely helpful in delineating if the attention deficit hyperactivity disorder (ADHD) symptoms are primary or secondary. For example, I often — but not always — hear parents of children who have ADHD describe hyperactivity and inattentive symptoms beginning very early on in life, with mood and anxiety symptoms occurring later. Additionally, defining the focus of anxious, worried thoughts or depressive thoughts can be very helpful. For example, if the worry or dysphoria is centered around performance or schoolwork, this presentation can often be suggestive of primary ADHD. Conversely, if the hyperactivity or attention problems tend to occur only in specific situations that also prompt significant anxiety — or if the anxiety symptoms occurred first and are generalized — such presentations would suggest the possibility that the anxiety symptoms are primary.

Use of a Multidisciplinary Team

In terms of treating these children, another theme — both in my practice, and in this chapter — will be that of a multidisciplinary team. I find that working with a therapist who can work both with the child and with the family in order to help with behavioral management techniques and strategies for helping maintain focus complements medication management. Also, as sensory issues can contribute to so many of the mood and behavioral issues that children on the spectrum experience, working with an occupational therapist who has experience and expertise working with children and teens on the spectrum, and who can provide treatment and support, can also be very helpful.

Medication Management

For medication management, I try to tailor the medication I recommend to the individual child. Stimulant medications may be useful at times but have some significant drawbacks. ADHD symptoms, especially in children who are hyperactive, impulsive, irritable, and have a difficult time sleeping, are not just problematic during the day. These symptoms can significantly impact home and social lives. Stimulants work best during school/work hours, and attempting to extend their duration can frequently lead to increased problems with insomnia and appetite loss. These side effects are two of the most common I see with these medications.

Psychiatric practices can vary greatly, and psychiatrists have individual styles regarding what they tend to prescribe more frequently, but I frequently use extended-release guanfacine in children with ADHD who are on the spectrum. This medication has the benefit of a 24-hour release, thus providing coverage not only during the day, but also in those first hours after awakening and those afternoon and evening hours which can be difficult to reach with some other medications. Additionally, the once-daily dosing aids in compliance and avoids students requiring doses of their medication at school. There is a different medication with similar mechanism of action called clonidine, that is available in a 12-hour, sustained-release formulation. In patients who also have quite a bit of anxiety, in addition to their ADHD symptoms, I have found Strattera can be quite useful. At times, I will also prescribe stimulants for patients on the spectrum, keeping in mind the problems associated with these medications I noted above. There are certainly other medications that can be used for treating ADHD in the context of autism spectrum disorder, but those go beyond the scope of this chapter.

In terms of general themes of medication management in autism spectrum disorder, I prefer to start at very low doses, often doses lower than I would start neurotypical children, and move up more slowly. For patients who have significant sensory issues and who struggle with rigidity, I find that they can often be very sensitive to changes in the way they feel internally. As such, utilizing more aggressive dosing strategies can trigger negative reactions that may not be experienced when initiating a medication more gradually.

Anxiety

I see anxiety present in several different ways in children and teens with autism. Many times, teens can express their anxiety and worry, or parents are able to perceive and relate this anxiety to the treatment team. However, there are times when anxiety presents more subtly. At times I see anxiety present with new or increased stereotypies, pacing, or self-stimming. Other times I see anxiety present as increased hyperactivity or inattention. Fairly frequently I see anxiety present as increased irritability, including aggression. I am a firm believer in the power of therapy for these patients, especially cognitive behavioral therapy, when possible. However, if therapy is resulting in limited success, or symptoms are severe, I have found medication can be quite helpful. The most common medication class I use to treat teens on the spectrum are the selective serotonin reuptake inhibitors (SSRIs: such as fluoxetine, citalopram, sertraline, and escitalopram). I have also had success with buspirone. Unfortunately, there are no Food and Drug Administration-approved medications for the indication of pediatric anxiety. While medications for ADHD, except for atomoxetine, tend to begin working quickly, medications for anxiety can take weeks or longer before benefit is achieved.

Parents often ask me about the risk of suicidal thoughts and behaviors with antidepressants. I inform them that suicidal ideation and behaviors are a real risk, and I have seen children develop such side effects in my practice. Additionally, I have seen children become manic, more aggressive, as well as disinhibited on these medications. However, the number of patients who have these side effects is small, in my experience, compared to the number of people who have benefited from such medication. However, risks cannot be minimized, and in the end, it is up to the family to decide whether the potential risks are worth the potential benefit.

Depression

My recommendations when it comes to treatment of depression in teens and adults on the spectrum are very similar to my recommendations for the treatment of anxiety. If possible, I prefer to see treatment utilizing an evidence-based psychotherapy approach as primary treatment. If such therapy is impossible or unsuccessful, or if symptoms are severe, utilizing a medication such as an SSRI might be helpful. As with any time I prescribe medication for these patients, I use the "start low and go slow" dosing philosophy.

While some patients may be able to verbalize their depression, other times, we see symptoms such as loss of interest and motivation, low energy, crying spells, decreased ability to enjoy things, isolation, hopelessness, and irritability. For both depression and anxiety, I strongly encourage people to exercise, as such activity can be helpful both from a physical and emotional standpoint.

Physical Health as Triggers for Symptoms

While I have not mentioned it yet, it is extremely important that physical health be taken into account when considering psychiatric/behavioral symptoms. For example, pain or discomfort, especially in someone who is nonverbal, can trigger a wide variety of symptoms. As such, psychiatrists must keep in mind non-psychiatric medical issues when assessing for psychiatric disorders and considering treatments. Referral to primary care can be helpful if a non-psychiatric medical issue is suspected, symptoms are of sudden onset or are atypical, or if symptoms are not responding to typical treatments.

Irritability and Aggression

By this point, I have mentioned irritability several times as a common theme and symptom of ADHD, anxiety, and depression. There are times, as a psychiatrist, that I am asked to treat a patient with irritability and subsequent aggression that is severe, but the patient does not have other symptoms which might suggest one of the above etiologies. In these situations, I have used medications from a family known as "atypical antipsychotics" or "second-generation antipsychotics," which includes such medications as Abilify, Risperdal, Seroquel, and numerous others. I generally try to use other medications first, given the side effects associated with these "atypicals," but there are times when other medications have not worked or symptoms are of a severity requiring intervention as soon as possible. While I have seen these medications work extremely well, they convey numerous risks including, but not limited to: weight gain, high cholesterol, high blood sugar, diabetes, muscle stiffness and spasms which can block the airway, restlessness which can be extremely uncomfortable, suicidal thoughts and behaviors, decreases in the white blood cell count, and movement disorders which do not necessarily go away even after the medication is stopped. Given the risks associated with these medications, regular blood work is necessary when prescribing these medications. Many times, when I have to resort to using such medications, I attempt to use them as a shorter-term strategy to assist in keeping things safe at home and at school until we can find another medication with fewer, long-term side effects, and/or until further non-medication, therapeutic interventions can take place.

Summary

When symptoms are mild, distress is mild, and disruption of functioning is minimal, I am reluctant to initiate medication unless there has been a significant trial of evidence-based psychotherapy. There have been plenty of times within my practice when I have seen a patient who has not had such a trial of psychotherapy, and – as a psychiatrist – it is always nice to be able to say that I do not think medication is indicated at this time. Other times, I see individuals who have been suffering with more severe symptoms and subsequently more severe disruptions in terms of their life and development, who potentially would have benefited from referral for psychiatric services earlier on in their treatment. A knowledgeable child and adolescent psychiatrist will assess the risks and benefits of treating with medication versus not medicating, and will not prescribe if the potential risks outweigh the potential benefits. They will also educate the patient and family regarding these potential risks in benefits, so that the family and patient can make an informed decision about their treatment.

Resources for Professionals

- Ji, N. Y., & Findling, R. L. (2015). An update on pharmacotherapy for autism spectrum disorder in children and adolescents. *Current Opinion in Psychiatry, 28*(2), 91–101. doi:10.1097/yco.0000000000000132
- Volkmar, F., Siegel, M., Woodbury-Smith, M., King, B., McCracken, J., & State, M. (2014). Practice parameter for the assessment and treatment of children and adolescents with autism spectrum disorder: Erratum. *Journal of the American Academy of Child & Adolescent Psychiatry, 53*(8), 931. doi:10.1016/j.jaac.2014.06.001

Resources for Families

- Parent's Med Guides, The American Academy of Child and Adolescent Psychiatry: http://parentsmedguide.org/

About the Author

Aaron G. Meng, MD, FAPA, is an Adult, Child and Adolescent, and Forensic Psychiatrist in Fort Collins, Colorado. He attended medical school at the University of Medicine and Dentistry of New Jersey, Robert Wood Johnson Medical School. He attended the Psychiatry residency program at Banner Good Samaritan Hospital in Phoenix, Arizona, and then completed his Child and Adolescent Psychiatry Fellowship at the University of North Carolina, Chapel Hill (and remains a devout Tar Heel fan). He attended his Forensic Psychiatry fellowship at University of Colorado, Denver. He has spent his career working in community mental health as well as in private practice.

29 Common Comorbid Conditions with Autism

Lauryn M. Toby

> *I first met Antwon in the inpatient unit at Johns Hopkins Hospital. He was a 14-year-old boy with autism and intellectual disability who was being discharged following a brief hospital stay for the treatment of facial wounds that were the result of severe self-injury. Specifically, Antwon would use his thumb and pointer finger on his right hand to poke and scratch at the area around his eyes until he caused significant tissue damage, bruising, and bleeding. His doctors were concerned about him causing vision damage should these behaviors continue to occur. My job following his discharge was to assess and treat the underlying cause of these self-injurious behaviors, starting with a detailed developmental history and clinical interview with his caregivers. I didn't know it at the time, but some of the most important information I would gather from that initial interview with his parents had to do with Antwon's medical history and associated health-related symptoms.*

Unfortunately, I often find that the importance of associated health conditions in individuals on the autism spectrum is often undervalued by clinicians in favor of more obvious behavioral symptoms related to the individual's primary disability. As a psychologist who conducts comprehensive psychological evaluations, I specialize primarily in assessment and subsequent diagnoses of a variety of neurodevelopmental disorders, specifically autism and related conditions. By the time families schedule an appointment for an evaluation with a psychologist, they have often lost countless hours of sleep, agonized over who to talk to, and fully researched all possible diagnoses and the best evaluators in town.

Across the individuals I evaluate and treat, the most distressing symptoms for families are often health-related. By far the most common comorbid health conditions I tend to observe in individuals with autism are sleep and feeding difficulties. These are discussed at length in previous chapters. However, medical conditions that are less often discussed – but just as important – are the presence of seizure activity, genetic disorders, and immunologic dysfunction such as allergies or asthma. Although secondary to the diagnosis of autism, these comorbid health conditions often have an additive or cyclical effect; that is, the presence of one appears to increase the severity of the other, and the more issues that are present the more impaired the individual will be. For example, a lack of sleep, poor diet, asthma, and the presence of seizure activity can lead to an increase in behavior concerns and difficulties in school and community settings. Unfortunately, research estimates that up to 70% of individuals with autism have multiple concurrent conditions (Lai & Baron-Cohen, 2015).

It is essential that these associated health symptoms are not overlooked. This section will describe three comorbid health conditions that I typically see in my patients with autism; discuss their prevalence and research-supported methods of treatment; and outline recommendations for when clinicians should refer out to other providers; we will also revisit Antwon's case.

Seizures

Research has established an increased risk for epilepsy in individuals with autism, but exact rates are unknown, with estimates ranging from 5% to almost 40% of those diagnosed on the autism spectrum. However, one of the most salient risk factors is the presence of comorbid intellectual disability in individuals with autism. In fact, the association between epilepsy severity and cognitive impairment is such that, as IQ decreases, epilepsy rates increase (Amiet et al., 2013). Also of interest when considering seizures is age of onset. Research has suggested that there may be two distinct presentations of epilepsy: one that peaks in early childhood and one that appears in adolescence (Parmeggiani et al., 2010). However, the risk does not decrease after adolescence, and may even continue into adulthood. One cross-sectional study estimated the prevalence of epilepsy in those with autism to be 12% in childhood, and up to 26% by adulthood (Viscidi et al., 2013).

Seizures come in many types and forms, and are typically classified as *focal seizures* or *generalized seizures*. Focal seizures refers to seizures that originate in a part of only one hemisphere, while generalized seizures describes a seizure originating simultaneously in both hemispheres (Berg & Millichap, 2013). Focal seizures are then further divided into simple focal seizures (i.e., without impairment of consciousness) and complex focal seizures (i.e., with impairment of consciousness). Generalized seizures are divided into *absence seizures* (i.e., brief lapses in consciousness), *minor motor events* (e.g., myoclonic, atonic), and *major motor events* (e.g., tonic, clonic, and tonic-clonic) (Hattier, Toby, & Williams, 2015). An in-depth discussion of these types of seizures is outside the focus of this chapter; however, most parents and caregivers can recognize a tonic-clonic or "grand mal" seizure when it occurs and can seek treatment accordingly. Absence seizures tend to be a different story. Although no one specific type of seizure has been clearly associated with autism, some research suggests individuals with autism are more likely to experience generalized absence seizures (Tuchman, Rapin, & Shinnar, 1991). Unfortunately, these types of seizures are also more challenging both to identify and treat.

Most often, a red flag for potential absence seizure activity arises in the context of caregivers describing concerns regarding attention and focus; they will note that their teenager engages in "staring spells" or brief periods of time when they appear unresponsive to others. During these periods, parents frequently note they are unable to redirect their child or gain their attention, despite various attempts to "snap them out of it." These spells are most often brief (10–30 seconds) in nature, and once the individual regains their focus, they do not have memory of the event. Many times, families associate these symptoms with the core symptoms of autism (i.e., lack of response to name, often in their own world), inattention, passive defiance, or just that their child is ignoring them. However, staring spells such as these could be an indicator of absence seizures, and the key as a clinician is when to know to refer a family for an electroencephalogram to rule out seizure activity. Specifically, I recommend that clinicians ask individuals or caregivers the following set of questions:

1. Are there periods of time of 10 seconds or more where the individual seems to "zone out" and you cannot redirect their attention?
2. Does the individual seem to suddenly "snap" back to awareness, with no recollection that you were attempting to talk to them or gain their attention?
3. Does the individual appear lethargic or tired after these episodes?
4. Do these episodes occur frequently throughout the day?

If the answers to more than one of the above questions are "yes," a referral to a neurologist may be appropriate. It is imperative that evaluation and treatment for individuals with autism and epilepsy should involve collaborative efforts among medical professionals, as the most common treatment is often antiepileptic medications, which require ongoing evaluation and monitoring.

Immunologic Dysfunction

Remember the case of Antwon and his severe self-injury outlined earlier?

> *After a detailed caregiver interview, it was revealed that Antwon's self-injurious behaviors were significantly associated with a certain time of the year, peaking around mid-April and lasting through August. It appeared that in August, the self-injurious behaviors would temporarily subside, with the lowest levels of self-injury present in the winter months. Upon further assessment and referral to an allergist, Antwon was found to have severe allergies to pollen and grass. His self-injury was an attempt to ameliorate the physical discomfort he was feeling but could not verbalize. Treatment with allergy-reducing medications resulted in a significant improvement in Antwon's overall quality of life, including a drastic reduction in his self-injury.*

Although Antwon's case is severe, it is not uncommon for individuals with autism to suffer from an increased prevalence of allergic symptoms. In fact, some research has found evidence for a seasonal pattern in significant behavioral changes among young adults with autism, with a worsening of symptoms typically occurring in April (cf., Boso et al., 2010).

Immunologic dysfunction is not unusual in individuals with autism, and typically refers to a variety of conditions such as gastrointestinal difficulties, respiratory allergy, skin allergy, food allergy, and asthma (Jackson, Howie, & Akinbami, 2013). Although research in this area is relatively scarce, a recent study of almost 200,000 U.S. children found a significant and positive association between food allergies and the presence of autism (Xu et al., 2018). A further study of individuals with high-functioning autism reported that various allergic responses were observed in 85% or more of autistic patients, compared to only 7% of age-matched neurotypical controls (Magalhães et al., 2009). There also may be a positive correlation between autism symptom severity and allergic manifestations (Mostafa, Hamza, & El-Shahawi, 2008).

Clearly, it is important for clinicians to investigate the presence of allergic conditions in their patients with autism in order to establish the need for appropriate referrals and testing, and to establish new therapeutic targets. Health care providers should likewise be alerted to any allergic-like symptoms in order to further secure appropriate referrals for treatment. Specifically, I recommend that clinicians ask individuals or caregivers the following set of questions:

1. Does the individual display frequent coughing or shortness of breath?
2. Does the individual display chronic nasal congestion?
3. Does the individual have a family history of eczema or skin rashes?
4. Does the individual complain of frequent headaches?
5. Does the individual have frequent allergic reactions or skin rashes?
6. Does the individual complain of vomiting or stomach aches after eating?

7. Are there behavioral concerns or symptoms that seem cyclical or worsen during certain times of the year?

Answering "yes" to two or more of these questions suggests the need for additional follow-up by a health care provider, who can subsequently make a referral to an allergist if needed.

Genetic Conditions

More than 30% of individuals with autism have identifiable genetic correlates that include several recognizable genetic disorders (Miles & Hillman, 2000). Specifically, fragile X, tuberous sclerosis, Angelman's syndrome, Phelan–McDermid, Down syndrome, Cornelia De Lange, and Smith–Magenis are just a few of the comorbid genetic disorders commonly seen in individuals with autism at the diagnostic clinic where I practice. Given the established association of genetic disorders and the presence of symptoms of autism, as a clinician the responsibility here is two-fold. Chiefly, when working with a client with autism and an already established genetic condition, understanding the symptoms associated with that condition is imperative in order to gain a better understanding of the presenting symptoms by knowing what is typical for that disorder. It would be a disservice to the individual you are working with to assume all symptoms and behaviors are a result of their autism.

Additionally, for individuals with autism who do not yet have a diagnosed genetic condition, it is important to determine if a referral for genetic testing may be warranted. Genetic testing, specifically a chromosomal microarray (CMA), is increasingly suggested for all individuals with an autism spectrum diagnosis. Certain conditions and abnormal physical features may indicate a higher concern for the prevalence of comorbid genetic conditions. Specifically, research suggests children with autism with abnormal features on physical exams are ten times more likely to have diagnosable genetic conditions (Miles & Hillman, 2000). Examples of abnormal physical features to look for include wide-set or droopy eyes, a flat face, and short fingers. Abnormal gait, growth issues, and developmental or intellectual disability are additional risk factors. Finally, a family history of genetic disorders may suggest a predisposition to a certain condition. Although the presence of one risk factor may not indicate a problem, multiple risk factors plus the presence of autism likely suggest the need for a referral for genetic testing.

Summary

Individuals with autism will likely face multiple comorbid health conditions during the course of their lives. In fact, as individuals with autism get older, they tend to acquire more comorbid conditions (Soke, Maenner, Christensen, Kurzius-Spencer, & Schieve, 2018). The adolescents at my clinic often present with at least three or more established health conditions, not including comorbid psychiatric diagnoses such as anxiety, depression, or attention deficit hyperactivity disorder. Unfortunately, due to difficulties with expressive language and a low tolerance for diagnostic medical procedures, individuals with autism also tend to be under-diagnosed for a variety of medical conditions with which they are afflicted (Jyonouchi, 2010). Therefore, the onus is on clinicians to effectively screen their clients for symptoms of comorbid health conditions when they present, and to subsequently refer to appropriate professionals for relevant assessment and treatment. Of particular importance is access to educational and medical records, as well as the completion of a detailed parent/caregiver interview at the onset of assessment and treatment to get a complete background/history. Ideally, ruling out medical causes for behavioral changes should occur prior to proceeding with typical therapeutic treatments for individuals with autism. Clinicians should establish a set of questions to ask during the assessment/clinical interview in order to flag for the presence of certain health conditions that may require additional follow-up or referral. The effective treatment of co-occurring medical conditions in individuals with autism will primarily help attenuate physical and behavioral symptoms, and in doing so will also help the individual's overall quality of life and facilitate their continued learning and development.

Recommended Resources for Professionals

* Wilkinson, L. (2014). *Autism spectrum disorders in children and adolescents: Evidence-based assessment and intervention in schools.* Washington, DC: American Psychological Association.
* Matson, J. L., & Matson, M. L. (2015). *Comorbid conditions in individuals with intellectual disabilities.* Cham, Switzerland: Springer International Publishing.

About the Author

Lauryn M. Toby, Ph.D., BCBA, is a licensed clinical psychologist and Board Certified Behavior Analyst at Little Star ABA Therapy Center in Carmel, Indiana. Her work focuses primarily on the assessment and treatment of children and adolescents with autism spectrum disorder. Lauryn has previously published in the *Journal of Applied Behavior Analysis* and has been a contributing author to multiple books on the topic of comorbid conditions in individuals with developmental disabilities. In her spare time, Dr. Toby enjoys reading, yoga, watching scary movies, and spending time with family.

References

Amiet, C., Gourfinkel-An, I., Laurent, C., Bodeau, N., Génin, B., Leguern, E., … Cohen, D. (2013). Does epilepsy in multiplex autism pedigrees define a different subgroup in terms of clinical characteristics and genetic risk? *Molecular Autism, 4*(1), 47. doi:10.1186/2040-2392-4-47

Berg, A. T., & Millichap, J. J. (2013). The 2010 revised classification of seizures and epilepsy. *Continuum: Lifelong Learning in Neurology, 19*(3), 571–597. doi:10.1212/01.CON.0000431377.44312.9e

Boso, M., Comelli, M., Emanuele, E., Podavini, F., Marini, M., Mancini, L., … Politi, P. (2010). Seasonal fluctuations in problem behaviors among young adults with autism and intellectual disability. *Medical Science Monitor, 16*(5), CR213–CR216.

Hattier, M., Toby, L., & Williams, L. (2015). Epilepsy. In J. L. Matson, & M. L. Matson (Eds.), *Comorbid conditions in individuals with intellectual disabilities* (pp. 195–236). Cham, Switzerland: Springer.

Jackson, K. D., Howie, L. D., & Akinbami, L. J. (2013). Trends in allergic conditions among children: United States, 1997–2011. *NCHS Data Brief, 121*, 1–8.

Jyonouchi, H. (2010). Autism spectrum disorders and allergy: Observation from a pediatric allergy/immunology clinic. *Expert Reviews in Clinical Immunology, 6*(3), 397–411. doi:10.1586/eci.10.18

Lai, M. C., & Baron-Cohen, S. (2015). Identifying the lost generation of adults with autism spectrum conditions. *The Lancet Psychiatry, 2*(11), 1013–1027. doi:10.1016/S2215-0366(15)00277-1

Magalhães, E. S., Pinto-Mariz, F., Bastos-Pinto, S., Pontes, A. T., Prado, E. A., & de Azevedo, L. C. (2009). Immune allergic response in Asperger syndrome. *Journal of Neuroimmunology, 216*(1–2), 108–112. doi:10.1016/j.jneuroim.2009.09.015

Miles, J. H., & Hillman, R. E. (2000). Value of a clinical morphology examination in autism. *American Journal of Medical Genetics, 91*, 245–253. doi:10.1002/(SICI)1096-8628(20000410)91:4<245::AID-AJMG1>3.0.CO;2-2

Mostafa, G. A., Hamza, R. T., & El-Shahawi, H. H. (2008). Allergic manifestations in autistic children: Relation to disease severity. *Journal of Pediatric Neurology, 6*(2), 115–123. doi:10.1016/j.bbi.2015.02.001

Parmeggiani, A., Barcia, G., Posar, A., Raimondi, E., Santucci, M., & Scaduto, M. C. (2010). Epilepsy and EEG paroxysmal abnormalities in autism spectrum disorders. *Brain and Development, 32*(9), 783–789. doi:10.1016/j.braindev.2010.07.003

Soke, G. N., Maenner, M. J., Christensen, D., Kurzius-Spencer, M., & Schieve, L. A. (2018). Prevalence of co-occurring medical and behavioral conditions/symptoms among 4-and 8-year-old children with autism spectrum disorder in selected areas of the United States in 2010. *Journal of Autism and Developmental Disorders, 48*(8), 2663–2676. doi:10.1007/s10803-018-3521-1

Tuchman, R. F., Rapin, I., & Shinnar, S. (1991). Autistic and dysphasic children. II: Epilepsy. *Pediatrics, 88*(6), 1219–1225.

Viscidi, E. W., Triche, E. W., Pescosolido, M. F., McLean, R. L., Joseph, R. M., Spence, S. J., & Morrow, E. M. (2013). Clinical characteristics of children with autism spectrum disorder and co-occurring epilepsy. *PloS One, 8*(7), e67797. doi:10.1371/journal.pone.006779

Xu, G., Snetselaar, L. G., Jing, J., Liu, B., Strathearn, L., & Bao, W. (2018). Association of food allergy and other allergic conditions with autism spectrum disorder in children. *JAMA Network Open, 1*(2), e180279–e180279. doi:10.1001/jamanetworkopen.2018.027

30 Autism Spectrum from the Inside Out

Cynthia Zuber

Hello! Welcome to my chapter! My name is Cynthia; I am a 44-year-old woman who was diagnosed as being on the autism spectrum at age 40. I am not a healthcare provider of any sort, but if the school of hard knocks due to multiple medical diagnoses and time in medical clinics counts for anything, I'd have honors degrees from Yale, Harvard, and Stanford! This is why I've been asked to write and share my experience *sans* official medical training. I want to give you an idea of what autism looks and feels like from the inside out, so you can understand the types of issues and feelings your clients may be dealing with on a daily basis. Through a combination of storytelling and guidance I am telling my story for you to understand the lived experience of myself and potentially other fellow autistics. I hope to help you bring greater compassion, awareness, and understanding to the autistics in your life or practice. We are an interesting and unique bunch for sure, with sensitive bodies, minds, hearts, and nervous systems. In being so sensitive I sometimes do not feel of this world. Not all autistics are this highly sensitive where the experience of being a human is so deeply painful and assaulting in multiple ways, but there is always some degree of sensitivity present in most autistics.

I was diagnosed with my first autoimmune disease at age eleven, type 1 diabetes. But this wasn't my first rodeo with illness. I came out of the womb ill, a colicky baby who never wanted to be held. I spent my childhood sick and eventually was diagnosed with other serious auto-immune diseases like endometriosis and Hashimoto's thyroiditis. These illnesses threw the quality of life I once enjoyed into the gutter. On a quest for wellness, I underwent several challenging surgeries and tried many potent pharmaceutical medications that left me with significant side effects. I struggled immensely, that is until I began exploring the wondrous benefits of holistic modalities of healing such as homeopathy, acupuncture, and herbs as well as nutritional and lifestyle strategies. I continue to grow and heal in every way and am so thankful for these alternatives.

Sensitivities of Individuals with Autism

I am very, highly, over-the-top sensitive. My sensitivity is woven into every part of my being. You've probably heard of psychologist Elaine Aron's book *The Highly Sensitive Person* (1997). I'm even more sensitive than this book depicts highly sensitive people! I remember writing on my intake paperwork for my autism assessment at my local autism society that, "I'm so sensitive it hurts to be alive."

Sensory Processing Issues

Before autism was even on the radar, I was referred to an occupational therapist where I was diagnosed with a severe sensory processing condition. My sensory sensitivities mean bright fluorescent lights and loud or unexpected noises are extremely painful for me, making me become dysregulated deep into my soul. Thankfully, through Pilates and yoga, I'm increasing my body awareness of where my body is in space, also known as *proprioception*, but the overwhelm of just being in the world for a day or even a few hours is extremely taxing for me.

I am highly sensitive physically to light and caffeine, both of which can throw off my sleep. What other people can get away with, I cannot. For example, with my blue light sensitivity I have poor sleep if I'm on electronics past 8:00 at night, or also if I have caffeine past 2:00 in the afternoon. If I stay up even thirty minutes past my latest bedtime of 10:30 p.m. I am groggy and completely out of it the entire next day.

Medication Sensitivities

For any medication I am prescribed, even in a minute dose, I will experience the side effects, often ten-fold, and usually some that aren't even on the side effect list! This is why I choose not to use many pharmaceutical medications except the ones to replace the hormones my body doesn't make on its own (insulin and thyroid hormone). Those on the autism spectrum may need to experiment with dosage of their pharmaceuticals. Temple Grandin, a popular autism advocate and animal sciences professor, notes that, for those on the autism spectrum, antidepressants may need to be prescribed at one-quarter to one-half the normal starter dose (Grandin, 2012) due to sensitivities that accompany an autism diagnosis.

Conversely for me, with some holistic treatments I need very potent doses, more than 99% of all patients! My homeopath says, "You come in here intense, so it makes sense you'd need a stronger homeopathic remedy!" Thankfully, she lets me listen to my own body and is willing to prescribe differently for me than any of her other patients. Sometimes a remedy dose that might stay effective in a traditional person's body for a month lasts for me less than 24 hours before I need another dose.

Taking a Deeper Look at Health Complaints

Food sensitivities are common for those with autism. Unfortunately, the awareness of how some of these foods can affect us in body, mind, and spirit is often sorely lacking among patients and providers. Many on the spectrum complain of such things as exhaustion, migraines, stomach aches, headaches, and pain of all kinds. While there may be other physical causes worth exploring, few may realize these quality-of-life-reducing symptoms may be caused or worsened by the very foods they are eating—many of which are eaten for comfort to deal with how distressing the autistic life can be!

While food sensitivities won't be the culprit of everyone's health issues, for those who feel unexplainably poor—not only with physical symptoms but also possibly depression, insomnia, anger, rage, and anxiety, and so on, the possibility of food sensitivities should be explored. Taking certain foods out of my diet per the suggestion of my healthcare team has improved my health immeasurably.

How Providers Can Help

When your autistic patient feels unwell and traditional doctors say there is nothing more they can do—it's what I heard for years, too, with respect to my depression and other troubling health issues such as digestive complaints and headaches—this is when a referral to a functional medicine provider or naturopath can be extremely beneficial.

Functional medicine practitioners can explore underlying food sensitivities, make diagnoses that other doctors may be overlooking, and suggest useful lifestyle and self-care strategies. There is always more that can be done to help your autistic patient feel their best. Don't underestimate them or give up hope. Just because we struggle or are disabled in some ways does not mean we should feel awful physically, too!

Relationships

Being in relationships can be painful with the many confusing and hurtful ways humans behave. This is most definitely intensified by an autistic's inability to interpret non-verbal and decipher communication due to our difficulty reading between the lines. When people act passive-aggressively, or cold, or are just not very verbally affectionate or warm, it can leave our heart and brain without the data we need to make sense of things. Conflict is difficult for many autistics to navigate and I often spend large chunks of my therapy appointments discussing social scenarios and figuring out how to navigate my way through them to find peace and happiness again. Many of us feel people are the most challenging part of life and that we would mostly get along just fine in the world if it were not for the demands non-autistic individuals sometimes place on us that we cannot live up to.

How Providers Can Help

It's important for providers to treat us as individuals. Be open to our differences and the unique insights we share. Textbook knowledge alone will never work in attuning to our specific needs and providing us the best care possible. This is why hearing autistic voices is so important through keeping up with various blogs and social media outlets where autistics openly share their stories and experience.

We are "out of the box" not only in our thinking, experiencing, and perceiving of the world, but in so many other ways, too. Even if you've never experienced x, y, or z with another patient, and it doesn't seem physically or scientifically possible for it to be happening to your autistic patient, don't be surprised it's occurring with us! Open your mind to what you've never experienced before! We really aren't the same; many of us feel like aliens dropped off on the wrong planet and often have a body, mind, and heart expressing themselves in extraordinary ways.

Armchair Researchers with High Attention to Detail

Know that autistics tend to be natural researchers. For me, this has put off a few doctors along the way and impressed the socks off others: one endocrinologist told me I'm smarter than any endocrinologist he works with! A doctor I saw last month who specializes in sleep paused me halfway into the appointment and said, "You sure have a lot of medical knowledge!" This extensive knowledge is because of my autism. Health, specifically holistic health and functional medicine, has become a special interest of mine and I'm quite educated about it, at least regarding the conditions I'm afflicted with. I can piece together random pieces of information and come up with theories about my body involving a complex interplay of symptoms, conditions, and treatments to make wild, often accurate hypotheses about what might be going on or what I need to move forward and heal. I'm often right. We can be more knowledgeable than our providers about some things, especially about our own bodies, and research is our strong suit. The challenge can be getting providers to listen to us.

Additionally, we are extremely thorough, detail-oriented, and conscientious. It might surprise you when we come to you with a long list of notes and go into extreme detail when describing a health situation or any other scenario that has come into our lives. I guarantee you, what feels like a million words to you is most likely only the tip of the iceberg for us.

How Providers Can Help

Know that those with autism are natural researchers, and often have had to research to make sense of our symptoms. Let us research and be educated, and don't be intimidated or frustrated by it. Our inquisitive mind is one of our greatest gifts, and this inquisitive mind is how we learn, process, and make sense of things. Know that our questions are not meant to challenge you, but to gain a deeper understanding which feels extremely comforting for us. In my case, the combination of my research and persistence is how I have attained the health I have, despite the serious conditions I live with.

Be thorough and conscientious yourself. Don't become frustrated with us for what is a natural ability. We cannot *not* be this way. As is sometimes said, "Autistics can find the needle in the haystack, but they cannot see the hay!"

Struggles with Executive Function

Executive function is an area of struggle for many of us. What does this mean? It means planning, organization, and time management are challenging for us. We may be late to our appointments despite disciplined effort to be on time. If we have any extra stress added to our lives, what little executive function we seem to have can be completely thrown out the window. This for me could be a poor night's sleep, too much socializing, or not enough transition or down time. These things tend to be extremely wearing for us and eat into our ability to be present and functional.

How Providers Can Help

Be patient and understanding with your autistic patients. We are not trying to be jerks! We most likely care very much, it's just that life is hard for us and we get stressed out easily! Being on time is challenging for many of us, as is being organized. Work on strategies to help us, but please be gentle in your approach. Keep in mind: if we have anything else going on (e.g., stressors, health challenge, poor sleep), any current challenging behaviors or improvements we've made might temporarily take a step back.

Sensitivity to Criticism

We are extremely sensitive to criticism and absolutely hate being misunderstood. This sensitivity to criticism is why we go into so much depth about everything, just to try to prevent the unpleasant feeling! If you assume you know what we will say or what we're about, this is infuriating for us! We are much more complex than you could probably wrap your mind around.

How Providers Can Help

Just listen and try to hear us without gathering too many assumptions upfront. There is so much pressure from the neurotypical world we need a place to rest, be ourselves, and be understood. Additionally, we are extremely adept at finding fault with ourselves, so if you have feedback, make sure to give it "sandwich style," as in, share a positive first before letting us know something we might need to improve on, and end again with a positive.

Intuitive Beings

We are intuitive. This might surprise you given how unaware we can seem about some other things. But we know things. We sense things. While we have our limitations in certain areas, in others we can have extraordinary abilities. After 13 years on my holistic journey to health, I have become deeply intuitive and insightful about my own body.

How Providers Can Help

Do not override our intuition or think it's silly or untrue. Understand that we are not made the same and some day when they can track our brains people will be amazed at our abilities and how we ever survived in the world the way we do. Trust us. For many of us our deep sense of knowing comes out to be true and spot on. It's like we have antennae, many of them, picking up what most people miss.

Summary

It has been a pleasure to outline some of the insights I've gained through living with autoimmune disease over three decades as an individual on the autism spectrum. I hope it has been helpful for you as you seek greater understanding of autistic individuals. Please keep in mind we are all unique! One thing I can say is autistics will challenge you, perplex you, and possibly frustrate the heck out of you at times. Know we also get frustrated with ourselves. But we are intensely loyal, loving, and interesting, and will always teach you something new and perhaps offer you, albeit unintentionally, a novel way to look at life. Be open to us and what we bring to the table: we may bring a more present, simple, and joyful approach! It is my hope you have gained a richer appreciation and understanding of what autism looks like so you can care for us in ways that feel nurturing and supportive. We appreciate your efforts tremendously!

Resources for Professionals and Families

- Autistic Not Weird: https://autisticnotweird.com/
- Spectrum Women Magazine: www.spectrumwomen.com/
- The Aspergian: https://theaspergian.com/
- The Yellow Ladybugs (Autistic Girls and Women): www.yellowlady bugs.com.au/

About the Author

Cynthia Zuber is an autism and autoimmune disease/holistic wellness writer from Minneapolis, Minnesota. She was diagnosed autistic at age 40 after a successful yet tumultuous life filled with so many questions and a profound sensitivity like no person she had ever known. Learning her lifelong challenges were due to a difference in brain wiring finally freed her to create a life she enjoys filled with peace, joy, and acceptance for herself in all her uniqueness. Honoring her life calling, she passionately shares her writing to an international audience in the tens of thousands where she guides and supports others in their journeys to wellness. You can find Ms. Zuber at The Neurodiverse Woman: https://m.facebook.com/theneurodi versewoman/.

References

Aaron, E. (1997). *The highly sensitive person: How to thrive when the world overwhelms you.* New York, NY: Broadway Books.

Grandin, T. (2012). Temple Grandin, Ph.D.: Frequently asked questions. Retrieved from www.templegrandin.com/faq.html

Part XI

Encouraging Health and Wellbeing

In the midst of chronic anxiety, sleeping and eating concerns, and medication changes, it can be easy to forget to ask about actual health and wellbeing. It is vital that we ask our clients about what is going well for them, and help them learn to find balance in life. Further, it is important to teach about the mind–body connection as well as the very functional aspects of hygiene and self-advocacy in the health care system.

In this part we hear from three leaders in the field about what they find to be vital to healthy living. We understand that folks on the autism spectrum have a unique biological makeup that needs to be addressed in medical offices, requiring patients to advocate for themselves. You may need to directly inquire about medical concerns in your office and help your clients access proper care. We also learn how to talk about hygiene-related concerns directly, something our clients sometimes need. Finally, we bring the mind and body together once more, remembering how much energy it takes to navigate the social world, coupled with techniques to self-soothe and center a person in a taxing situation. Health and wellbeing (the very thing all therapists want to access) will need to be directly discussed in your office.

31 I Got Fired by My Primary Care Physician

Anita Lesko

I have nearly 60 years of experience living on the autism spectrum; I didn't discover I was on the spectrum until the age of 50. As a therapist, you will be on the front lines of care for our unique population, and I'd like to enable you to provide top-rate care! However, as a healthcare provider who's autistic, I know inferior care lurks out there. Unfortunately, many of those on the autism spectrum avoid seeking health care because of past negative experiences. There is a valid reason for this. The vast majority of health care providers know little, if anything, about autism. In a large survey of health care providers, most admitted to lacking knowledge to properly care for this population (Zerbo, Massolo, Qian, & Croen, 2015).

They don't know what it's like living with it, they don't know how to communicate with us, or see the need for alternative routes to wellness, nor are they aware that many of us might not react to medications like the majority of neurotypical individuals do, instead causing numerous side effects, some life-threatening. It is not uncommon for those with autism to get treated with little or no respect by health care providers, brushed off as "crazy," marginalized, or even "fired" from the health care provider's care for various reasons.

Nearly two years ago I discovered I have diabetes. My primary care physician wrote out several prescriptions for the traditional medications to treat the condition and sent me on my way. I had numerous violent reactions to each one, rendering me homebound for days. I immediately went online looking for natural ways to treat diabetes. In fact, there *are* ways to naturally treat it with specific foods and walking 30 minutes a day. Several months later I returned to the physician for follow-up bloodwork, which was now normal. He thought I was taking all the pills. When I informed him that I wasn't taking any pills, but treated the diabetes naturally, thus no disastrous side effects, he flipped out. I explained what happened from the pills. He didn't want to hear it. I mentioned I have anxiety, which is part of having autism. That freaked him out too and he then stated that I don't need to see him any longer, and that I instead need to go to a psychologist instead of a doctor, so I was fired as his patient. By the faces he always made, it was obvious he was glad to be rid of me. The feeling was mutual.

How Therapists Can Help

As therapists, you can educate your patients on the need to find a health care practitioner who takes all the healing philosophies into account. The mind, body, and spirit all go hand in hand. All patients, particularly those on the autism spectrum, must be honored as an individual with unique biology, genetic makeup, and life circumstances. To approach health care with autism patients any other way is not simply unjust, it may be life threatening. Integrative medicine is what I *highly* recommend. This type of practitioner spends time with the patient to collect a full history and to understand the genetic, environmental, lifestyle, and any other factors which influence physical, mental, and emotional health. (Included in the *Recommended Resources for Professionals and Families* are three websites for your patients to locate an integrative medicine practitioner.)

Given that there are so many health care providers who lack the knowledge to provide care for those with autism, you need to teach your patients how to advocate for themselves within the health care system. Until they are able to locate an integrative care provider, they will have to navigate whatever is available to them. They must be encouraged to advocate for themselves, which may be difficult for some to do. In circumstances where the autistic individual is unable to advocate for themselves, you must teach their care-giver/family member how they can do this.

Teach Self-advocacy in the Medical Realm

First, you must instill in your clients that they have the *right* to receive health care just like anyone else. You can educate them to take steps to make the health care visit a more productive event. Most with autism will get overwhelmed by sitting in over-crowded waiting rooms which are brightly lit, noisy, filled by many different smells, with the TVs playing, and thus massive sensory overload. Tell the person to call the facility they are going to and directly request to be seated in an area away from all stimuli, and ask for a place to wait where it's quiet, with minimal people, and not so bright. If this phone call is made ahead of time, the facility can already be prepared for their arrival and they can be escorted to the separate area. Next, the autistic patient can request that anything that needs to be done (obtaining vital signs, bloodwork, any special test) be explained prior to the activity commencing. The autistic patient must also alert the facility of any special needs such as their desire to text their communication, possibly the need for time to process what the health care providers are saying to them, and to not marginalize them because they are different. All of these suggestions are discussed in my book *The Complete Guide to Autism & Healthcare* (Lesko, 2017). Until all health care providers are educated to care for the autistic population, each person is going to have to advocate for themselves. Once a person self-advocates several times in the medical realm, it will become second nature. Until then, you as their therapist must provide them with the information and encouragement to take the bull by the horns, as I like to call it.

Teach Awareness about Medication Sensitivities

In circumstances where health care providers want to prescribe medication for whatever reason, if the autistic patient has bad/unusual reactions to that medication (or any other) they must discuss this with the provider. If the provider isn't interested in listening to them and coming up with alternative methods/drugs to treat them, it's time to look for another provider. There are cases of autistic patients dying from drug-related reactions (Autism Research Institute, 2019). This must be taken seriously by health care providers, and it is up to the autistic individual or their caregiver/family member to advocate for their safety. Most commonly prescribed drugs have side effects that range from minor to severe to potentially fatal. Many on the spectrum suffer from seizures or are prone to seizures, and many of the drugs commonly prescribed to individuals on the autism spectrum may lower the threshold for having seizures. Additionally, many people with autism also have underlying mito-chondrial dysfunction issues (most don't even know they have these) (Siddiqui, Elwell, & Johnson, 2016), that also predispose them to having bad/serious/fatal reactions to otherwise commonly prescribed drugs.

Suggest Regular Check-Ins with a Preferred Provider

You can also emphasize to your autistic patients the importance of maintaining their health, including visiting a health care provider once a year for routine checkups and bloodwork. Raised blood pressure, diabetes, and other conditions might be silently occurring without displaying obvious symptoms. If there is something causing pain, or any unusual symptoms, autistic patients need to understand the importance of seeking health care immediately, and not putting it off until the situation becomes dire, which is typically the case. Hopefully you will develop a rapport with your autistic patient which will gain their trust in you, which in turn will give them the confidence they need to advocate for themselves.

Make Additional Accommodations for Visits in Health Care Facilities

You may also make suggestions to your clients with autism to take dark sunglasses along with them to their appointment to counteract fluorescent light. They might also consider bringing some kind of noise-cancelling device to minimize sound in case they have no other options of a quiet zone. During this time, while sitting there, they can be taught to use visualization to focus on a calming vision in their mind to take away anxiety and instead focus on the "happy place" they are visualizing.

Visualization and Neuroplasticity

In my book, *Becoming an Autism Success Story* (Lesko, 2019), I enlighten the reader of the powers of the mind; visualization can be extremely powerful for someone on the autism spectrum. Through the ability of the brain's way of changing, its neuroplasticity, I was able to re-wire my autistic brain. This enabled me to do things I otherwise would never have been able to do. For example, how many civilians do *you* know who got to fly in a U.S. Air Force F-15 fighter jet? Or have a 30-plus-year career as a Certified Registered Nurse Anesthetist which necessitates *extreme* executive functioning on all aspects? Your patients can learn the seven steps I clearly describe in great detail on how to learn to use visualization. They can use this to decrease anxiety, and also to enable them to achieve their dreams and goals. Almost everyone wants to have a productive and fulfilling life. Those on the autism spectrum are no different.

Sanctuary in the Saddle

Horses saved my life. I say this for a number of reasons, but the movement you experience when on the back of a horse is literally life-changing for an individual with autism. Obviously when I was young, I didn't know I was on the spectrum, thus my "horse therapy" wasn't formal and wasn't conducted by therapists. However, the results came from the very best teachers, the horses themselves. Each horse has a different gait. Some are very smooth, and others have huge, bouncy gaits. Guess which horses I was attracted to? The ones with the huge gaits! Unknowingly, the motion was stimulating my vestibular system, making me want more and more!

I can remember to this day the very first time I was in the saddle at age two. I can recall when the pony started walking, my whole world changed. I was mesmerized by the rhythmic movement. I focused all my attention to it, and tuned out the rest of the world. From that moment on, each time I rode a horse the world went away. That movement is what awakened my entire body, enabling me to start assimilating my arms and legs, and gaining total body awareness, in sharp contrast to the zero body awareness I had prior to riding. This is exactly what hippotherapy does for others. I highly recommend parents seek hippotherapy for their autistic child/adult if it is anywhere near them. The rewards are life-changing and priceless. Whether it's a child or adult, it is never too late to get involved with horses, though sooner is better. Being at the stable also got me out of my autism shell, because I wanted to start talking to others about my beloved horses. There are numerous studies about horse therapy autism, all showing positive results (cf. Gabriels, Zhaoxing, Guérin, Dechant, & Mesibov, 2018).

Virtually all aspects of being involved with horses will yield positive effects for your patient with autism. Individuals on the autism spectrum typically have an affinity for animals, making them in and of themselves very therapeutic. Horses especially seem to have this effect and can foster numerous positive changes. As most kids with autism are, I was *extremely* uncoordinated as a child. Over the years as I rode horses and worked around the stable, I gained mastery over my balance and my body. Horses can improve self-esteem and confidence, and enhance work ethic. I started working at the stable at age twelve through twenty-two as a working student. I not only worked my way up to becoming a top-level equestrienne who could make six-foot-high jumps, I developed life skills which enabled me to become a successful adult (cf., Lesko, 2016).

Summary

Those with autism need support and need to be active. Because I didn't learn I'm on the spectrum until the age of 50, I obviously never had *any* form of therapy, Individualized Education Programs, or other formal supports. However, the most helpful aspects of my development was that I was always out there *doing* stuff. Encourage your autistic patients to do exactly that! Get out there doing things, even as a child. Discuss with the parent the need to get the child doing various jobs around the house. This not only teaches work ethic, but with a chores allowance or other monetary award, it teaches the child the life skill of earning money, saving for something special, and purchasing it. Get them to try different sports, clubs, hobbies. When they find something they really enjoy, capitalize on it! It might be something that later turns into a life-long career. Suggest doing volunteer work in a hospital, a community project, a religious organization, a local food pantry/soup kitchen, and so on. Again, it might lead to a career. I became a volunteer at a local hospital in my late teens, which led to getting interested in earning my BSN for nursing, then becoming a nurse anesthetist. My good friend Temple Grandin, as most everyone knows, discovered her love for animals on her aunt's ranch, which led to her world-famous career in the meat industry.

Last but not least, enlighten your patients on the spectrum to the power they have within themselves, their power of the mind, to tap into it to achieve their best life possible. My husband is also on the autism spectrum. Early in our relationship I gave him a coffee mug with a saying on it which reads, "Life Begins at the End of Your Comfort Zone." This is very true for everyone on the autism spectrum, as routine is a safe zone. However, you will not get very far by staying in that safe zone, and therapists can help and support those with autism as they venture into the unknown.

Recommended Resources for Professionals and Families

*   Lesko, A. (2017). *The complete guide to autism & healthcare*. Arlington, TX: Future Horizons.

- Lesko, A. (2019). *Becoming an autism success story.* Arlington, TX: Future Horizons.
- Lesko, A. (2018). *Temple Grandin: The stories I tell my friends.* Arlington, TX: Future Horizons.
- Lesko, A. (2011). *Asperger's Syndrome: When life hands you lemons, make lemonade.* Bloomington, IN: Universe.
- Attwood, T., Evans, C., & Lesko, A. (2014). *Been there. Done that. Try this! An Aspie's guide to life on earth!* London, UK: Jessica Kingsley Publishing.
- Cook, B., & Garnett, M. (2018). *Spectrum women: Walking to the beat of autism.* London, UK: Jessica Kingsley Publishing.
- Anita Lesko: www.anitalesko.com
- American Hippotherapy Association: www.americanhippotherapyasso ciation.org
- Professional Association of Therapeutic Horsemanship International: www.pathintl.org
- Institute for Functional Medicine: www.ifm.org
- The American Board of Integrative Holistic Medicine: www.abihm. org/search-doctors
- Integrative Medicine for Mental Health: www.integrativemedicinefor mentalhealth.com/registry.php
- Autism Research Institute-Adverse Drug and Supplement Reactions: www.autism.org/adverse-drug-reactions/

About the Author

Anita Lesko is an internationally recognized autism activist since being diagnosed at age 50. A Columbia University graduate, Ms. Lesko has a 30-year career as a Certified Registered Nurse Anesthetist, specializing in anesthesia for neurosurgery, organ transplants, trauma/burns, and orthopedic joint replacement surgery. Ms. Lesko is an award-winning author, motivational speaker, member of the Autism Society of America's Panel of Spectrum Advisors, Board member of the International Board of Sensory Accessibility, Certified Executive/Life Coach, United Nations Guest Speaker, internationally published military aviation photojournalist, animal rescuer, and married to her soul mate, Abraham, also autistic. Visit Ms. Lesko at www.anitalesko.com or contact her at anitalesko1@gmail.com.

References

Autism Research Institute (2019). Adverse drug and supplement reactions. Retrieved from www.autism.org/adverse-drug-reactions/

Gabriels, R., Zhaoxing, P., Guérin, N. A., Dechant, B., & Mesibov, G. (2018). Long-term effect of therapeutic horseback riding in youth with Autism Spectrum Disorder: A randomized trial. *Frontiers in Veterinary Science, 5,* 156. doi:10.3389/fvets.2018.00156

Lesko, A. (2016). Sept 25). How childhood jobs prepared me for success as an autistic adult. Retrieved from https://themighty.com/2016/09/how-childhood-jobs-prepared-me-for-success-as-an-autistic-adult/

Lesko, A. (2017). *The complete guide to autism & healthcare: Advice for medical professionals and people on the spectrum.* Arlington, TX: Future Horizons.

Lesko, A. (2019). *Becoming an autism success story.* Arlington, TX: Future Horizons.

Siddiqui, M. F., Elwell, C., & Johnson, M. H. (2016). Mitochondrial dysfunction in autism spectrum disorders. *Autism-open Access*, *6*(5), 1000190. doi:10.4172/2165-7890.1000190

Zerbo, O., Massolo, M. L., Qian, Y., & Croen, L. A. (2015). A study of physician knowledge and experience with autism in adults in a large integrated healthcare system. *Journal of Autism and Developmental Disorders*, *45*(12), 4002–4014. doi:10.1007/s10803-015-2579-2

32 Why Good Hygiene and Grooming?

Mary J. Wrobel

For most of us good hygiene and grooming are givens. We know if we didn't bathe daily, apply deodorant, wear clean, appropriate clothing, and groom ourselves, people would assume there was something wrong with us (e.g., depression, mental illness, homelessness). Whether we go to school, work, and social events or just hang with friends, we make sure we are clean and look our best. We also know how to dress for any variety of social, formal, and work situations. As individuals, we may have our own style of dress, but how we groom and clothe ourselves is within the parameters of what is socially acceptable. Most people also pay attention to what is stylish, and update their clothes and hairstyle periodically. This is all about being acceptable to others.

For individuals on the autism spectrum, hygiene and grooming can be challenges. Before embarking on addressing grooming with autistic clients, the therapist needs to ascertain *why* the individual is having difficulties. Often, they are unaware of the importance of good hygiene and grooming. Other times, poor hygiene can be attributed to underlying depression and/or anxiety, which is prevalent with autistic individuals. Depression or anxiety can also cause clients to inadvertently appear belligerent and resistant to any changes. Before successfully addressing hygiene and grooming issues, as a therapist you must address any depression and anxiety with the client prior to embarking on hygiene education. Once any underlying depression and anxiety are addressed, your likelihood of successfully addressing hygiene will be markedly improved.

Pointing Out Hygiene Can Help Clients Meet Their Goals

Addressing hygiene and grooming with individuals with autism can be difficult, because they may be simply unaware of what they need to do on a daily basis. They may also not care how they look and smell, and see no reason for improvement. Perhaps they were dependent on others tending to their grooming needs and never developed a hygiene routine on their own. They may be comfortable in the clothes they wear, despite wearing clothes that are old, damaged, ill-fitting, and dirty. They may not know or care that their poor hygiene/grooming is off-putting to others, and hence they may resist change and even refuse to implement an appropriate hygiene/grooming routine. This can be a challenge for both families of the individual with autism as well as for the therapist.

However, it may be obvious to you that one of the reasons your client is unable to get or maintain a job and has few or no friends, including a lack of intimate relationships, is due to his/her poor hygiene and grooming. Unfortunately, this may not be obvious to your client with autism. In fact, your client will probably see nothing wrong with the way (s)he looks. One of the first steps you must take with such a client is to convince him/her that daily hygiene and a good grooming routine are important in order for them to meet their life goals.

One of the popular strategies for fitting in is for individuals with autism to pretend to be like everyone else, and that starts with looking like everyone else. When people are well dressed, any odd behaviors are more often overlooked than if their appearance is unusual or unkempt. When someone looks good, people may be more forgiving of odd or inappropriate behaviors. Being clean, smelling good, wearing nice clothes and accessories, and having an appealing and appropriate hairstyle all contribute to how we appeal to and impress others. You need to convince your clients with autism that if they want to get and maintain a job, find friends, and develop intimate relationships, they need to have good daily hygiene and grooming.

You can also point out that there are important health reasons for routinely washing, bathing, and maintaining good hygiene. Regular teeth brushing and flossing help to prevent cavities and gum disease (and extra trips to the dentist), as well as the added benefit of fresh breath. Washing our hands, body, and face/head helps to combat illness, viral and bacterial infections, and possible infestations.

As a professional, you may be concerned about bringing up the topic of bathing and grooming with a client on the spectrum. You may be one of the few people outside of the family willing to broach the topic, and you can do so successfully if you maintain a sense of respect and avoid shaming clients. Because your client has autism, you need to be direct and specific when addressing these issues. Keep your language clear and simple and avoid any subtlety and euphemisms. You can ask them questions related to what they do or should do. For example:

* How often do you shower? How do you feel about showering?
* Do you have a daily hygiene routine you follow? How do you feel about hygiene?
* How often do you wear different outfits? How do you feel about changing your clothes?

Developing a Hygiene Routine

Convincing an individual with autism to improve their hygiene and grooming won't be enough. It will likely be necessary that you help them develop a hygiene routine and teach them how to achieve steps toward successful grooming. Remember that individuals with autism need and want rules to follow. They do best when their day is structured with predictable routines. With your client's input, develop a daily hygiene routine checklist. Include everything they need to do. Advise them to hang the list in their bathroom or bedroom and check it every day to insure they have completed the routine. Use the example in Figure 32.1 as a guide.

If necessary, write Social Stories™ (Gray, 2000) or comic strip conversations with your client to help them better understand the steps, as well as the necessity of performing specific hygiene and grooming tasks. A Social Story™ will include a description of the task, specific steps or directives, and should also include the perspective or concerns of the client (cf., Wrobel, 2003). A Social Story™ provides a visual example of the desired behavior that involves the individual in the change process, and reinforces positive behavior.

Privacy Reminders

Remind clients that personal hygiene and grooming should be private, and not typically done in the presence of others (unless in a locker room/shower room). Certain hygiene or grooming behaviors would be viewed as inappropriate if performed in public. If such behaviors are done near others, people will not be forgiving of you and will typically be offended or grossed out. If you know your client performs certain inappropriate behaviors in public, emphasize the rules for privacy, discretion, and hygiene. The personal and private behaviors shown in Figure 32.2 should *not* be done in public, especially if others can see you.

Since many of these behaviors are unhygienic, not only are they not done in public, but your client should be reminded to wash hands after engaging in any behavior that is germy, gross, or dirty. Furthermore, remind your client that we don't talk about these private behaviors with others, as it would be offensive to most people.

Looking Your Best Is about Good Grooming

You may have a client who wants to look cool and attractive or just fit in with peers and co-workers. Grooming is the essential step to looking our best, but it starts with a clean body and clean clothes. No matter where you are or who you are with, good grooming is what makes you look and feel your best in any social situation. If your client is having a hard time getting a job and making friends, it might not be due to hygiene issues, but could be a result of poor grooming.

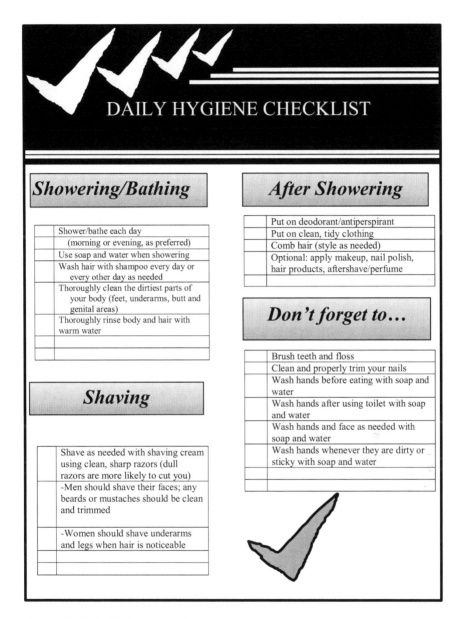

DAILY HYGIENE CHECKLIST

Showering/Bathing

Shower/bathe each day
(morning or evening, as preferred)
Use soap and water when showering
Wash hair with shampoo every day or every other day as needed
Thoroughly clean the dirtiest parts of your body (feet, underarms, butt and genital areas)
Thoroughly rinse body and hair with warm water

Shaving

Shave as needed with shaving cream using clean, sharp razors (dull razors are more likely to cut you)
-Men should shave their faces; any beards or mustaches should be clean and trimmed
-Women should shave underarms and legs when hair is noticeable

After Showering

Put on deodorant/antiperspirant
Put on clean, tidy clothing
Comb hair (style as needed)
Optional: apply makeup, nail polish, hair products, aftershave/perfume

Don't forget to...

Brush teeth and floss
Clean and properly trim your nails
Wash hands before eating with soap and water
Wash hands after using toilet with soap and water
Wash hands and face as needed with soap and water
Wash hands whenever they are dirty or sticky with soap and water

Figure 32.1 Daily Hygiene Checklist.

When it comes to grooming, a person's hair should be combed, styled, and be of appropriate length. If a client seeks assistance with his/her hairstyle, recommend them to first check out their peers and co-workers for hairstyles, and find a style that suits them best. A hairstylist can help

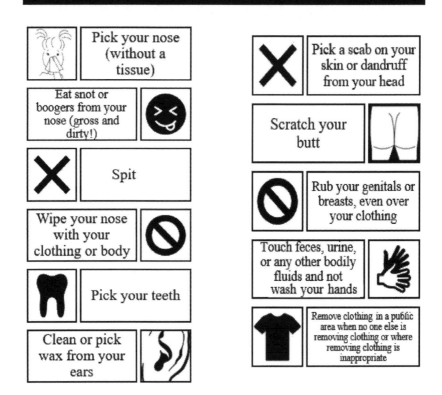

Figure 32.2 Personal Private Behaviors *Not* to be Done in Public.

determine and create an appropriate cut and style. Clean hair is a must, but if a client's hair is untidy, too long, or very outdated it may ruin their overall appearance. Figure 33.3 introduces a grooming checklist.

Clothes need to be neat and clean, but also fit well, and items need to match or at least go together. When approaching the subject of clothing, ask your client questions about his/her clothing decisions and preferences. Is your client even aware that the clothes (s)he chooses are inappropriate? The grooming checklist in Figure 33.3 may help your client stay on top of his or her hygiene and grooming needs.

My Grooming Checklist

Check the checkbox with a ✔ when a task is completed.

- I'm wearing clean clothes which are appropriate for the day's activities
- My clothes match or go well together
- My clothes are not too old, faded, or out of fashion
- My clothes look nice with no unwanted rips, holes, stains or broken zippers or missing buttons
- My shoes, socks, belt and other accessories go with my outfit
- My shoes and coat are clean
- My hair is clean, combed, and styled nicely
- My teeth are clean and my breath is fresh
- My face, hands, and nails are clean
- Any makeup I am wearing looks appropriate
- I look good!

Figure 33.3 Grooming Checklist.

What to Wear and When

Finally, remind your client that we dress for different events. There are rules to wearing clothes, including what to wear for specific events and situations. What a client wears in the privacy of his/her own home is up to

FASHION RULES FOR DRESSING

☑ Always wear clean, tidy clothes that fit you appropriately.

☑ Clothes, accessories and shoes should match or go together well.

☑ Clothing shouldn't be too worn out or damaged, unless you are painting, cleaning or gardening.

☑ Make sure clothes and shoes aren't too old or outdated compared to the ones your peers or co-workers are wearing.

☑ Make sure clothing is appropriate for where you are going, such as work, a date, sports event or wedding.

☑ Be sure you have a variety of clothes and shoes for everyday activities, such as work or school.

☑ Don't wear the same clothes every day, even if they are clean (the exception would be any uniform you need to wear for school or work).

☑ Don't wear the same pair of shoes every day and to every event (casual shoes are worn with casual clothes and formal shoes are worn with formal clothing).

☑ Try to wear individual shirts and dresses only once a week.

☑ Wear clothes that are similar to those of your peers and co-workers, and ask peers and family about what to wear to specific events.

☑ Check yourself out in the mirror before you leave home to be sure you look clean, tidy and ready for where you are going.

Figure 32.4 Fashion Rules for Dressing.

that person, but when your client leaves the house for work, school, or a special event or situation, he or she needs to dress accordingly.

We typically wear casual clothing when going to school or hanging out with friends. But people normally wear tidy, nicer clothes to work. People like to wear team logos and casual clothes to sports events, and specific outfits to special theme events. Funerals and weddings usually call for formal wear and suits. Any time we paint, clean, or work in the garden, we should wear old clothes we don't care about ruining. Many times, individuals with autism don't understand the rules to wearing clothes and as a result of their poor fashion sense they stand out and look odd. Unfortunately, people will judge them according to what they wear. Figure 32.4 introduces some fashion rules for dressing.

Remind clients of the rules of dress, and if they don't know what to wear for an event, they can ask family members or others who are attending the event with them. Women often ask other women what they are wearing to an event to help themselves decide what to wear. Tell your client to always check out peers and co-workers and pay attention to the clothing and fashions they wear. Your clients need to learn to dress like others, with a variety of clothing for different events.

Summary

For most of us, hygiene and grooming are something we give little thought to. Yet individuals with autism may need to be taught these important skills. Therapists need to be direct about hygiene and grooming needs. Not paying attention to these needs can stand in direct opposition to client goals, which may include increased autonomy and social acceptance. Therapists need to educate about specific hygiene routines, help develop checklists, help clients understand privacy rules, and know what specific clothing to wear and when. As you deal with some of these difficult client issues, you need to remember that part of your job is to help your client feel confident, accepted, attractive, and successful. Helping them to fit in with peers and co-workers by instilling good hygiene and grooming skills will assist them be more self-assured and successful with relationships and in life.

Resources for Professionals

- Attwood, T., Grandin, T., Bolick, T., Faherty, C., Iland, L., Myers, J. M. ... Wrobel, M. (2019). *Autism and girls: World-renowned experts join those with autism syndrome to resolve issues that girls and women face.* Arlington, TX: Future Horizons.
- Simmons, K. L. (2006). *The official autism 101 manual.* Sherwood Park, Alberta, CA: Autism Today.

Resources for Families

- Wrobel, M. (2003). *Taking care of myself: A hygiene, puberty and personal curriculum for young people with Autism.* Arlington, TX: Future Horizons.
- Wrobel, M. (2017). *Taking care of myself2: For teenagers and young adults with ASD.* Arlington, TX: Future Horizons.

About the Author

Mary Wrobel has written books and articles on autism and spoken nationally to parents, teachers, and various professionals/therapists for more than 25 years. Her first book, *Taking Care of Myself*, a hygiene, health, puberty, and personal safety curriculum for students with autism and related disabilities, won the Autism Society of America Outstanding Literary Work of the Year Award, Educational Division for 2004. Her most recent book, *Taking Care of Myself 2*, is a guide for teens and young adults with autism, and covers the topics of hygiene, health, public behavior, relationships, personal safety, and sex and sexual relationships. She has also contributed to two previously published books: *Autism 101 Manual* (Autism Today) and *Autism and Girls* (Future Horizons). Ms. Wrobel can be contacted at mary@autismtherapysite.com and on her website: www.autismtherapysite.com.

References

Gray, C. (2000). *Writing social stories with Carol Gray*. Arlington, TX: Future Horizons.

Wrobel, M. (2003). *Taking care of myself: A hygiene, puberty and personal curriculum for young people with autism*. Arlington, TX: Future Horizons.

33 Mentoring Successful Living in a Social-Energetic World

R. Vicente Rubio

You are complete as you are.

This message has been at the heart of my work with disenfranchised students since 1981—from street-smart survivors discarded by the system, to students with autism spectrum (AS) conditions, whom I have taught for years in my dance and aikido studios in New York, California, Hawaii, and Oregon. As an undiagnosed autistic child in the 1960s, I had to deal with everything going on within me internally, as well as the bewildering, raw hatred of racism externally. I was bullied, belittled, and shamed. Many of your clients have been, too. You can see it in their uncontrollable shakes and sweats, their darting eyes and panting short breaths, their oversensitivity to physical proximity, and their fight-or-flight response to others' touch, their sleepless nights, and their uneaten meals because of the fear of an up-coming social event—like going to school.

As someone diagnosed with autism as an adult in 2010, I also knew what it was like to struggle to connect, coordinate my body, and modulate my attention. I knew from deep within, too, to communicate to these students the same message I am now writing to you, the same message you must communicate to your clients: *You have what you need because you're a whole, complete person.*

The Social Energetic World

As one on the autism spectrum I have come to experience that being 'human' among other humans is a 'social-energetic' existence, unless I am living in a cave detached from the human world around me. The social experience is living, interacting, and creating a harmonious, meaningful, and successful life with other humans. 'Energetic' is defined in my practice as *life-force, manna, chi, and ki*—the underlining energy that allows living beings to thrive and prosper. This underlying energy also connects us to other life forms, nature, the earth, and the Universe.

Engaging socially with other humans requires energy. It takes energy to be mentally sharp when under stress. It takes energy to build and maintain physical stamina to stay calm when anxious. It takes energy to be clear in thoughts and language when communicating verbally or in writing. Living successfully amongst other humans is an energetic connection of giving and receiving energy from those around us. We exchange, gain, and lose energy when we interact with other life forms. It is a social-energetic world we live in. The health of our own energy, our life-force, allows us the opportunity to flow harmoniously in this highly charged social world that now exists.

It All Starts With a Relationship: Interpersonal Rapport, and Intrapersonal Mind–Body Connection

As a therapist, you already have extensive training in establishing rapport. You also know that many of your clients struggle with establishing relationships, or meeting the expectations that others impose on them. They may enter your office feeling broken, perhaps unskillful at relationships, even as you are starting to build a relationship with them. Your training has taught you that the basis of therapy is the establishment of a relationship, which creates the context for everything the therapist models and teaches. You are taught to use the relationship to teach skills, but without the relationship, you have nobody to teach. Your autistic clients require you to feel and see their pain, and see their bravery in the act of showing up to your office, and the many steps it took for that client to arrive in your office in that moment. As you begin to interface with them, they will interface with others. As you show compassion, they will show compassion to others. They will copy you, especially as you create opportunities for them to lead.

Once you have a strong relationship established, based on seeing your client as a whole, healthy, complete person, you can gently draw attention to how they experience the world, and how they can skillfully navigate their environment. You can teach your client to connect socially, and also how to read their physical body for clues, and modulate their attention. As a dance instructor and martial arts instructor, I have observed that making the mind–body connection is vital to human connection and a happy, healthy life.

When I was training to be a dancer in New York City, I began to learn how to understand the mind–body connection. I would sit on the steps of the Public Library on 42nd St and Fifth Avenue and watch people walk by. I would note how they carried their body weight, how they would lean to one side, or were hunched over, or lead with their head with their shoulder up by their ears. Later, in theater classes, I would learn how one carries their body to express joy, anger, depression, surprise, and so on. I learned how to use the 'facial mask' to express emotions, and was now able to 'read' the expressions of others through their facial expressions!

All the physical information I was learning on how to be a dancer/actor allowed me to begin studying myself. How was I breathing? Where did

I hold the energy of surprise? Or shame, anger, and sadness? Where did I go mindfully when I was stressed or anxious? Does my facial expression match the emotional message I am trying to convey?

Through constant self-evaluation and attention, I began to learn to 'read' the early bodily signs of a pre-meltdown in myself when under duress or experiencing fear. I acknowledged the heat building around my ears and back of my neck. My shoulders would hunch up for a fight. I noticed how my eyes darted around the room, not able to stay focused, scanning for a threat. At the same time, I would observe how I was cognitively expressing the anxiety and stress I was experiencing.

I began to notice the language and words I would use that would preempt a negative physical expression in me. I registered the negative thoughts of giving up, fleeing, or fighting. This observation check list allowed me time to *choose* to decompress or detach from what was making me anxious and stressed. Today, I live a life of constantly noting how I am feeling, processing, and expressing during any social event that I am engaged in. I learned also that when I am alone in a four-walled room with a door that can lock, then I can stand down and relax. This knowledge manifested in my work with students; consider the following case scenario.

Rene, a 13-year-old female client on the autism spectrum, was a 'cutter,' overeating from depression from body and social shaming, and physically aggressive and violent. Rene was a pudgy little girl with a beaming smile and glowing eyes when calm. Her arms and legs were laced with self-inflicted scratches and fine cuts. Highly imaginative and sturdy in frame, Rene hated herself and her world of constraints, being odd in her behavior of being bossy and commanding in social peer group interactions, experiencing uncontrollable anger when not getting her way, or feeling persecuted by her family and schoolmates who were the recipients of her destructive behavior.

I first aligned with Rene by understanding what she was experiencing, using the pain in my personal past as a guide to understanding. After I had honestly showed that the difficulties she was experiencing happen to all of us at one point or another, she relaxed. Once she relaxed, I was able to teach her breathing and stress reduction visualizations and games. As she responded to this approach, we developed a vision of what a healthy, safe, and happy self-image looked like for her. She realized she did not have to look as others do. She also realized that if she wanted to be connected with others, she needed to decrease her behaviors that alienated others. Over time, she learned to express her anger in healthy ways that people could 'hear' and respond to. She blossomed into a glowing young lady, losing her body armor (including losing actual weight), and having healthy relationships.

The Mind–Body Connection

As a young boy I was severely punished for simple things like spilling a cup of milk, dropping a bottle of catsup, being too slow to move, answering too slowly, and just being 'too stupid and spacy.' I could not throw a ball, catch a ball, dribble a basketball, or shoot a basketball; I never was asked to play in any school yard games or picked for any team sports. I was a team liability and a laughingstock. Needless to say, I was a loner at school recesses and play time.

Coordinating my mind (i.e., my intention) and my body (i.e., my physical manifestation into action) was a very daunting and confusing concept to grasp as a child. What seemed easy for other students to do was tremendously hard for me. Being beaten at home and bullied at school for the lack of a physical presence and fluidity in action did not make the learning process any easier for me.

Modulating my attention was wishful thinking for my parents and teachers. How was I supposed to modulate my attention (mindfulness) if I was not even connected to my physical body? I was an undiagnosed autistic child of the 1960s, inflicted at 4 years old with traumatic brain injury (TBI) to my frontal lobe area from a beating, and struggling with posttraumatic stress disorder (PTSD). I displayed severe stuttering when I spoke and nervous bodily twitches, I was easily startled by sound or physical touch, and was weak-lunged with a caved-in defensive body posture. I would quickly detach my mind from my body when being yelled at and physically hit. All these challenges kept me far from being grounded in the here and now, and fleeing to my secret place of the fantastical world of my wildly vivid imagination of peace and safety was my haven.

It took years, yet in the end, I would create and follow a path of self-discovery in helping myself understand how I processed the social/physical world; where I failed or was successful in my evolving life socially and physically with others; utilizing what activities and studies allowed me to be 'me,' and creating a career and livelihood outside the constraints of a 'normal' world where I did not fit in. And through the hardships and pain of many life trials by success and error, the sorrow of many failed relationships, and the depression of being alone, I learned how to focus my mind, how to build and strengthen my body, and how to be coordinated and graceful. Most importantly, my success spoke about my willingness to recognize the social and life skills challenges I faced without illusion; that I was aware I had many positive out-of-the-box choices to help me make changes for the better, and that I had developed the discipline and strength to marshal my procrastination and depression to achieve the successful completion of my goals.

Breathing

Through years of holistically observing my autistic clients and acknowledging my own autistic behaviors, I witnessed how breath can be altered by emotional, cognitive, and physical stimulation. Fear, shame, guilt, self-doubt, and anger can gut a healthy breathing cycle, creating a shallow, anaerobic wisp of respiration—yet as simple as this sounds: *breath is the essence of life for all animals, including humans.* Like a skipping stone on the water, cognitive information in therapy is pointless if a client is not mindful and in his energetic body: the information skips away into a powerless void. Thankfully, full, healthy breathing can be learned. Consider the following case scenario.

Lance was a 12-year-old client with major social anxieties who was reluctant to leave the house for fear of what others might think about him. I started slowly, introducing the awareness of his breathing when he was calm and when he would get stressed. Lance and I observed how, when he was faced with just the thought of engaging socially, he would begin to pant, grow anxious, then angry, and then become resistant to any and all suggestions. I found out that he never could play school-yard games and engage in social fun because he was physically uncoordinated and slow to understand games. In time, Lance slowly understood that, when he was calm in his breathing, his mind was relaxed and open, and the fictional anxiety in his head would subside. I helped change his language from, 'I am always this way' to 'I was this way in the past (one day ago, one minute ago, five years ago …) and I choose to be think/behave differently in this present moment.' This breathing work went hand in hand with training in developing his self-esteem and embracing his uniqueness of being on the spectrum through the visualization of how talented, creative, and resilient he actually was; and anchoring this mindful strength in his body by the physical training in things he hated: catching and throwing balls, running, and staying engaged in play even when frustrated and wanting to give up. His fears subsided when he understood how to manage the 'chattering monkey' in his mind by taking the time to pause, breathe, and trust himself—faults and all.

Mind

In my professional dance career (1980–2003), we practiced dry-running the piece first in our heads (vision). Then we physically rehearsed on stage (intention) to prepare for a successful performance (manifestation). Visualization is powerful—and you can use it with your clients to achieve diverse goals, from tackling a personal hygiene issue or learning a new social skills tool to physical acts like catching a rubber ball or learning to ride a bike (even as a young adult).

Most people on the autism spectrum are already out-of-the-box thinkers. With proper guidance, they can create proactive solutions to their challenges, so they can *live!* They can visualize each step in a process, clearly—

one step after another. Visualization clarifies intention, shapes articulation, and propels intention into vibrant, empowered, self-directed action.

In teaching visualization, I start with a simple exercise that shows anyone how easy it is practice visualization:

> Visualize or see in your mind's eye an apple. See it? Great! You did that quickly, didn't you? You see you have a library in your brain with many files, like your computer storage. You can easily go into your library and fetch or access the file on 'apples' and so you can 'see' or visualize an apple. OK! Let's try visualizing an orange; now try a tree. Simple! Good, now visualize yourself in a calm place where you are happy and in your confident and powerful self. See that place? It could be just the perfect place you want it to be. Is it in the water? Floating in the clouds? Under the earth? Just be playful with your imagination and let your creative self run wild! Great! So, in the future we will use this visualization tool to 'see' the plans and solutions to achieve your goals and continue to build your confidence and stamina for your growing life!

Body

It is a bewildering experience to grow up, not understanding autism. I didn't understand why I was different, nor how to fit in. I was bullied, beaten, shamed, and given insufficient compassion and support. It's thus no wonder that some children on the autism spectrum are traumatized around others and untrusting of the 'people world' around them. I have often heard from my autistic clients of the pain, embarrassment, and shame inflicted upon them by an ignorant society that devalues them for being who they are: a fellow human who experiences and processes the world through different lenses. And it is that pain, embarrassment, and shame they carry forward into their evolving life and see themselves through the perception of others who have bullied, insulted, abused, taunted, patronized, thrown away, and pushed away from the 'herd.' The only things left to a person on the autism spectrum are self-doubt, self-disgust, and self-ridicule.

Many of your clients have had this same experience. I had to find my own path out, but your clients have you for support!

Now, as a martial adept, I've trained to be consistent in applying the techniques I learned for successful outcomes. It was in consistent, hard, repetitious training in ballet and aikido that I learned these techniques 'old-school.' How I trained on the dojo mat was how my training would manifest on the street. How I trained in dance was how I would hit the stage when the curtains rose: performing fearlessly what I had uncompromisingly practiced—with joyful abandonment of self-doubt and low self-esteem.

'Dry-running,' reciting, or rehearsing anything with your client you wish him or her to try and practice when s/he is away from you is a great way of building confidence and empowering the self. This is also a perfect opportunity to strengthen executive skills functioning. For in the practicing and dry-running of anything you wish to express, there are clear steps and a structured way to accomplish the goal.

First, know that whatever you are introducing or wanting your client to learn will be broken down to the essential building blocks of that information: less is more. This is also the phase in which you co-create with your client a vision on how the client will practice calmly and safely on their own, taking breathing breaks to remain calm and anxiety-free.

Second, when instructing the client, slow down the tempo of your speech and find a comfortable tone of voice which is of a medium key—not too high or too deep in tone. Speak as if you are speaking to an alert and ready child: ready to process, learn, and needing a compassionate instructive presentation.

Third, repeat these instructions with patience and timing until the client has it down enough to repeat it with you. In time, as you use this teaching model, you will see your client slowly build self-confidence and self-esteem as they now 'own' for themselves what you are teaching them. You had helped your client to process the information at her/his pace and capabilities. They will get stronger emotionally and physically as their energetic stamina of self-esteem gains volume and identity.

To figure out the context we're in, the options we have, and what to do next, each of us carries forward our past experiences in our mind–body, looking for ways our experiences might be relevant. Being on the autism spectrum, I know how easy it is to allow the toxic and debilitating memories of my past failures and disappointments to pop up in my head before the 'good times' memories do. I have observed in my autistic clients a developed 'comfort zone'—that giving up before trying something is founded on memories of past failures and disappointment. It is an easy escape route to surrender to procrastination and stagnation because why try? 'I will fail anyway.' Drawing on positive memories or being detached from the emotional drama of negative memories is a matter of choice to do just that, to detach or attach. The choice to decide to choose peace over chaos can only be made when the mind–body is trained to be calm and confident.

Thankfully, seeing a traumatic experience on a tangible timeline can help anchor that experience in the past (relative to today), so it's less present in real-time interactions. Using a timeline, it's easier to shift language: 'I have been … ' rather than 'I am … '. It's easier to explore the reactions we've had, too—to envision new possibilities and to choose to deviate from past reactions.

Summary

Mind–body mentoring, like therapy, is about being a good listener and out-of-the-box thinker—even playful, like a child. For your clients and for yourself, compassion, presence, and perseverance are learned—so find a mentor if you need one. Then create a healthy, successful interface with your client—and enjoy the journey!

Resources for Professionals and Families

- Rubio, R. V. (2008). *Mind-body techniques for Asperger syndrome.* New York, NY: Jessica Kingsley Publishers.
- Rubio, R. V. (2014). *Odyssey of woolly mammoth boy: One man's journey through autism, racism, grief, and surviving the American dream.* Palo Alto, CA: Together Editing Press.

About the Author

R. Vicente Rubio is a fifth dan in aikido and a practitioner of the martial arts since 1980. He has worked in the field of autism in private practice and consulting since 1990, drawing upon his martial arts training, degree in dance from SUNY New Paltz, New York, and 23 years of experience as a professional dancer, and is the author of two books (see *Resources for Professionals and Families*, above). Today, Mr. Rubio's volunteer work includes tending public rose gardens, providing health-fitness classes to seniors, and teaching meditation and health classes to the economically disenfranchised. You can reach him for workshops or consultation at www.pathfindermentoring.com.

Part XII

Using Strengths to Drive Skill Growth

While we would all like to believe we are providing strengths-driven interventions, all of us sometimes get stuck on a particular symptom that is perhaps stubborn to treat. We can easily imagine a client with a clear interest in a topic who will revert to a monologue on that topic when anxious, and also imagine parents worried that their child will struggle socially because of that same topic. A savvy clinician will figure out how to invite that facet of personality, special interest, or symptom (depending upon your perspective) into a treatment plan to facilitate success.

In this part we see how some interests last a lifetime, and how these interests can be consistently employed to facilitate growth. We are reminded that resilience requires us to adapt to challenges in life. We see that neurodiversity should be celebrated, and that recognizing that exact neurodiversity may be a pathway to enhancing self-image and self-confidence, and even forming friendships or landing a job.

34 Combining Strength-Based Therapy with Behavior Analytic Approaches to Treatment

Autumn Vendramin and Patricia Belmas

From Einstein to Emily Dickinson, individuals on the autism spectrum can provide profound contributions to society. Learning how to assess for and harness these strengths while championing client special interests can be extremely helpful when applied to therapeutic treatment strategies. Strength-based intervention practices are vitally important to the therapeutic process to help make therapy more meaningful and engaging for the client.

The stressors associated with the responsibilities of adulthood while managing autism can be overwhelming for both the individual and their family. For clinicians in traditional mental health therapy settings, assessing skill deficits and strengths, identifying the function of behavior, choosing effective strategies, developing a collaborative treatment plan, and maintaining progress across environments for individuals with autism can be a daunting task. It is essential to have a comprehensive understanding of the individual's autism spectrum symptomology and choose evidence-based models to intervene successfully. In this chapter, traditional counseling methods are blended with applied behavioral analysis while incorporating client interests to drive increased client motivation.

Prior to starting therapy, it is recommended to conduct a thorough assessment of an individual's wellbeing across areas such as medical history, social, academic, career, family, and self as an important starting point. Effective behavioral and psychosocial interventions that target improvements in communicative and relational interaction skills include:

- **Incidental and responsive teaching**: create a teaching environment with typical activities where a client's interests are incorporated and emphasized in learning goals.
- **Peer and family-mediated interventions**: involve others in the prompting and practice of teaching a new skill.
- **Cognitive behavioral therapy**: utilizes strategies to produce changes in thinking, feeling, and behavior.

- **Acceptance and commitment therapy (ACT)**: ACT incorporates mindfulness techniques with behavior change strategies to increase resilience in thinking.

Incorporating Special Interests and Strengths Throughout Treatment

Individuals with autism commonly have strong topics of interest that can absorb their time and focus. Engaging in conversations and activities surrounding topics of interest can be a great source of happiness and comfort to a client with autism. Topics of interest can change periodically or can remain for a lifetime. Showing interest in and including a client's preferred interests can assist the client in feeling comfortable while engaging in the therapeutic process.

Intense interests can be expressed differently. Two people can both have an interest in geology but express that interest in unique ways. Some autistic individuals are great at logical thinking and rote memorization while others excel at visual thinking, or math/pattern thinking, or excel with more hands-on learning. Autistic individuals often feel positive emotions, including enthusiasm and pride, when actively engaged with their special interest.

Preferred interests can be encouraged by incorporating them into therapeutic and educational experiences. Explore ways to harness specific topics of interest that may be underutilized by the client, such as:

- Utilizing thoughts related to interests to assist in self-regulation and coping, or for a calming effect during stressful or crisis situations
- Advancing, launching, or changing a career or trade
- Attaining a college degree or taking college classes on the subjects of interest
- Enhancing social engagement by joining groups, conferences, workshops, or clubs that surround the topic(s) of interest
- Interacting with online chat forums or groups about special interests
- Creating an online blog or vlog on topic(s) of interest.

It is important to evaluate the intensity of the interest(s). Preferred topics of interest can become problematic when they interfere with the overall wellbeing and daily functioning of the individual. If it interferes with relationship development, relationship satisfaction, or family life, the clinician can assess and discuss this with the client. The client may not fully realize how much their special interest may dominate their time or attention, which may lead to the erosion of relationships over time. It may be helpful to have a spouse, partner, or other family members join sessions to address this topic in a family therapy context. Clinicians can also delineate between special interests and obsessive-compulsive behaviors, which could hinder growth and may need more specialized treatment.

Assessing Function to Guide Treatment Recommendations

Conducting a functional behavioral assessment (FBA) is helpful in the process of developing an effective treatment plan. An FBA is a procedure of determining the underlying purpose, or function, of a behavior so that effective intervention strategies can be developed. Discerning the function of a behavior (e.g., overworking to avoid family stressors), rather than just its form (e.g., overworking by 3 hours per day), leads to different and more personalized therapeutic interventions. Once the function is identified, the clinician chooses interventions that help to decrease concerning behaviors and increase desired behaviors.

An ABC (antecedent, behavior, consequence) assessment is one way to understand the client's context to assess the function of a behavior. *Antecedent* describes what happened before the behavior occurred. *Behavior* describes the client's behavior which is being targeted for assessment or change. *Consequence* describes what happened in the environment after the target behavior occurred.

Clinicians can easily create and individualize an ABC data sheet for a specific client to record targeted behaviors. Adult clients can complete the ABC sheet as a self-report document. When beneficial, a parent/guardian can complete it for an adolescent. Figure 34.1 shows an example of an ABC data sheet as entered by an adult client.

Date	Time	Antecedent	Behavior	Consequence
Date of incident	*Time of behavior*	*What happened before the behavior? What was the context, environment like?*	*Observable behavior. What did you do and say?*	*What happened after the behavior? What did you do after the behavior? What did others involved do?*
May 2	1:15 pm	My wife talked about our trouble conceiving. Attended family event where another couple announced pregnancy and just got back home. Wife keeps talking and crying.	I listened to my wife talk about having a baby. I yelled at her to just accept it!	Wife yells at me, says I'm "unbelievable" and "insensitive." She leaves the house. I watch my favorite show about fishing.

Figure 34.1 Example of ABC (Antecedent, Behavior, Consequence) Data Sheet.

By assessing these three conditions for targeted behaviors across environments and across several weeks, a clinician can gain valuable information as to what occurs in the environment when the client demonstrates the targeted behaviors. Once the context of the behavior or skill deficit is better understood, the clinician can determine the primary function of the behavior. The function of behavior helps a clinician assess "why" a person is engaging in a particular behavior.

As described by Iwata et al. (1994), the four main functions that maintain behaviors are:

- **Escape/avoidance**: The individual behaves in order to get out of doing something he/she does not want to do.
- **Attention seeking**: The individual behaves to get focused attention or access to relational reinforcers from others.
- **Seeking access to materials**: The individual behaves in order to get preferred items or to participate in a desirable activity.
- **Automatic reinforcement/sensory stimulation**: The individual behaves in a specific way because it feels good to them, and may not need others to accomplish.

As in the ABC data sheet example above (Figure 34.1), the clinician determines that a client's yelling at a spouse primarily serves to avoid an emotionally difficult topic. By yelling, the client avoids discussing the topic, and it temporarily gets the spouse to leave. The yelling behavior with the spouse functions as avoidance. Without the ABC information to help determine the function of yelling behavior, the function of avoidance may have been missed, or it may have taken much longer to determine why the client engages in verbal altercations with his spouse, resulting in less effective strategies being implemented.

Once the clinician assesses the primary function for the target behavior(s), the clinician can incorporate and teach effective replacement behavior(s) for each target behavior. An effective replacement behavior will serve a similar purpose for the client but be more socially or relationally appropriate. Using the previous example of yelling, the replacement behavior could be to teach the client to ask for a break or to self-soothe during difficult conversations.

Information obtained from an ABC data sheet can be used to address areas such as communication difficulties, behavioral challenges, school or work readiness, academic achievement, and adaptive skills. It is essential to collaboratively choose target behaviors with the client. The following should be considered when developing treatment plan goals:

- Select meaningful objectives with the client and start with attainable goals that the client is highly motivated to accomplish.
- Too many goals or goals that are too difficult initially can be daunting and can increase frustration with the therapeutic process.

- When choosing goals, choose no more than three at a time.
- Break down the skill or concept into small components.

Clinician's Role as a "Therapeutic Teacher"

It is important for the clinician to see their role as a "therapeutic teacher" who is an active participant in the change process. This is accomplished by understanding how to communicate and teach in a way that engages the autistic client.

Interpreting the subtleties of both verbal and non-verbal communication can be difficult for a client with autism. It may be helpful for the clinician to utilize a communication style that is clear and straightforward. The use of euphemisms, sarcasm, hyperbole, and allegory, and being too verbose, or even too loud in volume may be overwhelming to the client on the spectrum. This may lead to unintended misunderstandings; therefore, it is helpful to ask the client directly if any conversation styles are bothersome or cumbersome to them. This simple strategy can enhance the treatment process for the autistic client, and can provide valuable information to the clinician as to how the autistic client navigates the social world outside of the session room.

Clinicians can incorporate specific interests unique to the client while applying these interventions:

- **Visual supports**, such as pictures, written words, objects within the environment, schedules, or concept maps, and timelines help to organize and explain complex social and communicative concepts. Visual representation of concepts can be displayed on paper or digitally.

  For example, a young adult client will be living in a dorm room for the first time and is concerned about new daily tasks, such as walking to the shower from the dorm room. A list of pictures of essential items to gather before walking to the shower is developed with the client. The client likes anything to do with outer space; therefore, the clinician uses themed, galaxy paper to help make the visuals more appealing.

- **Social narratives** are an effective tool to teach social scenarios that help to explain complex relational scenarios. To create a social narrative:

  ○ Identify the social situation and setting to be practiced.
  ○ Identify the target behavior to teach and define it operationally.
  ○ With the client, collaboratively write a social narrative based on the client's unique needs, taking into consideration the client's cognitive level.
  ○ Use visual cues, including pictures, photos, or symbols, considering the client's unique interests and strengths.

- o   Read, discuss, and rehearse the social narrative with the client, and consider its application in the targeted setting.
- o   Review the data and results of the intervention that the client records when practicing in their natural setting.

For example, a client is having difficulties with casually speaking to coworkers. Using the steps above, the clinician incorporates the client's interest of pop culture by choosing several scenes from popular sitcoms to discuss and analyze how the characters are engaging with their coworkers. The client practices with the clinician and then tracks progress throughout the work week.

- **Task analysis** is a procedure where an activity or behavior is divided into small, manageable steps to teach each component of the larger skill. Between sessions, the clinician assigns skill practice through specific homework that is written and broken down into very small components. Ask the client to document progress during each step, including successes and barriers, and celebrate progress toward each step.

   For example, the client's goal is to learn to unpack and organize his backpack after school and a preferred interest is music. The clinician will assist the client in creating a task analysis by breaking the task into smaller steps. To incorporate a special interest, the clinician can insert each step into the client's favorite song melody and teach the song with the lyrics being each step of the task analysis.

- **Video modeling**, a visual prompting strategy, can be used to facilitate skill acquisition. This teaching method includes a client watching a video of someone completing an activity or skill and then imitating the activity themselves. The clinician develops a task analysis for the skill being targeted and then videotapes the client, clinician, or another person performing the task based on the task analysis. This strategy works well when the video can be played on portable devices so that it can be viewed immediately preceding the skill.

   For example, the client's topic of interest is football and the goal is to teach the individual to engage others in conversation without monopolizing it. The clinician creates a video showing conversations about many interests, including football. The video can be used to model how to have a conversation with the topic of interest present without dictating the conversation.

- **Self-management strategies** empower the client to take ownership of learning new skills. Self-management skills focus on the client discriminating between appropriate and inappropriate behaviors within a goal, monitoring and recording their own behaviors, and rewarding themselves for progress. There are two types of behavior changes with self-management: (1) something the client would like to do more frequently; and (2) something the client would like to do less frequently. Smaller components that are within reach should be encouraged, especially initially.

For example, a client wants to decrease social media use. The clinician can assist the client to assess usage habits, develop daily strategies to avoid social media use, and identify what can be used as reinforcers toward progress.

By incorporating these methods into practice, the clinician is increasing effectiveness by combining strong teaching practices with core therapeutic and supportive approaches.

Summary

Applying behavioral analytic techniques to a strength-based model of therapy yields better treatment results for clients. Finding creative ways to incorporate special interests and strengths enhances a client's motivation to develop new skills. Clinicians as "therapeutic teachers" can apply these techniques in treatment to improve client outcomes.

About the Authors

Autumn Vendramin, LMHC, BCBA and Patricia Belmas, LMFT, BCBA are dually licensed clinicians and co-owners of Life Strategies, LLC, an accredited Behavioral Health Center of Excellence operating out of three locations in Northern Indiana. Life Strategies, LLC, provides intensive Applied Behavior Analysis (ABA), behavioral consultation, and traditional mental health therapy, while specializing in the behavioral treatment of individuals with developmental disorders and autism. Learn more at https://life-strategies.net/.

Reference

Iwata, B. A., Pace, G. M., Dorsey, M. F., Zarcone, J. R., Vollmer, T. R., Smith, R. G., ... Willis, K. D. (1994). The functions of self-injurious behavior: An experimental-epidemiological analysis. *Journal of Applied Behavior Analysis, 27,* 215–240. doi:10.1901/jaba.1994.27-215

35 Motivation, Interests, and Activation

Susan L. Hepburn

As a clinical psychologist who works with individuals on the autism spectrum and their families, I believe our primary goal as clinicians is to promote resilience for the family and for all of the individuals within the family. Resilience has been defined in many ways; however, the definition proposed by renowned developmental psychologist, Ann Masten, has shaped my thinking on this topic: "Resilience is defined as the capacity of a system to adapt successfully to significant challenges that threaten its function, viability or development" (Masten, 2018, p. 1). Thus, whether acting as a diagnostician, therapist, or consultant, I try to keep this concept in mind. The emphasis on adapting to challenges is particularly important, as it implies that acceptance is happening – each individual in the family is endeavoring to accept the others for who they are, and each is trying (to varying extents) to adjust their expectations, behaviors, attitudes, and beliefs in a manner that helps the family to achieve balance and feel connected and supported by one another in a healthy way.

In my experience, resilient families struggle like other families, and they experience grief, loss, disappointment, and conflict like all families. But what distinguishes resilient families is that they are flexible when challenged and have learned to pivot to a different way of being that is consonant with their experiences. And this pivoting often requires letting go of long-practiced patterns of behavior and sometimes requires realigning values and priorities in an unexpected way. Pivoting to accept an unusual interest as a genuine enthusiasm can help to promote meaningful learning opportunities for people with autism. For example, consider the following case study that describes how a family's ability to embrace their son's unusual special interest led to several powerful social and emotional learning opportunities across his childhood, adolescence, and young adulthood.

Scott and the Lottery Numbers Game

As a house manager at a residential program for adults with autism, I once worked with a 26-year-old man (let's call him Scott) who was fascinated by state lotteries. He had kept a journal of the daily winning lottery numbers in several states in the Midwest throughout his childhood and adolescence. From the time he was in fourth grade, his parents, both busy lawyers, sat and listened to Scott read his lottery number lists for several minutes each morning. This routine calmed Scott immensely, and his parents reported that they often had a pleasant conversation with their son following this recitation, which meant a lot to them. If one of his parents was away on a business trip, Scott dictated the number list into a phone message. Neither of his parents had anticipated receiving cheerful recitations of Kansas' daily Powerball on their voicemail, but they adjusted to incorporate this interest into their daily routines; in other words, they pivoted quite well.

Accepting Scott's special interest allowed for several social learning opportunities. When Scott wanted to bring his lottery log book to middle school so that he could read his lists to a few classmates, his parents grew concerned that he would be bullied or teased for his unusual interest. They dissuaded him from taking his log book to school by relying on two reasons: (1) something could happen to his book – better for it to stay safely on his shelf; and (2) lottery numbers is a "family game." The second explanation led to a discussion about how different people like to play different games, and that as long as an interest didn't hurt anyone, whatever makes a person happy is fine to do – but in the right place and at the right time. Lottery numbers was a game for mornings with the family. It could be a game with friends, but it's not a game to play with people whose names you don't know. *This last rule gave Scott a very clear rule to consider when deciding whether or not to share his interest in lottery numbers. This particular rule has also been employed when teaching him how to adjust his behavior for familiar versus not familiar people (such as: when to hug/ kiss someone and when to shake hands or give a high-five).*

Many years later, when Scott moved into a residential program (where I met him), he maintained his log book with care and diligence. However, he only offered to read the numbers out loud to very few staff at his day or residential programs. Scott would gleefully announce if a staff person had earned access to his lottery numbers: jumping up and down excitedly, pointing his finger repetitively at the person he's thinking about. Using full names to identify the staff person and himself, he'd announce his proclamation in the voice of a game show host, laughing throughout: "Kevin Rhodes – you are the next listener on Scott (last name)'s Lottery Numbers Game!" His declarations were frequently met with cheers and applause from other staff and residents; his daily announcement became a house ritual we learned to expect and, like his parents, we enjoyed his joy, and appreciated his enthusiasm.

If not enough people were around to cheer, Scott might repeatedly say to several of us "Scott's Lottery Numbers Game is fun for family and friends, right? Yes … fun for family and friends," as if seeking reassurance. One of our social workers used that experience to teach Scott about disappointment, and repeating and rehearsing that word for how he felt when fewer people were around to hear his announcement helped to make the word concrete and meaningful, I think, as within a few months, Scott volunteered that he felt "disappointed at not-shotgun" (meaning that he didn't get to sit in the front seat). Learning to verbalize this instead of getting upset when it was another resident's turn to sit in the front seat was an important social-emotional skill for Scott, and his strong interest in lottery numbers provided a salient context for teaching these abstract concepts.

Scott also seemed to appreciate the autonomy and control his Lottery Numbers Game gave him within the busy residential program. Scott lived with three other young men with developmental disabilities, two of whom could be pretty disruptive at least a few times per week, sometimes throwing things or yelling or attempting to hit or kick staff. Thus, the program was heavily staffed, with two or three direct care providers in the home at all times. As an only child, Scott had grown up without needing to accommodate the behaviors of others, and this transition posed quite a challenge to his self-regulation. When another resident behaved in a way that bothered Scott, he would announce, "Jimmy Peirce will not be on the Lottery Numbers Game tonight?" He repeated this phrase a few times, but usually stopped when a staff person echoed the phrase back to him: "That is correct, Jimmy Peirce will not be on the Lottery Numbers Game tonight" – and then would add a positive phrase about a skill or behavior that would be more adaptive – "he needs to practice his inside voice." This last phrase was also frequently repeated by Scott a few times, and then usually closed the interaction. Thus, his special interest provided a salient vocabulary for expressing frustration with someone else's behavior and identifying a better alternative. Having a verbal routine – or script – around being frustrated by the behaviors of his housemates was very helpful in teaching Scott how to regulate his emotions in social interactions.

This same verbal routine eventually became a functional way for Scott to express his frustrations with a staff person. Direct care staff were focused on promoting independence and required more independence from Scott than he had been used to at home. So, like any of us being prompted by another person to do something, Scott sometimes became frustrated with his direct care staff. His initial response was to yell profanities and insults at the staff person, and when the staff person ignored these outbursts, his behaviors would escalate, making it difficult to coach him through the task. So, the behaviorist on the team suggested we shape his comments into his Lottery Numbers Game language and allow him to express his autonomy and feel some sense of control by deciding on game access. If a staff person prompted Scott to do a task or chore he didn't like and he started to yell, the staff person would say: "You can decide on the Lottery Numbers Game. Right now, please ... (clear your plate from the table)." This seemingly small intervention worked very well for Scott and he appeared to be satisfied expressing his resistance in this particular way. I can't say that the frequency of Scott's initial resistance to staff prompts decreased markedly during the two years I worked with him, but the intensity of his emotional reaction and his ability to regulate well enough to complete the task did improve.

How Can Parents or Professionals Identify a Relevant Strength and Utilize It in Instruction?

In Scott's case, his interest was readily apparent. There are certainly other situations where it is not easy to identify an interest that can be integrated into learning opportunities. A good question to ask a person (and/or his/her parents and providers) is some version of "If you had free time to do anything you wanted, what would you do?" or"Is there anything that you like to do (or talk about) more than other people?" If a verbal interview is not fruitful, consider taking the person to a place where different objects/interests are physically located in different parts of the space, such as a bookstore or toy store, and observe where the person goes and spends the most time. This is an approach that is often used in formal reinforcer probes, where potential rewards are positioned around a room and the person is allowed free access to all items, while an observer notes the number of times the person visits a particular area (e.g., light-up toys, building toys) and also notes the duration of interaction with specific items.

Sometimes, parents and caregivers are very aware of a person's interest, but view it as too unusual to be functional and may not mention it. Often, parents will report that it is really difficult to allow a child brief access to his favorite thing, knowing that leaving it will be problematic. As a result, families may actually avoid being in situations where their child's interest is explorable. For children with autism, who tend to have a limited repertoire of interests, missing the chances to pursue what makes them happy can contribute to irritability and difficulty motivating them to do things they do not intrinsically wish to do. In my experience, it can be very helpful to tackle how to engage and disengage from a special interest in a very deliberate manner. Once some routines are learned for managing leaving a favorite activity, those same structures can be brought to other transitions and contexts.

For example, Christopher is an 11-year-old boy I met when he and his parents came to clinic for a developmental evaluation. When I asked his parents what activities he enjoyed, they described how he didn't play with toys, and listed several specific age-appropriate toys he had rejected. When

I asked when he was happiest, his parents paused and looked at each other for a few seconds before the father said:

> You're going to think we're a little nutty but, Christopher loves fans – the bigger the better. On Sundays, he and I go to the landscape store really early so that he can visit the huge fan in the greenhouse. He'd stay there all day if we let him. He just stares at it, jumps up and down, flaps his hands a lot – we call it "doing the fandango." It's all good and he's really happy until it's time to go and then half the time he just falls apart. It's gotten so that I'm not even sure it's good for him to go there if he's going to have such a hard time leaving it.

In talking with Christopher's parents about his interest in fans and his challenges leaving after doing the fandango, we developed a plan for thinking about these Sunday field trips as times to practice appropriate transitions. We identified several ways to structure the fan visit routine to make it clear and predictable for Christopher. For example, his father used three picture cards to show a "first, second, third" sequence (first, look at fan; second, push cart; third, look at fan). By practicing two transitions within each routine, Christopher's father could encourage leaving the fan the first time, doing something else very briefly, and then returning to the fan. Thus, Christopher could practice leaving the fan without being completely done for the day.

Christopher's father also started using a consistent carrier phrase ("In two minutes, we will push the cart") to signal that the current activity will end soon. By using this phrase for easy transitions (e.g., "In two minutes, we will visit the fan") as well as the more challenging ones, the carrier phrase seemed to get Christopher's attention fairly quickly. Then, his father could wait a minute or so – using his judgment as to when Christopher's attachment to the current activity was beginning to wane – and then he'd announce the actual transition: "It's time to push the cart." The parents were encouraged to follow through once they said, "It's time to ..." but to allow for more warm-up time for the transition when giving the "In two minutes ..." instruction. For Christopher, practicing good transitions within this high-interest routine seemed to help him to learn those carrier phrases more quickly. His parents reported using similar verbal routines to coach him through many different transitions at home and in the community.

What are Some Ways that Interests Can Be Integrated into Activities at Home, in School, and in the Community?

There are a myriad of ways that a person's interests can be integrated into tasks or activities that are not necessarily inherently reinforcing. See

Table 35.1 for some real-life examples of infusing interests into tasks in different settings for persons of different ages and functioning levels. In each of these examples, a parent, teacher, or therapist considered the unique preferences of a person with autism and found a way to bring that interest into a particular learning task or used it as a reward upon completing the task.

Table 35.1 Examples of Ways to Integrate Interests into Non-Preferred Activities

Setting: Home

Task/Activity	Who?	Interest	How Interest was Integrated
Chores (rotating list of three daily chores posted on fridge: e.g., take out trash, feed dog, wipe table, and so on)	12-year-old boy	Insects	Found a plastic model of an insect that had three parts – head, thorax, abdomen; when he finished a chore on his list, he earned a piece of the model; when he earned all three pieces and built the model, he earned access to a set of "special" insect toys and books that were kept separately from his usual toys.

Setting: School

Task/Activity	Who?	Interest	How Interest was Integrated
Math worksheets (addition, subtraction) and attending school	Eighth-grade girl	Weather	Weather-related cues were used to frame worksheet problems; e.g., addition was about rainfall; subtraction was about temperature. This middle school student was offered the chance to do the morning weather report on the PA system each Friday, contingent on her attending school 3/4 days each week, which really helped counter her school refusals.

Setting: Work

Task/Activity	Who?	Interest	How Interest was Integrated
Filing papers alphabetically	25-year-old woman	Dolphins and other sea life	Learned to file alphabetically by filing papers with names of dolphin species and other marine life.
Breaking down computers into parts for recycling	38-year-old man	*Star Wars*	Practiced differentiating parts into bins labeled as different components for making R2D2 and other droids; picture cards of each computer part were labeled with terms from movies.

Summary

As professionals, it is our job to promote resiliencies in families with a member on the autism spectrum in the face of everyday challenges posed by the autism. One way to adapt to these challenges is to use the client's special interests in ways that help families feel connected. At times, families avoid the special interest in an effort to get their autistic family member to focus on other things, or because they fear what happens with the individual must shift gears from the special interest. However, special interests can be used productively to aid the individual in gaining a sense of autonomy and control. The interests can be an avenue for change, and if harnessed properly can be an exciting way to enhance clients and their families.

Recommended Resources for Professionals and Families

- Higashida, N. (2013). *The reason I jump: The inner voice of a thirteen-year old boy with autism.* New York, NY: Random House.
- Suskind, R. (2014). *Life, animated: A story of sidekicks, heroes, and autism.* New York, NY: Kingswell.
- Autism Certification Center: https://autismcertificationcenter.org/video-gallery/23
- Spark-Special Interests in Autism: https://sparkforautism.org/discover_article/special-interests-in-autism/
- Special Interests: www.autismspeaks.org/science-blog/autism-and-social-skills-complicated-role-special-interests

About the Author

Susan Hepburn, Ph.D. is a clinical psychologist and Professor in Human Development and Family Studies at Colorado State University. Dr. Hepburn directs the Strengthening Autism Identification Across the Lifespan (SAIL) projects at CSU, where she is actively involved in research, outreach, and consultation services focused on improving access to timely developmental evaluations for rural youth. Dr. Hepburn can be found at www.chhs.colostate.edu/bio-page?person=susan-hepburn-2370.

Reference

Masten, A. S. (2018). Resilience theory and research on children and families: Past, present, and promise. *Journal of Family Theory & Review, 10*(1), 12–31.

36 There Are Other Operating Systems besides Windows

Finding Strengths in Neurodiversity

Frank W. Gaskill

If a computer is not running Windows, does that mean it is broken? We need to change the way we think about autism, Asperger's, and everything in between. Therapy often focuses on fixing or getting rid of autistic symptoms, but what if we focus on understanding them? What if having a different operating system is a strength? What if being on the autism spectrum were not labeled or considered disordered? What if we embrace neurodiversity?

Our therapeutic work then begins with self-acceptance and a celebration of one's unique identity on the spectrum, with the focus of the strengths that come with this portion of an individual's identity. Those on the spectrum typically have a specific or obsessive interest such as the weather, dinosaurs, geology, history, stocks, or hundreds of other topics. Their interest in these subjects is hyper-focused in that they can concentrate and focus on something longer than most people are able. Such remarkable strengths accompany this crew: focus, concentration, persistence on task, and memory skills! The challenge for these talented neurodiverse individuals is to live in an allistic (i.e., not autistic) world that tends to pathologize even their amazing strengths.

Blend In or Stand Out?

Society continues to place social demands on all of us, demands which include conformity to an invisible set of rules, following a strict developmental timeline, and an emphasis on "blending in." If our brains are wired to do one or two things exceptionally well, and the mind is designed to engage in these interests for hours on end, why is socialization emphasized when there are far more interesting things in which to engage?

As you already know, people on the spectrum will not conform, and honestly, may not wish to blend in – and why should they? Rather than focusing on conformity, let's celebrate the special interests and help folks find their place in an overwhelming and confusing world. If we can remember and celebrate strengths, the path forward quickly becomes clear: use the strengths to provide cover for the area of concern.

Is It a Special Interest, or a Strength?

Many folks on the spectrum have special interest areas (SIAs). An SIA can be almost anything that grabs the person's attention, and about which they typically consume all of the available facts, experiences, and skills. When practiced productively, SIAs are what allow these individuals we diagnose based on deficiencies to excel in their field, making them the best game designer, software engineer, or history professor around. Without guidance, however, these areas can be unproductive, restrictive, and pervasive. Here are a few suggestions on how to help your specially talented clients capitalize on their SIAs.

Strengthening Self-Image Using SIAs

Children and adolescents with autism often define themselves by their SIA. When asked what is most important to them, they rank SIAs second only to family. By *engaging* in these areas, rather than dismissing them, or attempting to reprioritize the SIA, folks with autism feel more positively about themselves, find stability, and find a way to make sense of the world. By denying these, we are denying them; instead, we should support them and help them feel comfortable in their interests.

> *Jack is a young adult with a passionate interest in history, social justice, and some remarkable programming/GIS (geographic information system) skills. Jack is quick to engage a conversational partner in topics about his interests, sometimes to the point of alienating the listener. We can gently steer Jack toward an area where he could use these skills. For example, he may want to volunteer for a political campaign team of his liking. Folks who are campaigning need Jack's passion and his programming/GIS skills so that they can get the right message to the right audience. Jack can leverage passion and skill into a successful career, or a creative volunteer position. As Jack utilizes his interests to benefit a larger purpose, Jack is no longer talking at people; he is with his peers, making the world a better place, and has a sense of purpose.*

Strengthening Social Skills Using SIAs

Social communication improves when people with autism are engaged in SIAs. In these moments, they demonstrate better fluency, body language, eye contact, attention, and sensitivity to certain social cues. Because of this,

SIAs can be used as a social bridge. I often use video games, Lego, and table top games (e.g., *Dungeons and Dragons*) as a way to improve social skill development and provide my clients with a great environment to practice them and make friends.

Jill has quite a passion for Pokémon Go. Her parents are somewhat embarrassed by this passion and have quite clearly and repeatedly discouraged her from talking about Pokémon Go. Jill is now somewhat reluctant to talk about it, but when invited to discuss that topic, she lights up! She has better posture, is clearly engaged in the topic, and she is articulate on the topic, helping me understand how she processes information and codes (what she perceives to be) relevant data.

Jill is encouraged to go to the park to engage in a Pokémon Go raid at the local park, where she sees some folks she recognizes. They strike up a conversation. While they don't make any further plans or exchange contact information, Jill considers this a very successful outing as she feels less lonely and marginalized. (Of note, don't be asserting your goals in lieu of Jill's goals! She did what you wanted: she left the house and talked to someone. Don't make her conform to your newly revealed goals that she needs to also make a friend on that first outing!)

Using SIAs to Manage Emotions and Facilitate Coping

The more your clients positively engage in SIAs, the more likely they will have positive emotions. Additionally, SIAs can help your clients cope with negative emotions, reduce anxiety, and disrupt unwanted behaviors.

Pokémoning Jill is a good example of this. When she can get outside, walk around, get some sunshine and fresh air, and engage in Pokémon Go, she observes that on the whole she is less anxious. Sure, the first couple of times she was asked to try a new park she felt anxious, but she was able to try new things because she was also engaged in her passions.

When people, *all* people, engage in their passions, they are happier, less stressed, and healthier. You may need to be direct in coaching this skill to your clients, but it is truly worth it!

Using SIAs to Increase Skill Development

Folks with autism often have trouble with fine-motor and sensory skills (e.g., handwriting, tying shoes); however, SIAs have been shown to increase perseverance and task achievement (Attwood, 2007). Similarly,

SIAs help those on the spectrum persist through tasks that challenge sensitivity of senses (e.g., sticky glue and bad smells when building a model plane).

> *Imagine that Jack did indeed land a job in a political campaign, programming GIS information. It is brilliant fun. Unfortunately, he is asked to make some phone calls, a task that is remarkably distasteful for him. If forced to make these phone calls, he will consider quitting the job. (You already know what fictional Jack will be saying in your actual office: "I wasn't hired for this! Let me do the GIS, please! I could just send an email instead of making the phone call! Come on people, get with the program!") We can use Jack's passion to increase his motivation to learn skills around anxiety management, practicing some phone skills, and then practicing some negotiation skills at work!*

Using SIAs to Generalize School Performance into Job Performance

Integrating SIAs into school work can improve motivation, behavior, and academic skill development. Many of us use our passions to foster the development of a successful career path. Like Temple Grandin and her interest in livestock, many folks with autism pursue successful careers related to their SIA.

Because our clients can be so literal and can struggle to generalize, you can identify a clear path (preferably series of paths) from a person's passion to job opportunities. You can help your clients identify their strengths (strengths that they may take for granted, like memory, visual spatial skills, or innate poetry) and help them see how those strengths may be used in areas *other* than their passion.

> *Imagine that Jack gets frustrated with the politician's inability to grasp the data set that Jack provides. Jack churns out amazing data, but fails to recognize that his skills are far and above what the general public possesses. Further, Jack may think that his GIS skills can only be used with a political campaign. Ends up, GIS skills are great with Emergency Services organizations, including estimating response times, rerouting responders to open roads, and the like. Jack could have a career almost anywhere, but instead may limit himself to campaigns. You, the creative, bold therapist that you are, can help Jack generalize his skills, recognize his strengths, and use his innate talents to realize whatever goals he is brave enough to share in your office.*

Summary

Just because many computer systems come with Windows installed, and we are all used to it, does not mean there are not alternatives out there that might work better. In fact, some alternative computer systems might be faster, more innovative, and even more useful. Likewise, understanding our autistic clients' unique operating systems and strengths is imperative to successful treatment. These amazing clients have unlimited creative problem solving skills, though they have sometimes been asked to *not* tap into their strengths, may have been ashamed or embarrassed about their interests, and may be shy to share their strengths. It is your job to tease out the strengths, highlight them, and put the strengths to good use. Who knows, if you do your job properly, Jack and Jill can use their strengths, and then can you even imagine the possibilities? Maybe the Windows operating system we assume is the best is really not the best we have to offer.

Recommended Resources for Professionals

- Psychbytes. www.psychbytes.com/

Recommended Resources for Families

- Max Gamer: Aspie Superhero comic book series
- Autism/Asperger Network. www.aane.org/

About the Author

Frank W. Gaskill, PhD, is a licensed psychologist and co-founder of Southeastpsych.com and Shrinktank.com. He works with individuals on the autism spectrum and consults on the development of autism programs and private practice development across the country. Dr. Gaskill is the co-author of *Max Gamer: Aspie Superhero* as well as *How We Built Our Dream Practice: Innovative Ideas for Building Yours*. Dr. Gaskill's practice website is www.southeastpsych.com.

Reference

Attwood, T. (2007). *The complete guide to Asperger's syndrome*. London: Jessica Kingsley Publishers.

Part XIII

Animal–Assisted Interventions

A quality therapist will ensure that they are locating and using all of the resources available to improve a client's quality of life. Many therapists turn to animals, inside and outside the office, to help with the quality of life and therapeutic gains for clients on the autism spectrum. There is much confusion within the public at large about the use of animals and proper terms for animals (service animal, emotional support animal, therapy animal). As providers, we can start using these terms properly and making appropriate referrals for our clients.

In this part we learn about the difference between service animals and emotional support animals. We also learn about the types of questions we can ask our clients about readiness for an animal in the family or in the office. We also learn about the impact of animal-assisted interventions as well as a specific type of intervention called Animal Assisted Play Therapy. Gone are the days when a therapist could just bring her pet dog to work. We can all benefit from learning the legal definitions of animal interventions, and knowing when to make a proper referral.

37 To the Rescue

How Animals Can Assist People Diagnosed with Autism

Cyndie Kieffer

There are miraculous stories of how animals have transformed the lives of individuals with autism. How do professionals know when an individual on the autism spectrum would benefit from a service animal or emotional support animal? There are many considerations when recommending animal assistance to a client, such as the challenge of finding funding for service animals, locating a reputable training facility, helping families prepare for adding a new animal into their lives, and creating realistic expectations of change an animal may bring for an individual with autism. This chapter will aid therapists in understanding the difference between service animals and emotional support animals, inform how to assist clients who may benefit from animal assistance, and provide guiding questions to help determine which type of animal, if any, would most aid the client.

In advising individuals with autism about the viability of using an animal to assist in symptom management, the therapist should first understand the difference between *service animals* and *emotional support animals*. These terms are often misused, and there are differences both from a training perspective as well as from a disability law perspective. There is a great deal more training required for service animals as opposed to emotional support animals; in fact, only service animals are required to have formal training. From a legal perspective, according to the Americans with Disabilities Act, service animals can only be dogs or miniature horses; dogs, of course, are the most common. Emotional support animals are not restricted to dogs or horses, and provide companionship, relieve loneliness, and may help with certain mental health issues such as depression, anxiety, or phobias (ADA National Network, 2019).

To add to the confusion, *therapy animals* are mistakenly called service animals when in fact they are unable to be in businesses, hospitals, and other public spaces without invitation. Therapy animals may be used for therapeutic visitation in hospitals, nursing homes, and other facilities, or they may be used for animal-assisted therapy by a physical, occupational, or mental health therapist (National Service Animal Registry, 2019). They are trained to provide comfort for others, and typically require some sort of certification or registration prior to garnering access to public events or spaces (Smith, 2018). Many news stories perpetuate the confusion as the terms service animal and therapy animal are used incorrectly. While therapy animals do require training, they do not require the level of training that is needed for a service animal as they are not performing tasks for one specific person. In this chapter we will focus solely on the role of service animals and emotional support animals as potential assistance to clients with autism. A summary of differences between service animals and emotional support animals can be found in Figure 37.1.

Service Animals

Service animals are trained to complete specific tasks to assist a person with a physical, sensory, psychiatric, intellectual, or other mental disability. One such example is when a dog is trained to rest their head on the person's lap to aid in calming or providing a centering presence. Service animals are the only type of the three types of working animals (service, emotional support, and therapy) that has full access to public areas. The animal must pass a test that demonstrates reliable and safe behavior while in the public. This test is given after the animal has completed the necessary training to perform the tasks related to the disability.

Service animals can truly make a positive difference in the lives of the person diagnosed with autism. They often help to improve communication, improve the demonstration of empathy towards others, and improve the ability to transition from one activity to the next, as the animal acts as a constant or stabilizing being in those changing situations. Service animals have also helped improve regulation of emotions, improve confidence level, and facilitate grounding for those who elope (i.e., wander off), although a service animal is *not* a replacement for having a safety plan in place (AVMA Public Policy/Animal Welfare Division, 2017). Because dogs

Service Animals	Emotional Support Animals
• Formal training requirements	• No formal training requirements
• ADA law allows only dogs or miniature horses as service animals	• No restrictions as to type of animal; designated as an accommodation by ADA law
• Goal is for animal to complete specific tasks to assist person with physical, sensory, psychiatric, intellectual or other mental disability	• Goal is to provide companionship, relieve loneliness, or alleviate symptoms of mental health diagnoses
• Service animals have full access to public areas	• Emotional support animals have limited access to public areas
• Costly (in some cases over $10,000 depending upon training needed)	• Much less costly due to no specific training requirements

Figure 37.1 Service Animals vs. Emotional Support Animals. ADA, Americans with Disabilities Act.

communicate through body language, it often is easier for people with autism to relate to them and understand what is being communicated. The relationship that the person with autism has with their service dog can open up relationships with people as the skills are transferred in daily life.

> *Colton, a 14-year-old boy diagnosed with autism, is receiving counseling to address symptoms of anxiety. Colton consistently struggles with symptoms of anxiety when there are changes in his preferred routine; however, this school year has been particularly difficult. He has had an increase in symptoms of anxiety, including increased yelling, reluctance to attend school, attempting to leave situations where there are many people, and engaging in repetitive arm movements. His symptoms have been steadily getting worse and are negatively impacting his performance in school and relationships.*
>
> *The therapist encourages Colton's mother to contact several organizations to determine if a service animal might be of benefit. The therapist knows that a service animal could augment treatment and the animal would be able to apply deep pressure therapy during instances where Colton is quite anxious, provide behavior interruption when Colton begins to engage in repetitive movements, and act as an anchor in situations where there are many people and his feelings of anxiousness increase.*

Therapists can help prepare clients to gain access to a service animal. Questions for individuals/families to ask when considering obtaining a service animal include:

- Has the trainer previously trained service animals for people with autism and if so, how many animals, and with what rate of success?
- Are positive training methods used (positive training consists of the use of positive reinforcement methods and avoiding the use of physical punishment as well as fear)?
- What is the wait time for an animal?
- What is the cost and are there any suggestions for fundraising?
- Can the trainer provide references from families who have obtained service animals through their business?
- What tasks will the animal be trained for as the animal's training is individualized to the person's need(s)?
- Is there on-going support available to help with continued training? Often, once the animal joins the family in the home issues arise and further training or support is needed; knowing your trainer will be there for you helps ease the stress.
- What challenges should the family be aware of when getting a service animal?

While the process can be daunting, the therapist can support the family by helping them make informed choices along the way. When starting the process of acquiring a service animal, it is important to be thorough in getting references, completing background checks, and identifying the credentials of the trainer. At this time, there are no regulations on dog training, including service dog training, which allows *anyone* to advertise as a trainer. Better Business Bureau reports should be reviewed.

When deciding on a trainer it is prudent to ask where they received their professional credentials and then follow up with that agency to verify that the trainer remains in good standing. Sadly, many unscrupulous people take advantage of people in need of a service animal (Miller, 2019). Families should also check the validity of the organization that credentials the trainer. Two examples of credentialing agencies are Pet Professional Guild and International Association of Animal Behavior Consultants. While locating a reputable trainer can be a challenge, web sites such as Assistance Dogs International (included in the *Recommendations for Families* section below) offers a program search for accredited members of their organization. This is not a complete listing of trainers, but it does provide a start when researching where to turn when seeking a service animal.

When the family meets with the service animal trainer, they will want to think about the personality they wish for in the animal, and how those traits will ultimately help the autistic client perform tasks. The family will need to allow time for all members to develop a bond; once the animal has become part of family life, each member's life will never be the same in both expected and surprising ways. While out in the community, many times people will ask questions about how the service animal helps the family, sharing personal stories of their own or of someone they know, and the process of acquiring the animal, and may even pose intrusive questions such as why the animal is present. Establishments are only allowed to ask certain questions regarding a service animal, which include if the animal is required due to a disability and what tasks the animal is trained to do related to the disability.

Impediments and Contraindications for a Service Animal

Cost can be an impediment to getting a service animal. The cost varies greatly, with some service animals costing over $10,000 depending on the intensity of training needed. Given this cost, many families turn to fundraising to help offset the expense, such as GoFundMe, or other creative ways to help raise money. At this time, service animals are not covered by medical insurance; however, some expenses related to the service animal may be able to be deducted on taxes. Also, depending upon the training needed, there may be a wait list for the animal. Some people make the choice to train their own dog to become a service animal with help from an experienced trainer. This choice is not always the most appropriate decision, and the animal's personality and trainability must be taken into account.

Despite all of the wonderful benefits of having a service animal there are many times it is not appropriate for the person with autism or the family. If the family member with autism has sensory issues, the addition of an animal could be stressful as there will be increased noise, occasional slobbers, and different smells. There are instances where the person with autism does not like dogs; if they scream or choose to not be around the dog there may be little, if any, benefit. The cost of obtaining a service animal can be daunting; further, costs for caring for a service animal must be considered. When adding an animal to the family to provide support, it is important to remember that the animal is going to need routine care such as going outside to relieve themselves regularly, exercise, being groomed, regular veterinary care, and down time to rest. Often families/clients are already quite stressed with appointments, commitments, and so on, and adding a service animal or emotional support animal can create more stress. Additionally, if there is any family member with allergies to the animal, this will not be of benefit.

Emotional Support Animals

> *Abby is an 18-year-old young woman with autism who is seeing a counselor at the university she attends. Abby has been struggling with keeping up with her studies and admits to not sleeping well at night for nearly one month. Since moving out of her parents' home to attend college she has become anxious while in her apartment and unable to organize what needs to be done both for her home and school life. When Abby lived at home, her pet cat provided a great deal of support, and she did not exhibit any of these symptoms. Abby's counselor suggests that her pet cat become her emotional support animal, and after discussing the caregiving tasks that will need to be completed so her cat remains safe and healthy, a letter is written for Abby to provide to her landlord regarding her cat being an emotional support animal. Her cat will provide her the support while at home that is needed to improve her functioning.*

There are currently no limitations as to what types of animals can be emotional support animals, nor any specific training requirements for animals to become emotional support animals. While they are not recognized as service animals, these animals are categorized as an *accommodation* for a person diagnosed with a disability under the Fair Housing Act and the Air Carrier Access Act. A person obtains an emotional support animal by securing a letter from their physician (such as their psychiatrist) or a licensed mental health professional. Without being trained for specific tasks, an emotional support animal provides therapeutic benefit to a person who has been diagnosed with a mental or physical disability. There are currently no limits to the number of emotional support animals that a person can have in their possession. Often, people turn an animal that is already a family member into an emotional support animal, although the option to adopt an animal specifically for this purpose occurs as well. The timeline to secure an emotional support animal is much shorter than a service animal as there is no specialized training involved.

Benefits of an Emotional Support Animal for an Individual with Autism

The therapist can assist families in discovering whether or not an emotional support animal would benefit the family member with autism. It is important that everyone in the family honestly look at their situation when considering adding an emotional support animal to their home. Questions for individuals/ families to ask when considering obtaining an emotional support animal include:

* Is everyone on board in helping to care for the animal?
* How does the individual with autism feel about animals?
* How will boundaries around the animal and down time for the animal be determined?
* Have costs and time commitment been considered? Having an animal will mean vet visits and bills, providing care for an animal during vacations, and daily care is a commitment (e.g., walking a dog, cleaning a cat litter box).
* Is the family willing to understand the needs of the animal? It is beneficial for everyone in the family to learn how the animal communicates their needs, such as learning calming signals that dogs give to indicate their needs. This type of work can be stressful for animals and having their vest off to rest is extremely important.
* How will the family determine when the animal needs to be retired? At some point the animal will need or want to retire and it is prudent to consider this from the start of the process so there is a plan in place.

Impediments and Contraindications for Emotional Support Animals

Impediments to emotional support animals include allergies, dislike of animals, ongoing costs of care for the animal, and potential role overload if the animal increases family workload while providing little relief. There are no laws dictating what animals can be emotional support animals, thus the professional will need to educate themselves on an on-going basis dependent on the client's needs; some clients may choose animals that will not provide needed support and need guidance to find a good match between the client's needs and the type of animal that can provide that need (Human-Animal Interactions in Counseling Interest Network of the American Counseling Association, 2019).

There are situations where emotional support animals are not beneficial for a person. If the person is unable to meet the needs of the animal, including feeding, veterinary care, and humane treatment, this would be contraindicated. Since there are currently no specifications about what species can be an emotional support animal, it is important to know the specific needs of the animal. Some animals, such as dogs, need exercise and mental stimulation, and the person must be able to meet these needs.

Writing Letters of Support

Only licensed health care providers (including mental health care providers) can write letters of support for emotional support animals. Therapists should determine their policies and procedures on writing letters of support for clients and consider ethical obligations, including having knowledge of the human–animal bond. It is important that the professional learn about animal behavior to insure the humane treatment of the animal. It is appropriate to ask about how the person will care for the specific needs of the animal when exploring the need for an emotional support animal. The therapist should explore how the person plans to meet the animal's needs for exercise and veterinary care, and if they understand how the animal communicates stress. When a therapist is considering creating a policy about writing letters to back an emotional support animal, the following areas should be addressed in the policy.

Number of Therapy Sessions Required

It is important to determine if there will be a required minimum number of therapy sessions required before writing the letter and what assessments will be utilized, to insure this is an appropriate accommodation.

Assessments Required

Will the therapist require specific assessments in order to determine if an emotional support animal would benefit the client? For example, the World Health Organization Disability Assessment Schedule 2.0 (WHODAS, n.d.) assesses level of disability in six life areas. This assessment can be either self-administered or proxy-administered, and can help elucidate specific areas where an animal may be of assistance to the autistic client.

Need for the Emotional Support Animal

The letter should also indicate that an emotional support animal is necessary to assist with symptoms of the disability. The letter can utilize the assessment results discussed above as reasons why an emotional support animal is therapeutically indicated. The letter should specifically indicate that an emotional support animal is necessary to assist with symptoms of the disability.

Legal Requirements

The letter should state that the client has a disability that meets the definition under the Americans with Disabilities Act, the Fair Housing Act, and the Rehabilitation Act of 1973. Letters should indicate the date the letter is drafted and if there is a range of dates that the document is valid. While there is no law dictating the range of dates, it would be best practice to make the letter valid for one year, documenting this at the close of the letter.

Summary

Professionals who work alongside individuals with autism and their family have the opportunity to provide education regarding the role of service and emotional support animals, and the positive changes these animals can have in their lives. Service and emotional support animals can assist those with autism in countless ways, including greater independence, improved social skills, increased coping skills, and reduction in symptoms such as anxiety, depression, anger, or disruptive behavior. Therapists can aid families in determining which type of animal may be most beneficial in their situation, provide recommendations, and write needed support materials so the individual and their family can most benefit from animal-assisted intervention.

Recommended Resources for Professionals

- Ensminger, J. J. (2010). *Service and therapy dogs in American society: Science, law and the evolution of canine caregivers.* Springfield, IL: C.C.Thomas.
- Fine, A. (Ed.). (2010). *Handbook on animal-assisted therapy: Theoretical foundations and guidelines for practice.* San Diego, CA: Elsevier Science Publishing Co Inc.
- Pavlides, M. (2008). *Animal-assisted interventions for individuals with autism.* Philadelphia, PA: Jessica Kingsley Publishers.
- Tedeschi, P. (2018, May 24). Emotional support animals [Webinar]. In *Interconnected: A webinar series on the human-animal bond and its impact on public health and well-being.* Retrieved from www.du.edu/humananimal connection/resources/co-link-project.html

Recommended Resources for Families

- Aloff, B. (2005). Canine body language: A photographic guide interpreting the native language of the domestic dog. Wenatchee, WA: Dogwise.
- Arnold, J. (2011). *Through a dog's eyes*. New York, NY: Speigel & Grau.
- Assistance Dogs International: www.assistancedogsinternational.org
- Calmenson, S. (2007). *May I pet your dog? The how-to guide for kids meeting dogs (and dogs meeting kids)*. New York, NY: Clarion Books.
- Gross, P. D. (2006). *Golden bridge: A guide to assistance dogs for children challenged by autism or other developmental disabilities*. West Lafayette, IN: Purdue University Press.

About the Author

Cyndie Kieffer is a Licensed Clinical Social Worker in Illinois and Indiana who combined her passion for helping people with her love of dogs. Ms. Kieffer is a Certified Professional Practitioner of Animal Assisted Play Therapy through the International Institute of Animal Assisted Play Therapy. Ms. Kieffer enjoys helping others share their animal's unique talents through involvement with Pet Partners as an evaluator, instructor, and a handler. She has authored several articles about animal-assisted interventions. Additionally, she has spoken at many national, as well as state-level, conferences on the topic of animal-assisted interventions. She has over 20 years of experience in a variety of social work settings, including advocating for people with intellectual disabilities, hospice, and providing counseling for children and older adults. She provides contracting and consulting services through her business Sit.Stay.Heal. Ms. Kieffer can be reached at sit.stay.heal@hotmail.com.

References

ADA National Network. (2019). Service animals and emotional support animals. Retrieved from https://adata.org/publication/service-animals-booklet

AVMA Public Policy/Animal Welfare Division. (2017). Assistance animals: Rights of access and the problem of fraud. Retrieved from www.avma.org/KB/Resources/Reports/Documents/Assistance-Animals-Rights-Access-Fraud-AVMA.pdf

Human-Animal Interactions in Counseling Interest Network of the American Counseling Association. (2019). Emotional support animals human-animal interactions in counseling interest network steering committee position statement. Retrieved from www.ccu.edu/_files/documents/life-directions/human-animal-interventions-in-counseling-interest-network-position-statement.pdf

Miller, P. (2019, June). Service dog scams. *Whole Dog Journal, 22*, 8–10.

National Service Animal Registry. (2019). All about therapy animals. Retrieved from www.nsarco.com/qualify-therapy-dog.html

Smith, S. (2018, November 6). Service dogs vs therapy dogs. Retrieved from www.consumersadvocate.org/features/service-dogs-versus-therapy-dogs

World Health Organization. (n.d.). World Health Organization Disability Assessment Schedule 2.0. Retrieved from www.who.int/classifications/icf/whodasii/en/

38 Dogs, and Horses, and Cats, Oh My! Animal-Assisted Interventions for People with Autism

Laura A. Bassette

> *After returning home from a long week as an autism therapist, Ms. Jones sat down on the couch and her Golden Retriever, Sandy, immediately jumped up next to her, placed her head in her lap, and looked up at her with her big brown eyes. As Ms. Jones gently stroked Sandy, she thought, "People certainly have had animals on the brain lately!" First, she recalled how last week, the mother of one of her clients asked her how she could convince a service dog organization that her teenage son needed a dog as much as a younger child. Earlier this week, another parent shared that a friend's child spoke his very first word during "horse therapy" and asked her advice about this for her daughter, who was non-verbal. Then, just yesterday, one of her colleagues mentioned that a client asked how he could get their family cat "certified" so the cat would permitted in on-campus housing when he went off to college next year. As Ms. Jones reflected on her own love of animals, she came to the realization that she and most other providers she knew, as well as her clients and their parents, were probably not very familiar with the variations of animal-assisted interventions (AAI), the practical realities, and/ or the relevant research. She decided it was time to educate herself about all this buzz involving animals for people with autism!*

Overview of Animal-Assisted Interventions

In recent decades, there has been an increasing interest in utilizing animals for people on the autism spectrum. This field, broadly referred to as animal-assisted interventions or AAI, is defined as "any intervention that intentionally incorporates a live animal into the intervention" (O'Haire, Guérin, Kirkham, & Daigle, 2015, p. 2). These activities are frequently viewed as a complementary therapy, with approximately 25% of people with autism participating in some type of AAI (Christon, Mackintosh, & Myers, 2010). Proponents suggest AAI may be particularly impactful for people with autism due to the specific characteristics related to autism, such as social/communication deficits, stress, and anxiety, though research does suggest there are mixed results (O'Haire, 2017). Given the increased prevalence of programs, interest, and media coverage, there is a high likelihood that therapists who work with people with autism may be asked questions about AAI. Therapists will want to familiarize themselves with AAI so they can speak knowledgeably and be prepared to make referrals.

Impact of AAI for People with Autism

AAI can positively impact social concerns for clients with autism. For example, it is suggested that animals may serve as a facilitator, helping people with autism in engaging with others (Sams, Fortney, & Willenbring, 2006), and acting as a social buffer (Fine & Beck, 2015). While formal information on the interaction between animals and individuals with autism is limited, we know that anxiety during stressful social interactions for neurotypical individuals can be alleviated by the presence of animals (Polheber & Matchock, 2014). While the preliminary research on the impact of AAI is positive, the generalizability and impact on various other measures explored in people with autism (e.g., communication, problem behavior, motor skills, repetitive behavior) (O'Haire, 2017) are inconclusive to date. More study is needed to understand exactly how AAI can benefit individuals with autism.

Types of AAI

The field of AAI has worked to distinguish between the use of animals for "therapy" vs. "activities." Animal-assisted therapies (AAT) are when animals are included as part of a specific therapy plan by a licensed therapist to assist a client in achieving a specific targeted therapy goal. Animal-assisted activities (AAA), on the other hand, are conducted by trained professionals (i.e., not necessarily a licensed therapist) and the incorporation of the animal focuses on broader aspects such as motivation, quality of life, or education (AVMA, 2019). Typically, the animals used for AAA and AAT are not the client's pets; the animals do not live with the clients, and the clients do not provide for the day-to-day care for the animals.

AAI, by definition, includes live animals; however, the types of animals used, types of activities they are incorporated into, professional credentialing, and the certifying/accrediting bodies that oversee AAI vary greatly. The overwhelming majority of animals reported being used for AAI are horses and dogs, with other animals (e.g., guinea pigs) used to a lesser degree, and notably, the overall categorization of AAI is broad (O'Haire, 2017). For example, AAI with horses may be referred to as "equine-assisted activities," "hippotherapy," or "therapeutic horseback riding" (O'Haire et al., 2015), while AAI with dogs might be called "dog," "pet-facilitated," or "canine-assisted" therapy. In this chapter we will focus on AAI with horses and dogs.

AAI with Horses

> *To facilitate her understanding of AAI, Ms. Jones began Googling and found a wealth of information regarding the prevalence of horses in AAI and activities such as "therapeutic horse-back riding" (TR). She watched You-Tube videos of TR where a "PATH [Professional Association for Therapeutic Horsemanship]-certified riding instructor" worked on various skills with different riders with autism. First, she observed how the instructor prompted a rider, "What do you tell your horse?" and the rider confidently responded, "Walk on," in order to make the horse move forward. The video explained how the child previously engaged primarily in echolalic speech and when initially prompted, "Say, 'walk on,'" would repeat, word for word, "Say, 'walk on.'" Through working with her, the instructor taught the child that saying "Walk on" independently resulted in the horse moving, and this knowledge provided the child with motivation to speak.*
>
> *Another video demonstrated how a teenage rider diagnosed with Asperger's syndrome initially expressed anxiety when asked to get on the horse, but was ultimately empowered as she overcame her fear and learned to communicate aids to the horse (e.g., tell the horse "Whoa" and pull back on the reins to make it stop).*
>
> *A final video explained how a rider engaged in self-injurious behavior and bit his hands when stressed. As a way to interrupt the behavior, he was taught to hold the reins with his hands down and low near the horse's neck (since he could not simultaneously hold the reins and lift his hands up to bite them) and worked to increase the duration of holding the reins.*

PATH is one of the primary organizations in the field of AAI with horses that certifies professionals (e.g., therapeutic riding instructors) and accredits organizations (i.e., PATH Center Members, PATH Premier Accredited Centers). In 2017, PATH reported they served 706 people with autism and that autism was the most common disability type served by their centers (PATH, 2017). TR is one of the most common AAI with horses and is defined as an "activity" that contributes to the overall well-being of people with disabilities. Hippotherapy, on the other hand, is considered "therapy" and must be conducted by licensed professionals (e.g., occupational therapist, speech/language pathologist). Hippotherapy professionals are certified by the American Hippotherapy Certification Board (AHCB), where they learn strategies for incorporating horses into treatment plans. Hippotherapy professionals who work with people with autism intentionally use the movement of the horse (e.g., horse walking) to arouse or calm body systems, which assists in skill acquisition (e.g., speech, eye contact, posture). Other types of AAI with horses can include unmounted activities that focus on the interactions with horses to teach various skills and may be certified/accredited through other organizations (e.g., EAGALA).

> *As she continued her search, Ms. Jones came across the website of a local AAI organization that uses horses. She called up the director, who explained how the program collaborated with the local schools to get participants with autism "excited about learning." She also told Ms. Jones about an activity she frequently uses which requires the participant to catch their horse out in a large field. She explained how the activity provided motivation since the participants want to be with the horse; the activity teaches participants to effectively regulate their energy levels. She explained how participants whose energy is "too high" (e.g., they are too quick in their movements or display aggressive body language) will not be successful in catching the horses, since the horses will intuitively pick up on their energy levels and run away or not let the participant catch them. She explained how this helps participants learn to regulate emotions and behavior, which can then be applied in other areas of their lives.*

Given the inherent risks of working with horses it is important to consider the training and credentials of those conducting AAI with horses. Ensuring professionals/organizations are credentialed/accredited helps ensure quality and guarantees best practices are followed. This is important to protect participants and minimize risk to all involved. These oversights can also serve to promote the ethical treatment of the horses and provide guidance to assist with monitoring physical concerns (e.g., ensuring a client is not too heavy for a horse) as well as mental well-being (e.g., routine monitoring of the horses for signs of stress).

Summary

As the field of AAI continues to grow, therapists who provide services to people with autism may be asked about AAI. Therapists can note the many positive anecdotal benefits while emphasizing that the available empirically based evidence must be considered preliminary. Therapists should acknowledge that AAI appears to be most beneficial for people with autism in terms of improving social interaction, mood, and anxiety/stress, but there are still many unanswered questions. When making referrals, therapists should share information about the variety of AAI and importance of certification/accreditation. As the relationships that all people have with animals continues to evolve, it will be important to continue to monitor, assess, and explore the various ways animals may bring joy to everyone, including people with autism.

Recommended Resources for Professionals

- Ball State University, Center for Autism Spectrum Disorders: www.bsu.edu/academics/centersandinstitutes/center-for-autism-spectrum-disorder

- Fine, A. H. (Ed.). (2015). *Handbook on animal-assisted therapy: Foundations and guidelines for animal-assisted interventions* (4th ed.). San Diego, CA: Academic Press.
- Human Animal Bond Research Institute: https://habri.org/
- International Society for Anthrozoology: www.isaz.net/isaz/
- Purdue University Center for the Human Animal Bond: https://vet. purdue.edu/chab/

Recommended Resources for Families

- American Hippotherapy Certification Board: https://americanhip potherapyassociation.org/certification/
- Autism Quality of Life: https://autismqualityoflife.com/
- Autism Speaks Assistance Dogs Information: www.autismspeaks.org/ assistance-dog-information
- Ball State University, Center for Autism Spectrum Disorders': www. bsu.edu/academics/centersandinstitutes/center-for-autism-spectrum-disorder
- EAGALA: www.eagala.org/org
- Pet Partners: https://petpartners.org/
- Professional Association of Therapeutic Horsemanship: www. pathintl.org/

About the Author

Dr. Laura Bassette is an Assistant Professor of Applied Behavior Analysis/ Autism at Ball State University (BSU), serves as Director of Research at BSU's Center for Autism Spectrum Disorders, and is a Board Certified Behavior Analyst (BCBA-D). Dr. Bassette earned her Ph.D. in Special Education from Purdue University and completed a post-doctoral fellowship in severe disabilities at the University of Illinois. Dr. Bassette previously worked as a behavior analyst and developed behavioral interventions for adults/teenagers with autism/developmental disabilities in residential settings. She also taught therapeutic horseback riding to people with disabilities as an instructor with the Professional Association for Therapeutic Horsemanship (PATH) and conducted AAI research with both dogs and horses. In her free time, Dr. Bassette enjoys the companionship of her two cats and horse.

References

American Veterinary Medical Association (AVMA). (2019). Animal-assisted interventions: Definitions. Retrieved from www.avma.org/KB/Policies/Pages/ Animal-Assisted-Interventions-Definitions.aspx

Christon, L. M., Mackintosh, V. H., & Myers, B. J. (2010). Use of complementary and alternative medicine (CAM) treatments by parents of children with autism spectrum disorders. *Research in Autism Spectrum Disorders, 4*, 249–259. doi:10.1016/j.rasd.2009.09.013

Fine, A. H., & Beck, A. M. (2015). Understanding our kinship with animals: Input for health care professionals interested in the human-animal bond. In A. H. Fine (Ed.), *Handbook on animal-assisted therapy: Foundations and guidelines for animal-assisted interventions* (4th ed., pp. 3–10). San Diego, CA: Elsevier Inc.

O'Haire, M. E. (2017). Research on animal-assisted intervention and autism spectrum disorder, 2012–2015. *Applied Developmental Science, 21*(3), 200–216. doi:10.1080/10888691.2016.1243988

O'Haire, M. E., Guérin, N. A., Kirkham, A. C., & Daigle, C. L. (2015). Animal-assisted intervention for autism spectrum disorder. *HABRI Central Briefs, 1*(6), 1–8.

Polheber, J. P., & Matchock, R. L. (2014). The presence of a dog attenuates cortisol and heart rate in the Trier Social Stress Test compared to human friends. *Journal of Behavioral Medicine, 37*(5), 860–867. doi:10.1007/s10865-013-9546-1

Professional Association of Therapeutic Horsemanship (PATH). (2017). *2017 fact sheet.* Rate in the Trier Social Stress Test compared to human friends. *Journal of Behavioral Medicine, 37*, 860–867. doi:10.1007/s10865-013-9546-1. Retrieved from www.pathintl.org/images/pdf/about-narha/documents/2017-fact-sheet.pdf.

Sams, M. J., Fortney, E. V., & Willenbring, S. (2006). Occupational therapy incorporating animals for children with autism: A pilot investigation. *American Journal of Occupational Therapy, 60*, 268–274. doi:10.5014/ajot.60.3.268

39 Animal Assisted Play Therapy®

Risë VanFleet

Josh had been mistakenly diagnosed with oppositional defiant disorder when he was younger, largely because of incidents of throwing things when he became angry. There had been delays in his language development, and his frustration tolerance was low. Eventually he was diagnosed with autism. He functioned well in school except when in social situations where he sometimes had been teased. He rarely spoke or replied during conversations, even with his parents. He was referred for Animal Assisted Play Therapy (AAPT: a form of animal-assisted intervention, or AAI) after a school incident when he was in a mainstreamed sixth-grade classroom; he was 11 years old at that time. A classmate had asked Josh why he wore black clothes all the time, and Josh reacted by trying to hit the boy and throwing books and pens at other classmates in the vicinity. Josh had always expressed interest in animals, so the school counselor thought that AAPT might work well for him.

Josh cooperated with the introductions to the author's AAPT dog, Kirrie. In early sessions, he did not want to touch her or look at her, but he did toss treats on the floor for her after asking her to sit, stay, lie down, turn around, pick up (a toy), and a number of other cues. He was given the option of using gestural (hand) cues and/or verbal ones. He did not interact with the therapist, but he showed that he was listening to what she said.

During the fourth AAPT session, Josh put on a grooming glove and petted Kirrie for the first time. He also played an eye contact game with her, giving her treats after she made eye contact with him. The therapist reassured him, empathically reflected his reactions, and encouraged him as he interacted with the dog. By the fifth session, he began glancing at the therapist when Kirrie engaged in some humorous behaviors, and he began using some verbal cues spontaneously. In the sixth session, he entered the room and told the therapist about a dog his neighbor had recently adopted. It was the first conversation anyone had ever heard him initiate. He continued to make progress and eventually invited his family to watch a trick that he had taught Kirrie from

> start to finish. He arranged their seating so they could see well and shyly smiled a couple times when they praised what he had done. His family noticed improvements in his social interactions at home, and continued therapy resulted in fewer problems in school. His work with Kirrie in AAPT seemed to create a sense of safety and acceptance for him through which he could express himself and grow in his social and emotional development.

Many children with autism have an affinity for, or at least a curiosity about, nonhuman animals. Social interactions with humans can arouse anxiety for them, but animals seem to pose fewer problems, perhaps because animals have fewer expectations of people. Increasingly, therapists are using AAI with children, teens, and adults with autism as a means of conducting mental health, allied health, and educational interventions. The use of service or assistance dogs for children with autism has blossomed, and the benefits and problems associated with that are discussed in VanFleet and Colţea (2012). Because fully trained assistance dogs can be extremely expensive and sometimes add stress to the family, other options for engagements with animals can be very useful. While family pets can also be useful, the stress of caring for animals while negotiating the therapies and needs of a child with autism can be significant (VanFleet & Colţea, 2012). One way to explore a client's reactions to animals is through the use of therapy dogs (or cats, horses, or other properly selected and prepared species). This contribution looks at the use of animal-assisted therapy coupled with play therapy, in the form of AAPT, to help clients of all ages with autism. Play therapy systematically uses play interventions and a playful climate to help create an emotionally safe experience while allowing for the expression of feelings, problems, and mastery that can be nonverbal or verbal in nature. Play is the language. Integrating these two modalities is a unique way in which to connect with the child to enhance almost any form of therapy, including mental health, occupational, physical, and speech therapies, as well as for some educational plans.

In the sections that follow, a description is provided of AAPT, its principles and goals, as well as when one might include it in a client's treatment plan. Considerations for referrals to practitioners of AAPT (and more broadly, AAI) are outlined, and some guidelines are provided for determining the qualifications of those conducting AAI with young people on the spectrum and their families. AAPT is particularly well suited for children and teens living with autism.

AAPT emphasizes the centrality of relationships among all participants (client–therapist–animal), the use of play-based interactions, and the continuous attention to both client and animal well-being. It is described in depth in VanFleet and Faa-Thompson (2017). AAPT represents a full integration of concepts, skills, and methods from several fields, including play therapy, psychotherapy, animal-assisted therapy, ethology, animal behavior, animal handling, group therapy, professional ethics, and animal welfare. As such, it requires considerable training and supervision. This is largely true of AAI, too. It is neither safe nor ethical to simply bring one's family-friendly pet into the therapy situation. There are scope-of-practice issues that are discussed briefly in this contribution, and much more fully elsewhere (Stewart, Chang, Parker, & Grubbs, 2016; VanFleet & Faa-Thompson, 2017).

AAPT is defined as:

> the integrated involvement of animals in the context of play therapy, in which appropriately trained therapists and animals engage with clients primarily through systematic playful interventions, with the goal of improving clients' developmental and psychosocial health, while simultaneously ensuring the animals' well-being and voluntary engagement. Play and playfulness are essential ingredients of the interactions and the relationship.
>
> (VanFleet & Faa-Thompson, 2017, p. 17)

A climate of playfulness and affirming humor helps create the emotional safety necessary for clients to work through their troubling emotions, developmental issues, and social and behavioral problems in therapy. AAPT can be conducted with clients in individual, family, and group formats, and it can be used by mental health practitioners who ascribe to virtually any theoretical orientation, including integrative models. At its core, AAPT is a form of relationship therapy. It helps create the conditions under which clients can feel safe in their relationships, allowing them to express themselves and work on various challenges they face. It is flexible and can be adapted to suit the needs of the client while involving the special abilities of animals to build trust, connection, and relationship, as well as specific skills (VanFleet & Faa-Thompson, 2017).

Before considering how AAPT can help with clients with autism, it is important to understand the principles that guide it. Not all AAI programs are equal – some are excellent, and some are poorly conceived and executed, with everything in between. Increasingly, as competencies and position statements are being constructed for the major mental health organizations in the United States, it is clear that those used by AAPT fit nicely with the direction in which the broader field is moving.

Principles and Goals

AAPT is based on principles evidenced in all interactions and interventions. They are described in VanFleet and Faa-Thompson (2017). In short, they are listed below:

- Respect – equal and reciprocal respect of clients and animals
- Safety – physical and emotional safety for all
- Enjoyment and choices – always the option of nonparticipation for clients and animals; and for the animals, enjoyment rather than resignation
- Acceptance – of the client and the animal for who they are
- Training – use of only positive reinforcement, noncoercive, animal-friendly methods
- Relationship – the primary focus of all; reciprocal, empathic, playful
- Empowerment – encouragement of growth, independence, competence, and confidence for clients and animals alike
- Process – more important than any single outcome; unexpected events are expected and woven into the therapeutic process
- Foundations – grounded in well-established theories and practice, animal welfare and well-being in the forefront, guided by research.

AAPT can help address a wide range of goals for clients, and it can be used to help children with autism function more fully in many areas. Sometimes children with autism and their families have a full schedule of therapies, and when a playful tone and a willing animal are involved, it can build motivation and create a sense of safety that is valuable for clients on the spectrum. The five major mental health goal areas are listed and briefly described below (VanFleet & Faa-Thompson, 2017).

Self-efficacy

This area gives clients opportunities to develop their capabilities, including various life skills and the ability to protect themselves from harm. Interventions aimed at self-efficacy help clients feel competent and confident, assisting with a sense of empowerment. Clients with autism can benefit by developing their areas of interest, learning about animals, and having skills to understand animal emotions and behaviors. These are all areas that can assist in their relationships with humans as well.

Attachment and Relationship

Very often, social relationships can be challenging for clients with autism. Work with an animal and a therapist in AAPT can help clients feel safer trying out new social skills. The focus on the relationship with the animal has direct parallels with human relationships, yet the animals often feel safer to clients who are still learning about social interactions.

Empathy

Empathy refers to the ability to see the world through another's eyes or viewpoint. In AAPT, an emphasis on understanding the animal's body language and how to interpret it in the context of the situation can help develop skills useful in understanding human expressions and emotions. Again, the safety of trying this with an animal who seems accepting and happy to be involved can ease a client's fears and allow for greater relaxation while learning.

Self-regulation

Interacting with animals can assist clients as they learn to manage their own emotional reactions and the dysregulation that can occur when things do not go as expected. Play and playfulness can effectively assist with self-regulatory processes, and the need to interact safely with the animals helps clients modify their reactions and behaviors. Because animals give "honest" reactions, a skilled therapist using AAPT can help the client understand when their behavior brings the animals closer or when it moves them away. (Animals at no time are expected to "put up with" inappropriate behaviors of clients, and they often work off-lead so they can always move away at will.). When animals seek out the clients of their own volition, it can have a powerful impact on clients who might feel disengaged from other beings. Sometimes animals can help with difficult transitions as well.

Specific Problem Resolution and Skill Development

There are many specific goals with which AAPT can be used. Learning to communicate better with a dog can assist learning to communicate better with humans. Helping an animal overcome a fear (with the guidance of the therapist) can provide new tools for facing and overcoming human fears. AAPT can also be used for client goals such as overcoming a fear of dogs, tactile defensiveness, fine motor movements (e.g., to give the animal a treat), or pronouncing certain phonemes more clearly (e.g., when giving the dog verbal cues to perform a certain behavior). It is useful for building attentiveness, reducing anxiety, and building friendships with the skills and knowledge gained in this work.

All of these goal areas can be merged with other forms of treatment for clients with autism, too. For example, AAPT goals and methods can be readily adapted for use with AutPlay Therapy, which is a multimodal, comprehensive, and family-oriented approach designed specifically for children and adolescents with autism (Grant, 2017a, 2017b).

Factors Related to Clients with Autism in AAPT

Clients with autism and their families present in many different ways during therapy. They can have sudden outbursts of emotion, resist change, exhibit some odd physical movements, or recoil from the touch of an animal's hair or fur. Practitioners of AAPT should first be well trained and experienced in their professional field. Adding an animal complicates the process because there is much to attend to. Even so, once one is confident in the core therapy competencies, there are innumerable ways that animals can help.

There is never a need to push clients with autism into certain behaviors or types of interactions. For example, while an AAPT therapist might suggest that a client play the Eye Contact Game (VanFleet & Faa-Thompson, 2019) with a dog, there would never be pressure to do it if the client resisted. Emotional safety is maintained at all times. Similarly, clients who struggle with language need not speak to the animals. They can learn and use gestural signals which the animals have learned and readily understand. Very often, when the pressure to perform behaviors that feel foreign to these clients is removed, they more willingly try to engage in social interactions and communication (VanFleet & Colțea, 2012).

Therapy should not be rule-heavy. Starting with a list of rules can increase the anxiety of clients. It is far better to teach clients how to interact with the animals at the start, and then to handle behaviors that might frighten or harm animals as they arise. All clients in AAPT learn how to ask permission to meet a dog, not only from the owner but also how to ask the dog (i.e., assuming a position that invites the dog to come to them rather than approaching or intruding on the dog). The same can be done with horses, cats, goats, and other animals involved in this work. Clients also learn how to avoid things that the animals dislike and *what to do instead* (e.g., instead of hugging a dog around the neck – which is unsafe and the source of many facial bites in children – how to stand or sit parallel and scratch the shoulder, under the neck, and on the chest). These early "lessons" help clients feel safe, give them tools that will ensure better relationships with the animals, and structure interactions to ensure success for everyone involved. If a client engages in an unsafe behavior, the therapist can set boundaries, empathically listen to emotional reactions, and/or move the animal away until the situation is safer for all once again.

Patience is key, and the AAPT practitioner must know the client and the animals well, and have a range of options to help engage the client in interactions that are comfortable for all. Different activities can help build client skills for interacting, training, touching, and building a relationship with the animals.

As the AAPT process helps clients reach individual goals, it can be broadened to include family members or friends. Clients have, in essence, developed some expertise in interacting with the animal, and they can be invited to share that with their parents, peers, or classmates. A case example of this follows.

Case Example

Sarah Gordon is a special needs teacher in England. She is also certified in the use of AAPT. With her Newfoundland dog, Frank, she has developed a program that has been highly successful (personal communication, October 15, 2017). Because Frank is large and completely black in color, Sarah has created a cardboard cut-out that looks like and is the same size as Frank. With her clients with autism, she first introduces them to the cut-out so they can be better prepared to meet Frank. After they meet Frank and learn how to interact with him in ways that he enjoys, they learn his various cues and behaviors, how to give him treats, how to stand with him, and how to handle it if he has some trouble following directions. Only humane, positive methods are used. While the child's focus is often on the dog and the skills, much relationship building occurs during this time, both with Frank and with Sarah.

After several weeks of working with Frank, the client decides which classmate they will invite to a later session to teach the classmate about Frank. This can create considerable anxiety, so Sarah works with the client to prepare for the meeting when the classmate/friend comes. Eventually the client welcomes the classmate/friend, teaches and demonstrates how to interact with Frank for some simple behaviors, helps the friend do it correctly, asks the friend to help with some aspect of the interaction, and enjoys being able to use new-found social skills to communicate and give positive feedback to the friend. Clients who are nonverbal can demonstrate the entire lesson nonverbally for their classmate and friend if so desired, but most seem to prefer speaking if they are able. (Speech therapy can even be incorporated, as the dog can be trained to respond to unique cues that include phonemes and speech patterns that the client is working on.) It is common for clients to experience great pride and excitement when achieving this milestone.

Developing Competence in AAPT

AAPT requires considerable training and supervision for therapists to master, as well as care in the selection of an appropriate animal, training using positive methods, and building a solid relationship between therapist and animal. All of this needs to occur prior to working with an animal using this modality with any client, including those with autism. A description of the training process, competencies, and full certification can be found in VanFleet and Faa-Thompson (2017) and at www.iiaapt. org. This approach offers the emotional safety required by clients with autism as well as a wide range of versatile methods to help with many of the challenges faced by clients with autism.

Referrals for AAPT or AAI

Because of the time it takes to develop skills and full certification in AAPT, as well as the need to have animals of one's own to involve, some therapists might wish to refer their clients with Autism to other AAPT or AAI programs. This requires care and a bit of homework.

First, one must consider the timing of such a referral. If the client is seriously dysregulated and unable to follow directions, or has numerous and unpredictable emotional episodes, moving into some form of animal-assisted therapy can be counterproductive. Animals are unpredictable, even if they have been thoroughly vetted and trained, and something as small as a lick to the hand might be extremely uncomfortable to the child. Conversely, if the child is prone to grasping and pulling hair, it is unfair to ever expect an animal to experience that. In cases such as this, initial therapies can help prepare the client for later involvement with animals. The use of animal books and toys can help pave the way as well.

Second, the animals must be appropriate. Some children are drawn to dogs, others to horses, cats, or even goats, pigs, and donkeys. Animals involved in the therapy must be well suited for the type of AAI they are being asked to perform. This does not mean that the animals must be completely docile and tolerant. Animals who eagerly and freely approach and interact with children can be very helpful in building social relationships, provided they are still under therapist control. Active animals are not ruled out, but the "goodness of fit" between animal and therapeutic tasks must be well established. AAPT uses a goodness-of-fit model for the wide range of interventions in which animals can participate. Animals must also be prepared for the work using positive reinforcement-based training methods. Punishment and corrections have no place in the therapeutic environment. Not only do they fail to consider the animals' well-being, they also provide a very poor model and metaphor of human behavior in relationships!

Third, one must determine if the AAI therapist is well trained in the treatment of autism and is willing to coordinate their work with others involved with the client. It is important that therapists first and foremost know how to do the therapeutic work with this population, and then later have had training in how to incorporate the animals into their work.

Fourth, before referring to someone for an AAI program, clinicians should become familiar with the competencies that those involving therapy animals must have (Stewart et al., 2016; VanFleet & Faa-Thompson, 2017). Some certifications are based on demonstrated competencies (such as that for those certified in AAPT; see certification manual and directory at www.iiaapt.org). Others require primarily online or reading work, but very little hands-on experience. It can be beneficial to ask the other therapist what

(1) training, (2) supervision, and (3) experience they have had, as well as (4) their model of intervention when involving animals.

Fifth, it is reasonable to ask the AAI therapist if you can visit the program and the animal. What *sounds* good in their descriptions of their programs does not mean that they *are* good, so it is good to see as much as you can for yourself. Trust your own observations more than what the person says. How do they handle the animals? Do they pull the animal around to do their bidding? Do they scold the animal or make harsh noises to correct the animal? Or (better indicators) do they keep a loose leash or no leash at all so that the animal can move away as desired? Do they have a "safe space" where the animal can go and not be followed by people? Does the animal seem friendly and eager to interact with people? Is the animal well behaved overall? Or (not so good indicators), does the animal jump up, ignore requests of the handler, bark a lot, startle easily with sounds or quick movements, look sad or anxious, lean away from people, or seem hesitant to interact? All of these are clues about the AAI therapist's skill and the appropriateness of the animal.

Summary

While various forms of AAI can be an excellent adjunct to the therapies required of children and young people with autism and their families, caution is needed. Due to the rocketing popularity of animals in therapy, there are some cautions to consider along the way when referring to other programs. The commitment to training and supervision needed to develop the competencies that have been defined for therapists is considerable. Even so, when the right animals and well-trained therapists with skill in treating individuals on the autism spectrum are in place, many wonderful benefits can attend.

Often, there are breakthroughs that many years of therapy have not afforded. The client with autism first learns what it means to be in a safe relationship and opens up more fully. Clients can then learn to trust humans using some of the same skills and approaches they learn with the animals. The process can be fun for them, when AAPT is used by a skilled therapist. In some of the author's cases, as well as those she has supervised, full natural play has occurred with the animals, often the most play that parents and caregivers have ever seen. Parents often express surprise and gratitude at the combined power of play and animals in helping their children as well as their own relationships with their children.

Recommended Resources for Professionals

- VanFleet, R., & Faa-Thompson, T. (2017). *Animal Assisted Play Therapy*. Sarasota, FL: Professional Resource Press.
- Grant, R. J. (2017). *Play-based interventions for autism spectrum disorder and other developmental disabilities*. New York, NY: Routledge.

Recommended Resources for Families

- Animal Assisted Play Therapy- Playful Pooch Program: http://risevan fleet.com/aapt/

About the Author

Risë VanFleet, PhD, RPT-S, CDBC is a Licensed Psychologist, Registered Play Therapist-Supervisor, and Certified Dog Behavior Consultant in Boiling Springs, Pennsylvania. She trains and supervises therapists in play therapy, Filial Therapy, and AAPT throughout the world. She is the author of numerous books, articles, and chapters on these topics as well. Her coauthored book with Tracie Faa-Thompson (cited in this chapter), *Animal Assisted Play Therapy*, was recognized with a 2018 Maxwell Award as the best book on the human–animal bond category. She can be reached through www.iiaapt.org.

References

Grant, R. J. (2017a). *AutPlay therapy for children and adolescents on the autism spectrum: A behavioral play-based approach* (3rd ed.). New York, NY: Routledge.

Grant, R. J. (2017b). *Play-based interventions for autism spectrum disorder and other developmental disabilities.* New York, NY: Routledge.

Stewart, L. A., Chang, C. Y., Parker, L. K., & Grubbs, N. (2016). *Animal-assisted therapy in counseling competencies.* Alexandria, VA: American Counseling Association, Animal-Assisted Therapy in Mental Health Interest Network.

VanFleet, R., & Colţea, C. (2012). Helping children with ASD through Canine Assisted Play Therapy. In L. Gallo-Lopez, & L. C. Rubin (Eds.), *Play-based interventions for children and adolescents with autism spectrum disorders* (pp. 39–72). New York, NY: Routledge.

VanFleet, R., & Faa-Thompson, T. (2017). *Animal Assisted Play Therapy.* Sarasota, FL: Professional Resource Press.

VanFleet, R., & Faa-Thompson, T. (2019). *Manual of Animal Assisted Play Therapy techniques.* Boiling Springs, PA: Play Therapy Press.

Part XIV

Legal and Financial Planning

There are a few topics we don't discuss in mixed company: religion, politics, and money. As a professional, you probably end up hearing about all three of those forbidden topics, but you really need to be able to initiate and encourage conversations about money and legal rights. Families rarely *want* to discuss topics such as money, financial planning, guardianship, or how their child will make decisions when their parents are not around. But you already know that not wanting to have the discussion doesn't make the need to have the discussion magically disappear.

In this part we discuss money and decision-making. We learn about the philosophy of an abundance model, how that shapes financial decisions, and about creating a financial plan that invites optimistic life goals into the conversation. We also learn about specific tools available such as the ABLE (Achieving a Better Life Experience) account and Social Security Disability Income (SSDI). (If you haven't had an SSDI conversation in your office in a while, you really need to be initiating these fun conversations!) Finally, we learn about supported decision-making – a way to conceptualize how adults make decisions, and how to help adults make decisions as independently as possible.

Money – it is a thing that is on our minds, but rarely are we given permission to discuss it directly. Please allow conversations about money to be invited into your office, and please help these families by making timely referrals to financial and legal professionals.

40 Options for Adulthood

How to Support Decision-Making and Independence for People with Autism

Melissa L. Keyes

We make thousands of decisions every day – some more complex than others. Regardless of the decision, each one involves the same process: understanding the issue; gathering information; identifying possible choices; determining a course of action; making or implementing your choice; and evaluating the consequences. Sometimes these steps happen instantaneously, for example, when deciding what to wear or what to have for lunch. Other times, we are much more deliberate, like when deciding whether to take a new job or where to live. No matter what choice we make, as adults with presumed capacity, those decisions are generally respected. We have self-determination, or control, over the direction our lives are taking. Unfortunately, not everyone has the same right. People on the autism spectrum or others who may have difficulty making decisions due to disability may be prevented from exercising self-determination and independence to the greatest extent possible. Think of a time where someone has made a choice for you – even a simple one like what to eat for dinner – and how frustrating that can feel. Imagine someone making your major decisions – where to live, how to spend your free time, whether you can spend your money – and keep that feeling of frustration in mind as we explore various ways to support people with autism exercise as much self-determination as possible.

Decision-Making on the Spectrum

There exists a body of research suggesting that people with autism have different approaches to decision-making than their neurotypical peers (Luke, Clare, Ring, Redley, & Watson, 2011). For example, people with autism have demonstrated more erratic patterns of choice and a greater motivation by fear of failure than sensitivity to reward (Luke et al., 2011). A survey study found that, compared with neurotypical individuals, people with autism reported experiencing greater anxiety, exhaustion, problems engaging in the decision-making process, and a tendency to avoid decision-making altogether (Luke et al., 2011). Anecdotally, people with autism report becoming "locked up" or freezing when faced with making a decision (Luke et al., 2011). These tendencies may present challenges for people with autism to make decisions in the moment or when under stress. Fortunately, there are ways to support or accommodate someone in the decision-making process to help address these challenges.

Options to Support Decision-Making

There is a growing civil rights movement centered on the proposition that all people should be able to exercise self-determination. This means that people should have control, input, and an ability to make decisions affecting their lives to the greatest extent possible. One way to enhance self-determination is to embrace the concept of supported decision-making. In its most basic understanding, supported decision-making is a way to accommodate the decision-making process. The core principle of supported decision-making is that the person uses "supporters" – generally trusted friends, relatives, or caregivers – to help them through the decision-making process, but the person retains the ultimate decision-making authority. The concept itself is not new. Indeed, most of us consult friends, family members, or professionals when faced with a complex decision. However, the formalization and legal recognition of supported decision-making as a valid way for someone to make a decision are gaining traction nationwide. For people with autism, supported decision-making may be a good tool to help address challenges in the decision-making process. For example, if a person with autism "locks up" when faced with a decision (a problem in gathering information or implementing a choice, perhaps), the supporter could assist with behavioral strategies the person needs to "unlock," enabling the person to make the decision. The following is an example to put the concept into context.

Alex is a 22-year-old male with Asperger's syndrome. He lives at home with his parents and has a job working as a stock clerk at an electronics store. He is of average intelligence, and while he is capable, relies on his parents to oversee most of his affairs. Alex's parents do this informally and they do not have guardianship over him.

Alex injures his knee at work and the course of treatment is presented as either surgery or a trial of physical therapy and anti-inflammatory injections – neither of which sound appealing and the options are causing Alex a great deal of anxiety. Alex is unsure what decision to make and as his anxiety increases, he begins exhibiting self-stimulating behavior in the doctor's office. Alex's mom, serving as a supporter, recognizes that Alex needs some assistance and takes him outside for some fresh air. She helps to ease his anxiety by writing down the options and helps him create a visual list of pros and cons for each choice. Ultimately, Alex is able to make the decision himself and communicate that decision to his doctor.

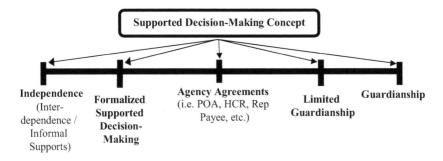

Figure 40.1 Spectrum of Support. POA, Power of Attorney; HCR, Health Care Representative; Rep Payee, Representative Payees.

This is an example of supported decision-making. It can be a powerful tool to promote independence and self-determination (Blanck & Martinis, 2015). Had Alex not used a supporter in this situation, it is possible that his behavior and inability to make a decision would lead the doctor to perceive that he is unable to make a decision and thus needs a guardian to decide and consent to treatment.

The goal with any intervention, even one focused on decision-making, is to intervene in the least restrictive manner possible. There are several options available to provide support for decision-making and promoting independence. The following is a brief discussion on several types of tools, ranging from least restrictive to most restrictive (Figure 40.1).

Informal Supports

Informal supports are tools to help fill gaps in someone's needs with minimal intrusion into their life. These supports generally take the form of technology, tools, or help from friends or family. In the example above, Alex's parents provide informal support in helping to manage his affairs. There are infinite creative ways to support someone's needs using informal supports or technology; for example, using smart home apps to help someone who forgets to lock doors or close garages, or using credit cards with low spending limits or store-specific gift cards to help someone with budgeting. Even a simple paper calendar can help a person better organize their time and tasks. The key is thinking creatively and capitalizing on the person's strengths and interests to find ways to support their independence.

Formalized Supported Decision-Making

As mentioned previously, the concept of supported decision-making is a way to support the decision-making process, but the person makes the choice themselves. Formalization of supported decision-making generally means writing that plan into a document called a supported decision-making agreement. In formalized supported decision-making, the person chooses the areas where they need support – for example, finances, health care, or employment. The person also chooses who they want to serve as supporters and how they want that support to be given. In the example above, Alex's supported decision-making agreement might include his mother as a supporter and outline the strategies he wants to use if he "locks up" and is unable to make a decision (i.e., remove him from the situation if he starts to become anxious and help him better articulate the pros and cons of the available options). Some states that recognize supported decision-making in statute require the agreements to be on a specific form or to adhere to specific rules; however, generally a court does not need to approve a supported decision-making agreement in order to use one. The agreements are flexible and are under the control of the person using them.

Agency Agreements

There are many types of agency agreements. The one most people are familiar with is a power of attorney (POA) document. In general, agency agreements allow a person to appoint someone else to make decisions or act on their behalf in certain situations. These arrangements can be revoked by the person (so long as they are still competent) and do not require court oversight. The scope of the documents varies greatly depending on the type of support being provided. Some common examples, in addition to powers of attorney, are health care representative (HCR), representative payees (Rep Payee) to oversee social security or veteran's benefits, or trustees overseeing trust accounts. These tools are considered slightly more restrictive because in fact the decision is being made by the agent or attorney, not the person – compared to supported decision-making, where the person makes the decision. These tools are important as part of sound advanced planning; however, they should not be used as a way to supplant the choice of the person and should work to further the person's wishes and best interest.

Guardianship

Guardianship in any form requires court involvement. Each state has its own laws regarding guardianship. In some states, being under guardianship removes the person's ability to vote, to marry, to choose where to live, what job to have, or whether to attend college. Guardianship, while a necessary tool for those who need it, is a significant infringement on a person's civil rights and should only be used if the person truly lacks capacity to make decisions.

There are different types of guardianships – temporary, limited, and full (also called plenary). Temporary guardianships allow someone to make decisions for a person for a short period of time. The guardianship automatically goes away after that time period expires. A limited guardianship allows someone to make decisions for a person only in the areas specifically outlined by the court. The person retains the right to make decisions in all other areas of their life. Generally, limited guardianship is over just the person – meaning decisions relating to health care or living arrangements; or the estate – meaning decisions relating to finances or property. Full or plenary guardianship means that the guardian makes all decisions allowed by law. Guardianships can be difficult and costly to terminate, so it is important to consider the least restrictive option available to support someone. The concept of supported decision-making can be used even by those currently under guardianship as a way to develop decision-making skills, which may lead to the ability to use a less-restrictive option.

There are other tools not specifically discussed here that could also help people in certain situations, including protective orders, psychiatric advanced directives, shared or team-based decision-making, and living wills. Many of these tools can be used in combination or change over time to provide individualized support. Readers are encouraged to talk to an attorney in their state to learn more about different tools that might be available and what state-specific requirements exist to use them.

Role of the Therapist in Decision-Making

As therapists, you have great influence over someone's ability to make decisions. You may be called upon to provide medical testimony about a person's capacity to make decisions in a guardianship proceeding. You may be presented with a client in your office who needs some assistance in making decisions. When determining a person's ability to make decisions, whether for purposes of guardianship or informed consent to treatment, keep the importance of self-determination in mind. Self-determination has been linked to positive outcomes in living independently, managing finances, and employment (Blanck & Martinis, 2015). Lack of control over one's life, on the other hand, has been associated with decreased quality of life and poorer health outcomes (Blanck & Martinis, 2015). Decision-making is a skill that can be learned, refined, and supported. You can counsel families to seek out information about options available to support their loved one; you can advocate for more appropriate treatment goals and encourage active participation by the person in treatment planning. Finally, you can support them when they make a decision by respecting their choice. Because no one likes having decisions made for them, even if it is only dinner.

Recommended Resources for Professionals

- Indiana Disability Rights: in.gov/INSDM
- American Bar Association: www.americanbar.org/groups/law_aging/resources/wings-court-stakeholder-partnerships.html
- National Resource Center for Supported Decision-Making: www.supporteddecisionmaking.org

Recommended Resources for Families

- Indiana Disability Rights: in.gov/INSDM
- Autistic Self-Advocacy Network: https://autisticadvocacy.org/policy/toolkits/choices/
- Justice for Jenny Hatch Project: http://jennyhatchjusticeproject.org/
- American Bar Association: www.americanbar.org/groups/law_aging/resources/wings-court-stakeholder-partnerships.html
- National Resource Center for Supported Decision-Making: www.supporteddecisionmaking.org

About the Author

Melissa L. Keyes is the Legal Director for Indiana Disability Rights, the state's protection and advocacy agency which provides legal services to individuals with disabilities. Ms. Keyes received her law degree from Indiana University McKinney School of Law. She was the Editor-in-Chief for the *Indiana Health Law Review*, and was selected as a Program on Law and State Government Fellow. During law school, Ms. Keyes served as a research and policy consultant to the Autism Society of Indiana. Before becoming an attorney, Ms. Keyes worked at Riley Hospital in the autism clinic, at which time she earned her Master's degree in clinical psychology. Ms. Keyes has an interest in advocating for options to support decision-making in adulthood. She represented Jamie Beck in becoming the first person in Indiana to have a guardianship terminated in favor of supported decision-making and regularly speaks on the subject both locally and nationally. Ms. Keyes can be reached at mkeyes@indianadisabilityrights.org.

References

Blanck, P., & Martinis, J. G. (2015). "The right to make choices": The National Resource Center for Supported Decision-Making. *Inclusion*, *3*(1), 24–33. doi:10.1352/2326-6988-3.1.24

Luke, L., Clare, I. C. H., Ring, H., Redley, M., & Watson, P. (2011). Decision-making difficulties experienced by adults with autism spectrum conditions. *Autism*, *16*(6), 612–621. doi:10.1177/1362361311415876

41 Planning for the Financial Future of Individuals with Autism

Clayton Olson

Planning for our own financial future can be a daunting task for most people. When can I retire? How much money do I need to have saved before I can retire? How many years of retirement need funding? How much money should I save and what types of accounts should I use? How will I pay for my children's college education? Who would be impacted financially if I were to become disabled and could no longer work? If I died unexpectedly what financial position would my family be in? There are many questions with no easy answers and a lot of variables between today and the future.

Now imagine that in addition to planning for your own financial future, there is a person who is dependent on your support physically, emotionally, and financially. They will probably outlive you and still need the support that you have provided for them, but you will no longer be there to give it. You will need to make sure that the people who will provide that support are identified, educated, and involved in the life of your child, so that when they need to take on the support role, the transition will be as smooth as possible. You will also need to make sure that the financial resources to pay for the things that they need are in place so that the life to which they are accustomed can continue even when you are gone.

This is the situation that families with a person diagnosed on the autism spectrum find themselves facing. While each situation is unique based on the severity of the symptom presentation, and each family's situation has unique strengths, there are many similarities to the solutions that each family needs. You may ask yourself, "What can I do as a therapist to help them be prepared and find the resources for these types of decisions?" That is a great question and it is what we will explore in this chapter.

We can separate financial planning for an individual with autism and their family into three main components: income, assets, and people. How these three things interact will be different, though, based on age (supporting a minor child versus an adult), and the financial situation of the parents.

Meet Michael

Michael is a 17-year-old male with autism. He lives at home with both of his parents and a younger brother, Steve, who is in elementary school. He also has a sister, Jackie, who is 23 and is attending college out of state. His father, John, is 53 years old and is employed as a software engineer for a large tech company; his mother, Cindy, is 51 years old and is employed as an office manager at a dental office. Michael enjoys school and has a good social circle there, but his parents feel that, while he will be able to work in the future, he will continue to need a moderate level of ongoing support; they hope that some day he will be able to live in supported independence outside their home. Based on their family income and the fact that John and Cindy have always been able to pay for the services Michael needs, they have never investigated what government assistance is available for Michael, and they assumed that they would not qualify for any government support based on their income. Michael's older sister Jackie adores him, and she is John and Cindy's first choice to be Michael's caregiver if something were to happen to them.

Income

While Michael is a minor, the income used for any qualification of benefits would be his parents' household income. This will change once Michael reaches the age of 18 and is an adult. He would then qualify for any benefits based on his own income and not his parents', even if he is still living at home. There are income limits for Michael to qualify for Supplemental Security Income (SSI) and Medicaid that John and Cindy will need to be aware of. Earned and unearned income sources for Michael are also treated differently when calculating eligibility for any potential benefits for Michael.

What is considered income and how it is treated can be found on the Social Security website at Understanding SSI (see *Recommended Resources for Professionals and Families*, below). Qualification for government benefits like SSI and Medicaid is used as a gateway qualification for many other government benefits that are available in order to reduce the complexity of determining eligibility for different programs.

If there is a change in earnings or Michael were to start or stop working, it must be reported to Social Security no later than the 10th day of the month after the change. Since Michael was diagnosed prior to age 22, when John and Cindy reach retirement age and begin drawing their social security benefits, Michael would be able to qualify for a benefit from Social Security Disability Income (SSDI) based on either John or Cindy's earnings history and he would no longer need to qualify for SSI.

Assets

While Michael is a minor, the assets used for any qualifications of benefits would be his parents' assets. This will change once Michael turns 18 and is an adult. He will then be evaluated for eligibility based on assets that are titled in his name only. It is important that John and Cindy take steps to keep the countable assets in Michael's name under $2,000 so that he can qualify for government benefits.

The Social Security website documents what they consider to be countable and non-countable assets.

There are a few options available to help John and Cindy keep his countable assets under $2,000, even if Michael is working. The first option is an ABLE (Achieving a Better Life Experience) account. ABLE accounts are a relatively new account for persons who were diagnosed with a disability prior to age 26. The money invested in these accounts is not countable as an asset for Medicaid and SSI (up to $100,000). The money in these accounts grows tax-deferred, meaning no taxes are paid on an annual basis while it is growing. If the money in the ABLE account is used to pay for a qualified disability expense (QDE), then the distribution does not count as income to the beneficiary and there are no income taxes due on the distribution. The definition of a QDE is intentionally very broad, affording latitude and flexibility regarding the use of these funds.

There are annual contribution limits for an ABLE account, and a maximum amount that can be held in the account.

The ABLE National Resource Center is a great place for John and Cindy to get more information about the ABLE account in their state. Michael can direct the spending of the money in this account if he retains the capacity to make financial decisions.

Another resource is *Practical Money Skills* by VISA (see *Recommended Resources for Professionals and Families*, below). Available in 19 languages, *Practical Money Skills* has lesson plans and materials that teach concepts like making decisions, making money, budgeting, shopping, living on your own, banking and credit, protecting your money, and saving and investing. This is a free resource to teach financial literacy and is geared towards students with special needs.

A special needs trust (SNT) is also a tool that can also be used safeguard funds for individuals. There are different types of SNT to be considered, depending on whether the assets to be moved into it are coming from the person with the disability, such as from a settlement or inheritance; or if the assets are coming from a third party, such as parents or other family members. The assets inside the SNT are not countable towards Medicaid or SSI qualification, and there is no maximum limit on the dollar amount that can be placed into these types of trusts. These assets are controlled by a trustee, and the beneficiary has no control over how the assets are used; that said, the assets can be used for almost anything that benefits the beneficiary. An attorney is needed to set up an SNT, and this is typically done in conjunction with the parents doing their own estate planning so that the plans are integrated together.

People

One of the biggest challenges we see in planning for individuals with disabilities is finding the successor caregivers for their child. Many parents stop looking for a successor caregiver when they find a (singular!) person who says yes. The reality is that there needs to be two or three back-up successor caregivers, and the list needs to be updated on a regular basis. Circumstances change over time, and willing volunteers may find that they can no longer serve as a caregiver.

> *For example, even though Jackie adores her brother, she may end up living in a different state than Michael and her parents. If something happened to her parents, moving Michael to a different state could disrupt his benefits and pull him away from his support network. There may be waiting lists in the new state for services that he is already receiving in the state he lives in. Given career and family obligations, Jackie may not able to move back to take care of Michael in the state he lives in and there may be too many negative consequences to moving Michael to a new state. Jackie may have health concerns that would prohibit her from taking care of Michael for a time or indefinitely. In addition to having multiple people identified to support Michael if something were to happen to John and Cindy, they also need to make sure that those people understand Michael's situation.*

One tool to help with this is called a letter of intent (LOI). An LOI is a document that is created to communicate what the next caregiver would need to know to take care of an individual and to minimize the negative effects of a transition. The LOI covers things such as personal information, health history, likes and dislikes, routines, important relationships, current benefits and services, locations of important documents and anything else that would help them understand and take care of an individual better. While this is not a legal document, the future caregivers for a person will generally follow the LOI unless in their judgment something needs to be done differently due to changes in circumstances.

Summary

It indeed takes a village to raise a child. That concept most certainly applies to helping individuals who have been diagnosed with autism reach their full potential. The collaboration of the important people in their lives is essential to helping them grow as individuals.

While you do not need to be an expert in financial planning for your clients, it is important to know that they need a plan in place to make sure that the people and resources their child needs to succeed will be there throughout their lives. You can help your clients and their families discuss the planning that is necessary to ensure a successful transition of people and resources to take care of their child. Many families are overwhelmed in their daily routines and most of us are not comfortable initiating these conversations, nor seeking a professional who can help them solve these financial and legal puzzles. Clients tell us that they value the introductions that the people they already trust in their lives can give them. This is where your community connections come in to play: being connected to your community and making timely referrals is one more way you make a difference in the lives of those you serve.

The best place to get an introduction to an attorney or financial planner is to connect with the organizations in your community that serve those with disabilities and ask for referrals to people they have used and trust. If you have not been able to establish relationships, then there are also organizations to which attorneys and financial planners belong that focus on planning for families with special needs, such as the Special Needs Alliance or the Academy of Special Needs Planners.

Recommended Resources for Professionals and Families

- Morton, D. A. (2019). *Nolo's guide to social security disability* (9th ed.). Berkeley, CA: Nolo.
- Urbatsch K., & Fuller-Urbatsch, M. (2017). *Special needs trust: Protect your child's financial future.* Berkeley, CA: Nolo.

- Wright, H. (2013). *The complete guide to creating a special needs life plan: A comprehensive approach integrating life, resource, financial, and legal planning to ensure a brighter future for a person with a disability.* London, UK: Jessica Kingsley Publishers.
- Social Security, Understanding SSI: www.ssa.gov/ssi/text-understanding-ssi.htm
- ABLE National Resource Center: www.ablenrc.org
- Practical Money Skills: www.practicalmoneyskills.com/teach/lesson_plans/special_needs
- Center for Parent Information & Resources: www.parentcenterhub.org
- The ARC: www.thearc.org
- Special Needs Alliance: www.specialneedsalliance.org
- Academy of Special Needs Planning: www.specialneedsanswers.com

About the Author

Clayton Olson is a Financial Advisor in Fort Collins, Colorado with Global View Capital Advisors. He has 18 years of experience working with families to help them identify and solve the financial challenges they face while raising a family and preparing for retirement. Mr. Olson is an active member of Rotary, enjoys spending time outdoors, and has a passion for helping children. He is married to Tonya; he says he is still not sure why she said yes to his marriage proposal, but he is eternally thankful! They have seven children and three grandchildren. Most of their time outside of work is spent chasing kids from one activity to another, which they thoroughly enjoy! You can find Mr. Olson at www.gvcnoco.com.

42 Financial Planning for Families with Children with Autism

Phillip Clark

"How can we feel secure in our entire family's financial future while also planning for a secure future for our child with autism?"

"How do we make sure our financial plan provides enough funding for our child with autism in the event that we are no longer here to care for them?"

"How do we financially plan for the needed resources and experiences that our child needs today that will allow them to thrive now – and in the future?"

Questions like these, and many others, frequently concern parents who have a child on the autism spectrum who will potentially need supplemental financial support for the rest of his or her life. Planning seems overwhelming, frustrating, and confusing since there are often so many unknowns about their child's future, yet every family needs to plan. Families who have a child with autism must address many challenges in planning for their family's successful financial future. Many of these financial challenges are faced by every family, regardless of whether there is a special needs diagnosis or not. Here are some financial mistakes I have seen families make, and some solutions I encourage.

Not being as efficient as possible. Most families, because of inefficiencies in their planning, are losing assets out of their financial model. Inefficiencies can include poor decisions around acquiring and paying down debt, investments that don't align with your overall goals, paying unnecessary taxes, and owning insurance products that are too expensive or don't cover your risks appropriately. This often occurs without them even knowing they are losing cashflow.

The solution? Because increasing cashflow is vital to achieving future goals, the first step in any successful financial plan is to find inefficiencies, fix those inefficiencies, and put that "found money" back into monthly cashflow. Finding extra cashflow and putting it back to work in a sound financial model, compounded over time, can make a tremendous difference in a family's future security.

Not making financial decisions by following a rules-based approach. Most families don't have an overall strategy for how they make future planning decisions. Instead, they work with many different financial institutions and advisors (e.g., banks, insurance agents, credit card companies, retirement accounts). As a result, they often implement many *different* strategies that conflict with one another. Unless families have established their own rules for their own unique financial goals, it's likely that these institutions will make decisions independently that are not aligned with the overall goals and priorities of the families.

The solution? It is vital that all financial strategies families implement work together for the overall long-term success of their financial plans. For this to happen, families need to think about what matters most to them and what rules and strategies they want to utilize across all of their financial planning considerations. By beginning with their preferred rules in mind, families can ensure that every financial decision they make reflects the goals and priorities they have predetermined are appropriate for their family situation.

Not emulating the financial strategies of successful institutions. Financial institutions are among the most successful and secure sectors of our economy because they have an approach to managing their own money that allows for one dollar to accomplish multiple goals and grow efficiently. However, the advice financial institutions offer to typical families is often contrary to the institution's own financial strategies. Think about a bank, for example. A bank will encourage you to store your money in various savings accounts and systematically add to those accounts to save for the future. But the bank's strategies for growing their own assets are quite different. Any inflows of assets that the bank gets, instead of sitting and accumulating in an account, are redeployed to produce multiple revenue streams for the bank.

The solution? In order to be successful with money, families must think differently from what they have been taught in the past. Instead of simply putting all of their savings in a bank account and letting the money sit, families need to follow the same strategies successful financial institutions utilize and enable every dollar they earn to do more than just one thing to benefit the family. Working with a financial advisor who understands the family's unique situation as well as the strategies used by financial institutions can be helpful to make sure families are able to think differently and plan better.

Not having an organized and coordinated approach to managing their finances. Many families' organizational method for keeping track of their financial strategies is simply stuffing all of their receipts in a shoe box. Other families go a step beyond this and keep their financial documents in a file cabinet that they might rifle through once a year. Very few families have an organizational method that allows for the clear coordination of each of their financial strategies. Since each independent financial decision can affect the family's overall financial picture, it is important for families to understand the details.

The solution? Use technology and get organized! Web-based platforms, like Intuit Mint (www.mint.com), can allow families to see a basic snapshot of their personal financial picture. National organizations, like JarredBunch Consulting (https://jarredbunch.com), provide more comprehensive tools that help families get organized and predict how decisions made today will impact their family's financial future.

Additional Hurdles

In addition to these common challenges, there are three additional hurdles that families who have a child with autism must address and find solutions for as they plan financially, including:

- Depending upon the level of disability, the family may need to plan for support for their loved one for his or her entire life – not just until they turn 18 (this often equates to planning for an extra retirement).
- The family may have waited too long to begin planning. Many families don't begin planning until they reach a state of urgency. Financial problems that could have easily been solved through planning conversations are often impossible to fully tackle at this late stage in the game.
- The family approaches financial planning with a limited mindset. Families who believe that "Financial planning is only for wealthy people" or "Planning is only for what happens when we die" often delay planning conversations or avoid them entirely. Then, when something does happen and they are unable to care for their child with autism, the situation gets even more complicated and difficult to ameliorate.

It is vital for families to find a way to overcome the financial challenges they often face as they plan for a secure future for their loved one with autism as well as make financial plans for their entire family unit. Therapists can gently encourage families to have difficult conversations so that their long-term goals of independence and fulfillment can be met. Consider the following case of Tyler and his family.

Tyler and His Family

Tyler is a 30-year-old male with autism. When he was young, Tyler's parents were concerned by certain behaviors and tendencies that they witnessed in their son. After consulting with their doctor, a local specialist, and various therapists, Tyler was diagnosed with autism. The delivery of this diagnosis began with the words, "I'm sorry...." Instead of receiving information about the positive impact Tyler could have on others' lives, Tyler's parents were bombarded by limited expectations for his life from the doctor and therapists.

When they received the diagnosis, Tyler's parents were only vaguely familiar with autism, so this news was devastating for them and negatively impacted their outlook for Tyler's life. Their hopes and dreams for the future were instantly shattered. Tyler's parents knew they needed a plan. Local autism organizations advised them to create a special needs financial plan. They quickly learned that traditional financial planning professionals only focused on helping them answer the question of "What happens to Tyler when we die?" At this point in their life, Tyler's parents were young and healthy, and with all of the new emotions swirling around in their heads from the autism diagnosis, they didn't feel like they could even begin to think about what would happen to their son if they died prematurely, never mind what Tyler might need decades from then. No family ever wants to think about worst-case scenarios. So, Tyler's parents delayed the much-needed planning conversations they knew they needed to have. They told themselves: "We'll get to it later."

As Tyler grew, his parents were introduced to other families in their community who also had children with autism. To their surprise and excitement, they discovered that many of these families had rejected the limited expectations that doctors and other professionals had placed upon their children. Instead of seeing autism as a negative that would burden their child and family, other parents had found ways to think abundantly about their children's potential and future. These attitudes were much different than how Tyler's parents had been thinking for years.

Over time, Tyler's parents became especially close to a family who had a daughter with autism, Lauren, several years older than Tyler; this family had a very abundant vision for Lauren, a teen who was working part-time at a local animal shelter, was actively involved in the family's church, and even volunteered at a local nursing home occasionally. Tyler's parents found that Lauren and her parents were a source of encouragement during difficult times. Lauren's family's mindset about Lauren's abilities and the future intrigued Tyler's parents, and they often asked questions about the path this family had taken to enable their daughter to develop such a meaningful life.

Through the course of the relationship, Lauren's parents eventually probed Tyler's parents about what strategies they had put in place that would allow Tyler to live out a full and abundant life, no matter might happen now or in the future to his parents. Tyler's parents were a little embarrassed to admit that they had not even begun their planning journey, sharing that it was just too overwhelming and difficult to plan for today, let alone think about a long-term plan to ensure Tyler was taken care of.

Lauren's family empathized with these emotions − they'd been there, too. But they were also quick to explain that their abundant vision for their daughter's life and their belief that she could live a life that meaningfully impacted others were what propelled them to create a plan for the future. To them, financial planning, and special needs planning more broadly, was not only about what would happen to Lauren when they died, but rather should be focused on helping their family become as efficient as possible so that they could provide Lauren with all of the opportunities and resources now, so that she could live a great life every day and reach her full potential.

Tyler's parents had not previously thought that planning could help them have peace of mind today − they always thought it was just about preparing for bad things that might happen in the future. With this shift in their mindset about planning, Tyler's parents were able to focus on finding time for planning and felt more motivated than ever to create a plan to enable their son to live his best possible life. This abundant mindset was the missing piece of the puzzle that had prevented them from planning previously. However, after meeting with a financial planner, they began to embrace an abundant vision for Tyler's life. This change in perspective allowed the family to plan for a purposeful and impactful future for Tyler.

The Limited vs. Abundant Mindset

A family's mindset concerning the future could be the most impactful determining factor of a family's ability to create a successful financial plan. The previous case study shows how mindset can clearly impact financial decision-making and overall outcomes for families with children with autism.

While financial planning for families with loved ones with autism does need to address the tough conversation of what happens in the future, it is just as important (if not more important) that financial planning conversations also focus on helping families become efficient, strategic, well organized, and coordinated *today* so that they are able to provide their loved ones with every opportunity to live unique lives of purpose and impact. This includes enacting strategies that allow families to save resources, and access to accounts that will allow their child to receive supplemental income while not being disqualified from receiving various government benefits (e.g., Supplemental Security Income [SSI] and Medicaid) that are vital to their ongoing support and development. Holistic financial planning provides parents with peace of mind, knowing that their loved one's security is well planned for, no matter what life events transpire.

> *Because Tyler's family was finally able and willing to adopt an abundant mindset about Tyler's life, they began viewing obstacles and challenges differently than they had before – including developing a financial plan for his future. Tyler's parents knew that every time they were able to successfully overcome a challenge through planning, they were taking one step closer to allowing Tyler to live the abundant life that they had come to envision for him.*

A holistic special needs planning process will help families make this mindset shift and transition to viewing the future of their son or daughter in a positive way.

While a family's mindset about planning might not *seem* like it impacts their financial planning decisions, cultivating an abundant mindset impacts the family in the following ways:

1. An abundant mindset helps families overcome the challenge of delaying or avoiding planning for the future (that is, thinking that planning is only about answering the "What happens when we die?" question that they'd prefer to avoid considering). Families with abundant mindsets know that planning is about answering the question of "How can we create a plan that enables our loved ones to live a purposeful, impactful life today – and every day in the future?"
2. Cultivating an abundant vision for the child's life by discussing the family's hopes and dreams and the child's many abilities, and documenting what a great life could look like, provides families with the motivation they need to not only create a financial plan, but to put that plan into action and follow the strategies they have enacted.
3. Finally, families with an abundant mindset about planning and the future are able to plan effectively, providing both current and future opportunities for their child to thrive, while simultaneously feeling secure in their *own* plan for the future, including retirement.

Financial planning for families with a child with autism should enable both the child and the family to be successful today – and every day in the future. Both plans (child and retirement) have to work together seamlessly, no matter what happens. A financial advisor who specializes in serving families with children with autism can help families evaluate their plans to determine that they work together and will continue working regardless of changing circumstance.

Questions for Therapists to Ask Clients and Families about Financial Planning

As a professional, you can encourage families to prepare in ways that help them feel secure about their own futures, as well as their children's futures.

Here are a few basic questions to help you start a conversation about financial planning:

1. Do you have a detailed plan in place to financially care for your child if something happened to you?
2. Have you calculated the amount of money (literal dollar value) required for your child with special needs to have the quality of life you envision for him or her – throughout his or her entire life?
3. Does your family's financial plan (including retirement plans) align with and complement the choices you've made through your special needs planning process, so that both plans will succeed, no matter what happens?
4. Are you confident that the financial plan you've designed is aligned with all government policies, so that your son or daughter will never be disqualified from receiving his or her government benefits?
5. If something happened to you, are there other people who know about and understand your overall financial plan for your child's life?

Therapists can make referrals to qualified financial planners to help the family attain their long-term goals of a prosperous life for their child, and peace of mind for themselves. To determine whether a financial planner is qualified to help a family with their special needs planning, the therapist should ask them the following five questions:

1. Do you specialize in guiding families through a holistic special needs planning process that addresses more than just planning financially for the future?
2. How long have you been helping families plan for their children with special needs?
3. Why do you work with families who have children with special needs?
4. How do you and your team make the client experience unique for families who have children with special needs?
5. Do you and your team collaborate with other professionals serving the special needs community? If so, how do your clients interact with these professionals?

Summary

Many families do not plan well financially, and the outcome can be particularly distressing when there is an individual with autism. Families must think about the financial future of their child with autism, especially for those on the spectrum who may encounter employment challenges or those who are disabled to the degree they cannot work. Having these difficult conversations can be rewarding when financial planning results in peace of mind, and a plan for a prosperous future for the autistic client. A holistic special needs planning process will help families make this mindset shift and transition to viewing the future of their son or daughter in a positive way. At the end of the day, special needs planning should enable an individual with autism to live a purposeful, impactful life today – and every day in the future. Having a secure financial plan in place is one piece of this holistic planning process that every family needs to complete.

Resources for Professionals

- Dweck, C. (2007). *Mindset: The new psychology of success.* New York, NY: Ballantine Books.
- Hampton, K. (2013). *Bloom: Finding beauty in the unexpected – A memoir (P.S.).* New York, NY: William Morrow Paperbacks.
- Leaf, C. (2013). *Switch on your brain: The key to peak happiness, thinking, and health.* Grand Rapids, MI: Baker Books.
- Gordon, J. (2013). *The energy bus for kids: A story about staying positive and overcoming challenges.* Hoboken, NJ: John Wiley & Sons.

Resources for Families

- Duckworth, A. (2016). *Grit: The power of passion and perseverance.* New York, NY: Simon & Schuster, Inc.
- Financial Planning tools: https://jarredbunch.com/
- Financial Planning Webinar: www.youtube.com/watch?v=L3O8K87 XYFU&t=13s
- HOW TO: Create a Special Needs Plan that Allows Your Child to Live a Purposeful, Impactful Life Webinar: www.youtube.com/watch?v=CeFiwd3kTW8&t=1116s
- Life Planning Video: www.youtube.com/watch?v=Xw0-hoyo1as&t=1s
- Olson, J., & Mann, J. D. (2013). *The slight edge: Turning simple disciplines into massive success and happiness.* Austin, TX: Greenleaf Book Group Press.
- Special Needs Planning information: https://enablesnp.com/

About the Author

For over a decade, Phillip Clark has helped families with their special needs planning. He is the Founder and President of ENABLE Special Needs Planning, an organization that serves families nationwide, helping families create truly *comprehensive* special needs plans for their loved ones with autism and other special needs. Because of personal experiences growing up with a younger sister with Down syndrome, Mr. Clark has a unique approach to planning that focuses on enabling our loved ones to live purposeful, impactful lives *today* – and every day in the future. Mr. Clark is frequently invited to speak at national and statewide conferences. You can learn more about Mr. Clark at https://enablesnp.com/.

Part XV

Moving towards Adulthood

An Important Developmental Step

Launching, adulting, finding your way … is a crucial developmental shift. No matter *when* this shift happens chronologically, the process of becoming an adult is fascinating. As therapists, we often hear the pleas from parents starting in about the junior or senior year in high school – what will become of my child? Simultaneously, we often see these very "children" either develop some skills for adulthood, *or* start to backslide under the pressure. Adulthood, increased personal responsibility, and increased freedom happen for all of us. As therapists, we can help our clients grow skills in a timely manner, rather than allow our clients to suffer.

In this part we learn about the "services cliff" that happens when individuals leave the relative safety of the educational system and drop into the adult system, perceiving themselves to be without a safety net. We hear about the power of coaching, the power of the word *yet*, about growing self-awareness skills, and accessing guided practice. Finally, we hear from a writer who breaks the model of launching and re-creates a model of a ramp, highlighting the need for interdependence, not independence. No matter what you call it – launching, ramping, adulting – it is going to happen. Help your clients prepare to navigate this wonderful period of life.

43 Launching into Adulthood

Transitioning with the Youth at the Center

Matt Cloven

Parenting, no matter who your child is, has one end goal – preparing that child to lead the best quality of a life possible once they enter adulthood. For all parents, this goal of launching our children into adulthood with the skills they need to be both successful and happy is a challenge. This task often feels more challenging when raising a child who lives on the autism spectrum. Parents of a child who lives with autism must focus on getting them to/from extra-curricular activities, or making it through high school, but as the child shifts into adulthood, different questions arise. Parents begin to ask questions such as: Can my child live independently when they are an adult? Will they have the skills to make safe decisions? Will they have friends or social outlets and not just hide out in their room or apartment? Will they be able to get and hold a job?

What Is the Professional's Role in the Launching Process?

As professionals who are working with families and individuals who live with autism, it is imperative that we consciously be a support and conduit for parents to help them plan for their youth's future and help create a vision of what that future can look like. As professional advocates, we are in a role of trust and looked upon to help bring focus and guidance into areas of life they may not fully see or understand themselves. Each child's launching into adulthood will be unique. One of our roles is to recognize the personal strengths, interests, and barriers that an individual lives with, then help translate those qualities into assistance about resources, identifying which areas need to be focused on, and where and to whom to turn. Advocates can assist by taking a positive, strength-based approach to goal setting when advancing this transition to the future.

As an advocate who has worked directly with families and youth transitioning into adulthood, one phrase I have consistently heard from parents is, "My child is almost 18 and about to leave public school. What should I do or what should I be focusing on?" The youth themselves may also be asking this question. The transition from high school can be a frightening transition for families, as they are now required to ponder uncertain answers to questions about their future. Typical concerns are about the youth's social life, job/career, and ability to live independently. The unique context of how autism influences the youth's social, emotional, behavioral, executive functioning and neurological processing, adaptive behavior, and other impacted needs will influence the transition into adulthood. Therapists can help identify the need to plan and prioritize for the future goals into adulthood. Therapists can help the youth and their family by helping them develop a plan in response to the question: "What does being an adult look like and what skills are needing to be developed?"

Unfortunately, all too often, questioning, processing, and planning for launching into adulthood come at the eleventh hour, where questions about independent living skills, residence, finances, public support services, social isolation, education, or employment will become a reality in a few short months. It is imperative that we are asking questions about what adulthood looks like early on, and not assume that this planning has already taken place. No matter what the child's age, transitions require planning and preparing, knowing what questions to ask, and having time to find the right resources specific to the child's needs.

Formulating the Question for Parents and Young Adults

For transition planning, the right time to be thinking about this is now! Age 3 is appropriate; age 7 is also appropriate; by age 14, it is vital. It is imperative we highlight the tasks of preparing for adulthood with the parent or individual, then direct them to those who can help with transition planning and goal setting. Clear goals will help the team determine what skills the youth needs to learn so they can be successful and as independent as possible later in life. Helpful questions to ask parents are:

- Where do you see your child when they are 25? 35? When you are no longer here?
- What do you see them doing or wanting to do when they are an adult? Where are they living? Who is in their life and what supports do you see them needing?
- What are your child's natural strengths and interests?
- In what areas does your child genuinely need help?

These questions generally set the stage for opening the door to helping identify what is important for both the parents and the youth, helping assess the youth's goals, interests, strengths, and areas of concern or struggle.

Knowing what questions to ask is often the biggest barrier for individuals and/or families when they are being asked to imagine their own or their child's future as an adult. When asking, "What do you want or see as your child becomes an adult?" a common response I hear from parents is, "I want them to be happy and safe." In asking a young adult who lives with autism, the common response is that they want friends (social), want to do the things they are interested in (independence), and want to go to school or make money (purpose). As you already know, "What do you want out of life?" or "What do you want your life to be?" are not simple questions with clear answers. It is often our role as professionals to help parents tease out the details of what a happy, safe, social, independent, purposeful life means for them and/or their child. In planning for transition into adulthood, these questions can be simplified into two main questions:

- What do you see you or your child doing after high school graduation?
- What do you see as the biggest barriers to you or your child living an independent, quality life with social outlets, employment, housing, and/or higher education?

The second question is vital, as it helps highlight the most common topics that we as professionals need to discuss. I cannot emphasize this enough: we as advocates, therapists, educators, or other professionals cannot assume these questions have been asked or adequately explored when discussing transition planning into adulthood with individuals or parents of youth who live on the autism spectrum. You are strongly encouraged to initiate these conversations and deal with the fear and anxiety that are often laced into the responses (or lack of responses). Therapists can guide families by breaking down these questions into five domains to encourage more detailed planning:

- **Domain 1 (finances, daily living skills)**. Will the youth/young adult live on their own?
- **Domain 2 (social, social recreation)**. What does their community engagement look like?
- **Domain 3 (employment, volunteering, higher education, community classes)**. Will they work or continue their education?
- **Domain 4 (self-determination and health/safety)**. Will they make safe decisions and advocate effectively for themselves?
- **Domain 5 (community and professional resources to help the planning process)**. Who is involved already to help with the transition planning and process? Does the family want/need resources to help?

The first four domains (finances/daily living skills, social/recreational, employment/volunteering/higher education/community classes, self-determination/health and safety) are the framework to work from in exploring the unique strengths and needs for a youth launching into adulthood. The fifth domain (community and professional resources to help the planning process) is a vital question to help us professionals know who is involved in the individual's life (the circle of support), and if we need to help by referring the individual or family to another professional who specializes in transition planning. Keep in mind that transition-planning professionals are as varied as any profession, including case managers, special education teachers, financial planners, and attorneys. When helping a family or an individual identify professional supports, you are seeking a facilitator who can help them talk through the *dynamics* of the transition into adulthood. This includes talking openly and objectively about opportunities, identifying goals around what successful independence looks like across life domains (community, education, living, financial, legal), and creating an action plan with clear, realistic steps for that future. It is these qualities and facilitation skills that you will be looking for in a professional resource. If you are uncertain, call and interview the professional about what their experience is in working with people who live with autism and what their transition/life-planning process looks like for an individual or family.

What Does Transition Planning Look Like?

The first step in creating a transition plan is to start by identifying what specific skills the client already has, including independent living skills, community and social skills, and vocational skills. One effective method for determining these skills is to utilize a Transition Planning Inventory (TPI). These tools are generally comprehensive questionnaires that allow the parent and youth to consider current abilities and focus on specific areas that could be worked on towards greater independence. Some examples of domains explored include: Do they know how to cook using a microwave? Do they know how to balance a checkbook? Can they navigate public transportation? Can they identify recreational opportunities and are they able to attend independently? Using a TPI tool is a good first step for taking the next leap into transitioning into adulthood, the actual plan. These are also great tools to help therapists and other professionals become familiar with what questions you may want to be asking your clients when talking about if they need help with launching into adulthood. There are many TPI formats that you can find online.

Perhaps one of the most powerful tools to help plan for a youth or young adult's launch into adulthood is to create what is called a *Person-Centered Plan* (PCP). There are several structured formats to help create the PCP, including *Planning Alternative Tomorrows with Hope* (PATH), and *Making Action Plans* (MAPS) (see *Resources for the Professionals and Families* below for more information).

A person-centered approach will give you the structure to start identifying specific goals and steps toward achieving those goals based on who the focus person is and can become from a whole-life perspective. Person-centered planning is effective because it empowers the person's voice and perspective, and allows us to envision a future through the individual's eyes and experiences. In doing so, we shift the conversation from one of what services will be able to meet a youth's needs when they are an adult, to the identification of *their* dreams and goals, what action steps need to be taken, and who needs to be involved to support attaining these goals and dreams (both natural supports and paid professional supports). Person-centered planning gives the structure for this conversation to unfold in a powerful and meaningful way. As professionals who know the person in transition, you may want to be part of this dynamic process and participate in transition meetings. If so, you may want to ask permission to join the conversation outside your office, and consider playing a more active role beyond just making a referral to a person-centered planning facilitator.

Importance of Perspective in Transition Planning

When we think about transition planning, we are assembling a team: the client, the family, the transition planner who facilitates the process, and possibly you, the therapist. We must begin and end with the central belief that *every person has a gift and the ability to contribute meaningfully to their community*, regardless of their diagnosis or ability. Whether through paid employment, volunteering, being part of social or recreational groups, or other ways, the transitioning youth/young adult's gifts and dreams need to be at the center of the conversation about their transition into adulthood. They have ideas and a voice. Though their voice may need support to develop the ideas and details, or support to bring to light health or safety concerns, the planning process should be creative, open, and always focused on what will help the youth/young adult to be successful and happy, and live the best quality of life possible.

As a therapist, your perspective is a meaningful contribution to this conversation. You can be an influential person in both the youth's perspective of themselves, as well as the perspective of the parents regarding what they should be focusing on and what their child needs in the way of support and other services. Like anyone, professionals come with a perspective lens specific to their field of expertise and personal experiences. This professional perspective is why parents and individuals seek professional guidance.

Summary

Planning for the launch into adulthood requires professionals to evaluate an individual's level of independence, daily living skills, finances, and social relationships. Therapists need to be able to facilitate an understanding of the individual's purpose, and how they wish to live their adult life in an enriched and safe manner. Identifying outside sources of help to aid in the transition-planning process will be imperative. In planning for a youth's launching into adulthood, as a professional you get to be part of this conversation as support and a creative resourceful voice of experience, conversations that guide and set the stage for the greatest potential. In my experience this is an exciting and dynamic series of conversations. It is also one of the most important conversations we can have and should be having. Too many times I have seen transition planning be forgotten or under-emphasized, with the result being an increase in stress for the parent and lost opportunity for the youth. Transition planning requires a team, time, tools, and the ability to plan from a person-centered approach.

Resources for the Professionals and Families

- Planning Alternative Tomorrows with Hope (PATH): www.imagine better.co.nz/what-we-offer/planning/path/
- Making Action Plans (MAPS): https://inclusive-solutions.com/person-centred-planning/maps/
- Exploring and Implementing and Person Centered Approach: www.facs.nsw.gov.au/__data/assets/pdf_file/0008/591362/193-DADHC_PersonCentred201208-accessible.pdf
- Person Centered Planning: www.autism.org.uk/professionals/health-workers/person-centred-planning.aspx

About the Author

Matt Cloven operates a private disability-focused advocacy and consultation practice in northern Colorado. He has worked directly with individuals who live with intellectual and developmental disabilities (I/DD) and their families since 2002. His areas of expertise include special education, justice, child welfare, and person-centered planning. He has trained and presented on a variety of topics to professionals and community, including disability awareness, disability in correctional facilities, special education, and disability in child welfare. The focus of Mr. Cloven's work is centered on how to facilitate the voices, dreams and aspirations of the adults, youth, and families, including ways to increase and maintain independence and inclusion into their community. You can find Mr. Cloven at www.peace wolfadvocacy.com.

44 Countdowns, Mis-launches, and Birds in Flight

Jan Starr Campito

"Adulting" is hard – for anyone. In our culture, we have lost sight of how very many complex skills being an adult requires. The last months of high school double as a countdown to a launch into the adult world, for which many of our graduating teens are unprepared. The launch can be especially difficult for young adults with an autism spectrum profile. In my private practice, I work as a life coach for young adults with autism and other executive function, communication, and confidence-building challenges. The frustration and fear I hear from the parents who reach out for my help are real. "He's so isolated. He says he wants friends, but when I suggest he go out, he says it's too much trouble." Or, "She had a decent first semester at community college, but she seems to be crashing now. I keep telling her she should go for help, but she doesn't." "He graduated from college two years ago, but can't find a job. He's so discouraged; I think he's given up even trying."

After coming so far, making it through all the obstacles posed by the K-12 school system and maybe even some post-secondary education, it is extremely disheartening to get stuck *now* on the real-life part. The parents weren't prepared for this, and neither were their young adults. What I'm seeing in my practice are the mis-launches. These young men and women, typically somewhere in their twenties, feel beaten down. They are often heartbreakingly hard on themselves for their lack of easy flight into adulthood. They shut down, and their parents don't know what else to try. Addressing this frozen defensiveness and learned helplessness is one of the first steps in my coaching work.

And yet ... Carol Dweck, a psychologist who studies motivation, speaks about the power of that little three-letter word, "yet." Can't fly yet doesn't mean you can't fly. It just means you can't fly, *yet*. You haven't found a way that works for you, *yet*. "Yet" recognizes the possibility for growth and change. I coach my clients to change their language and their outlook by introducing them to the power of *yet* and the possibility that working together we can maybe achieve a different outcome. But for change to happen, the client first must stop being passive. Preparation for eventual success includes an attitude shift in my clients.

In their book, *Come to Life!*, Thomas Iland and his mother Emily Iland describe Thomas's life-changing realization that, instead of waiting for the life he wanted to somehow appear, he could control its manifestation by seeking it out and by taking steps to make it happen (Iland & Iland, 2017). For some of our clients, this freedom and its accompanying personal responsibility are a new and dizzying perspective, and they need help adjusting to the view. Many of my clients tell me that they've never given much thought to their future. Coaching helps the client explore themselves and what they would like to see in their lives in five or ten years, even if they aren't ready (yet) to commit to a positive vision of next year. To get them to dream, we also have to work to replace their existing image of themselves as damaged and failed with an image of a whole, complex individual. I laughed as I told one client, "You have some serious delusions of incompetence." But I couldn't have been more serious, and so my work with him involved helping him see himself the way I see him, as a person of capability and deserving of a rich, fuller life.

"Yes, but …" I hear from my clients. Yes, but it's hard. Yes, but I don't like doing that, it's boring. These "yes, buts" put the brakes on change; the words actually translate into "no!" These "yes, buts" result in a continued lockdown in the self-protective defense mode that has their parents so concerned. The coaching work here is to help our socially isolated folks in on the big secret. It can be hard, or boring, at times for everyone. Everyday life throws lots of things at all of us that we don't like or don't want to do. Taxes, anyone? Cleaning the oven? The trick in coaching is to change what we string after the "yes, but." Do we end it with the effort-deadening restatement of difficulty or distaste? Or do we substitute the positive version of "yes, but?" "Yes, but beyond this icky step is something you really want." Or, "Yes, but it'll get better; here is what we can do to help make it more manageable for you."

When I first went into coaching individuals on the spectrum, I expected most of my work to be teaching a set of skills. And in addition to helping change attitudes towards personal responsibility, teaching does play an important role in my work. But it is a different form of teaching than they may have encountered in the past. Listening carefully to my clients and probing further with nonjudgmental questions teaches me what it is they need to learn. There is a huge difference between abstract health class lessons on puberty, and individualized practice on applying that knowledge to tracking one's own menstrual cycle, taking one's birth control pills properly, or developing good, consistent personal hygiene. I find a lot of my coaching work involves discovering what my clients already know, and what are the things that none of us have thought yet to teach them – the missing pieces that they don't even realize are missing.

The most common areas that I work on with my clients are time management, emotional regulation techniques, self-knowledge of needs and how to support those needs in the context of daily life, and finally, social, communication, and employment-related skills. For example, almost all my clients struggle with the executive functioning skills needed to take control of their time. They don't effectively use planners and to-do lists, or know how to break down tasks into manageable parts that can be prioritized and scheduled. My clients almost universally note how difficult mornings are for them, and how many of their emotional and energy "spoons" they use up before they have even begun that day's real tasks. They don't know how to set up and maintain a routine that might relieve some of this exhausting burden. As their coach, I listen to what they describe and we explore what modifications they could make that might free precious resources for other things that matter to them.

Some of my clients are very informed about autism and have a great deal of self-awareness. But others, especially the younger ones, don't yet have a good grasp of how their neurology impacts their needs. They are still struggling to understand themselves, and sometimes are still wrestling with erroneous dichotomies of competence vs. flaws. Valerie Gaus' book, *Living Well on the Spectrum* (2011), contains valuable questionnaires for building self-awareness. I sometimes use these to open a dialogue with my clients. Self-knowledge is essential also for finding a job fit that works for them. Unemployment and underemployment are commonly recognized problems for individuals with disabilities, including even some of our most obviously able adults on the autism spectrum. My clients often need to address gaps in their job search preparedness before they can effectively use the agencies designed to help with their employment. How do you write a resume if you don't have an awareness of your strengths and applicable experience? How do you put in perspective whether you are qualified for a job when you are hypercritical of yourself and others, and literal in your interpretation of the job description? You may need practice developing a script for likely interview questions, using the telephone, or creating and following through on a more effective job-search strategy.

So far, all of my clients have spoken of their desire to make social connections, to find others who might share their interests and to be companions for activities, or even possible romance. Although many are introverted individuals by nature, the degree of their social isolation feels uncomfortable, even to them. It deprives them of the sources of information, perspective, and natural support that can come from being surrounded by others. I find this is one of the slowest areas to change, especially for individuals who may feel social anxiety or have had unpleasant, damaging social interactions in their past. Many of the individuals I work with are aware that they lack some social skills that they need, and yet it is very difficult to find professionals who teach these skills to adults. Having reciprocal conversations, making social plans and following through with them, dealing with criticism or conflict, and understanding the social thinking and complexities of dating and relationships are inadequately supported needs for many of our launching adults.

What can a family do to help their young adults launch and thrive? First, it takes conscious work on both sides to break the cycle of dependency that often exists between young adult and parent. We have to start to shift the parenting role away from doing for the young adult, or always directing them in what to do. We have to give the young adult space and tools so that they can move into the leading role, with the parent more in the background for backup support as needed. This shift in expectations is often facilitated when the young adult moves into employee or volunteer roles within the community, outside of the parent's immediate sphere. But it can also begin in the home by increasing personal responsibility for managing meals, shopping for clothing and personal items, medications, appointments, and household chores. In the age of YouTube and the Internet, I don't worry about adding a dedicated curriculum to teach the young adult a huge list of the discrete skills that they will need for independent living. But some of our individuals may benefit from participation in a multi-year, intensive transition program, such as the College Internship Program, or Transitions. It is useful for parents and young adults to be aware of this possible (although often expensive) resource.

I encourage parents to see mis-launches as indicative of the need for a prolonged period of guided practice – an apprenticeship to life skills. I also encourage parents and young adults to adjust their expectations. The parents who seem best equipped for helping their young adults launch are those who have already recognized that the initial launch countdown was not applicable to their own young adult's needs. An alternate timetable factoring in more extensive mentoring and financial support is actually just a different type of normal for many young adults.

My clients often don't have much of a vision of their future, much less a plan for what the steps to getting there might look like. High school transition Individualized Education Program meetings tend to address this only superficially, focusing on immediate post-graduation goals. They don't address the bigger questions of how the individual will create the adult life they might want. As parents, we are still thinking of our young adults as children, and we often don't realize the greater needs of launch planning until much later, long after our supportive high school teams and resources are gone. Then we stumble from agency to agency, trying to figure out on our own what adult supports for independent living are available, and how to work the various convoluted systems to access them. All of this takes a huge amount of time to get right, and sometimes appropriate supports and resources for a particular individual or circumstance do not even exist at all. In my dream society, transition teams would continue to be available through the schools for an extended time beyond graduation. Somehow, we have to help our folks find a space in which they can be safe, encouraged, and supported in their own individualized path towards greater independence.

Life coaching can help clarify what is important for the individual, generate practical strategies to move the client towards their goals, enhance problem-solving ability, foster independence and self-confidence, and lower anxiety by building on success. It can help provide practical mentoring, to bridge the transition between the world of the dependent child, to the world of the inter-dependent adult. Part teacher, part ally, and even part therapy dog, as a life coach I work with my clients to help them create a systematic, manageable plan that works for their life and their goals. "I think I'm starting to get the hang of this adult stuff," one young man recently told me. I know it's starting to work when I see them glance up at the sky, fluff their wings, and prepare to give it another go.

Recommended Resources for Professionals

- Gaus, V. L. (2011). *Living well on the spectrum: How to use your strengths to meet the challenges of Asperger syndrome/high-functioning autism.* New York, NY: Guilford Press.
- McManmon, M. P. (2016). *Autism and learning differences: An active learning teaching toolkit.* Philadelphia, PA: Jessica Kingsley Publishers.
- Reducille, D. (2017, April 3). The twentysomething cliff is much worse when you're autistic! *Slate.* Retrieved from https://slate.com/technology/2017/04/the-twentysomething-cliff-is-much-worse-when-youre-autistic.html
- Guare, R., Guare, C., & Dawson, P. (2019). Richard Guare, *Smart but scattered—and stalled: 10 steps to help young adults use their executive skills to set goals, make a plan, and successfully leave the nest.* New York, NY: Guilford Press.
- Bissonnette, B. (2013). *The complete guide to getting a job for people with Asperger's syndrome: Find the right career and get hired.* Philadelphia, PA: Jessica Kingsley Publishers.

Recommended Resources for Families

- Bédard, R. (2018, February 22). Redefining adulting: A brief primer for different brains. *Different brains.* Retrieved from www.differentbrains.org/adulting-brief-primer
- Campito, J. (2007). *Supportive parenting: Becoming an advocate for your child with special needs.* London, UK: Jessica Kingsley Publishers.
- Dweck, C. (2014, September). The power of believing that you can improve [Video file]. Retrieved from www.ted.com/talks/carol_dweck_the_power_of_believing_that_you_can_improve
- Iland, T. W., & Iland, E. D. (2017). *Come to life! Your guide to self discovery: Helping youth with autism and learning differences shape their futures.* Porterville, CA: Porterville Press.

- Asperger Experts. (2018). *7 easy ways to motivate someone with Asperger's.* Seattle, WA: Author.
- Asperger Autism Network. Retrieved from www.mightycause.com/ organization/Asperger-Autism-Network (this site has various webinars and forums offered, withself-advocacy Adults with Asperger's online support forum and the Parents of Adults with Asperger's forum).

About the Author

Jan Campito, M.S., M.Phil. is the parent facilitator of a large family support program for families living on the autism spectrum in the Capital District, New York. She is a former college instructor in educational psychology, the author of *Supportive Parenting: Becoming an Advocate for Your Child with Special Needs* and a frequent speaker on issues and concerns of individuals and families in the autism community. She is certified in the LifeMap coaching method employed by the Asperger Autism Network. A graduate of New York State Partners in Policy-Making, her work with adults is heavily influenced by their positive vision for a full, person-centered life. Jan can be reached at jan.campito@gmail.com.

References

Gaus, V. L. (2011). *Living well on the spectrum: How to use your strengths to meet the challenges of Asperger syndrome/high-functioning autism.* New York, NY: Guilford Press.

Iland, T. W., & Iland, E. D. (2017). *Come to life! Your guide to self discovery: Helping youth with autism and learning differences shape their futures.* Porterville, CA: Porterville Press.

45 The Launching

Dena L. Gassner

Autistic adolescents and adults are at higher risk for suicidal ideation and attempts (Cassidy et al., 2014) and for non-suicidal self-injurious behavior (Maddox, Trubanova, & White, 2016), and have higher than usual rates of co-occurring eating disorders (Baron-Cohen et al., 2013; Huke, Turk, Saeidi, Kent, & Morgan, 2013; Mandy & Tchanturia, 2015; Pooni, Ninteman, Bryant-Waugh, Nicholls, & Mandy, 2012; Rastam, 2008). They also experience barriers to accessing healthcare (Burke & Stoddart, 2014; Croen et al., 2015; Fortuna et al., 2015; Nicolaidis et al., 2013). In some of the most startling recent research, it has been found that autistics have a significantly higher mortality rate than non-disabled peers, with the average age of demise a mere 37 years (Cassidy et al., 2014; Hirvikoski et al., 2016). These concerns are what keep parents up at night.

Launching our autistic persons into the world of adulthood is often fraught with misinformation when it comes to figuring what adulthood looks like. Adulthood is often framed in ableist, time-constricted demands that are not useful or productive for the autistic person. One must become "independent" despite the reality that no one else is truly self-sufficient; in reality we all rely on support systems. One must aspire to work 40 hours a week, even if the emotional and ensuing physical costs are exorbitant. When viewed in this manner, launching can seem like an unattainable goal. However, with some savvy networking, research, and respecting the individual's capacities, *The Launching* can happen. There is no set timeline for *The Launching* as each person develops at their own pace with their own unique skills. While the purpose of this chapter is addressing the transition to adulthood, learning about one's autism, understanding the shared experiences surrounding it, and maximizing services in light of this understanding can happen at any age. As therapists, you have the privilege to help families navigate this journey toward adulthood and/or individual self-efficacy in a healthy, resourced manner.

The Big Lie: Independence

The first challenge that disabled persons experience in navigating *The Launching* is the very idea of independence. In reality, independence is a tremendous double standard and is very intimidating for autistic persons. The goal *should be* to foster *interdependence and a collaborative* capacity so that the autistic person can learn to ask for and receive support from someone other than parents, teachers, and support staff. As a therapist, your job is to reduce the stress associated with the false goal of independence, to promote interdependence, and to assist the autistic person in seeing and understanding that others are interdependent and are help seeking, too.

For literal-thinking autistics, *independence* can represent the idea that they can't ask family, friends, staff, or teachers to help any more. The reality is, most adults have networks and friends or community mates that can assist with everyday needs. Learning to navigate those key relationships between disabled persons and non-disabled folks in the social network can be a very doable and necessary goal.

Many autistic teens (particularly those who reject their autistic identity or those from whom their identity has been withheld) can sabotage or disintegrate in the last transition years to avoid these unreasonable and extraordinary demands. For autistics without intellectual disability, the transition to adulthood can be met with an alarming decline in functioning, as the first paragraph illustrates. Studies reflect an overall decline or regression after high school as "Youth who did not have an intellectual disability evidenced the greatest slowing in improvement," and women were particularly vulnerable to these declines (Lounds-Taylor & Seltzer, 2010, p. 1431). Gender expectations also may influence this process: males are often encouraged to try new attempts (employment, post-secondary situations) if they fail, but families will tend to hold girls/young women closer to home in an effort to protect and shield them.

Teaching Autistics to Engage in Help Seeking

There are several steps in help seeking that need direct instruction. Helping your client and their family understand that *everyone* needs and accepts help is critical. Autistics can live amongst those receiving help from friends, family, and co-workers and never take notice. Help them *notice* this natural and informal way of help seeking and receiving in real time, as you model it. It is very useful to demonstrate that help seeking is a natural part of the human experience and not a "disability thing."

Therapists can offer direct instruction and "homework" to help the autistic client to *see* the help seeking and, more importantly, to see that people *are happy to give it*! It helps to destigmatize asking for help. The goal is not independence – it's interdependence and collaboration. Schools and parents should encourage autistic persons to learn these less overt lessons in human engagement via the transition plan within the Individualized Education Plan (IEP).

Changing the Phrasing from Cliff to Ramp

We often hear the phrase "transition cliff," which occurs when a student graduates from public education and then suddenly finds themselves without access to a great number of services. This can be a very stressful time for the autistic individual and their family. It would be wise to move away from the metaphor of a "cliff" and replace it with the more useful one of a "ramp." There *are* many resources, but few parents or providers are aware of what's available and how resources vary by state, and even fewer families know how to navigate these systems.

The transition to adulthood begins with many "ramps" that start well before adult age commences. One ramp could be when a child independently orders their own meal, or creates their own daily schedule. These changes don't occur because clients march across a magical chronological threshold. They may start with an old-school laminated sequence in the shower, a whiteboard by the front door, and repetition from the very beginning. It's incremental, and a slow, gently rising ramp is less overwhelming, less intense, and can be achieved with smaller, more proactive steps.

The ramp ideally occurs with an early diagnosis, and the capacity based on the diagnosis to seek tools, resources, and community. A later diagnosis can cause some autistic individuals to lack access to formal planning for skills acquisition, or cause these individuals to delay learning about and understanding their autism. Additionally, when there are undiagnosed symptoms it can lead to traumatizing situations for the individual, which may need to be addressed before growth can occur. However, no matter when an individual is diagnosed, an individualized ramp can be developed.

The Foundation for the Ramp

In achieving wellness with a diagnosis of autism, therapists can help these individuals and their families understand how to live with autism. This understanding helps us construct the ramp to adulthood. There are four key questions that I find helpful to gain this understanding and provide a foundation for growth:

- First and foremost, *what is autism?* This means discovering what autism means to your client and his/her family. How has it positively and negatively impacted them?
- How does your autistic client *perceive the world uniquely through their lens of autism?*
- How do *others perceive your client's expression of autism?*
- What tools, adaptations, modifications, supports, and choices can be made with insights from the first three questions?

Based on this foundation of an evolving, but cohesive and comprehensive, understanding of self, providers can help the family and your client to identify what scripts, tools, strategies, entitlements, and laws can be used close the gap that blocks the person from maximizing existing strengths. They need to learn that *not* using accommodations is a certain way to fail. Using accommodations is the way to achieve with the least fatigue. This does not generally come naturally – it needs to be directly taught, yet we tend to think autistic people just know this.

Immersion in the autism community through support groups, conferences, and with neurotypical peers can support the ramp to adulthood in a naturalistic way. Assistance can come in many forms. It can be family, friends, and community-based groups (for my son, church pals, hockey teammates, and his three sisters helped with the ramp to adulthood). Without this self-awareness, clients tend to freefall in this seemingly never-ending sense of bewilderment, with autism happening to the client; instead we want the client to know it is just something they need to learn to live with.

Systems Navigation

Our goal continues to be fostering and teaching interdependence and collaboration. As an individual reaches adulthood, there continue to be many systems to navigate. Clients need to be allowed to direct the trajectory of their growth, genuinely learning what they truly want, as compared to being swept into an ableist series of insurmountable goals. What clients need is to prioritize achieving personal wellness and balance, having community, and having something that drives them. It is our job to help them get there by providing multiple options, experiences, and possibilities, and then following that lead. It's our job to maximize the systems and supports to make sure they achieve the goals *they've* set. We have to become systems navigators, and teach them these important skills. Mandating that clients/parents just figure this out for themselves is a sure way for the family/autistic person to fail.

In systems navigation, you are a partner, working in conjunction with the individual/family to work through the systems. As a partner, you participate by identifying the system, making the calls hand in hand, and facilitating followthrough. It's knowing the system from the local resources through the regional, state, and national resources. Executive function, social anxiety, social networking demands, expressive language, perfectionism, and regulation issues are just a few of the barriers that block people from navigating systems successfully. You don't have to be an autism expert to navigate; you just need to care and unconditionally accept the need is real.

There are a variety of systems out there to help people, such as the school transition programs under the Individuals with Disabilities Education Act (IDEA), Social Security Disability, and Vocational Rehabilitation. Some states also have Board of Developmental Disabilities. Any family/ individual would be overwhelmed by these complex, ever-changing tasks, made even more challenging by the fact that they often house "hidden curriculums" (i.e., unspoken and implied rules and lessons). Therapists can help in navigating systems in the following ways:

- **Know your limits.** If you are not an autism expert, become knowledgeable enough to know when to refer. Launching an individual on the spectrum is a group effort!
- **Develop expertise with frequently used systems.** If your clients are involved with the Division of Vocational Rehabilitation, for example, learn the system, get to know the case managers, and become the go-to person in your office for this expertise.
- **Understand that systems have limitations.** The various government agencies that deliver day-to-day services for our clients are divided, with different roles within different agencies. This means that they have inherent limitations as to what they can do, and it may feel that there are inconsistencies between outward appearances and reality. Therapists need to find a balance between advocating for services and understanding and accepting what is available.
- **Be patient with the client and their family.** Realize that you may not be dealing with just an autistic teen/adult, but also with a parent or parents with a broad phenotypic expression (some features, not all) or a full-on undiagnosed case of their own autism. Be kind and gentle while providing needed support.

Summary

Success in launching will mean different things for different clients. It could be they refrain from self-harm, it could be getting and retaining a job, or it could be defending a dissertation. Achieving one's personal best is doable for all. Clients will not "outgrow" autism, but they can grow *into* it and use these services to become their own authentic personal best. An important part of the therapist's job is to help autistic individuals and their families realize that success does not have to be measured by ableist, time-constricted demands that society thrusts on us. Part of this is helping the autistic individual understand their view as a competent, able, individual with autism, and providing direct help in navigating support systems they need to access in order to be successful for *The Launching* into adulthood.

Recommended Resources for Professionals and Families

- Conway, F., Haines, K., Frey, A., McHenry, E., Nagler, M., Gassner, D., Kelty, P., Magro, K., Mooney, M., Grandin, T., McLaughlin, K., Best, C. T., Minutella, S., Damilatis, D., & Coniglaiaro, A. L. (2015). *College for students with disabilities: We do belong.* London, UK: Jessica Kingsley Publishers.
- Elcheson, J., Stewart, C., Lesko, A., Willey, L. H., Craft, S., Purkis, J., Ross, K., Jurkevythz, R., Mayne, T., Campbell, M., Gassner, D., Morgan, L., & Jenkins, C. (2018). *Spectrum women: Walking to the beat of autism.* London, UK: Jessica Kingsley Publishers.
- Gaus, V. L. (2018). Cognitive-behavioral therapy for adults with autism spectrum disorder. New York, NY: Guilford Press.
- Perner, L. (2012). *Scholars with autism achieving dreams.* Sedona, AZ: Auricle Books.

About the Author

After spending 20 years navigating systems for her autistic son, Dena Gassner's private practice focuses on systems navigation. She is the 2019 winner of the Cathy Pratt Professional of the Year award from the Autism Society of America. She holds seats on the Board of Directors for The Arc US, and the advisory board of the Asperger/ Autism Network of New York. She has spoken internationally, and provided key testimony in Washington and the United Nations. Ms. Gassner has contributed chapters to *Scholars with Autism Achieving Dreams* and *College for Students with Disabilities: We Do Belong.* She is a wife, mother, and grandmother and lives an authentic autistic life. You can find her on Facebook at the Center for Understanding and at www.denagassner.com.

References

Baron-Cohen, S., Jaffa, T., Davies, S., Auyeung, B., Allison, C., & Wheelwright, S. (2013). Do girls with anorexia nervosa have elevated autistic traits? *Molecular Autism, 4*(1), 24. doi:10.1186/2040-2392-4-24.

Burke, L., & Stoddart, K. P. (2014). Medical and health problems in adults with high-functioning autism and Asperger syndrome. In F. R. Volkmar, B. Reichow, & J. C. McPartland's (Eds.), *Adolescents and adults with autism spectrum disorders* (pp. 239–267). New York, NY: Springer Publishing.

Cassidy, S., Bradley, P., Robinson, J., Allison, C., McHugh, M., & Baron-Cohen, S. (2014). Suicidal ideation and suicide plans or attempts in adults with Asperger's syndrome attending a specialist diagnostic clinic: A clinical cohort study. *The Lancet Psychiatry, 1*(2), 142–147. doi:10.1016/S2215-0366(14)70248-2.

Croen, L. A., Zerbo, O., Qian, Y., Massolo, M. L., Rich, S., Sidney, S., & Kripke, C. (2015). The health status of adults on the autism spectrum. *Autism:*

The International Journal of Research and Practice, *19*(7), 814–823. doi:10.1177/ 1362361315577517.

Fortuna, R. J., Robinson, L., Smith, T. H., Meccarello, J., Bullen, B., Nobis, K., & Davidson, P.W. (2015). Health conditions and functional status in adults with autism: A cross-sectional evaluation. *Journal of General Internal Medicine*, *31*(1), 77–84. doi:10.1007/s11606-015-3509-x.

Hirvikoski, T., Mittendorfer-Rutz, E., Boman, M., Larsson, H., Lichtenstein, P., & Bolte, S. (2016). Premature mortality in autism spectrum disorder. *The British Journal of Psychiatry: The Journal of Mental Science*, *208*(3), 232–238. doi:10.1192/ bjp.bp.114.160192.

Huke, V., Turk, J., Saeidi, S., Kent, A., & Morgan, J. (2013). Autism spectrum disorders in eating disorder populations: A systematic review. *European Eating Disorders Review*, *21*(5), 345–351. doi:10.1002/erv.2244.

Lounds-Taylor, J. L., & Seltzer, M. M. (2010). Changes in the autism behavioral phenotype during the transition to adulthood. *Journal of Autism and Developmental Disorders*, *40*, 1431–1446. doi:10.1007/s10803-010-1005-z.

Maddox, B. B., Trubanova, A., & White, S. W. (2016). Untended wounds: Non-suicidal self-injury in adults with autism spectrum disorder. *Autism: The International Journal of Research and Practice*, *21*(4), 412–422. doi:10.1177/1362361316644731.

Mandy, W., & Tchanturia, K. (2015). Do women with eating disorders who have social and flexibility difficulties really have autism? A case series. *Molecular Autism*, *6*(1), 6. doi:10.1186/2040-2392-6-6.

Nicolaidis, C., Raymaker, D., McDonald, K., Dern, S., Boisclair, W. C., Ashkenazy, E., & Baggs, A. (2013). Comparison of healthcare experiences in autistic and non-autistic adults: A cross-sectional online survey facilitated by an academic-community partnership. *Journal of General Internal Medicine*, *28*(6), 761–769. doi:10.1007/s11606-012-2262-7.

Pooni, J., Ninteman, A., Bryant-Waugh, R., Nicholls, D., & Mandy, W. (2012). Investigating autism spectrum disorder and autistic traits in early onset eating disorder. *International Journal of Eating Disorders*, *45*(4), 583–591. doi:10.1002/eat.20980.

Rastam, M. (2008). Eating disturbances in autism spectrum disorders with focus on adolescent and adult years. *Clinical Neuropsychiatry*, *5*(1), 31–42. doi:2008-07906-005.

Index